THE KLEINMAN EDITION

לימוד יומי

A Daily Dose of Torah

A Torah theme for every day of every week, blending profound perspectives from all areas of Torah literature – Scripture, Mishnah, Jewish Law, Mussar/Ethics, Tefillah/Prayer, and Hashkafah/Jewish Thought – collected for daily study.

ArtScroll Series®

THE KLEINMAN EDITION

A TORAH THEME FOR EVERY DAY OF EVERY WEEK
FROM ALL AREAS OF TORAH LITERATURE —
COLLECTED FOR DAILY STUDY

Rabbi Yosaif Asher Weiss
General Editor

SERIES TWO

OF TORAH

VOLUME 6

DAILY STUDY FOR THE WEEKS OF

כי תשא - ויקרא

KI SISA – VAYIKRA

Published by
ArtScroll ❖ **Mesorah** Publications, ltd

FIRST EDITION
First Impression ... February 2009

Published and Distributed by
MESORAH PUBLICATIONS, LTD.
4401 Second Avenue / Brooklyn, N.Y 11232

Distributed in Europe by
LEHMANNS
Unit E, Viking Business Park
Rolling Mill Road
Jarow, Tyne & Wear, NE32 3DP
England

Distributed in Australia and New Zealand
by **GOLDS WORLDS OF JUDAICA**
3-13 William Street
Balaclava, Melbourne 3183
Victoria, Australia

Distributed in Israel by
SIFRIATI / A. GITLER — BOOKS
6 Hayarkon Street
Bnei Brak 51127

Distributed in South Africa by
KOLLEL BOOKSHOP
Ivy Common
105 William Road
Norwood 2192, Johannesburg, South Africa

ARTSCROLL SERIES®
THE KLEINMAN EDITION — LIMUD YOMI / A DAILY DOSE OF TORAH
SERIES TWO — VOL. 6: KI SISA – VAYIKRA
© Copyright 2009, by MESORAH PUBLICATIONS, Ltd.
4401 Second Avenue / Brooklyn, N.Y. 11232 / (718) 921-9000 / www.artscroll.com

---

ALL RIGHTS RESERVED
The text, prefatory and associated textual contents and introductions
— including the typographic layout, cover artwork and ornamental graphics —
have been designed, edited and revised as to content, form and style.

No part of this book may be reproduced
IN ANY FORM, PHOTOCOPYING, OR COMPUTER RETRIEVAL SYSTEMS
— even for personal use without written permission from
the copyright holder, Mesorah Publications Ltd.
except by a reviewer who wishes to quote brief passages
in connection with a review written for inclusion in magazines or newspapers.

THE RIGHTS OF THE COPYRIGHT HOLDER WILL BE STRICTLY ENFORCED.

ISBN 10: 1-4226-0599-X (hard cover)
ISBN 13: 978-1-4226-0599-8 (hard cover)

Typography by CompuScribe at ArtScroll Studios, Ltd.
Printed in the United States of America by Noble Book Press Corp.
Bound by Sefercraft, Quality Bookbinders, Ltd., Brooklyn N.Y. 11232

DEDICATION OF THIS VOLUME

This volume is dedicated in honor of one of the truly visionary couples of modern philanthropy

Ira and Ingeborg Rennert

They take the lead in supporting Torah causes and needy families throughout the world.

Quietly and generously, the Rennerts have earned a prominent place atop the honor roll of Torah patrons. Their generous support of ArtScroll and the Mesorah Heritage Foundation is unlocking Talmud Yerushalmi for countless thousands of our fellow Jews.

Thanks to this volume of A Daily Dose of Torah, myriad Jews will enjoy the rich treasury of Torah knowledge during minutes they never realized were free.
This dedication is a fitting tribute to one of the first families of Torah dissemination.

THE KLEINMAN EDITION

To our fathers and grandfathers, daily Torah study was the first priority.
It is fitting, therefore, that we dedicate this Limud Yomi Series in their memory

Avrohom Kleinman ז״ל
ר׳ אברהם אייזיק ב״ר אלכסנדר ז״ל
נפ׳ י״ב שבט תשנ״ט

After years of slave labor and concentration camps — years when he risked his life to put on *tefillin* every day! — he courageously rebuilt. Wherever he was — in DP camps, Poughkeepsie, Borough Park, or Forest Hills — he was a one-man *kiruv* movement, before "*kiruv rechokim*" was a familiar phrase. Everyone was drawn to his enthusiasm for Yiddishkeit.

His home was open to anyone in need, even when there was barely enough for family.

All his life he felt close to his Rebbe, the Nitra Rav, and to the father-in-law he never knew; their *sefarim*, *Naos Desheh* and *Lechem Abirim*, were part of our Shabbos table. He was a caring and gentle man whose life was defined by his love of learning Torah, *gemillas chasadim*, *kiruv* work, *hachnasas orchim*, *askanus*, and love for his family. He left a noble legacy that we are honored to perpetuate.

Mendel Indig ז״ל
ר׳ מנחם דוד ב״ר מרדכי שמואל ז״ל
נפ׳ ט׳ אדר ב׳ תשס״ג

"It was as if a *maloch* protected us," he used to say about the dark years of Churban Europa. He lost almost everything — even the *tefillin* that he put on every day until the very end — but he kept his spirit, his *emunah*, his dedication to Torah, and his resolve to rebuild.

He became a living legend of Torah, *chesed*, and service to his Bensonhurst community. His home was open to anyone in need, and there was always enough room for guests. His *succah* was the largest in the neighborhood, and he always found a way to bring endangered relatives to America and help them become established.

After he retired, he devoted himself to learning and bringing others close to Yiddishkeit, especially immigrants from the former Soviet Union, teaching them to put on *tefillin* and reuniting them with the Judaism of their ancestors. It is our privilege to carry on his glorious legacy.

We pay tribute to our mothers

Ethel Kleinman תחי׳
Rose Indig תחי׳

To us and our children and grandchildren — and to all who know them — they are role models of *emunah*, *chesed*, love and wisdom.

Our mothers שיחיו and our fathers ז״ל planted seeds of Torah in America and produced magnificent *doros* of children, grandchildren, and great-grandchildren following their example. May Hashem continue to bless our mothers with good health and many nachas-filled years.

Elly and Brochie Kleinman and their children
Deenie and Yitzy Schuss   Yossie Kleinman   Aliza and Lavey Freedman
and families

PATRONS OF LIMUD YOMI / A DAILY DOSE OF TORAH
SERIES TWO

With dedication to the principle that Torah study should always be available,
the following generous and visionary patrons
have dedicated volumes of this series:

VOL. 1: BEREISHIS-VAYEIRA / בראשית-וירא
Mrs. Sara Perlstein
Judah and Miriam Perlstein   Tzali and Esther Weiss
Sholie and Bruchi Perlstein   and families
In memory of their husband and father
Heshy Perlstein ז"ל — צבי אריה ב"ר יצחק ז"ל
נפ' כ"ו תשרי תשס"ה

VOL. 2: CHAYEI SARAH-VAYISHLACH / חיי שרה-וישלח
in honor of
Stanley and Ellen Wasserman

VOL. 3: VAYEISHEV-VAYECHI / וישב-ויחי
Chaim Yehoshua and Dini Klein
in memory of their grandmothers
יענטא בת יהודה חיים ע"ה
נפטרה כ"ט אייר תשס"א

חבלה מרים בת אברהם משה ע"ה
נפטרה כ"ה טבת תשנ"ז

הענא פייגא בת דוד אריה ע"ה
נפטרה ד' חנוכה תשל"ב
and ולהבחל"ח in honor of our dear friend
Elly Kleinman

VOL. 4: SHEMOS-BESHALACH / שמות-בשלח
dedicated in memory of the Kedoshim of Mumbai הי"ד
Rabbi Gavriel Noach Holtzberg הי"ד
Rebbetzin Rivka Holtzberg הי"ד
Rabbi Aryeh Leib Teitelbaum הי"ד
Rabbi Benzion Kruman הי"ד
Norma Rabinovitch הי"ד
Yocheved Orpaz הי"ד

VOL. 5: YISRO-TETZAVEH / יתרו-תצוה
in memory of
ז"ל **Rabbi Heshel Ryzman** — הרב יהושע השיל ב"ר חיים ז"ל
נפטר עשרה בטבת תשס"ט

VOL. 6: KI SISA-VAYIKRA / כי תשא-ויקרא
in honor of
Ira and Ingeborg Rennert

PATRONS OF LIMUD YOMI / A DAILY DOSE OF TORAH
SERIES TWO

VOL. 14: THE RABBINIC FESTIVALS AND FAST DAYS / חגים, צומות ושאר ימים מצויינים
in tribute to
Raine and Stanley Silverstein

PATRONS OF LIMUD YOMI / A DAILY DOSE OF TORAH
SERIES ONE

With dedication to the principle that Torah study should always be available, the following generous and visionary patrons have dedicated volumes of this series:

VOL. 1: BEREISHIS-VAYEIRA / בראשית-וירא
Elly and Brochie Kleinman and family
In memory of their fathers
Avrohom Kleinman – ר' אברהם אייזיק ב"ר אלכסנדר ז"ל ז"ל
Mendel Indig – ר' מנחם דוד ב"ר מרדכי שמואל ז"ל ז"ל
and יבלח"ט in tribute to their mothers שתחי' לאוי"ט
Ethel Kleinman
Rose Indig

VOL. 2: CHAYEI SARAH-VAYISHLACH / חיי שרה-וישלח
Motty and Malka Klein
for the merit of their children שיחי'
Esther and Chaim Baruch Fogel Dovid and Chavie Binyomin Zvi
Elana Leah and Natan Goldstein Moshe Yosef Yaakov Eliyahu
In honor of his mother שתחי'
Mrs. Suri Klein לאוי"ט
In memory of his father
Yidel Klein – ר' יהודה ב"ר דוד הלוי ז"ל נפ' כ"ז אדר ב' תשס"ג
In memory of her parents
Anchel Gross – ר' אשר אנשיל ב"ר משה יוסף ז"ל נפ' ג' שבט תשנ"ט
Suri Gross – שרה בת ר' חיים אליהו ע"ה נפ' כ"ד סיון תשס"א
And in memory of their grandparents who perished על קידוש השם in the Holocaust
Klein – ר' דוד ב"ר יעקב הלוי ע"ה ופערל בת ר' צבי ע"ה הי"ד
Klein – ר' מרדכי ב"ר דוד הלוי ע"ה ולאה בת ר' יעקב הלוי ע"ה הי"ד
Gross – ר' משה יוסף ב"ר בנימין צבי ע"ה ומלכה בת ר' יחיאל מיכל ע"ה הי"ד
Gartenberg – ר' חיים אליהו ב"ר מרדכי ע"ה וויוטא בת ר' שלמה אליעזר ע"ה הי"ד

VOL. 3: VAYEISHEV-VAYECHI / וישב-ויחי
Leon and Agi Goldenberg
Mendy and Estie Blau — Efraim, Rivka, and Chava
Shiffie Grossman — Chanie, and Rikki
Abi and Shoshana Goldenberg — Yehudis
Tzvi and Leilie Fertig
and Yitzy Goldenberg
In memory of their fathers and uncle
Abba Goldenberg – ר' אברהם אבא ב"ר צבי ז"ל ז"ל
Joseph Brieger – ר' יוסף אליעזר ב"ר יעקב יצחק ז"ל ז"ל
Yaakov Shlomeh Lebovits – ר' יעקב שלמה ב"ר משה הלוי ז"ל ז"ל
and יבלח"ט in tribute to their mothers שתחי' לאוי"ט
Chaya (Sicherman) Goldenberg Malka (Karfunkel) Brieger
and their aunt — Faiga (Sicherman) Lebovits

PATRONS OF LIMUD YOMI / A DAILY DOSE OF TORAH
SERIES ONE

VOL. 4: SHEMOS-BESHALACH / שמות-בשלח
Yossi and Bella Essas (Los Angeles)
Noam Zvi   Hillel Avraham   Adina Batya   Ashira Miriam
In honor of his parents
Rabbi Eliyahu and Anya Essas שליט״א

VOL. 5: YISRO-TETZAVEH / יתרו-תצוה
Edward J. and Rose F. Leventhal
in honor of their children,
Alison, Martin and Bonnie,
and in honor of their parents
Eddie and Irma Muller,
and Ruth Leventhal,
and in beloved memory of his father,
ז״ל ברוך בן משה ז״ל — Bernard E. Leventhal

VOL. 6: KI SISA-VAYIKRA / כי תשא-ויקרא
Drs. Mark and Barbara Bell (Shavertown, PA)
in honor of their children,
Ben, Mory and Adina Kayla,
and in honor of their parents
Drs. Isadore and Viola Evelyn Kreel שיחי׳
Rabbi Tzvi Alexander and Renah Bell שיחי׳
and grandparents
Rabbi Moses and Magda Mescheloff שיחי׳
and in memory of their grandparents
Kreel — בן ציון בן אליה ז״ל ונחמה רבקה בת דוד ע״ה
Hornstein — יוסף חיים ז״ל וטאניה ע״ה
Schonfeld — הרב אליעזר בן הרב משה ז״ל
Furth — וקיילא שרה בת הרב אפרים ע״ה
Bell — ראובן בן יחזקאל ז״ל ואיידל בת יעקב שמשון ע״ה

VOL. 7: TZAV-METZORA / צו-מצורע
Lawrence Uri and Barbara Skolnik (Toronto)
Brian Benjamin and Marni Skolnik
Allen and Mindy Smith
and families
in honor of their mother and grandmother
Mrs. Masha Skolnik שתחי׳
in memory of their parents and grandparents
ז״ל יוסף בן משה ז״ל — Joe Skolnik ז״ל
ז״ל ניסן בן מנחם מענדל ז״ל — Norman Chousky ז״ל
ע״ה מאטל גיטל בת בנימן ליפא ע״ה — Mildred Chousky ע״ה
and in memory of their brother and uncle
ז״ל ברוך ירחמיאל בן יוסף ז״ל — Prof. Barry Skolnik ז״ל

PATRONS OF LIMUD YOMI / A DAILY DOSE OF TORAH
SERIES ONE

VOL. 8: ACHAREI-BECHUKOSAI / אחרי-בחקתי
in honor of
R' Zvi and Betty Ryzman (Los Angeles)

VOL. 9: BAMIDBAR-SHELACH / במדבר-שלח
Mark and Chani Scheiner
Dr. Jonathan and Vicki Scheiner
in memory of
שלמה טוביה בן יהושע מנחם הלוי ע"ה — Sol Scheiner
אליהו ב"ר חיים ע"ה — Elihu Brodsky
יונה בת ר' פינחס ע"ה — Vera (Greif) Brodsky
in honor of
Rhoda Scheiner

VOL. 10: KORACH-PINCHAS / קרח-פינחס
Jeffrey and Leslie Bernstein
for the merit of their children
Gideon, Hadassah, and Josiah
And in memory of all those who have perished *Al Kiddush Hashem*
defending the Children of Israel and the Land of Israel,
with a special tribute to
Major Ro'i Klein הי"ד and
Lieutenant Colonel Emanuel Moreno הי"ד

VOL. 11: MATTOS-VA'ESCHANAN / מטות-ואתחנן
in honor of
Jay and Jeanie Schottenstein
Joseph and Lindsay — Jacob Meir
Jeffrey   Jonathan

VOL. 12: EIKEV-KI SEITZEI / עקב-כי תצא
Clive R. and Eva H. Ginsberg
in honor of our children
Sacha and Aaron
in honor of our mothers
Mére Ginsberg
and Saida Shamai
and in beloved memory of
יעקב ב"ר אפרים נח ז"ל — Jack Ginsberg ז"ל
אהרן בן אברהם ז"ל — Haroun Abraham Shamai ז"ל

VOL. 13: KI SAVO-VEZOS HABERACHAH / כי תבוא-וזאת הברכה
in memory of
Saul Schottenstein ע"ה — ישראל בן אפרים אליעזר ע"ה
נפ' שבת קודש פרשת ראה, כ"ז מנחם אב תשס"ז

PATRONS OF LIMUD YOMI / A DAILY DOSE OF TORAH
SERIES ONE

VOL. 14: THE FESTIVALS / מועדי השנה

The Teichman Family (Los Angeles)

In memory of their parents and grandparents

Sam Teichman — שמואל ב"ר יששכר דוב ז"ל ז"ל

Lujza Teichman — ליבה בריינדל בת ר' יהושע הלוי ע"ה ע"ה

Rose Teichman — רחל בת ר' אלכסנר סנדר ע"ה ע"ה

Isaac Nae — יצחק אייזיק ב"ר אברהם חיים ז"ל ז"ל

and to the memory of our recently departed brother

Steve Teichman — שלום נחמן ב"ר שמואל ז"ל ז"ל

DEDICATION OPPORTUNITIES

We are gratified by the
very enthusiastic response to this
new program for daily Torah study.
It is yet another demonstration
of the strong and growing desire
to make Torah part of every Jew's life,
seven days a week, fifty-two weeks a year.

Each volume of the
KLEINMAN EDITION
A DAILY DOSE OF TORAH
will carry individual dedications.
Many visionary families have already
undertaken to dedicate volumes
in memory or in honor of loved ones.
Additional dedication opportunities are available.

For further information, please call:
718-921-9000,
write to:

ArtScroll · Mesorah Publications, ltd
4401 Second Avenue · Brooklyn, NY 11232
or e-mail: DailyDose@artscroll.com

◈§ Publisher's Preface

King David said: גַּל עֵינַי וְאַבִּיטָה נִפְלָאוֹת מִתּוֹרָתֶךָ, *Unveil my eyes that I may perceive wonders from your Torah* (Psalms 119:18).

Shammai said: עֲשֵׂה תּוֹרָתְךָ קֶבַע, *Make your Torah study a fixed practice* (Avos 1:15).

Rav Saadiah Gaon said: The Jewish people is a nation only by virtue of the Torah.

The first series of **The Kleinman Edition: Limud Yomi / A Daily Dose of Torah** — all fourteen volumes — has been completed to great acclaim. More important, it has become a daily Torah staple in the lives of many thousands of people — in their private learning, in telephone *chavrusas*, and in discussion groups. We are deeply gratified, and very proud to embark on the second fourteen-volume series.

The Torah is the essence of the Jewish people, and not a day should go by without Torah study. How much learning should there be? Just as the Torah itself is infinite, there is no limit to the effort to master its contents. The task does not end when one bids farewell to the academy and enters the world of work and business. All over the world, study halls are filled before dawn and after dark with men plumbing the depths of the Talmud and other works. Before and after their workdays, they overcome fatigue with a relentless desire to absorb more and more of God's word.

To such people, **The Kleinman Edition: Limud Yomi / A Daily Dose of Torah** will be a welcome supplement, an enrichment that offers glimpses of additional topics and a means of filling the day's spare minutes with nourishment for the mind and spirit.

To those who as yet have not been able to savor the beauty of immersion in the sea of study, the Daily Dose is a vehicle to enrich their every day with an assortment of stimulating Torah content.

We are gratified that the volumes of the first series have been phenomenally well received. Many people have told us how they are filling once-empty gaps in their day with these "daily doses," and how they are stimulated to do further research. As King Solomon said, תֵּן לְחָכָם וְיֶחְכַּם־עוֹד הוֹדַע לְצַדִּיק וְיוֹסֶף לֶקַח, *Give the wise man and he will become wiser; make known to the righteous and he will add [to his] learning* (Proverbs 9:9).

Each "Daily Dose of Torah" includes selections from a broad spectrum of Torah sources (see below); in combination they provide a multi-dimensional study program. Each selection can stand on its own, or, ideally, serve as a vehicle for further research and enrichment. These components are:

❑ *A Torah Thought for the Day*, focusing on a verse in the weekly *parashah*. The discussion may revolve around various classic interpretations or offer a selection of insights and lessons that are derived from the verse. This section will draw from a wide gamut of early and later commentators, and will enhance the reader's appreciation for the wealth of Torah interpretation and its lessons for life. [Every day, there will be a challenging "Question of the Day," related to the theme of the day. The answers for the questions will come at the end of each week.]

❑ *The Mishnah of the Day,* presenting a Mishnah selection every day, with text, translation, and concise commentary, adapted from the classic ArtScroll Mishnah Series and the Schottenstein Edition of the Talmud.

❑ *Gems from the Gemara,* presenting some of the Talmud's discussion of the daily Mishnah. Thus the reader will "join the academy" of the Talmud's question-and-answer clarification of the laws and underlying principles of the Mishnah.

❑ *A Mussar Thought for the Day,* building upon the theme of the *Torah Thought for the Day*, it presents an ethical or moral lesson drawn from the masters of Mussar, Hashkafah, and Chassidus. This selection stimulates thought and growth — and is a welcome source of ideas for times when the reader is called upon to speak at a *simchah*.

❑ *The Halachah of the Day,* presenting a practical, relevant halachic discussion, adapted from the popular and authoritative works of Rabbi Simcha Bunim Cohen and Rabbi Binyomin Forst, which are part of the ArtScroll Series. [These brief discussions are not intended to be definitive. Questions should be directed to a qualified rav.]

- ❏ *A Closer Look at the Siddur,* broadening the reader's understanding of the rich tapestry of *tefillah*/prayer. The Shabbos Daily Dose will focus on the Shabbos prayers. And once a week, this section discusses such universal themes as the Thirteen Principles of Faith or the Six Constant Commandments.
- ❏ *A Taste of Lomdus,* a special weekly feature that presents a brief in-depth discussion of a Talmudic subject, in the tradition of the Torah giants whose reasoning and novellae are the basis of study in advanced yeshivas.

Each volume of the Daily Dose of Torah Series will present a capsule study program for twenty-eight days. The annual cycle will be comprised of thirteen four-week volumes, covering all fifty-two weeks of the year, and a fourteenth volume devoted to festivals and special days in the calendar. We are confident that the complete series will bring the excitement of Torah study to countless people, and will be a springboard to further learning, both independently and by joining *shiurim*.

The Kleinman Edition: Limud Yomi / A Daily Dose of Torah is dedicated by **ELLY AND BROCHIE KLEINMAN**, in memory of their fathers ז״ל and in honor of their mothers שיחיו. The Kleinmans have long distinguished themselves as generous and imaginative supporters of Torah and *chesed* causes. With warmth and kindness, they have opened their home countless times to help institutions and individuals. They have richly earned the respect and affection of all who know them, and we are honored to count them not only as major supporters of our work, but as personal friends. They and their family bring honor to the legacy of their parents.

The editor of this new series is **RABBI YOSAIF ASHER WEISS**, Rosh Yeshivas Ohr Hadaas, Staten Island, who is a distinguished editor of the Schottenstein Editions of the Talmud Bavli and Yerushalmi. His reputation as a noted scholar and educator has been embellished by the Daily Dose Series.

We are grateful to **RABBI RAPHAEL BUTLER,** the dynamic and innovative founder and president of the Afikim Foundation, who conceived this concept and was significant in its development. We are proud of his friendship.

We are grateful to the outstanding *talmidei chachamim* who are contributing to this series: **RABBI YOSEF GAVRIEL BECHHOFER, RABBI REUVEN BUTLER, RABBI ELIYAHU COHEN, RABBI ASHER DICKER, RABBI YOCHONON DONN, RABBI MOSHE YEHUDA GLUCK, RABBI AARON MOSHE HOBERMAN, RABBI GIDONE LEIB LANE, RABBI BORUCH LEFF, RABBI MOSHE ROSENBLUM, RABBI BERYL SCHIFF, RABBI MORDECHAI SONNENSCHEIN, RABBI MOSHE UNGAR, RABBI YISROEL DOV WEISS,** and **RABBI YITZCHOK ZELIG WEISS.** The quality of their scholarship shines through every page. We thank **RABBI SIMCHA SHAFRAN** for allowing us to use his *sefer Maadanei Simchah* as a source for some of the Questions of the Day.

The beauty and clarity of the book's design is yet another tribute to the graphics genius of our friend and colleague **REB SHEAH BRANDER.** As someone once said in a different context, "I can't put it into words, but I know it when I see it." It is hard to define good taste and graphics beauty in words, but when one sees Reb Sheah's work, one knows it.

ELI KROEN, a master of graphics in his own right, designed the cover with his typical creativity and good taste. **MOSHE DEUTSCH** had an important hand in the typesetting and general design. **MRS. CHUMIE LIPSCHITZ**, a key member of our staff, paginated the book. **TOBY GOLDZWEIG, SURY REINHOLD,** and **DEVOIRY WEISBLUM** typed and corrected the manuscript. **MRS. ESTHER FEIERSTEIN** proofread the final copy.

MRS. MINDY STERN proofread and made many important suggestions. **AVROHOM BIDERMAN** was involved in virtually every aspect of the work from its inception, and **MENDY HERZBERG** assisted in shepherding the project to completion.

As this series goes into its second stage, we express our great appreciation to our long-time friend and colleague **SHMUEL BLITZ**, head of ArtScroll Jerusalem. His dedication and judgment have been indispensable components of virtually every ArtScroll/Mesorah project.

We are grateful to them all. The contributions of ArtScroll/Mesorah to the cause of Jewish life and Torah study are possible because of the skill and dedication of the above-mentioned staff members and their colleagues.

It is a great privilege to be instrumental in bringing Torah to the people of Torah. There are no words to express our gratitude to Hashem Yisbarach for permitting us to disseminate His Word to His children.

Rabbi Meir Zlotowitz / Rabbi Nosson Scherman

Adar 5769 / February 2009

פרשת כי תשא

Parashas Ki Sisa

פרשת כי תשא

A TORAH THOUGHT FOR THE DAY

SUNDAY

PARASHAS KI SISA

כִּי תִשָּׂא אֶת־רֹאשׁ בְּנֵי־יִשְׂרָאֵל לִפְקֻדֵיהֶם וְנָתְנוּ אִישׁ כֹּפֶר נַפְשׁוֹ לַה׳ בִּפְקֹד אֹתָם וְלֹא יִהְיֶה בָהֶם נֶגֶף בִּפְקֹד אֹתָם. זֶה יִתְּנוּ כָּל־הָעֹבֵר עַל־הַפְּקֻדִים מַחֲצִית הַשֶּׁקֶל בְּשֶׁקֶל הַקֹּדֶשׁ עֶשְׂרִים גֵּרָה הַשֶּׁקֶל מַחֲצִית הַשֶּׁקֶל תְּרוּמָה לַה׳

When you take a census of the Children of Israel according to their numbers, every man shall give HASHEM *an atonement for his soul when counting them, so that there will not be a plague among them when counting them. This shall they give — everyone who passes through the census — a half shekel of the sacred shekel, the shekel is twenty gerahs, half a shekel as a portion to* HASHEM (*Shemos* 30:12-13).

The *parashah* begins with the mitzvah of *machatzis hashekel* — the method of properly conducting a census of the Jewish people. The Torah tells us that if it is done correctly, it will be כֹּפֶר נַפְשׁוֹ, *an atonement for [one's] soul;* incorrectly, and יִהְיֶה בָהֶם נֶגֶף, *there will be a plague among them.* The Midrash relates that Moshe Rabbeinu had some difficulty with a certain aspect of this mitzvah. As the Midrash states: "R' Meir said: The Holy One, Blessed is He, took the likeness of a coin of fire from under the כִּסֵּא הַכָּבוֹד, *Throne of Glory,* and showed it to Moshe: 'Like this shall they give!' " (*Midrash Rabbah, Bamidbar* 12:3).

This Midrash — a version of which is cited by *Rashi* — is perplexing. Had Moshe never seen a coin? Was he not aware of the form of a half-*shekel?* Also, what was the implication of the coin being made of fire — ultimately, the mitzvah would be fulfilled with standard metal coins! Finally, what was the significance of the location of this coin of fire — why was the likeness of this coin under Hashem's Throne of Glory?

The Gemara (*Menachos* 29a) relates that Moshe Rabbeinu was troubled by three things — the Menorah (see *Bamidbar* 8:4), Rosh Chodesh (see *Shemos* 12:2), and *sheratzim* (see *Vayikra* 11:29-31) — until Hashem showed them to him (the configuration of the Menorah, the phases of the moon, and the characteristics of the *sheratzim*). R' Yosef Shalom Elyashiv (in *Divrei Aggadah*) cites *Tosafos* (*Chullin* 42a), who ask a question on this Gemara: Why doesn't it mention the coin of fire Hashem showed Moshe to demonstrate to him the mitzvah of *machatzis hashekel?*

Tosafos offer a cryptic answer to their question: "Moshe did not

SUNDAY
PARASHAS KI SISA

have difficulty with understanding *machatzis hashekel;* rather, he was taken aback, 'What can one give as a כֹּפֶר נֶפֶשׁ, *an atonement for one's soul?'* Hashem showed him the coin of fire so that Moshe would mark it well, and inform Israel."

R' Elyashiv explains that Moshe's wonderment was because he thought, "How can one possibly atone for his sins through a coin — money that brings people to destruction!" Hashem, answering Moshe's question, told him that coinage can be like fire — destructive: burning everything in its path; or productive: warming, illuminating, and useful.

This dichotomy is illustrated by the story of King Munbaz (*Bava Basra* 11a). When a famine struck his nation, he disbursed his dynastic treasure — his own and his ancestors' accumulated wealth — to the needy. His relatives attacked him, exclaiming, "Your forbears added to their predecessors' wealth, while you squander it!" He responded with a lengthy rebuttal, which included the argument, "My forefathers stored their treasure in a place where it could be harmed. I store my treasure in a place untouchable by humans, as the verse (*Tehillim* 89:15) says: צֶדֶק וּמִשְׁפָּט מְכוֹן כִּסְאֶךָ, *Righteousness and justice are Your throne's foundation.* My treasure is hidden in the foundation of Hashem's Throne of Glory."

Hashem specifically showed Moshe a fiery coin that He took from under His Throne of Glory, because this was the kind of coin that is an atonement for one's sins. As *Tosafos* explain, Moshe was to mark it well — that is, to pay attention to the difference between "kosher" and "nonkosher" money — and to inform Israel of the type of money that they should have in their possession.

It is up to each individual, concludes R' Elyashiv, to determine how to use each coin. Money can cause a person to sin — whether through robbery, fraud, or even murder! On the other hand, one can use money to feed the poor, dress the needy, and to save lives; it is this kind of money that is stored under Hashem's Throne of Glory, and this is the money that is able to serve as כֹּפֶר נֶפֶשׁ, *an atonement for one's soul.*

QUESTION OF THE DAY:
Why was everyone required to donate a half-shekel rather than a complete shekel?

For the answer, see page 68.

פרשת כי תשא

MISHNAH OF THE DAY: BEITZAH 2:10

SUNDAY
PARASHAS KI SISA

The Mishnah discusses the *tumah* and *muktzeh* status of another implement:

עֲגָלָה שֶׁל קָטָן — *A child's* toy *wagon*[1] טְמֵאָה מִדְרָס וְנִטֶּלֶת — is susceptible to *midras contamination*;[2] וְאֵינָהּ נִגְרֶרֶת אֶלָּא עַל בַּשַׁבָּת — *it may be moved on the Sabbath*,[3] גַּבֵּי כֵלִים — *but it may be dragged only over clothing*.[4] It may not be dragged on a dirt floor, lest the wheels of the wagon dig out furrows in the dirt.[5] רַבִּי יְהוּדָה אוֹמֵר — *R' Yehudah disagrees and says:* כָּל הַכֵּלִים אֵין נִגְרָרִין — *No utensil may be dragged* on the ground, חוּץ מִן הָעֲגָלָה מִפְּנֵי שֶׁהִיא כּוֹבֶשֶׁת — *except a wagon because it* only *presses*.[6]

---NOTES---

1. A toy wagon in which the child sits and is moved about for his entertainment (*Rashi;* cf. *Tosafos*).

2. If someone who is *tamei* as a result of a bodily function [e.g., a *zav* (a man who has become *tamei* because of a specific type of seminal emission; see *Vayikra* 15:1-15) or a *niddah* (see ibid. vs. 20-22)] sits or leans on a bed, couch, or chair, it acquires the same level of *tumah* as the person from whom the *tumah* emanates. The *tumah* of objects upon which one of these people rests or leans is called *tumah* of *midras*.

In our Mishnah, if the child is a *zav*, making him an *av hatumah* (someone with primary *tumah* contamination), the wagon will also contract that degree of *tumah*, because it is used for sitting. Even when the wagon is used as a toy, the child leans on it, and leaning is also a manner of transmitting *midras* contamination. If the wagon was primarily used for another purpose, the fact that the child happened to sit or lean on it would not give it *midras* contamination (*Rashi* as explained by *Lechem Shamayim*).

3. It is considered a utensil [and consequently, it is not *muktzeh*] (*Rav*).

4. The term *keilim* includes clothing (*Rashi* on 18a). *Rashi* adds that this ruling, like the previous one, applies to the Sabbath (cf. *Tosafos Yom Tov; Meleches Shlomo*).

5. This is forbidden as a subcategory of the *melachah* of חוֹרֵשׁ, plowing (*Rav*).

6. Although furrows appear as it is moved, the wagon does not remove any earth from its place. Its wheels only depress the earth over which it passes; this does not constitute an act of חוֹרֵשׁ (*Rashi*).

GEMS FROM THE GEMARA

Our Mishnah cited the opinion of the Tanna Kamma, that the wagon of a child may be dragged over clothing. The Gemara analyzes this ruling:

The Mishnah ruled that dragging the wagon over clothing is permitted,

פרשת כי תשא

SUNDAY — PARASHAS KI SISA

the implication being that dragging it on the ground is not permitted. What is the reason for this prohibition? It must be because the wagon makes a furrow when it is dragged on the ground. [As noted in the Mishnah, the digging of a furrow is forbidden due to the prohibition against *plowing*.]

The Gemara seeks to identify the author of the Mishnah:

Who is the Tanna that this ruling follows? It is R' Yehudah, who stated that an unintended labor is prohibited; because if it is R' Shimon, why, he has stated that an unintended labor is permitted! For it was taught in a Baraisa: R' Shimon says: A person may drag a bed, chair, or bench as long as he does not intend to make a furrow.

When one intends to perform a permitted act (i.e., dragging a wagon) and a second, prohibited act (i.e., making a furrow) may occur incidentally, R' Yehudah's view is that the permitted act may not be performed. R' Shimon disagrees with R' Yehudah and is of the opinion that unintended *melachah* is permitted. Therefore, our Mishnah, which prohibits dragging a wagon on the ground because of the possibility of incidentally making a furrow, must follow R' Yehudah's stringent opinion.

The Gemara questions this deduction:

But according to this, how will you explain the end of our Mishnah, which said: R' Yehudah disagrees, and says: No utensils may be dragged on the ground on the Sabbath, except a wagon because it only presses. This is permitted because the wagon presses, from which we may infer: But it does not make a furrow. However, the Gemara earlier deduced that the beginning of the Mishnah also followed the opinion of R' Yehudah, and there it implies that one *may not* drag a wagon on the ground because the wagon does indeed make a furrow!?

The Gemara concludes:

The two sections of our Mishnah follow two Tannaim who disagree about what R' Yehudah would rule in the case of a wagon.

A wagon generally depresses the ground as it is pushed without digging up any earth; that would be permitted even according to R' Yehudah. However, the Tanna Kamma of our Mishnah prohibits pulling a wagon, because sometimes a wheel does not turn properly and gets dragged, causing it to dig up the ground. According to R' Yehudah, this would be prohibited despite the fact that it is an unintended labor. The Tanna's view cited at the end of our Mishnah is that it is unlikely for a wheel to get stuck, and it is consequently permitted, even according to R' Yehudah, to pull the wagon (*Rashi*).

פרשת כי תשא

A MUSSAR THOUGHT FOR THE DAY

SUNDAY

PARASHAS KI SISA

The pursuit of money is often a necessary part of our lives. As R' Alexander Moshe Lapides (in his *Divrei Emes, Kuntres HaAnavah VeHaYirah* 3) — a contemporary of R' Yisrael Salanter — notes, one may not rely upon miracles, saying, "I will sit in the *beis hamidrash* and learn Torah, serving Hashem night and day, and whatever Hashem decrees upon me shall come to pass!" The decree of בְּזֵעַת אַפֶּיךָ תֹּאכַל לֶחֶם, *By the sweat of your brow shall you eat bread* (*Bereishis* 3:19), obligates man to work. Yet, a God-fearing person who is forced to work long hours can still serve Hashem. R' Lapides applies to this situation the dictum of R' Yehudah HaNasi: יֵשׁ קוֹנֶה עוֹלָמוֹ בְּשָׁעָה אֶחָת, *Some earn their portion in the World to Come in one moment.* If we translate the word שָׁעָה, *moment,* according to its literal meaning, *hour,* we can explain R' Yehudah HaNasi's statement as: *Some earn their portion in the World to Come with one hour* — that is, with one hour of daily Torah learning.

R' Lapides elaborates: One who can learn Torah for only one hour daily, but does so with intent to fulfill the Torah he learns, is considered as if he were occupied with Torah learning for the entire day! In the second verse of *Tehillim*, David HaMelech writes: כִּי אִם בְּתוֹרַת ה' חֶפְצוֹ וּבְתוֹרָתוֹ יֶהְגֶּה יוֹמָם וָלָיְלָה. One can explain the verse as follows: *But his desire is in the Torah of Hashem,* yet due to the circumstances facing him he can only learn for an hour each day. Still, he is considered as if *in His Torah he meditates day and night*!

Elsewhere, David HaMelech states: לְכוּ־בָנִים שִׁמְעוּ־לִי יִרְאַת ה' אֲלַמֶּדְכֶם, *Go, O sons, heed me, I will teach you the fear of Hashem* (ibid. 34:12). We may ask: Why does the Psalmist tell his sons (or students — *Radak*) to *go* and *I will teach you the fear of Hashem*? Generally, when one teaches, he tells the student to *come,* not to *go*! The verse should have begun *Come, O sons, heed me . . .* R' Lapides infers from this anomaly that the verse is teaching us that even one who needs to *go* — to his business, to his occupation — must do so with the requisite יִרְאַת ה', *fear of Hashem.* He will then certainly set aside time to perform kindness and to teach his children to live a Torah-directed life. And when he does learn Torah, in the specific times he sets for himself daily, it is considered as if he fulfills the directive: וְהָגִיתָ בּוֹ יוֹמָם וָלַיְלָה, *you should contemplate it day and night* (*Yehoshua* 1:8) — that he learns *all* day and night.

Ultimately, one must fulfill the dictum of the verse in *Mishlei* (3:6): בְּכָל־דְּרָכֶיךָ דָעֵהוּ, *In all your ways know Him.* One should both mentally

SUNDAY
PARASHAS KI SISA

and verbally reiterate, "I am going to work so that I can provide for myself and my household, and then I will be able to serve Hashem — by designating time to learn Torah and to perform the mitzvos, and by giving *tzedakah* to the needy. I will support my family and guide them in the good and proper path, and be able to hire teachers to teach my children Torah."

Although one must work to make money, one must also not lose sight, says R' Lapides, that working more or harder does not necessarily mean that one will make more money. Not all who engage in commerce profit, nor does every wise person become wealthy! As we see from the Gemara (*Kiddushin* 82b), there is no craft that does not have both rich and poor people working in it. If Hashem decrees that a person should be poor, none of his endeavors or increased exertion will make him rich. Even if one is of the impression that his intensified application to his business matters will net him more money, he should realize that it is not as it appears. Hashem has many messengers to implement His wishes, and if a person is destined to remain poor, He will cause him to lose money in other areas.

HALACHAH OF THE DAY

Today, we will continue yesterday's discussion of the paragraph of מִזְמוֹר לְתוֹדָה. Since the recital of this paragraph is a reflection of the sacrificial service of the *korban todah* that took place in the *Beis HaMikdash*, it follows that it is not to be recited on days that the offering itself could not have been brought. On Shabbos and Yom Tov, only communal offerings were brought; consequently, an individual was unable to bring a personal *todah*-offering on those days. Thus, we do not recite this paragraph on Shabbos or Yom Tov. The *todah*-offering included forty loaves, some of which were *chametz;* it therefore could not be brought from Erev Pesach until after the entire festival. For this reason, we do not recite מִזְמוֹר לְתוֹדָה during this period. The *todah*-offering was also not brought on Erev Yom Kippur, because one would have to cease eating its meat once the fast of Yom Kippur begins. Since there is a prohibition against causing the meat from a sacrifice to be left over beyond the time frame during which it may be eaten, we refrain from bringing the sacrifice at a time when the window of opportunity to eat it is shortened. Thus, we do not recite מִזְמוֹר לְתוֹדָה on Erev Yom Kippur.

We will continue our discussion of *Pesukei D'Zimrah* with *Ashrei*.

The Gemara (*Berachos* 4b) teaches us: R' Elazar said in the name

פרשת כי תשא

SUNDAY

PARASHAS KI SISA

of R' Avina: One who recites תְּהִלָּה לְדָוִד, *a psalm of praise by David* (*Tehillim* Ch. 145), three times each day can be sure that he will merit a portion in the World to Come. What is the reason? Because it contains the verse: פּוֹתֵחַ אֶת־יָדֶךָ וּמַשְׂבִּיעַ לְכָל־חַי רָצוֹן, *You open Your hand and satisfy the desire of every living thing* (v. 6).

The above Talmudic passage is referring to the prayer known as אַשְׁרֵי, because of the first word of the two introductory phrases that the Sages attached to this psalm. The prayer of *Ashrei* is one of the centerpieces of *Pesukei D'Zimrah*, and we recite it at other points in our prayers as well.

The Gemara cited above explains the reason for the exalted status given to this psalm: It contains the verse, פּוֹתֵחַ אֶת־יָדֶךָ וּמַשְׂבִּיעַ לְכָל־חַי רָצוֹן, *You open Your hand and satisfy the desire of every living thing*. This is an especially important verse, for it addresses Hashem as the One Who, in His mercy, supplies sustenance to every single living being. Because of the status conferred upon this verse, it is essential that one recite it with great concentration, reflecting upon its meaning during its recital. If one did not say this verse with proper concentration, he must repeat all the verses from פּוֹתֵחַ אֶת־יָדֶךָ until the end of אַשְׁרֵי. This ruling holds true even if one did not realize his lapse until he has already concluded the *Shemoneh Esrei*.

Some people have the custom to raise their hands to Heaven while reciting this verse.

A CLOSER LOOK AT THE SIDDUR

Rambam (*Hilchos Dei'os* 3:3) famously enunciates an important principle of Judaism: An action can sometimes be a mitzvah, while the same action — performed with different intent — is not. For example, one who takes care to remain healthy, guarding his body from illness and being vigilant about his diet, receives no merit for his behavior. But, if he acts in exactly the same way except that he also keeps in mind, "I am endeavoring to stay healthy so that I can serve Hashem properly, with a healthy body and a calm mind," then his healthy living regimen is part of his service of Hashem!

Similarly, someone who engages in business with the intent that he should have the financial wherewithal to serve Hashem is performing a mitzvah through his otherwise mundane business activity. Even inaction, says *Rambam*, can be a mitzvah! If one goes to sleep keeping in mind that it be for the purpose of keeping his mind clear and body

SUNDAY — PARASHAS KI SISA

healthy so that he should not fall ill and be unable to perform the Torah obligations incumbent on him, his sleep, too, is service of Hashem! This kind of behavior is mandated in *Mishlei* (3:6): בְּכָל־דְּרָכֶיךָ דָעֵהוּ וְהוּא יְיַשֵּׁר אֹרְחֹתֶיךָ, *In all your ways know Him, and He will smooth your paths.*

The Gemara (*Berachos* 63a, with *Ein Yaakov*) applies this verse to prayer in a very interesting way. The Gemara there — the source for *Rambam's* principle — says that the verse בְּכָל־דְּרָכֶיךָ דָעֵהוּ is a "short passage upon which all the principles of the Torah depend." Rava, elaborating on this, says that the verse includes even sinful matters. The commentators (see *Maharatz Chayes* and *Hagahos Yaavetz*) on the Gemara explain that this refers to a person who sins for the sake of heaven, with positive intent. We find this a number of times in the Torah, such as in the episode of the daughters of Lot (see *Bereishis* 19:30-38), or of Yael (see *Shoftim* 4:17-22). But the next words of the Gemara (found in *Ein Yaakov's* text of the Gemara, and as a variant reading in standard editions of the Gemara) add another layer of nuance to this subject. According to this reading, the Gemara continues: "R' Pappa says: That is what is meant by the common adage: 'A thief, at the mouth of his tunnel, calls out to Hashem.'" The implication is that even if one is, unfortunately, a sinner — he should still pray to Hashem for success in his misdeeds! Perhaps this is because by praying, he will remain connected to and aware of Hashem, and ultimately repent, fulfilling the end of the verse: וְהוּא יְיַשֵּׁר אֹרְחֹתֶיךָ, *and He will smooth* (or straighten) *your paths.* [A similar point is made by *Iyun Yaakov*, although he gives no indication as to whether he had *Ein Yaakov's* reading.]

Based on the principle enunciated by *Rambam*, *Turei Zahav* (*Shulchan Aruch, Even HaEzer* 25:1) explains a verse in the series of *Shir HaMaalos* recited after the Shabbos *Minchah* prayers. The verse (*Tehillim* 127:2) says: שָׁוְא לָכֶם מַשְׁכִּימֵי קוּם מְאַחֲרֵי־שֶׁבֶת אֹכְלֵי לֶחֶם הָעֲצָבִים כֵּן יִתֵּן לִידִידוֹ שֵׁנָא, *It is vain for you who rise early, who sit up late, who eat the bread of sorrows — for indeed, He gives His beloved ones restful sleep.* The *Turei Zahav* explains that the verse refers to Torah scholars. One scholar might *rise up early* and *sit up late* so as to be able to spend as much time as possible learning Torah. Another scholar, though, makes sure to sleep enough so that he has the strength and clarity of thought to be able to learn Torah properly. The second scholar, observes *Turei Zahav*, can learn in one hour what the first needs two hours to understand well!

It is certain, concludes *Turei Zahav*, that both scholars receive the

SUNDAY

PARASHAS KI SISA

same Heavenly reward for their efforts in learning the Torah. If that is the case, then why should one exert oneself to learn for so long, when he can ensure that he sleeps enough and learns the same amount of Torah in less time? That is the intent of the verse: *It is vain* — for no purpose — *for you* Torah scholars *who rise early, who sit up late, who eat the bread of sorrows* so as to maximize the amount of time in which you learn Torah — *for indeed, He* [Hashem] *gives* the same amount of Torah knowledge to *His beloved ones* — who make sure to have enough *restful sleep* so as to be able to learn Torah with a clearer mind.

A TORAH THOUGHT FOR THE DAY

פרשת כי תשא

MONDAY
PARASHAS KI SISA

רְאֵה קָרָאתִי בְשֵׁם בְּצַלְאֵל בֶּן־אוּרִי בֶן־חוּר לְמַטֵּה יְהוּדָה. וָאֲמַלֵּא אֹתוֹ רוּחַ אֱלֹהִים בְּחָכְמָה וּבִתְבוּנָה וּבְדַעַת וּבְכָל־מְלָאכָה

See, I have called by name: Bezalel, son of Uri, son of Chur, of the tribe of Yehudah. I have filled him with a Godly spirit, with wisdom, insight, and knowledge, and with every craft (Shemos 31:2-3).

As *Ramban* notes, the Torah — here and in the next *parashah* (36:30-34) — seems to give an inordinate amount of attention to Hashem's choice of Bezalel as the chief architect and designer of the Mishkan. The reason for this, explains *Ramban,* was to draw attention to Hashem's preparation for the construction of the Mishkan, a building to be devoted solely to the glory of Hashem. Indeed, when we look at the list of Bezalel's talents, we realize the extraordinary range of his capabilities! It is rare — in any era — to find a person who is skilled in all of the separate and distinct crafts of goldsmithing, silversmithing, shaping gemstones, carving wood, weaving, and embroidering! When we add that Bezalel was enslaved in Egypt, we have to wonder how — in the midst of the horrors of slavery — he was able to acquire all these skills.

That is why — explains *Ramban* — Hashem emphasized to Moshe (who, in turn, relayed this message to the Jewish people) that Hashem had bestowed upon Bezalel the capability to perform all the craftsmanship necessary for the Mishkan. Since Hashem had intended that the Jews build a Mishkan, He saw to it that there be born among them a person with supernatural talent and the ability to oversee the work.

There was, though, another facet to Bezalel's skill. The Gemara (*Berachos* 55a) relates: "Bezalel knew how to combine the letters with which the heaven and earth were created." *Ramban* explains this by saying that all the details of the Mishkan and its utensils alluded to profound secrets of heaven and earth, and Bezalel understood these secrets. R' David Povarsky (*Mussar VeDaas,* Volume 1:15) explains the significance of this knowledge: When a person does a mitzvah with the proper intent, the result is not two entities: a mitzvah and a separate מַחֲשָׁבָה (the thought containing the holy intent and contemplation involved in performing the mitzvah). Instead, there is just one entity — a mitzvah in which the מַחֲשָׁבָה, the thoughts accompanying it, are inherently part of the physical action of the mitzvah.

MONDAY

PARASHAS KI SISA

Similarly, the *Torah SheBichsav* (the Written Torah) and the *Torah SheBe'al Peh* (the Oral Tradition of Torah) are not two separate entities, with the written portion a dry, simple reading of law and history and the oral portion a vibrant record of the reasoning behind the law together with a vast repository of halachah. In truth, the תּוֹרָה שֶׁבִּכְתָב has inherent in it — in one of Hashem's wondrous compositions — the vast volume of the teachings of the תּוֹרָה שֶׁבְּעַל פֶּה.

This, explains *R' Povarsky,* is what the *Ramban* means when he cryptically states (20:30) that the תּוֹרָה שֶׁבִּכְתָב and the תּוֹרָה שֶׁבְּעַל פֶּה parallel the heaven and the earth. The wisdom that Hashem used in creating the loftiest parts of heaven is the same as the wisdom He used to create the lowliest part of the most insignificant creature on earth. And the secrets inherent in that creation are the same as those inherent in the highest of angels. Thus, the relationship of the heaven to the earth is the same as that of the תּוֹרָה שֶׁבְּעַל פֶּה to the תּוֹרָה שֶׁבִּכְתָב.

Now we can explain the importance of Bezalel's knowledge of the secrets of the creation of heaven and earth. Bezalel was required to make sure that he had the proper intent in the process of building the Mishkan and its utensils. This does not mean, as one might think, merely that he was required to have the proper thoughts in mind. Rather, he needed to make the intent an actual part of — something inherent in — the holy Mishkan and all its related equipment, just as the heaven is an inherent part of the earth and just as the תּוֹרָה שֶׁבְּעַל פֶּה is intrinsic to the תּוֹרָה שֶׁבִּכְתָב.

Bezalel was not simply performing the actions of weaving or carpentry. Every single action necessary in the building of the Mishkan needed to be attached to and imbued with the Heavenly influences that were appropriate to the item being worked with. This knowledge — the same as how the heaven and earth were created — was the talent Bezalel needed to build the Mishkan properly.

MISHNAH OF THE DAY: BEITZAH 3:1

As we have already seen several times (for example, above, Mishnah 1:2), the Torah generally permits forms of labor that are forbidden on the Sabbath to be performed on Yom Tov, when that labor is necessary in the preparation of food. However, not all forms of labor are permitted. The coming Mishnah considers the law in regard to trapping animals, fish, or fowl that would be eaten on a Yom Tov:

פרשת כי תשא

MONDAY

PARASHAS KI SISA

אֵין צָדִין דָּגִים מִן הַבִּיבָרִין בְּיוֹם טוֹב — *We may not catch fish from a fish pond on a Yom Tov,*[1] וְאֵין נוֹתְנִין לִפְנֵיהֶם מְזוֹנוֹת — *nor may we place food before them.*[2] אֲבָל צָדִין חַיָּה וָעוֹף מִן הַבִּיבָרִין — *But we may trap animals or fowl from enclosures,*[3] וְנוֹתְנִין לִפְנֵיהֶם מְזוֹנוֹת — *and we may put food before them.*[4] רַבָּן שִׁמְעוֹן בֶּן גַּמְלִיאֵל אוֹמֵר לֹא כָל הַבִּיבָרִין שָׁוִין — *Rabban Shimon ben Gamliel says: Not all enclosures are the same.*[5] זֶה הַכְּלָל כָּל הַמְחֻסָּר צִידָה אָסוּר — *This is the general rule: Any animal that lacks trapping*

--- NOTES ---

1. It would seem that catching fish, as a step in the preparation of food (אוֹכֶל נֶפֶשׁ), should fall into the category of labor that is permitted on a Yom Tov. However, not all forms of forbidden labor are permitted on a Yom Tov. Reaping (i.e., harvesting) remains Scripturally prohibited. Moreover, the exclusion of reaping is not specific to that labor, but is applicable to all similar forms of forbidden labor. Accordingly, all forms of labor that are more removed from actual consumption of food, as is reaping — viz., those forms of labor involved in *procuring* food, as opposed to *preparing* it for eating — remain prohibited. Only those forms of labor that are preparatory to the *actual* consumption of the food — e.g., kneading, slaughtering, and cooking — are permitted. This category includes all forms of labor that are classified as trapping — including the catching of fish (*Rav; Tosafos;* see *Shitah Mekubetzes;* cf. *Rashi; Rosh* and *Ran,* who explain that forms of labor such as reaping and trapping remain forbidden for the same reason that some forms of grinding remain forbidden on a Yom Tov [see above, Mishnah 1:7]; cf. also *Rambam, Commentary* and *Hil. Yom Tov* 2:7, and *Meiri,* who explain that catching fish is prohibited on account of *muktzeh*).

2. Since fish can subsist on the food they find in the water, feeding them is considered unnecessary effort, and is consequently prohibited (*Rav; Rashi;* see *Rosh Yosef;* cf. *Rambam, Commentary* and *Hil. Yom Tov* 2:17; *Tosafos* to 23b; *Rashba, Avodas HaKodesh* 1:9; *Meiri*).

3. I.e., from the enclosures designed for the purpose of stocking animals (*Rambam Commentary; Rashi* on *Rif*).

4. Because these animals depend upon their owner for food during the winter — and sometimes even in the summer, if they can find no pasture — he is allowed to feed them (*Rav; Rashi*). [The reasons given by other commentators for the prohibition against feeding fish do not apply here either. There is no fear that he may violate the labor of trapping, because the animals are considered previously trapped. *Muktzeh* does not apply because these animals may be slaughtered and eaten on Yom Tov.]

5. Rabban Shimon does not disagree with the previous Tanna. He is merely clarifying the law. The animals may be taken from the enclosures only if the enclosures are small enough that the animals in them can be considered trapped from the time that they were placed in these enclosures (*Rav;* see, however, *Gems from the Gemara* to our Mishnah).

MONDAY

PARASHAS KI SISA

is prohibited to be caught or fed;[6] וְשֶׁאֵינוֹ מְחֻסַּר צֵידָה מֻתָּר — *while any* animal *that does not lack trapping is permitted* to be caught and fed.[7]

───────── NOTES ─────────

6. I.e., an animal that cannot be caught without resorting to special tactics or strategies. As the Gemara (*Shabbos* 74a) puts it: Whenever one would say: הָבֵא מְצוּדָה וּנְצוּדֶנּוּ, *bring a trap* [*or net*] *and let us catch it* (*Rav*).

7. I.e., an animal that one can reach and catch in one lunge is considered trapped, and may be taken on a Yom Tov (*Rav* from Gemara 24a).

GEMS FROM THE GEMARA

*R*av to this Mishnah adds an important condition to the permit given in the Mishnah to take animals from an enclosure — viz., they may be taken only if they had been designated for slaughter prior to Yom Tov; otherwise they are *muktzeh*. *Rav's* position is evidently derived from a divergent version in *Rashi* (23b): Our text of *Rashi* states that the animals must be הַמְכוּנָסִים, *those that have been ingathered*. *Rav's* version was evidently הַמּוּכָנִים, *those that have been prepared* (see *Meiri* with notes ad loc. and *Ohr Zarua* 2:352).

Rambam, on the other hand, in his ruling (*Hil. Yom Tov* 2:7), paraphrases our Mishnah in a manner that clearly indicates his opinion that the issue of trapping is moot, for the animals are automatically considered prepared (מוּכָן) by virtue of their presence within an enclosure erected for the purpose of stocking animals for consumption. Nevertheless, *Mishnah Berurah* (497:20) rules in accordance with *Rav's* view without indicating his source and without mention of divergent opinions.

Later in his commentary, *Rav* states that there is no difference of opinion between the Tanna Kamma of our Mishnah and Rabban Shimon ben Gamliel, and that the latter's intent is to expand on the law stated by the former. However, *Rashi* (24a) indicates that there is disagreement among the Tannaim (see *Maharsha*; *Maharam Schif*). Assuming the premise that there is a disagreement, it centers around the criteria to be used in judging an animal to be considered trapped. According to the first Tanna, one of the criteria (as stated in the Gemara) is that he be able to reach it with one lunge (דְּמָטֵי לֵיהּ בְּחַד שְׁחִיָּא). If this requirement is met, the enclosure is considered small and the animals may (according to the first Tanna) be caught. Rabban Shimon, on the other hand, disagrees, and prohibits catching the animal even in such a case, as long as the situation is one in which a person is likely to ask for a trap with which to catch it (*Rashi* 24a); i.e., if the enclosure is large enough so that even though he can seize the animal with one lunge if he so pleases, he nevertheless prefers to do so with a trap, he may not take an animal from there on a Yom Tov.

פרשת
כי תשא

**MONDAY
PARASHAS
KI SISA**

Rambam (*Hil. Yom Tov* 2:7), as explained by *Maggid Mishneh* (ad loc.), maintains that there is a disagreement, but interprets it differently: According to the first Tanna, the criterion that one must be able to seize the animal with one lunge (or that he does not generally ask for a trap to capture the animal) applies only to animals and fowl, but not to fish — those one may not catch in any event. Rabban Shimon, however, applies this criterion to fish, as well as to animals and fowl. He thus rules more leniently than the Tanna Kamma. *Rambam* (from Gemara 24a) decides the law in accordance with Rabban Shimon, and accordingly rules that one may catch fish from a small pool (see *Rama, Orach Chaim* 497:1).

A MUSSAR THOUGHT FOR THE DAY

In *A Torah Thought for the Day* we discussed one explanation of the Gemara's comment (*Berachos* 55a) that Bezalel knew how to combine the letters with which the heaven and earth were created. R' Shimon Schwab (in his *Maayan Beis HaSho'evah*) has a different perspective on this Gemara.

The letters of the Hebrew alphabet have an intrinsic order. *Aleph* (א), comes before *beis* (ב), which comes before *gimmel* (ג), and so on. In addition, the letters have numerical value — א is one, ב is two, ג is three, and so on. The Torah was written with these letters — which have a rational order to them — to signify that we need to learn and understand the Torah through our reason and intellect.

R' Schwab explains that when the Gemara (*Kiddushin* 30a) says that the scholars of earlier generations were called *Sofrim* — literally "counters" — because they would count all the letters of the Torah, it has the same meaning: They had an intellectual grasp of the entire Torah, just as numbers grow ordinally in an understandable progression.

But Hashem's understanding of the Torah is on an entirely different level — the letters in the "heavenly Torah" are not in any order, and are not fathomable by the human mind. To understand it, one must experience a transcendent revelation on the soul's level — as the mind does not possess the tools to fathom the "heavenly Torah" on an intellectual level.

MONDAY

PARASHAS KI SISA

When the Mishkan — which was where Hashem's presence was to be manifest on earth — was being built, it needed to be built on the level of the "heavenly Torah." To this end, Hashem said of Bezalel (31:3): וָאֲמַלֵּא אֹתוֹ רוּחַ אֱלֹהִים, *I have filled him with a Godly spirit.* Bezalel knew how to combine the letters — the letters of the "heavenly Torah" — through which heaven and earth were created.

[Based on this, says R' Schwab, we can understand an enigmatic Mishnah in *Shekalim* (3:2). The Mishnah records a disagreement as to the proper procedure for removing the *machatzis hashekel* money from its storeroom in the *Beis HaMikdash*. The prevailing opinion is that the money was moved to three large containers, marked *aleph, beis, gimmel* — א׳ ב׳ ג׳. R' Yishmael disagrees — he says that the boxes were marked with the Greek letters *alpha, beta, gamma*. At first glance, R' Yishmael's opinion seems bizarre — in the holiest place in the world, the *Beis HaMikdash*, why should one use a language foreign to Judaism? But, says R' Schwab, R' Yishmael was making precisely this point: The *Beis HaMikdash* — just like the Mishkan — was also above the level of the intellect. Using the Hebrew alphabet would have demonstrated an order, an ability to comprehend that was not appropriate for the level of holiness in the *Beis HaMikdash*. Thus, other letters were deliberately used.]

Although the Torah's essence is Hashem's wisdom, incomprehensible on our own level, when we learn Torah we attempt to fathom its wisdom to the best of our abilities. We delve deeply and work at uncovering the true meaning of the Torah. It is true that there are higher levels of learning the Torah — which are dependent on the soul's comprehension — but our obligation is to learn the Torah based on our individual intellects.

Tehillim 119 is a long paean of praise for learning Torah, and it is structured as an eightfold repetition of an *aleph-beis* acrostic. On Friday evening we recite אֵשֶׁת חַיִל (*Mishlei* 31:10-31), a poem interpreted metaphorically by the Sages as praise for the holy Torah. It, too, is constructed around an *aleph-beis* acrostic. This symbolizes, explains R' Schwab, this very message: The primary Torah learning to which one should apply oneself is on the intellectual level, orderly and sensible as the *aleph-beis*.

QUESTION OF THE DAY:

Why does the Torah say that Hashem "called" Betzalel?

For the answer, see page 68.

HALACHAH OF THE DAY

פרשת
כי תשא

**MONDAY
PARASHAS
KI SISA**

Continuing our discussion of *Pesukei D'Zimrah*, we arrive at the paragraph of וַיְבָרֶךְ דָּוִיד, *And David blessed*. One should stand from the beginning of this paragraph until after he recites the words: אַתָּה הוּא ה' הָאֱלֹהִים. While one is required to stand while reciting these phrases, most people are accustomed to stand from the beginning of וַיְבָרֶךְ דָּוִיד until after the recitation of *Borchu* following *Yishtabach*.

Some customarily give charity when saying the words וְאַתָּה מוֹשֵׁל בַּכֹּל, *And You rule over all . . .*, that appear in the prayer of וַיְבָרֶךְ דָּוִיד.

The prayer of אָז יָשִׁיר, the song that the Bnei Yisrael sang at the splitting of the Reed Sea, should be recited with great joy and happiness. While reciting these verses, one should imagine that he himself has just crossed the Reed Sea that very day, and is singing praises to Hashem in thanks for his salvation. Indeed, the authorities tell us that joyful recitation of אָז יָשִׁיר is helpful in attaining pardon for one's sins.

One should recite the blessing of יִשְׁתַּבַּח immediately upon concluding the recitation of the *Pesukei D'Zimrah*. This remains true even if he has concluded his recitation of *Pesukei D'Zimrah* ahead of the congregation and he will now have to wait for the congregation to catch up to him. This is because, as we have learned, the blessing of יִשְׁתַּבַּח serves as the closing blessing of *Pesukei D'Zimrah*. This being the case, it would be improper to allow a lapse of time to interrupt between the recitation of *Pesukei D'Zimrah* and the blessing.

However, while the above is true, an exception is made in regard to the one who will be leading the services after יִשְׁתַּבַּח. The *chazzan* is required to recite the *Kaddish* prior to *Borchu;* and the halachah stipulates that there be no interruption between the *Kaddish* and יִשְׁתַּבַּח. Therefore, the *chazzan* should not recite יִשְׁתַּבַּח until he is prepared to recite the *Kaddish*.

Similarly, if the congregation began the services before a full *minyan* arrived in the synagogue, the *chazzan* should not recite יִשְׁתַּבַּח until a full *minyan* has arrived.

One who has concluded יִשְׁתַּבַּח before the *chazzan* is ready to recite *Kaddish* may respond with בָּרוּךְ הוּא וּבָרוּךְ שְׁמוֹ and אָמֵן to any *berachah,* as well as to *Kaddish*. He may also recite all of the responses to *Kedushah*.

פרשת כי תשא

MONDAY
PARASHAS KI SISA

Some authorities permit the recital of *Tehillim* at this point. Likewise, if for any of the reasons that we will discuss further, someone omitted parts of *Pesukei D'Zimrah*, he may recite them now. All authorities agree that one may study Torah silently while waiting for the *chazzan* to conclude *Pesukei D'Zimrah*.

A CLOSER LOOK AT THE SIDDUR

We recite the *Ashrei* prayer three times each day — twice in *Shacharis* and another time before *Minchah*. The main portion of אַשְׁרֵי is the entire Chapter 145 of *Tehillim*, which begins with the words תְּהִלָּה לְדָוִד, *A psalm of praise by David*, and it is by those words that the Gemara (*Berachos* 4b) identifies it: "R' Elazar said in R' Avina's name: 'One who says תְּהִלָּה לְדָוִד three times each day can be sure that he will merit a portion in the World to Come.'" The Gemara seeks to find the reason for such a blanket statement, and suggests that perhaps it is because the verses of this chapter are arranged in an alphabetical acrostic. It counters that if that is the reason, why not recite *Tehillim* Chapter 119, which has an eightfold alphabetical acrostic? The Gemara suggests further that perhaps תְּהִלָּה לְדָוִד is unique in that it contains the verse (v. 16): פּוֹתֵחַ אֶת־יָדֶךָ וּמַשְׂבִּיעַ לְכָל־חַי רָצוֹן, *You open Your hand, and satisfy the desire of every living thing*. The Gemara objects: One can instead recite *Tehillim* Chapter 136, which contains a similar sentiment (v. 25): נֹתֵן לֶחֶם לְכָל־בָּשָׂר כִּי לְעוֹלָם חַסְדּוֹ, *He gives nourishment to all flesh, for His kindness endures forever!* The Gemara concludes that the reason תְּהִלָּה לְדָוִד is special and that one who recites it thrice daily will merit a portion in the World to Come is because it possesses both these attributes — it is in alphabetical acrostic format and contains the verse פּוֹתֵחַ אֶת־יָדֶךָ, *You open Your hand*.

R' Shimon Schwab, continuing the thought we discussed in *A Mussar Thought for the Day*, asks the obvious questions: What does the alphabetical order of the psalm have to do with Hashem's making food available to all life, and why is the merit of underscoring this connection so great that through it one can obtain a portion in the World to Come?

He explains that *parnassah*, livelihood, has a dual nature. On the one hand, one's *parnassah* is totally dependent on Hashem's will. Hashem's methods for distributing wealth and sustenance are beyond our comprehension. One person is poor, while his friend is rich; one works many hours each day and still is short of money, while another has to put a minimum of effort into seeing to his livelihood. [R' Schwab suggests an illustration of his point, based on R' Samson Raphael Hirsch's translation of וּמַשְׂבִּיעַ לְכָל־חַי רָצוֹן, *and satisfies every living thing according to its grace*: if a pauper finds grace in the eyes of a philanthropist, he will receive more alms. Should merchandise find more grace in a buyer's eyes, it will command a higher price; and a job-seeker's salary is commensurate to the grace his employer finds in him. All these are examples of situations where one's livelihood is not dependent on any rational factor, but a metaphysical grace that Hashem either does or does not bestow upon a person.]

MONDAY
PARASHAS
KI SISA

On the other hand, we find that when one seeks sustenance, he must do so according to the laws of nature and common sense (see *Berachos* 35b). On this level, one's livelihood is very much a rational pursuit, both in the sense of the actual work and in keeping to the Torah's strictures regarding forbidden behaviors such as theft and usury. [Should one, for example, not keep proper books, one may soon find himself overcharging his clients.]

In sum, we find that in the matter of *parnassah* there is a dichotomy: The intellectual level — where one tries to subsist according to the natural course of events; and the super-intellectual level, the level of the soul — where one has to recognize that ultimately his or her livelihood is dependent on Hashem's will.

תְּהִלָּה לְדָוִד teaches both these lessons: It is composed along an alphabetical acrostic, denoting order and rationality, as we discussed earlier. It also contains the verse: פּוֹתֵחַ אֶת־יָדֶךָ וּמַשְׂבִּיעַ לְכָל־חַי רָצוֹן, *You open Your hand, and satisfy the desire of every living thing,* the recital of which indicates one's recognition that ultimately one's *parnassah* is in Hashem's hands. One who repeats תְּהִלָּה לְדָוִד three times daily, concludes R' Schwab, while recognizing that one's service of Hashem should encompass both points of view, certainly does deserve a portion in the World to Come.

פרשת כי תשא

A TORAH THOUGHT FOR THE DAY

TUESDAY
PARASHAS KI SISA

וְאַתָּה דַּבֵּר אֶל־בְּנֵי יִשְׂרָאֵל לֵאמֹר אַךְ אֶת־שַׁבְּתֹתַי תִּשְׁמֹרוּ כִּי אוֹת הִוא בֵּינִי וּבֵינֵיכֶם לְדֹרֹתֵיכֶם לָדַעַת כִּי אֲנִי ה׳ מְקַדִּשְׁכֶם

Now you, speak to the Children of Israel, saying, "However, you must observe My Sabbaths, for it is a sign between Me and you for your generations, to know that I am Hashem, *Who makes you holy" (Shemos 31:13).*

In this verse, Hashem instructs Moshe to teach the Jewish people the importance of Shabbos, and its significance as a sign between Him and His nation. The wording of the verse, though, is puzzling. Hashem tells Moshe to begin his lesson about the importance of Shabbos with the word אַךְ, *however,* implying that Shabbos is being contrasted with something else. What is this word supposed to teach us?

Rashi to the verse addresses this question, and bases his approach on a *Yerushalmi* (*Berachos* 9:5) that states that whenever the words אַךְ, *however,* or רַק, *only,* are used in the Torah, the implied intent is to exclude something. Here, says *Rashi,* the Torah means to exclude the work of the Mishkan, which is discussed in the previous section (31:1-11) of the *parashah. Rashi* explains: "Even though you should be diligent to complete the work, do not push Shabbos away because of it!" Thus, Shabbos supersedes even the holy work of building the Mishkan.

Ramban, however, argues with *Rashi's* explanation. According to *Rashi,* although one might think that the observance of Shabbos does not apply during the work of the Mishkan, the word אַךְ teaches that one must always observe Shabbos. This, says *Ramban,* indicates that *Rashi* is misapplying the *Yerushalmi's* rule. Whenever that rule is used, he says, it comes to exclude something from the subject the word אַךְ or רַק is written about. Here, the word אַךְ is written about Shabbos — it should be excluding some observance of Shabbos. But according to *Rashi's* understanding, אַךְ actually expands the scope of Shabbos observance, and constrains one's obligation of building the Mishkan.

Ramban therefore explains that the verse must be understood on two levels. At the basic level — the actual meaning of the words — the verse is a continuation of the previous section, saying what *Rashi* indicated: "Perform the work necessary for the building of the Mishkan, אַךְ, *however,* still always observe My Shabbos." This does not address the exegetical rule of the *Yerushalmi;* that, says *Ramban,* must be used for a different lesson — one that diminishes the obligation of Shabbos. As examples, he suggests that the word אַךְ might be excluding situations of *Bris Milah,* circumcision, which is permitted on Shabbos; alternatively, it could be referring to a situation of potential danger to human life, where the strictures of Shabbos do not apply. Indeed, *Yerushalmi* (*Yoma* 8:5) specifically designates this verse as the source for this latter rule.

[The commentaries struggle to defend *Rashi* from *Ramban's* attack. See, for example, *Mizrachi, Divrei David,* and *Tosfos Berachah.*]

Chasam Sofer (in *Toras Moshe*) observes that as *Ramban* understands it, we see from the proximity of this verse to the previous section that one *may not* violate Shabbos to build the Mishkan, yet we use the word אַךְ to teach us that one *may* violate the Shabbos to save a human's life. We see, then, that Shabbos is more important than building the Mishkan, but saving a life is even more important than Shabbos! This is, explains *Chasam Sofer,* an indication of the great holiness inherent in the Jewish soul, and demonstrates the strong love Hashem has for each and every one of His people. Indeed, this is what the verse means when it concludes: לָדַעַת כִּי אֲנִי ה' מְקַדִּשְׁכֶם, *to know that I am* HASHEM, *Who makes you holy.* A Jew's life is more important than Shabbos because, "I, Hashem, make you holy — and since My holiness is in you, you are more important than building the Mishkan, or even than Shabbos itself!"

MISHNAH OF THE DAY: BEITZAH 3:2

After clarifying in the previous Mishnah the issues involved in the trapping and feeding of fish, animals, and fowl, the coming Mishnah follows with a discussion of laws governing the use of animals on Yom Tov in cases in which the issue of trapping is not a concern. Our Mishnah considers the issue of *muktzeh*:
מְצוּדוֹת חַיָּה וְעוֹף וְדָגִים שֶׁעֲשָׂאָן מֵעֶרֶב יוֹם טוֹב — *Traps for animals, fowl, or fish that were set prior to Yom Tov,* and upon returning on Yom Tov, one found animals caught in these traps, לֹא יִטֹּל מֵהֶן בְּיוֹם טוֹב — *one may not take* the animals *from them on Yom Tov,*[1] אֶלָּא אִם כֵּן יוֹדֵעַ שֶׁנִּצּוֹדוּ מֵעֶרֶב יוֹם טוֹב — *unless he knows that they were* already

---- NOTES ----

1. If the animals had become trapped on Yom Tov they would be *muktzeh,* and it would be forbidden to eat or even move them. Although in this case it is questionable whether they became trapped on Yom Tov or prior to the onset of the Yom Tov, they are nonetheless forbidden (*Rav*).

TUESDAY
PARASHAS KI SISA

וּמַעֲשֶׂה בְנָכְרִי אֶחָד — *trapped on the eve of Yom Tov.*[2] שֶׁהֵבִיא דָגִים לְרַבָּן גַּמְלִיאֵל — *And there was an incident with a certain non-Jew who brought fish to Rabban Gamliel* on Yom Tov, and it was not known whether the fish had been caught prior to the onset of the Yom Tov. וְאָמַר מֻתָּרִין הֵן אֶלָּא שֶׁאֵין רְצוֹנִי לְקַבֵּל הֵימֶנּוּ — *And* Rabban Gamliel *said, "They are permitted* to be eaten, *but it is not my will to accept* them *from him."*[3]

─── NOTES ───

2. I.e., they are prohibited on account of *muktzeh. Ramban* explains that although *muktzeh* is a Rabbinic ordinance, and Rabbinic decrees normally do not apply in questionable circumstances (סְפֵיקָא דְרַבָּנָן לְקוּלָא), our Mishnah nevertheless prohibits the trapped animals on the basis of the principle (Gemara 4a) that דָּבָר שֶׁיֵּשׁ לוֹ מַתִּירִין, *an item that will be permissible* — e.g., an object prohibited because of the Sabbath, but which will become permissible after the Sabbath — remains prohibited even when the prohibition in question is in doubt, and even in cases in which only a Rabbinic prohibition is involved. Accordingly, since the prohibition of *muktzeh* will no longer apply after the Yom Tov, the animal is forbidden *on* the Yom Tov even where its *muktzeh* status is questionable (*Milchamos, Shabbos* 151a; cf. *Derush VeChiddush R' Akiva Eiger* 3b; *Tos. R' Akiva* here; see also *Tos. Yeshanim* 3b; *Meiri;* and *Raaviah* 3:763).

3. I.e., although the fish were not *muktzeh,* Rabban Gamliel nevertheless refused them because he was not on friendly terms with this non-Jew (*Rav; Rashi*). The Gemara (24a) explains that obviously there is a segment missing in the text of the Mishnah immediately preceding Rabban Gamliel's statement. It should have read: סָפֵק מוּכָן אָסוּר — *Objects of questionable preparation are prohibited* [as is evident from the words of the first Tanna], וְרַבָּן גַּמְלִיאֵל מַתִּיר — *but Rabban Gamliel permits* [*them*]. The incident is then cited to demonstrate Rabban Gamliel's position. Accordingly, Rabban Gamliel evidently offered his explanation for not taking the fish because he did not want his refusal of the present to be construed as an approval of the first Tanna's decision prohibiting questionable *muktzeh* (*Rav;* see *Gems from the Gemara* to this Mishnah).

GEMS FROM THE GEMARA

As we saw in our commentary to this Mishnah, the Gemara (24a) states that a segment is missing in the text of our Mishnah immediately preceding Rabban Gamliel's statement. It should have read: סָפֵק מוּכָן אָסוּר — *objects of questionable preparation are prohibited* [as is evident from the words of the first Tanna], וְרַבָּן גַּמְלִיאֵל מַתִּיר, *but Rabban Gamliel permits* [*them*]. According to this reading, Rabban Gamliel disagrees with the first Tanna and permits any *muktzeh* of questionable status.

On the other hand, the Gemara (24b) also tells us that Rabban Gamliel concedes that questionable *muktzeh* may not be eaten. He only permits it to be moved (טלטול מוקצה).

פרשת כי תשא
TUESDAY
PARASHAS KI SISA

In light of this Gemara, Rabban Gamliel's disagreement with the first Tanna must be clarified. If Rabban Gamliel agrees that eating the fish is prohibited, why does he disagree on the question of moving the fish?

As we also saw in our commentary to this Mishnah, *Ramban* states that the Tanna Kamma prohibits the fish on account of *muktzeh* — even though its *muktzeh* status is in doubt — on the basis of the principle of דָּבָר שֶׁיֵּשׁ לוֹ מַתִּירִין, *an item that will be permissible* at a later time. Accordingly, *Tzlach* (24b) and *Tos. R' Akiva Eiger* explain that this principle is applicable only to the issue of eating the item in question. They reason that since you can eat something only once, this principle mandates that this specific act be deferred to a time when no question of *muktzeh* exists. On the other hand, you can move an item repeatedly. As moving it another time is by definition an act that is distinct and separate from the act of moving the item that one had contemplated earlier, to defer such an act is not to delay it, but to lose one of the opportunities to move it altogether. Since the act of moving the item tomorrow is distinct and separate from the act of moving the item on Yom Tov, moving doubtful *muktzeh* on Yom Tov is not an act that will become permissible after Yom Tov when no question of *muktzeh* exists.

Following this logic, we have two possible explanations for Rabban Gamliel's disagreement with the first Tanna: (1) Rabban Gamliel accepts this fine distinction between eating and moving *muktzeh,* while the Tanna Kamma rejects it; (2) the first Tanna agrees with this distinction, but he argues that the de facto prohibition against eating the questionable *muktzeh* in itself renders the object *muktzeh* concerning moving. This latter possibility is in accordance with a rule formulated by *Rosh* and *Rif* (here) that anything that may not be eaten on a Yom Tov is automatically *muktzeh* in regard to moving it as well (*Tzlach; Rosh Yosef; Simchas Yom Tov*).

[The Gemara (24b) also applies the logic of this Mishnah to fruit that is brought by a non-Jew to a Jew on Yom Tov. As long as there is a possibility that it was picked on Yom Tov, in which case it would be *muktzeh,* the fruit is prohibited.]

QUESTION OF THE DAY:
What do we learn from the word לָכֶם, *"for you," in this verse?*
For the answer, see page 68.

פרשת
כי תשא

TUESDAY
PARASHAS
KI SISA

A MUSSAR THOUGHT FOR THE DAY

The Gemara (*Shabbos* 10b) makes a very interesting statement based on the verse we discussed in *A Torah Thought for the Day*. It says: "The Holy One, Blessed is He, said to Moshe, 'I have a good gift in my hidden vaults; it is called Shabbos. I wish to give it to Israel — go inform them.' " The Chofetz Chaim (*Kuntres Beis Yisrael* 2) explains this Gemara using a parable. We know, he says, that there are many different varieties of gemstones and jewels, some worth more than others. A moderately well-to-do individual can afford some, even though they are expensive. Others are more valuable, and only an affluent person can afford them. There are some jewels, though, that are so costly and rare that only aristocrats or the very richest of people can afford to acquire them, and even they are more than likely not to have a complete collection of all the types of the most valuable gems. It stands to reason that the most powerful ruler would have the most extensive and valuable hoard in his vaults.

Hashem, who is the King of kings, certainly has more numerous and more valuable treasures than any earthly king! And of them all, which is the one He calls "a good gift" and designates it with a special name — only Shabbos! There certainly is no limit, then, to the goodness and importance of Shabbos. Hashem gives this gift to His people through their observing the Shabbos, and accordingly, a person needs to long to observe Shabbos properly, so as to be able to take part in this wonderful gift.

After understanding this, says the Chofetz Chaim, we can comprehend how foolish are those people who — through their actions and speech — desecrate the Shabbos. They are destroying the portion they have in Hashem's most valuable treasure. Unfortunately, sometimes as a person becomes more tolerant of his own חִלּוּל שַׁבָּת, *desecration of Shabbos*, he does not refrain from desecrating it even in public. Such behavior severs a person's relationship with the Jewish nation, as one who desecrates Shabbos is denying the validity of the entire Torah (*Chullin* 5a, *Rashi*). Why is this so? Chofetz Chaim explains with another parable:

A craftsman will put a sign outside his place of business to indicate to all passersby the nature of his work. As long as the sign is up, one knows that the craftsman still works there — even if at the moment he happens not to be present. If the sign should be removed, though, one knows that the craftsman has moved on.

TUESDAY PARASHAS KI SISA

Shabbos is the sign that bears testimony that Hashem created the world in six days and rested on the seventh. It is also a sign for the Jew who keeps it that he or she believes that Hashem is the Master of all that exists, and that we are obligated to follow His will to the best of our capability. One's belief in Hashem engenders holiness in one's heart, so Shabbos — signifying belief in Hashem — is the cause for a Jew's holiness: כִּי אוֹת הִוא בֵּינִי וּבֵינֵיכֶם לְדֹרֹתֵיכֶם לָדַעַת כִּי אֲנִי ה׳ מְקַדִּשְׁכֶם, *for it is a sign between Me and you for your generations, to know that I am* Hashem, *Who makes you holy* (*Shemos* 31:13).

The "sign" that one is a Jew remains even when one sins. Just as one knows that the craftsman is still available, one knows that the Jew still remains true to Hashem. But if one's sin is desecration of Shabbos, then he or she has taken down the "sign" — demonstrating that the belief in Hashem and His sovereignty is no longer present in one's mind. That is why one who violates Shabbos is considered to have denied the validity of the entire Torah. If other sins might be compared to one's arm or leg, then a sinner is like an amputee. But Shabbos is like the heart — and one cannot live without a heart.

HALACHAH OF THE DAY

As we have learned, it is proper that one recite the words of *Pesukei D'Zimrah* with concentration and great care, as if he were counting money. In order to accomplish this, one should strive to arrive at the synagogue early enough to ensure that he will be able to recite his *tefillos* in an appropriate manner, while still being able to keep pace with the congregation. In this way, not only will he be able to recite the *Pesukei D'Zimrah* in a befitting manner, he will also be able to recite the *Shemoneh Esrei* together with the congregation.

If one arrived at the synagogue late, and the recital of the full *Pesukei D'Zimrah* will now preclude his reciting the *Shemoneh Esrei* together with the congregation, some authorities permit him to omit parts of *Pesukei D'Zimrah* in order to catch up to the congregation and fulfill the requirement of *tefillah b'tzibbur* (praying with the congregation). However, it should be noted that this is a remedy for one who unfortunately arrives late on an infrequent basis; it is not a formula that is to be relied upon regularly.

The formula that allows for omissions in *Pesukei D'Zimrah* may also be utilized in order to recite *Shema* and *Shemoneh Esrei* within the proper time frame specified for them by halachah.

TUESDAY

PARASHAS KI SISA

There are sections of *Pesukei D'Zimrah* that may not be skipped — even for the above given reasons. We will now discuss what may be omitted and what may not be omitted, and how one should prioritize his recitation of the various sections of *Pesukei D'Zimrah* in concert with the amount of time he has available for its recital.

As we have seen, *Pesukei D'Zimrah* is made up of an opening blessing, בָּרוּךְ שֶׁאָמַר, and a closing blessing, יִשְׁתַּבַּח, both of which surround the actual *Pesukei D'Zimrah* — verses of praise — themselves. This basic formula, established by the Sages, must be kept intact. Therefore, neither one of these blessings may be skipped at any time for any reason.

In regard to the various chapters of *Tehillim* and other verses of praise that make up the *Pesukei D'Zimrah,* the halachah divides them into groups, with higher priority given to some, and lesser priority to others. The most important section is the paragraph of אַשְׁרֵי. Just as the two blessings may never be skipped, אַשְׁרֵי likewise must always be recited. Thus we see that these three prayers — יִשְׁתַּבַּח, בָּרוּךְ שֶׁאָמַר, and אַשְׁרֵי — form the essence of the *Pesukei D'Zimrah.*

Tomorrow we will discuss how one should proceed if time allows him to recite additional portions of *Pesukei D'Zimrah.*

A CLOSER LOOK AT THE SIDDUR

The full text of the Shabbos morning *Kiddush,* known as קִדּוּשָׁא רַבָּא, *Kiddusha Rabba,* is composed of four parts. The first section consists of two verses from *Yeshayah* (58:13-14). It is followed by two verses in *Parashas Ki Sisa* (*Shemos* 31:16-17); these verses follow almost immediately after the verse we discussed in *A Torah Thought for the Day.* The third part of the *Kiddush* consists of four verses from the *Aseres HaDibros,* the Ten Commandments, in *Parashas Yisro* (*Shemos* 20:8-11). The fourth — and most important — part of the *Kiddush* is the *Borei Pri HaGafen* blessing, recited over the *Kiddush* wine or grape juice. [One who recites *Kiddush* over a different beverage substitutes *Shehakol Nihyeh Bidvaro;* see *Mishnah Berurah* 288:8-9.] There are various customs regarding which of these verses one recites and their order, before one says the *Borei Pri HaGafen,* with some beginning as late as the second half of the last verse (... עַל־כֵּן בֵּרַךְ ה׳, *therefore* HASHEM *blessed*), and others beginning from the verses in *Yeshayah* or *Shemos.* [It is noteworthy that the *Mishnah*

Berurah (288:2) frowns upon the practice of beginning from עַל־כֵּן, because of the Talmudic dictum (*Taanis* 27b): "We do not divide any verse not already divided by Moshe Rabbeinu."]

פרשת כי תשא
TUESDAY
PARASHAS KI SISA

Various interpretations are given by the commentators as to the reason why this *Kiddush* is called *Kiddusha Rabba*, literally, *the great Kiddush*, and the reason these particular verses were selected by the Sages to be included here. R' Moshe Cordovero (in his *Tefillah LeMoshe*) explains that the verses from *Yeshayah* are included because — aside from their obvious connection with Shabbos — they parallel the words זָכוֹר, *Remember* (*Shemos* 20:8), and שָׁמוֹר, *Safeguard* (*Devarim* 5:12), which, in the Ten Commandments, refer to Shabbos. The first verse stresses refraining from forbidden activity on Shabbos, paralleling שָׁמוֹר, *Safeguard,* which implies a negative commandment: "Do not desecrate Shabbos." The second verse stresses the positive actions one takes to honor Shabbos, paralleling זָכוֹר, *Remember.*

Shaar HaKollel explains both the reason why we call this *Kiddush* "great" as well as why we insert the verses from *Shemos*. He says: Anything that — through Hashem's great Name י-ה-ו-ה — keeps the world in existence is called "great." We usher the Shabbos in with the Friday evening *Kiddush,* but the Name י-ה-ו-ה does not appear in it. In the Shabbos morning *Kiddush,* though, we conclude עַל־כֵּן בֵּרַךְ ה' אֶת־יוֹם הַשַּׁבָּת וַיְקַדְּשֵׁהוּ, *therefore* Hashem *blessed the Sabbath day and sanctified it.* Since we mention Hashem's Name י-ה-ו-ה, we call the *Kiddush* "the Great *Kiddush,*" or קִדּוּשָׁא רַבָּא.

The reason there is a difference between Shabbos eve and Shabbos day is because the Jewish people have a hand in the beginning of Shabbos — they add on to it with *tosfos Shabbos,* beginning Shabbos a bit early, and to that end Hashem gives them an extra soul, a *neshamah yeseirah,* through which the holiness of Shabbos is channeled. But on Shabbos day, the holiness comes solely through Hashem. That is why we begin the daytime *Kiddush* with the verses from *Shemos* (31:16-17), which talk about the Jews' observance of Shabbos: וְשָׁמְרוּ בְנֵי־יִשְׂרָאֵל אֶת־הַשַּׁבָּת, *and the Children of Israel observed the Sabbath.* In these verses the holy Name י-ה-ו-ה is mentioned only in connection with Hashem's creating the world in six days.

We then continue with the verses from *Shemos* (20:8-11): זָכוֹר אֶת־יוֹם הַשַּׁבָּת לְקַדְּשׁוֹ, *Always remember the Sabbath day to hallow it . . .* These verses, too, speak of the obligation of the Jew in making Shabbos holy. It is only at the final words (v. 11) that we reach the *Kiddusha Rabba* aspect — that Hashem, through His great Name י-ה-ו-ה

TUESDAY
PARASHAS KI SISA

makes the Shabbos day holy — עַל־כֵּן בֵּרַךְ ה' אֶת־יוֹם הַשַּׁבָּת וַיְקַדְּשֵׁהוּ, *therefore* Hashem *blessed the Sabbath day and sanctified it.* [*Shaar HaKollel* concludes by explaining that it is because of this that the words עַל־כֵּן... are written in the *siddur* in a larger type size than the first half of the verse. He is referring to the *Siddur Nusach Ari,* but presumably one can extend this to many other *siddurim* that also print these words in a larger type.]

A TORAH THOUGHT FOR THE DAY

פרשת כי תשא

WEDNESDAY
PARASHAS KI SISA

וַיִּפֶן וַיֵּרֶד מֹשֶׁה מִן־הָהָר וּשְׁנֵי לֻחֹת הָעֵדֻת בְּיָדוֹ לֻחֹת כְּתֻבִים מִשְּׁנֵי עֶבְרֵיהֶם מִזֶּה וּמִזֶּה הֵם כְּתֻבִים. וְהַלֻּחֹת מַעֲשֵׂה אֱלֹהִים הֵמָּה וְהַמִּכְתָּב מִכְתַּב אֱלֹהִים הוּא חָרוּת עַל־הַלֻּחֹת

Moshe turned and descended from the mountain, with the two Tablets of the Testimony in his hand, Tablets inscribed on both their sides; they were inscribed on one side and on the other. The Tablets were God's handiwork, and the script was the script of God, engraved on the Tablets (Shemos 32:15-16).

The preceding verses tell of the Jews' sin against Hashem — while Moshe Rabbeinu was receiving the לֻחֹת הָעֵדֻת, *the Tablets of Testimony*, they fabricated the Golden Calf. When Hashem informed Moshe of this sacrilege and His intention of utterly destroying them, Moshe prayed, successfully, that He forgive His nation. Now, the verses tell of Moshe's subsequent action — he descended the mountain holding the Tablets of Testimony, the *Luchos*.

The commentators take note of the wording describing Moshe's descent: וַיִּפֶן וַיֵּרֶד מֹשֶׁה מִן־הָהָר, *Moshe turned and descended from the mountain*. As *Ohr HaChaim* asks, was it proper for Moshe to turn his back upon leaving Hashem's presence? And, as R' Yaakov Kamenetsky points out, it is clear from Moshe's retelling of the incident in *Devarim* (9:15) that Hashem's presence was still on the mountain!

Rabbeinu Chananel avoids this difficulty by explaining that the word וַיִּפֶן in this context does not mean *and he turned*, but comes from the same root as פָּנִים, *face*. In fact, the verse indicates that Moshe did not turn around, but he remained facing the presence of Hashem as he descended the mountain: *Moshe faced [Hashem's presence] and descended from the mountain*. [In an interesting aside, *Rabbeinu Chananel* explains that this is similar to the universal custom when completing one's *Shemoneh Esrei* prayers — one remains facing the direction toward which one prayed and steps back three steps. See *A Closer Look at the Siddur*.]

Ohr HaChaim is of the opinion that the word וַיִּפֶן does indicate turning, so to answer his question he suggests that the word is not referring to a physical act of wheeling around, but to Moshe's behavior with the people. When Moshe was beseeching Hashem not to destroy His nation, he was careful to minimize the sin, saying (32:11):

WEDNESDAY
PARASHAS KI SISA

לָמָה ה׳ יֶחֱרֶה אַפְּךָ בְּעַמֶּךָ, *Why, Hashem, should Your anger flare up against Your people?* Now, acting as their leader, Moshe changed his tone when he approached his charges (32:30): אַתֶּם חֲטָאתֶם חֲטָאָה גְדֹלָה, *You have committed a grievous sin!* The Torah is underscoring this change — this *turn* — in attitude.

Other commentators understand the word וַיִּפֶן literally — Moshe did turn his back on Hashem's presence. But why would he do so? Even a student, upon leaving his teacher, is enjoined from turning his back toward him (see *Yoma* 53a)! R' Naftali Tzvi Yehudah Berlin (the *Netziv*), in his *Haamek Davar*, suggests a novel interpretation: We see from earlier (19:14) that when Moshe Rabbeinu descended the mountain he did back away — otherwise the Torah would have told us there, also, that he turned. Why did he turn here? It must be, explains the *Netziv,* that although Moshe did not fear for his personal safety — perhaps he would trip on a rock or some other obstacle — when backing away from Hashem, that was only when he was the only one at risk. Now, he was holding the *Luchos,* and he was afraid that should he stumble as he backed away, they would — Heaven forbid — fall from his hands. That was justification enough for Moshe to turn, and face away from Hashem's Presence as he descended the mountain.

R' Kamenetsky answers this question differently. He suggests that Moshe Rabbeinu was actually fulfilling Hashem's command by turning! In Moshe's retelling of the episode of the Golden Calf (*Devarim* 9:12), he quotes Hashem as instructing him: קוּם רֵד מַהֵר מִזֶּה, *Arise, descend quickly from here.* It would be impossible for Moshe to *descend quickly* while backing away! That was why Moshe *turned and descended from the mountain,* instead of backing away as he normally would have done.

MISHNAH OF THE DAY: BEITZAH 3:4

The coming Mishnah considers the details of examining the blemish of a *bechor* and slaughtering it on a Yom Tov.

The Torah requires every בְּכוֹר, *firstborn* [to his mother] *male* of a kosher animal that is suitable to be brought as a sacrificial offering (viz., a cow, sheep, or goat), to be given to a Kohen (*Shemos* 13:12). It is then incumbent upon the Kohen to bring the animal to the Holy Temple, where it is slaughtered, and its specified portions offered on the Temple Altar. Only then may the Kohen eat the remaining meat of the animal (*Bamidbar* 18:17-18). However, a *bechor* that becomes

WEDNESDAY
PARASHAS KI SISA

blemished — i.e., afflicted with a permanent מוּם, *blemish* or *imperfection* — is disqualified from being offered upon the Altar (see *Devarim* 15:21-22). In such a case, the *bechor* may be slaughtered and eaten outside of the Temple. The blemish must be examined and certified by a מֻמְחֶה, *expert,* who is specifically ordained to judge these matters.

The laws of *bechor* apply even now, in the absence of the Temple, for even though a *bechor* cannot be brought to the Temple, it nevertheless possesses the sanctity of a sacrificial offering. Accordingly, any *bechor* that is born in the herd or flock of a Jew may not be slaughtered outside of the Temple unless certified as blemished by an expert.

רַבִּי יְהוּדָה — בְּכוֹר שֶׁנָּפַל לְבוֹר — *A firstborn* animal *that fell into a pit,*[1] אוֹמֵר יֵרֵד מֻמְחֶה וְיִרְאֶה — *R' Yehudah says: An expert should go down* into the pit *and see* the blemish. אִם יֶשׁ בּוֹ מוּם יַעֲלֶה וְיִשְׁחֹט — *If* the expert finds that *it has a* permanent *blemish, he may bring it up and slaughter* it;[2] וְאִם לָאו לֹא יִשְׁחֹט — *but if not,*[3] *he may not slaughter it.*[4] רַבִּי שִׁמְעוֹן אוֹמֵר כָּל שֶׁאֵין מוּמוֹ נִכָּר מִבְּעוֹד יוֹם אֵין זֶה מִן הַמּוּכָן

— NOTES —

1. When an animal falls into a pit, there is the possibility that it will suffocate and die there. The owner therefore wants to hoist the *bechor* out of the pit. This specific *bechor* is one concerning which it was known prior to the onset of the Yom Tov that it had a blemish, but that blemish had not yet been examined by an expert to determine whether it is permanent. Since the blemish has not yet been certified, the *bechor* is not currently suitable for slaughtering, and hence it may be *muktzeh.* Accordingly, to hoist it would violate the prohibition of moving *muktzeh* on a Yom Tov (*Rav* from Gemara 26a).

2. The expert must descend into the pit to examine the blemish. Once he determines that the blemish is permanent, it is clarified that the animal is suitable for slaughtering on Yom Tov and therefore not *muktzeh* (*Rav, Rashi;* see Gemara 26a).

3. I.e., if the expert did not determine that the blemish was permanent.

4. The Gemara (26a) asks why this clause of the Mishnah is necessary: If the blemish was not permanent, then surely it goes without saying that the animal remains a sacrificial offering and may not be slaughtered. The Gemara answers that the Mishnah here teaches us that even if the animal had developed a *different* permanent blemish, but had developed it subsequent to the onset of Yom Tov, it may not be slaughtered. For although the new blemish effectively removes the prohibition against slaughtering a *bechor* outside the Temple, one may still not slaughter it on Yom Tov because it was not anticipated before Yom Tov; the animal therefore remains *muktzeh.* Moreover, even if the blemish was present prior to the onset of the Yom Tov, but at that point was only a temporary blemish, becoming permanent only after Yom Tov began, it is also forbidden on account of *muktzeh* (*Rav*).

WEDNESDAY
PARASHAS KI SISA

R' Shimon says: In any case in which the blemish was not detected when it was yet day,[5] it is not considered to be from that which was prepared.[6]

---- NOTES ----

5. I.e., the day before, prior to the onset of the Yom Tov.

6. I.e., it was not prepared to be designated as a blemished animal, and therefore may not be hoisted up on Yom Tov. However, it is not on account of *muktzeh* that R' Shimon rules stringently (for this is one of the forms of *muktzeh* that R' Shimon rejects — see our prefatory remarks to Mishnah 1:1 above). Rather, R' Shimon's position is that passing judgment on the validity of a blemish is equivalent to adjudicating a lawsuit (דָּן אֶת הַדִּין), an activity that is prohibited on Yom Tov (see below, Mishnah 5:2). Therefore, even if the *bechor* was known to have had a blemish prior to the onset of a Yom Tov, and is therefore not *muktzeh*, it is still forbidden for the expert to examine it that day. Moreover, even if the expert goes ahead and examines the blemish on Yom Tov and certifies it to be permanent, his determination is considered null and void. Hence, this animal cannot possibly be eaten, and therefore it is forbidden to hoist it from the pit on Yom Tov (*Rav* from Gemara 26b).

GEMS FROM THE GEMARA

The Gemara (27a) cites an incident that is related to the dispute in our Mishnah: Ami from Vardena was the resident expert in the house of the *Nasi* (the leader of the Jewish community in the Land of Israel), who would examine any blemish that would occur in a *bechor*. Once, he refused to examine a *bechor*'s blemish on a Yom Tov. Some people who were evidently upset by this went and complained to R' Ami. R' Ami said to them: "He is acting properly in not examining blemishes on [Yom Tov]."

The Gemara asks: But did not R' Ami himself examine blemishes on Yom Tov!? Why did he praise Ami from Vardena for acting stringently?

The Gemara answers that R' Ami would examine the blemish on the previous day, prior to the onset of Yom Tov, to see if it was a permanent or temporary blemish, without issuing a verdict. Subsequently, on Yom Tov he would ask the *bechor*'s owner how the blemish occurred.

[R' Ami needed to determine how the blemish occurred, because the Gemara (*Bechoros* 35a) tells us that on account of the great bother and expense involved in caring for a *bechor* until it develops a blemish, a Kohen is suspected of having himself inflicted the blemish on the animal. (At a time when there is no Temple in which to offer the *bechor* as a sacrificial offering, the animal is put out to pasture, to graze until it

פרשת כי תשא

WEDNESDAY
PARASHAS KI SISA

develops a blemish.) A Kohen is therefore not believed if he reports that a blemish developed naturally, but is required to substantiate this claim with the testimony of a disinterested witness. If he cannot substantiate his claim, he is penalized in that the *bechor* is not permitted on the basis of this particular blemish. When R' Ami would be too busy prior to the onset of a Yom Tov to investigate the circumstances under which the blemish developed, he would just examine the *bechor* to determine if its blemish was permanent, as this determination could not be delayed until Yom Tov. R' Ami would then ask the owner to return on Yom Tov for the investigation of the circumstances under which the blemish developed. (This procedure did not require further examination of the animal.) Upon ascertaining that the Kohen did not inflict the blemish, R' Ami would pronounce the *bechor* blemished (*Rashi*). Since the main part of the judgment — the determination that the blemish is permanent — had been determined before Yom Tov, there is no prohibition against investigating the origin of the blemish on Yom Tov (*Meiri*).]

The Gemara (27b) then tells of another Amora who conducted himself in a similar manner — viz., an incident in which a Kohen brought a *bechor* before Rava in the afternoon of the day before Yom Tov, while Rava was sitting and scrubbing his head in preparation for Yom Tov. Rava lifted his eyes, examined the blemish, and told its owner, "Go now and return tomorrow [for a ruling]." When the owner came the next day, Rava asked, "How did this [blemish] occur?" The owner answered, "Barley was strewn on one side of a thorn fence and [the *bechor*] was on the other side. When it wanted to eat [the barley], it thrust its head [through the fence] and a thorn split its lip." [This is a permanent blemish that renders the animal unfit for sacrificial offering.] Rava asked him, "Perhaps you caused this?" [By deliberately placing the barley on the other side of the fence so that the *bechor* should injure itself in its attempt to reach it.] The owner answered Rava, "No!" [Presumably, he offered some proof to this effect (see *Rashi*). The Gemara goes on to derive from Scripture (*Vayikra* 22:21) the prohibition to deliberately cause a blemish to a *bechor*.]

QUESTION OF THE DAY:
Where else do we find that one must back away from holiness, as Moshe backed away from הַר סִינַי?
For the answer, see page 68.

פרשת כי תשא — A MUSSAR THOUGHT FOR THE DAY

WEDNESDAY
PARASHAS KI SISA

In *Avos* (6:2), R' Yehoshua ben Levi famously interprets one of the verses we quoted in *A Torah Thought for the Day*: וְהַלֻּחֹת מַעֲשֵׂה אֱלֹהִים הֵמָּה וְהַמִּכְתָּב מִכְתַּב אֱלֹהִים הוּא חָרוּת עַל הַלֻּחֹת, *The Tablets were God's handiwork, and the script was the script of God, engraved on the Tablets.* אַל תִּקְרָא חָרוּת אֶלָּא חֵרוּת שֶׁאֵין לְךָ בֶּן חוֹרִין אֶלָּא מִי שֶׁעוֹסֵק בְּתַלְמוּד תּוֹרָה, *Do not read "engraved"* (חָרוּת) *but "freedom"* (חֵרוּת), *for you can have no freer man than one who engages in the study of the Torah.*

At first glance, this statement is puzzling. If the Torah imposes restrictions on a person's choices, how can one who studies Torah be considered the freest of all men?

R' Yitzchak of Volozhin (in a comment on his father's *Nefesh HaChaim*, 4:32) explains by means of a parable. Suppose one should fall ill, and is instructed by his doctor exactly what means of medicine and behavior would effect his cure. Would he consider substituting the doctor's directions with his own ingredients and dosages? Certainly not! The doctor is an expert in both the disease and its cure; it would be the height of foolishness to disregard him.

The Gemara (*Kiddushin* 30b) relates that Hashem tells us, "My children! I created the *yetzer hara*, the Evil Inclination, and I created the Torah as the countermeasure — if you engage in Torah study, you will not be ensnared by it." This, explains R' Yitzchak of Volozhin, is what the Mishnah is teaching us: Hashem tells us: "Don't mistakenly think that you can figure out strategies of your own to be free of the *yetzer hara's* influence! I created it, and I, alone, know its weakness — and I have created the Torah to counteract the harm it is capable of!" One is truly free of the influence of the *yetzer hara* when one is immersed in Torah study; that is the only medicine appropriate for the disease.

R' Eliyahu Eliezer Dessler (*Michtav MeiEliyahu*, Vol. 1, pp. 116-117) approaches this Mishnah from a different perspective. He states: Philosophers call mankind's ability to make decisions בְּחִירָה חָפְשִׁית or "free will." But this term is not always applicable. True, one can exercise his free will in matters that present him with a choice — but often one really does not have the option to choose. At times, one's *yetzer hara* so strongly influences him that he really does not have the ability to deny it its wish — and has no choice but to sin. At other times, one's will to do good (his *yetzer tov*) has so influenced him that he has no choice — he has put himself under Hashem's dominion — and he must perform the mitzvah that is presenting itself.

פרשת
כי תשא

**WEDNESDAY
PARASHAS
KI SISA**

One can reach this latter state by instilling in himself a true fear of Heaven, *yiras Shamayim*. And when he does reach this level, he will realize that until that point he had not been free. Earlier he had mistakenly thought of himself as free, but how can one imagine he had freedom to choose when the choice was between good and evil? When he thought that he had that choice he was not truly free, but he did not recognize that until he reached the level of fearing Hashem.

In fact, a person's goal in life should be to abandon his free will. That is, one should strive to raise himself above the level where doing good and evil seem to be equal possibilities. Instead, one should be so aware of Hashem's existence that doing evil is not an option.

An even higher level, though, is for one to not only feel that he does not have the capability of doing evil, but to actually love doing good. At that level, one does not anymore feel an *obligation* to do good, because one cannot feel obligated to do something unless he feels opposition toward it. Since he loves doing Hashem's will, he feels no opposition to it, and does not feel obligated to do it — and that is the true freedom! This is what the Mishnah means, "You can have no freer man than one who engages in the study of the Torah." One who is engaged in Torah, that is, he loves it to the degree that he feels no opposition to fulfilling it — he is truly free.

HALACHAH OF THE DAY

We continue our discussion of one who has arrived at the synagogue late, and needs to omit sections of *Pesukei D'Zimrah* in order to ensure his ability to recite *Shemoneh Esrei* together with the *minyan* (or in order to ensure his recital of the *Shema* and *Shemoneh Esrei* in their proper times).

As we have learned, one must, at minimum, recite both בָּרוּךְ שֶׁאָמַר and יִשְׁתַּבַּח, with אַשְׁרֵי recited between them. In this way, the basic formula of *Pesukei D'Zimrah* — opening blessing, praise of Hashem, and closing blessing — has been preserved. If one has additional time available for the recitation of more praise, he should first try to ascertain how much time he has, and how much of the *Pesukei D'Zimrah* he feels he will be able to recite. In order of priority, first preference is given to the last of the paragraphs that begin with the word הַלְלוּיָהּ. If one has time to recite another paragraph, he should recite the third הַלְלוּיָהּ (reciting them in order, first the third and then the last). If one

WEDNESDAY
PARASHAS KI SISA

has even more time, he should attempt to recite all of the paragraphs that begin with הַלְלוּיָהּ, giving the rest of them priority based upon the order in which they appear in the *siddur*.

The next addition would be the series of verses beginning with וַיְבָרֶךְ דָּוִיד and ending with the words לְשֵׁם תִּפְאַרְתֶּךָ.

What to add next is dependent upon whether one is following the structure of *Nusach Ashkenaz* or *Nusach Sefard*. According to *Nusach Ashkenaz*, the compilation of verses that begins with הוֹדוּ is recited after בָּרוּךְ שֶׁאָמַר, and is therefore an integral part of *Pesukei D'Zimrah*. Thus, one who follows *Nusach Ashkenaz* would, if time allows, next give priority to the series of verses beginning with הוֹדוּ and ending with the verse of וְהוּא רַחוּם located in the middle of הוֹדוּ.

According to those who follow *Nusach Sefard*, הוֹדוּ is recited before the blessing of בָּרוּךְ שֶׁאָמַר, and it is therefore not seen as being an essential part of *Pesukei D'Zimrah*; therefore, everything that comes after the blessing is given priority over it.

The rest of the *Pesukei D'Zimrah*, i.e., all of the paragraphs and verses not mentioned in the above list, should be prioritized in order of their appearance in the *siddur*.

[Please note: When following the above guidelines, one should first ascertain how much time he will have and then, using the above instructions, choose the paragraphs and verses he feels he will have time to recite and then *recite them in order*. One should not, however, first recite a higher priority paragraph, and then, seeing that he has more time, add another paragraph out of order.]

A CLOSER LOOK AT THE SIDDUR

In *A Torah Thought for the Day* we quoted *Rabbeinu Chananel*, who said that Moshe's backing away from Hashem was akin to our custom of stepping back after the *Shemoneh Esrei*. The source for our practice is the Gemara (*Yoma* 53b) that says that after one recites the *Shemoneh Esrei*, he should take three steps back and then take leave of Hashem (עֹשֶׂה שָׁלוֹם...). The Gemara concludes, "If one did not do this, it would have been better had he not prayed." Although this seems like a harsh statement, *Levush* explains that it is perfectly logical: Should a servant leave his master's presence without permission, he shows that he does not respect his master. After this display of disrespect, the master will surely not trouble himself to grant his servant's wishes! Likewise, if someone does not display the proper reverence upon leaving Hashem's presence, he might as well not have prayed — because Hashem will not listen to his prayers.

פרשת כי תשא
WEDNESDAY
PARASHAS KI SISA

What do the three steps parallel? A number of suggestions are offered by the halachic authorities. *Beis Yosef* (*Orach Chaim* 123) quotes the *Orchos Chaim* who says that the three steps parallel the three *milin* (a unit of measure — a bit more than half a mile) that the Jewish people retreated from Mount Sinai at the giving of the Torah. [Other sources, such as *Rashi* to *Shemos* 20:14 and Gemara *Shabbos* 88b, give the measurement as twelve *milin*, obviously negating this as a source for the custom. It is possible, though, that the text of the *Orchos Chaim* should read, "The three *parsaos* that the Jewish people retreated from Mount Sinai at the giving of the Torah." Three *parsaos* are exactly equal to twelve *milin*, and would reconcile both the custom and the other texts.] Another reason (also cited in *Orchos Chaim*) is that Moshe Rabbeinu encountered three different levels of separation when he ascended Mount Sinai: חֹשֶׁךְ עָנָן וַעֲרָפֶל, *darkness, cloud, and thick cloud* (*Devarim* 4:11). When he descended the mountain he left through these three levels, and we take three steps backward paralleling that.

Beis Yosef also quotes from *Shibbolei HaLeket*, who suggests a different reason for stepping back: since one was standing in the presence of the *Shechinah*, Hashem's manifestation of His Presence on earth, when one is finished praying one must physically remove himself from this holy place. According to this reason, the three steps do not necessarily parallel something; rather, they are the amount the Sages felt were appropriate to be considered as having left Hashem's Presence.

Rabbeinu Manoach (also quoted by *Beis Yosef*) explains that the three steps correspond to the verse (*Yechezkel* 1:7): וְרַגְלֵיהֶם רֶגֶל יְשָׁרָה, *their legs were a straight leg*, describing the attributes of the angelic *Chayos*. רַגְלֵיהֶם — the plural of leg — parallels two steps, and the word רֶגֶל teaches us of the third. Others, also quoted by *Rabbeinu Manoach*, read further in the verse: וְכַף רַגְלֵיהֶם כְּכַף רֶגֶל עֵגֶל, *and the sole of their feet was like the sole of a rounded foot*. This supplies us with the source for three more steps, for a total of six steps. This is still consistent with the Gemara, because they interpret the Gemara as requiring that one move both legs once to count as one step. Thus, six leg movements equal the three steps of the Gemara. [This custom is still practiced by some.]

Magen Avraham (*Orach Chaim* 123:1) presents another reason. The *Zohar* (Volume 1, p. 202a) recounts how Nebuchadnezzar merited to

WEDNESDAY

PARASHAS KI SISA

destroy the *Beis HaMikdash* — by virtue of the three steps he took to retrieve a letter that was addressed: "Peace to Chizkiyahu, king of Yehudah, peace to the great God, and peace to Jerusalem!" He substituted a letter placing Hashem's Name first: "Peace to the great God, peace to Jerusalem, and peace to Chizkiyahu!"

We try to counteract Nebuchadnezzar's merit by taking three steps back, and then immediately praying that the *Beis HaMikdash* be rebuilt: שֶׁיִּבָּנֶה בֵּית הַמִּקְדָּשׁ בִּמְהֵרָה בְיָמֵינוּ, *that the Holy Temple be rebuilt, speedily in our days!*

A TORAH THOUGHT FOR THE DAY

פרשת כי תשא

THURSDAY
PARASHAS KI SISA

וַיֹּאמַר הַרְאֵנִי נָא אֶת־כְּבֹדֶךָ. וַיֹּאמֶר אֲנִי אַעֲבִיר כָּל־טוּבִי עַל־פָּנֶיךָ וְקָרָאתִי בְשֵׁם ה' לְפָנֶיךָ וְחַנֹּתִי אֶת־אֲשֶׁר אָחֹן וְרִחַמְתִּי אֶת־אֲשֶׁר אֲרַחֵם. וַיֹּאמֶר לֹא תוּכַל לִרְאֹת אֶת־פָּנָי כִּי לֹא יִרְאַנִי הָאָדָם וָחָי.

He said, "Show me now Your glory." He said, "I shall make all My goodness pass before you, and I shall call out with the Name HASHEM before you; I shall show favor when I choose to show favor, and I shall show mercy when I choose to show mercy." He said, "You will not be able to see My face, for no human can see Me and live" (Shemos 33:18-20).

After Moshe Rabbeinu beseeched Hashem for forty days to forgive the Jewish people, Hashem instructed him (34:1): פְּסָל־לְךָ שְׁנֵי־לֻחֹת אֲבָנִים כָּרִאשֹׁנִים וְכָתַבְתִּי עַל־הַלֻּחֹת אֶת הַדְּבָרִים אֲשֶׁר הָיוּ עַל־הַלֻּחֹת הָרִאשֹׁנִים, *Carve for yourself two stone Tablets like the first ones, and I shall inscribe on the Tablets the words that were on the first Tablets.* Thus, the Bnei Yisrael would once again be privileged with receiving Tablets similar to those that had been broken, as well as the Torah that the Tablets had contained. At this time of exceptional closeness with Hashem, Moshe made another request (33:18): הַרְאֵנִי נָא אֶת־כְּבֹדֶךָ, *Show me now Your glory.*

The *Malbim* offers insight into Moshe's petition. The final Mishnah in *Pirkei Avos* tells us: כָּל מַה שֶּׁבָּרָא הַקָּדוֹשׁ בָּרוּךְ הוּא בְּעוֹלָמוֹ לֹא בְרָאוֹ אֶלָּא לִכְבוֹדוֹ, *All that the Holy One, Blessed is He, created in His world, He created solely for His glory.* Thus, the aim and goal of the entire world is only to reveal Hashem's glory. When Moshe asked that he be shown Hashem's *glory,* he was in fact asking that he be able to fully understand the intricate manner in which Hashem manages the world, and how the myriads of creations come together to achieve Hashem's will.

Appreciating Hashem's glory through His creations may be achieved in a number of ways. On a basic level, man may examine each individual creation and use its inherent beauty, as well as the flawless perfection in which its different parts are meticulously arranged, as a means of recognizing the glory and greatness of its Creator. There is a deeper manner as well in which Hashem's creations may be used to better appreciate Him. When we examine the world that surrounds us and remember that it is Hashem Who is managing every facet, we may use that which we see and the events that occur to better understand

THURSDAY
PARASHAS KI SISA

Hashem's *middos*, the qualities that He displays of Himself. For example, seeing that every single living being in the world finds precisely the type of food that it needs to survive allows us to grasp that Hashem is the ultimate Sustainer. Furthermore, this continuous flow of sustenance also reveals that Hashem is the "Master of *chesed*," for much of this bounty is freely provided.

Another way in which man may use the world to better comprehend Hashem is by seeing how He uses the entirety of creation to achieve His plans. A person who studies world history carefully will find evidence of Hashem's great wisdom, for he will begin to perceive how Hashem mysteriously lays foundations many, many years in advance, in preparation for events that will not take place for quite some time. [A remarkable example of this idea was evident in the opening months of the Second World War, when the lives of many Jews in Eastern Europe were miraculously saved by the Soviet Union's declaration in 1939 that they would soon return the city of Vilna from recently conquered Poland to Lithuania. This announcement allowed masses of Jews to flock there during the weeks and days before this transfer, without the need for documents and permission to actively cross the normally sealed border. In recounting this miracle, the Mirrer *Mashgiach*, R' Yechezkel Levenstein, exclaimed that it is clear that Hashem had prepared this salvation twenty-one years earlier, when, in 1918, He arranged that Lithuania be granted her independence. However, the purpose of this new state did not become clear to man for another two decades, when Lithuania proved to be a temporary haven for thousands of refugees fleeing from Russian and German persecution, allowing them several months of time in which many were able to plan their next step, and eventually reach permanent safety.] Through each perspective that a person uses to recognize Hashem's involvement in the world, the *glory* of His open goodness becomes clearer and clearer.

Malbim explains that when entreating Hashem to show him His glory, Moshe was in fact making a threefold request. First, he asked to be shown the hidden Kabbalistic realities of Hashem's essence, as it were. Second, he requested to be allowed to understand the principles that govern how this hidden essence of spirituality interacts with the world. Third, Moshe asked to be allowed to understand *how* Hashem's plans to actualize these principles are realized, by being shown how the fullness of creation and the wide array of events that Hashem arranges all work together to bring His glory to fruition.

Malbim explains how Hashem answered each of Moshe's requests.

**THURSDAY
PARASHAS
KI SISA**

The first one, to fully understand the totality of Hashem's essence, was refused, for Hashem told him (33:20): לֹא יִרְאַנִי הָאָדָם וָחָי, *no human can see Me and live.* However, Hashem promised (v. 19): אֲנִי אַעֲבִיר כָּל־טוּבִי עַל־פָּנֶיךָ, *I shall make all My goodness pass before you.* All My goodness, explains *Malbim,* is a euphemism for all of creation, which came into existence only in order to provide Hashem with a forum for fulfilling His desire to provide *good* for others. Thus, in this statement, Hashem agreed to show Moshe — or *pass before him* — all the areas and events of creation so he would see how they work together in seamless fulfillment of the goals that Hashem intends to achieve.

Moshe's final request was that beyond seeing how each item in creation is used in actualization and fulfillment of Hashem's will, he also be told the principles that Hashem uses to guide and govern these many happenings. Hashem, in telling him (v. 18): וְקָרָאתִי בְשֵׁם ה' לְפָנֶיךָ, *I shall call out with the Name* HASHEM *before you,* agreed to fulfill this request. Hashem told Moshe: I shall explain to you My Name — or Attribute — of HASHEM, which denotes an outlook based on the quality of constant and everlasting kindness and mercy.

The specific principles of this Attribute — or the explanation of this overarching quality of Divine mercy and kindness in greater detail — were taught to Moshe in the following chapter, where the י״ג מִדּוֹת הָרַחֲמִים, *Thirteen Attributes of Mercy,* are detailed. For example, one aspect of the mercy and kindness with which Hashem interacts with the world is that He is רַחוּם, *Compassionate,* which, explains *Sforno,* means that even during times of punishment, He will lighten the blow that must be meted out if He is appealed to in prayer. Another is אֶרֶךְ אַפַּיִם, *Slow to Anger;* Hashem will delay punishment in order to allow the person to return to Him in *teshuvah.* In total, Hashem revealed to Moshe the thirteen different principles of kindness and mercy that provide the blueprint for His intricate management of the world.

We shall discuss these Attributes in greater detail in *A Mussar Thought for the Day.*

QUESTION OF THE DAY:

What great kindness was Hashem promising with the words: וְחַנֹּתִי אֶת־אֲשֶׁר אָחֹן, *"I shall show favor when I choose to show favor"?*

For the answer, see page 68.

פרשת כי תשא

THURSDAY

PARASHAS KI SISA

MISHNAH OF THE DAY: BEITZAH 3:5

The coming Mishnah continues the previous Mishnah's consideration of the status of a consecrated animal on Yom Tov:

בְּהֵמָה שֶׁמֵּתָה לֹא יְזִיזֶנָּה מִמְּקוֹמָהּ — *A* consecrated *animal that died, one may not move it from its place* on Yom Tov.[1] וּמַעֲשֶׂה וְשָׁאֲלוּ אֶת רַבִּי טַרְפוֹן עָלֶיהָ וְעַל הַחַלָּה שֶׁנִּטְמְאָה — *And there was* once *an incident, and they asked R' Tarfon about this matter and about challah that had been rendered tamei.*[2] וְנִכְנַס לְבֵית הַמִּדְרָשׁ וְשָׁאַל וְאָמְרוּ לוֹ לֹא יְזִיזֵם מִמְּקוֹמָם — *And he entered the house of study and asked. And [the Rabbis]* that were there *said to him: "He may not move them,"* i.e., the dead animal and the *challah* that became *tamei, from their places."*[3]

---NOTES---

1. From the juxtaposition of this case and the case in the latter part of the Mishnah — viz., that of *challah* — the Gemara (27b) infers that just as *challah* is consecrated dough, so too the animal in this case is one that has been consecrated — viz., as a sacrificial offering. When an animal that has been consecrated as a sacrificial offering dies, it is considered totally useless, for it cannot be redeemed. [The option of redemption (פִּדְיוֹן), whereby the carcass will be rendered *chullin* (non-sacred) and fit for use as feed has no validity here, because (1) a consecrated animal can be redeemed only while it is alive; (2) one may not redeem sacred items if the only use for these items will be as animal food (אֵין פּוֹדִין אֶת הַקֳּדָשִׁים לְהַאֲכִילָן לִכְלָבִים); and (3) redeeming sacred items is regarded as a business transaction and is forbidden on Yom Tov (*Rashi* 27b).] It is forbidden to derive any benefit from an unredeemed consecrated item; it cannot even be fed to dogs. Therefore, the carcass may not be moved, for like any item that has no use (e.g., sticks and stones), it is considered *muktzeh* (*Rav*).

2. *Challah* is a portion that must be separated from the dough and given to a Kohen (*Bamidbar* 15:17-21; see above, Mishnah 1:6). *Challah* is subject to the same laws as *terumah,* the portion of the unprocessed grain that is also given to the Kohen (*Challah* 1:9). Accordingly, a non-Kohen may not eat *challah.* Once the *challah* becomes *tamei,* it may not be eaten at all, and must be burned. In itself, this law would not render *challah* that is *tamei* useless, as it can be burned in a manner in which it serves as fuel for illumination or for cooking, etc. However, it is nevertheless considered *muktzeh,* for the law also states: אֵין שׂוֹרְפִין קָדָשִׁים בְּיוֹם טוֹב, *one may not burn consecrated items* (such as *terumah* or *challah,* even once they have become *tamei*) *on Yom Tov.* Accordingly, on a Yom Tov, *challah* that has become *tamei* is useless (*Rav; Rashi*).

3. R' Tarfon was unsure of the law, because he thought that perhaps these two items may be moved because of the reverence due to them as consecrated items, even after they have died or become *tamei;* leaving the dead sacrificial animal or the *challah* that has become *tamei* in an open area might be considered a desecration of consecrated items. The Rabbis rejected this consideration, and ruled that these items are *muktzeh* (*Tos. Yeshanim*).

GEMS FROM THE GEMARA

פרשת
כי תשא

**THURSDAY
PARASHAS
KI SISA**

After inferring that our Mishnah refers exclusively to a consecrated animal that died, the Gemara (27b) observes that if it is specifically on account of this animal having been consecrated as a sacrificial offering that when it died on Yom Tov it is *muktzeh,* we may infer that if it were an *ordinary,* non-sacred animal that died on Yom Tov, it would be permitted (see *Rav*).

The Gemara therefore asks: This is fine according to Mar the son of Rav Yosef in the name of Rava, who says that R' Shimon disagreed with R' Yehudah even in regard to healthy animals that died on the Sabbath or Yom Tov, holding that they are permitted; according to him, our explanation of the Mishnah works out well. [I.e., according to this view, we can say that our Mishnah, which implies that an ordinary animal that dies is not *muktzeh,* follows R' Shimon, who rules leniently in the laws of *muktzeh* (*Rashi*).] But according to Mar bar Ameimar in the name of Rava, who said that R' Shimon concedes that healthy animals that died on the Sabbath or Yom Tov are prohibited, to whom can the ruling of our Mishnah be attributed? Our Mishnah implies that non-consecrated animals are not *muktzeh*! This follows neither the opinion of R' Shimon nor that of R' Yehudah!?

The Gemara answers that the case we are discussing in our Mishnah is a case of an animal that was dangerously ill when Yom Tov began. The Mishnah therefore conforms to all views of R' Shimon's opinion. [I.e., both Mar bar Ameimar and Mar the son of Rav Yosef agree that R' Shimon permits the use of the carcass of an animal that was near death at the onset of Yom Tov and subsequently died on Yom Tov. It is only because the dying animal is consecrated that the Mishnah deems its carcass to be *muktzeh* (*Rashi*). R' Yehudah, on the other hand, considers the carcass *muktzeh* even if the non-consecrated animal was close to death at the onset of the Sabbath. Since the Mishnah cannot possibly accord with R' Yehudah's opinion, we are compelled to explain that the Gemara's statement, "and [it] conforms to all views" — a phrasing that normally implies universal agreement — refers here narrowly to both Mar bar Ameimar and Mar the son of Rav Yosef, who had differing explanations of R' Shimon's view (*Chidushei HaMeiri;* cf. *Ran, Maharam*).]

This is the second and final approach presented by the Gemara. The conflicting opinion maintains that according to R' Shimon, whose rulings regarding *muktzeh* tend to be lenient (in comparison with those of R' Yehudah), even the carcass of an animal whose death was not

THURSDAY

PARASHAS KI SISA

anticipated is not *muktzeh*. Consequently, the Mishnah need not (in this view) refer exclusively to a deathly sick animal, for it may represent R' Shimon's view (according to R' Yehudah such a carcass is surely *muktzeh*). Furthermore, there is debate among the *Rishonim* (see *Rif* with *Ran*; *Rambam, Hil. Yom Tov* 2:16 and 1:17; *HaMaor, Rashba,* and *Meiri*) whether R' Yehudah would consider the carcass of an animal deathly ill prior to Yom Tov *muktzeh*. If he does not consider it *muktzeh,* the statement of the Mishnah can even be interpreted to agree with R' Yehudah's view. (For a discussion of the law on these points, see *Shulchan Aruch, Orach Chaim* 518:6; *Mishnah Berurah* and *Beur Halachah* ad loc.)

A MUSSAR THOUGHT FOR THE DAY

We continue from *A Torah Thought for the Day,* where we learned that Hashem taught the י״ג מִדּוֹת הָרַחֲמִים, *Thirteen Attributes of Mercy,* to Moshe in fulfillment of his request that he understand the principles that Hashem employs in His guidance and management of the world. However, beyond simply allowing Moshe the unbelievable opportunity to better understand Hashem and His deeds, the Gemara tells us that Hashem's explanation of these principles allowed Moshe another gift as well. When promising (33:19): וְקָרָאתִי בְשֵׁם ה׳ לְפָנֶיךָ, *I shall call out with the Name HASHEM before you,* Hashem also stated: וְחַנֹּתִי אֶת־אֲשֶׁר אָחֹן וְרִחַמְתִּי אֶת־אֲשֶׁר אֲרַחֵם, *I shall show favor when I choose to show favor, and I shall show mercy when I choose to show mercy. Malbim* explains that Hashem was telling Moshe that when these Attributes — which openly highlight Hashem's qualities of kindness — are invoked by man, the result will be an occasion of Divine *favor* and *mercy*.

The Gemara in Rosh Hashanah (17b) discusses the role that the Thirteen Attributes play in achieving Divine favor. When teaching the Attributes to Moshe, Hashem, as it were, appeared to him as a *shliach tzibbur,* or *chazzan,* enwrapped in a *tallis,* and demonstrated how these hallowed words — which speak of the very principles of Hashem's guidance of the world — may be used as a prayer formula in times of trouble. If the Jews will sin and deserve to be punished, Hashem told Moshe, let them perform this procedure before Me, and I will forgive them, as I have forgiven them at this time for the sin of the Golden Calf. [We will discuss the use of the Attributes in prayer in *A Closer Look at the Siddur.*]

Some commentaries, such as the *Alshich* and *Sefer HaChaim* (4:8),

THURSDAY
PARASHAS KI SISA

explain that when the Gemara states that all that Jews must do is invoke the Attributes before Hashem and they are assured of forgiveness, this does not mean that all they must do to win forgiveness is to simply utter these words. Indeed, these authorities comment, we have sadly heard of many congregations that have recited these words of prayer many, many times, and nevertheless suffered harsh decrees and punishments. Rather, a more precise reading of the Gemara shows that Hashem's promise to Moshe was not *Say* this procedure before Me and I shall forgive them, but *Perform* this procedure before Me and I shall forgive them. The way in which this procedure works, explains these authorities, is by our emulating Hashem's aspects of mercy that these Torah verses describe. [This approach does not mean that the Attributes are not to be included in *tefillah*. Rather, the purpose of their recitation is to serve as an inspiration for us to include these principles in our lives.] *Alshich* points out that the ability to avert a harsh decree by internalizing these Attributes is a great Divine benefit as well; the gift of the Attributes is that by simply emulating Hashem's qualities of mercy and kindness when dealing with other people, it is possible to avert great amounts of painful punishment.

Explaining how man can emulate Hashem's Attributes of Mercy is the focus of the opening chapter of the work *Tomer Devorah*. In this *sefer*, R' Moshe Cordovero elucidates how each of these Thirteen Attributes are expanded on by the prophet Michah (*Michah* 7:18-20), and how man may internalize each of these qualities of Hashem.

Let us study one example of *Tomer Devorah's* theme. One of the Attributes is אֶרֶךְ אַפַּיִם, *Slow to Anger;* as we learned in *A Torah Thought for the Day,* Hashem will delay punishment in order to allow a sinner to return to Him in *teshuvah*. In the Attributes as said by Michah, this quality is termed לִשְׁאֵרִית נַחֲלָתוֹ, (*Who pardons iniquity and overlooks transgression*) *for the remnant of His heritage.* Alternatively, לִשְׁאֵרִית נַחֲלָתוֹ may be understood as *the heritage who are His close kin.* This is how the *Tomer Devorah* understands the phrase. He explains that the reason Hashem is *Slow to Anger* in His relationship with the Jewish people is because He views us as His own, His heritage, who are inherently bound to Him. It is for this reason that Hashem is Slow to Anger and always prepared to accept those who return to Him in repentance. *Tomer Devorah* tells us that Hashem, as it were, says: How am I to punish the Jewish people? Our relationship is likened to that of a close relative; any punishment that I administer to them will, as it were, impact on Myself as well.

The way in which man may emulate this Attribute is by realizing that

THURSDAY
PARASHAS KI SISA

just as the entire Jewish people are tightly bound with Hashem, so too, we are also all inherently connected with each other. We must realize that the entire Jewish people are spiritually related, for we all share one *neshamah* (soul). With this outlook, it becomes immeasurably easier to provide each other assistance, for just as one brother will automatically help another because his brother's pain truly becomes his *own,* we will realize that in helping — or being more patient — in the manner of *Slow to Anger* when dealing with our fellow Jew, we are in fact assisting ourselves.

HALACHAH OF THE DAY

Yesterday, we discussed how one should prioritize the various chapters and verses of praise that make up the *Pesukei D'Zimrah,* in terms of what to recite and what to omit when there is not enough time available for the full recitation.

On Shabbos and Yom Tov, there are additional verses of praise that are added to the daily *Pesukei D'Zimrah*. Of these, the chapter of נִשְׁמַת has the same status as אַשְׁרֵי; it may not be omitted for any reason. Thus, on Shabbos and Yom Tov the *Pesukei D'Zimrah* has four required components: בָּרוּךְ שֶׁאָמַר, אַשְׁרֵי, נִשְׁמַת, and יִשְׁתַּבַּח. One who has time for the recitation of more than these chapters should first follow the guidelines given yesterday for the regular weekday *tefillos*. [These take precedence over any additions for Shabbos or Yom Tov.] If he has still more time and is able to recite at least some of the additional praises, one who follows *Nusach Ashkenaz* should add as many paragraphs as possible assigning priority based upon appearance in the *Siddur*. One who follows *Nusach Sefard* should grant priority first to the paragraph of לַמְנַצֵּחַ (Psalm 19), then the paragraph of לְדָוִד (Psalm 34), followed by the paragraph beginning רַנְּנוּ (Psalm 33), and then the rest of the Shabbos/Yom Tov additions in order of their appearance in the *siddur*.

One who did omit parts of *Pesukei D'Zimrah* for lack of time should, if possible, recite them after the conclusion of the prayers.

As we have noted previously, once one has recited בָּרוּךְ שֶׁאָמַר, he is not permitted to talk until after the conclusion of the *Tachanun* portion of the services (according to some, this prohibition extends until the end of the services). However, one is permitted to utter certain responses and blessings during this time. The particular prayers or blessings to which one may respond differ, depending upon which section of the prayers one is currently reciting.

Once one has uttered the words בָּרוּךְ אַתָּה ה׳ of the final part of either the blessing of בָּרוּךְ שֶׁאָמַר or יִשְׁתַּבַּח, he may not utter any responses or prayers at all until the end of the blessing. Upon the conclusion of the בָּרוּךְ שֶׁאָמַר blessing, one must immediately begin the *Pesukei D'Zimrah*. Thus, no interruptions may be made between בָּרוּךְ שֶׁאָמַר and הוֹדוּ (in *Nusach Ashkenaz*) and between בָּרוּךְ שֶׁאָמַר and מִזְמוֹר לְתוֹדָה (in *Nusach Sefard*). [As we noted previously, however, one may answer אָמֵן to another's recital of בָּרוּךְ שֶׁאָמַר.]

THURSDAY
PARASHAS
KI SISA

Tomorrow we will discuss responses that remain permitted even in the midst of *Pesukei D'Zimrah* itself.

A CLOSER LOOK AT THE SIDDUR

We learned in *A Mussar Thought for the Day* that the Gemara in *Rosh Hashanah* (17b) tells us that when teaching the Thirteen Attributes of Mercy to Moshe, Hashem, as it were, appeared to him as a *shliach tzibbur*, or *chazzan*, enwrapped in a *tallis*, and taught him these principles that He employs in His management of the world. If the Jews are to sin, Hashem told Moshe, let them perform this procedure of the Thirteen Attributes before Me, and I will forgive them. It is for this reason that these Attributes are a central theme of the *Selichos* prayers that are recited from before Rosh Hashanah until Yom Kippur, as well as on public fast days. Additionally, people who pray according to *Nusach Sefard* include the Attributes as part of the daily *Shacharis* and *Minchah* prayers, by saying them prior to the recitation of *Tachanun*.

Remarkably, the Gemara tells us that if the Torah would not have told us of Hashem's revealing the Thirteen Attributes to Moshe and instructing him to use them in *tefillah*, we would not have been able to fathom that this episode indeed occurred. The commentaries offer several approaches as to specifically which aspect of this episode we would never have been able to envision if not for the Torah's clear statement that it took place. *Ritva* understands that this statement is referring to Hashem's revealing Himself to Moshe in the guise of a *shliach tzibbur*. [The Torah states (34:6): וַיַּעֲבֹר ה׳ עַל־פָּנָיו, Hashem **passed** before Him, which is related to the term used to describe a prayer leader: הָעוֹבֵר לִפְנֵי הַתֵּיבָה, (literally) *one who **passes** before the ark*. From the similarity of these words we learn that Hashem appeared this way when teaching the Attributes to Moshe.]

Teshuvos HaRashbash (*Siman* 191) [see also *Teshuvos HaRashba*

THURSDAY
PARASHAS KI SISA

(1:211)], however, understands differently; the aspect of this episode that we never would have thought possible had the Torah not have clearly told us is the very recitation of the Attributes themselves. We might have thought that these words, since they are the very principles that allow man to understand Hashem in the clearest way, are not permissible for man to say (just as it is forbidden to utter certain Names of Hashem). Accordingly, concludes *Teshuvos HaRashbash,* since these hallowed words may be recited only in the forum of a *minyan* with a prayer leader (for the Gemara specifically tells us that Hashem appeared to Moshe in the guise of a *shliach tzibbur*), an individual is in fact not allowed to recite this *tefillah* on his own. [See *A Taste of Lomdus* for further discussion of this ruling.]

Why is it that the Attributes may be recited only when one is praying as part of a *minyan*? Perhaps it is because an individual, who by definition sees things from only one limited perspective, is simply unable to relate to the total array of this thirteen-fold spectrum that Hashem employs in His management of the world. Thus, it is impossible for someone who is praying on his own to truly understand this wide variety of qualities that Hashem employs. However, a *minyan,* which is a community of people who join together, is an entity that includes all of these aspects; some of the people can relate to Hashem's quality of רַחוּם, *Compassionate,* while others have experienced, or can better understand, His role as רַב חֶסֶד, *Abundant in Kindness.* [Similarly, based on what we discussed in *A Mussar Thought for the Day* — that the true purpose of the Attributes is not merely to say them but to internalize them — *Sefer HaChaim* explains that the reason the Attributes are said only by a congregation is because it is rare, if not impossible, for one person to exemplify all of these traits. When a congregation joins together, however, one person may typify one quality and someone else another. The group is therefore better able to emulate Hashem in every respect.] It is thus only when praying as one element of a multi-faceted *tzibbur* that these descriptions, which relate to Hashem's totality, may be said.

A TASTE OF LOMDUS

Shulchan Aruch (*Orach Chaim* 565:5) tells us that the Thirteen Attributes of Mercy may be recited only in the presence of a *minyan.* In this sense, the Attributes are similar to many other parts of the communal *tefillah* that are not said by a person who is praying alone, such as the prayers of *Kaddish, Kedushah,* and *Borchu.*

פרשת
כי תשא

THURSDAY
PARASHAS KI SISA

However, we find several differences between the laws of *Kaddish, Kedushah,* and *Borchu,* and those of the Thirteen Attributes. One difference is the permissibility to interrupt one's prayers when in the middle of *Pesukei D'Zimrah,* or the *berachos* which precede and follow *Krias Shema,* in order to respond to *Kaddish, Kedushah,* or *Borchu* together with the congregation. *Shulchan Aruch* (*Orach Chaim* 66:3) tells us that a person is permitted, and in fact required, to pause in his personal prayers in order to answer *Kaddish, Kedushah,* and *Borchu.* However, R' Shlomo Kluger (*Orach Chaim, Siman* 65; see also *HaElef Lecha Shlomo, Siman* 44) rules that the blessings of *Krias Shema* may not be interrupted to recite the Thirteen Attributes with a congregation who is doing so. R' Moshe Feinstein (*Igros Moshe, Orach Chaim* III, *Siman* 89) tells us of another, similar, distinction between the Attributes and *Kaddish, Kedushah,* and *Borchu.* The *Rama* (*Orach Chaim* 126:2) rules that a person who has already prayed and, while present in a synagogue, hears *Kedushah* being said by a congregation, is required to pause and answer to the *Kedushah.* However, R' Moshe tells us that strictly speaking, even if a person is not involved in prayer or Torah study, no obligation exists to recite the Attributes a second time.

The difference between the laws of these two sets of prayers lies in the reason that each of them is said only with a *minyan. Kaddish, Kedushah,* and *Borchu, Tur* (*Orach Chaim* 565) tells us, are דְּבָרִים שֶׁבִּקְדֻשָּׁה, *matters of sanctity.* Since, explains the Gemara in *Berachos* (21b) [see also *Rambam* (*Hilchos Tefillah* 8:6)], the Torah states (*Vayikra* 22:32): וְנִקְדַּשְׁתִּי בְּתוֹךְ בְּנֵי יִשְׂרָאֵל, *I should be sanctified among the Bnei Yisrael,* we may understand that prayers said for the purpose of *sanctifying* Hashem — such as publicly declaring His blessing in *Borchu,* or His Holiness in *Kaddish* and *Kedushah* — must be recited only in the presence of an assembly of the Bnei Yisrael, and not by an individual who is standing alone. Additionally, explains R' Moshe, the Torah's statement of וְנִקְדַּשְׁתִּי בְּתוֹךְ בְּנֵי יִשְׂרָאֵל, *I should be sanctified among the Bnei Yisrael,* mandates that when the opportunity to do so arises, a person is *required* to publicly sanctify Hashem. The very opportunity of hearing *Kedushah* being said in a *minyan* — which is a public forum *among the Bnei Yisrael* — implicitly creates an obligation upon a person to respond and to fulfill the mitzvah of offering added praise to, and thereby *sanctifying,* Hashem.

However, nowhere do we find that the purpose behind our saying the Thirteen Attributes is to praise or sanctify Hashem, for, on the contrary, these words are a prayer in which we implore Divine mercy. The only

פרשת כי תשא
THURSDAY
PARASHAS KI SISA

reason, explains *Teshuvos HaRashbash* (*Siman* 191) [see also *Teshuvos HaRashba* (1:211)], why the Attributes may not be said by an individual is because of the reason we discussed in *A Closer Look at the Siddur;* had Hashem Himself not, as it were, shown Himself as enwrapped in a *tallis* in the manner of a *shliach tzibbur* leading the Jewish people in prayer, we would never have thought it possible for mankind to recite these hallowed words. Accordingly, we have no right to extend this prayer to any area in which we have not been explicitly permitted, and since the vision in which Hashem taught Moshe this prayer was that of a *shliach tzibbur* leading its recitation, we have no permission to grant an individual the permission to say these words.

This being the case, R' Moshe explains that in contrast to דְּבָרִים שֶׁבִּקְדֻשָּׁה, where the very presence of a *minyan* implicitly requires a person to respond with added words of praise of Hashem, the reason why a *minyan* is needed to recite the Thirteen Attributes is only because this is the required venue for this *tefillah*. Thus, the role that the *minyan* serves is only to allow this prayer to be said. On the other hand, when it comes to דְּבָרִים שֶׁבִּקְדֻשָּׁה, someone who has already recited *Kedushah* is required to do so a second time and beyond, for each of these new occasions creates a new opportunity to sanctify Hashem that is wholly unrelated to the first. However, a person who has already fulfilled his responsibility of prayer using the Thirteen Attributes is not required to do so again. Similarly, a person is required to interrupt *Pesukei D'Zimrah* and the blessings of *Krias Shema* only when presented with the immediate obligation to fulfill the mitzvah of sanctifying Hashem. However, no reason exists to interrupt these prayers in order to recite a different one, such as the Thirteen Attributes.

R' Moshe concludes that although a person is under no obligation to say the Attributes a second time, and thus should not do so if he is engaged in prayer or Torah study, people are nevertheless accustomed to recite these words if they hear a congregation doing so. The reason for this is as we explained; the Attributes are not words of praise, but words of prayer, and the power of prayer is such that every person who participates in a group of people who are praying adds to, and therefore strengthens, the prayers of the entire group. Therefore, R' Moshe explains that participating in these prayers even when not obligated to do so is an act of *chesed* to the people who are praying, for this added participation will help the prayers of the entire group elicit a positive response from Hashem.

A TORAH THOUGHT FOR THE DAY

פרשת כי תשא

FRIDAY
PARASHAS KI SISA

וַיְכַל מֹשֶׁה מִדַּבֵּר אִתָּם וַיִּתֵּן עַל־פָּנָיו מַסְוֶה.
וּבְבֹא מֹשֶׁה לִפְנֵי ה' לְדַבֵּר אִתּוֹ יָסִיר אֶת־הַמַּסְוֶה
עַד־צֵאתוֹ וְיָצָא וְדִבֶּר אֶל־בְּנֵי יִשְׂרָאֵל אֵת אֲשֶׁר יְצֻוֶּה

Moshe finished speaking with them and he placed a mask on his face. When Moshe would come before HASHEM to speak with Him, he would remove the mask until his departure; then he would leave and tell the Children of Israel whatever he had been commanded (Shemos 34:33-34).

Earlier (v. 29), the Torah related how Moshe's face was radiant after he descended from Mount Sinai. As *Abarbanel* explains, this was a parallel to the giving of the first pair of the Tablets of the Testimony, the *Luchos HaEdus*; the Torah attests there that the people saw the glory of Hashem (*Shemos* 24:17): וּמַרְאֵה כְּבוֹד ה' כְּאֵשׁ אֹכֶלֶת בְּרֹאשׁ הָהָר לְעֵינֵי בְּנֵי יִשְׂרָאֵל, *The appearance of the glory of* HASHEM *was like a consuming fire on the mountaintop before the eyes of the Children of Israel.* Now, after the sin of the Golden Calf, the nation had to suffice with the radiance of Moshe's face; even that, though, was too much for them (see *Shemos* 34:30). As the Torah now tells us, Moshe would cover his face with a mask at all times — except while speaking with Hashem and then relaying His message to the nation. As the next verse tells us, when Moshe finished teaching the people, he then replaced the mask until the next time Hashem spoke to him.

The commentators give many reasons to explain why Moshe wore a mask. *Ibn Ezra* (*HaAruch*) says that one explanation given is based on the fact that the radiance on Moshe's face would become renewed each time he went into the Mishkan to speak with Hashem. The radiance would remain until Moshe completed giving Hashem's teachings over to the Jewish nation, and then it would disappear until the next time he spoke with Hashem. If the nation were to see Moshe's face without the radiance they had come to associate with it, they might — incorrectly — think badly of him! Therefore, Moshe would cover his face with a mask so that it wouldn't be apparent that the radiance was not there, and remove it only in order to absorb the radiance again upon his next conversation with Hashem.

The above explanation is predicated on the premise that the radiance on Moshe's face was not constantly present. But the consensus of the commentators is that the radiance remained on Moshe's face until

FRIDAY
PARASHAS KI SISA

his death, and this is supported by a *Pesikta Zutresa* (*Devarim* 34:7) that states that Moshe's face did not change — even after his death — from the radiant appearance that it had assumed on Mount Sinai. Indeed, Moshe looked "as if he were still alive, standing in service before the Living God."

Ibn Ezra, continuing, quotes Rav Hai Gaon, who also opines that Moshe's face remained permanently radiant. He gives a practical reason why Moshe kept his face covered: Since he was involved in adjudicating the Jewish people's legal proceedings, he worried that because of the radiance of his face a litigant might be fearful or abashed when speaking to him, and might not properly present his case!

While agreeing with Rav Hai Gaon about the permanence of the radiance, *Ibn Ezra* offers a different explanation for Moshe's mask. He posits that the mask was necessary so that the radiance should not be constantly visible, something necessary to ensure proper respect for this Divine manifestation.

In a similar vein, *Chizkuni* notes that if the people of Israel would have been able to constantly see the radiance on Moshe's face, habit would have dulled their perception of the extraordinary. They would have stopped noticing that the radiance came from Hashem's *Shechinah,* a manifestation of Hashem's very presence.

However, while Moshe was teaching the people, and while he was talking to Hashem, he would remove the mask, fulfilling the intent of the verse (*Yeshayah* 30:20): וְהָיוּ עֵינֶיךָ רֹאוֹת אֶת־מוֹרֶיךָ, *and your eyes will behold your Teacher.* When Moshe was conversing with Hashem he would remove the mask so there should be no obstruction between him and his Teacher, and when he was teaching the nation he would remove the mask so that they could see him — their teacher.

MISHNAH OF THE DAY: BEITZAH 3:6

The previous Mishnah completed a series of Mishnayos that considered the laws that apply to the various aspects of trapping and slaughtering animals on a Yom Tov. The coming Mishnah and Mishnah 8 below consider the laws of buying and selling the meat of animals on Yom Tov. [Although the purchase of meat is used as an illustration, the same laws apply to buying any article on a Yom Tov.]

While the prohibition against conducting business on the Sabbath or on a Yom Tov is a Rabbinic decree, *Rashi* (27b) points out that it is of very ancient origin, and is already mentioned in the Bible. At the end of the book (13:15-18) that is named after him, we find Nechemiah being appalled at the desecration of the Sabbath in the Jerusalem of his times through commerce, a practice that he proceeded to outlaw. The basis of Nechemiah's consternation, explains *Rashi* (37a), is the verse in *Yeshayah* (58:13) that states: ... וְכִבַּדְתּוֹ מִמְּצוֹא חֶפְצְךָ וְדַבֵּר דָּבָר, *and you shall honor* [the Sabbath] ... by *not pursuing your business or discussing the forbidden.*[1]

FRIDAY
PARASHAS KI SISA

As commerce is defined as the exchange of money or its equivalent for a commodity, it is permitted to buy on credit on a Yom Tov. The coming Mishnah teaches that this is so only if the transaction is based on mutual trust — a price may not be mentioned explicitly (see *Mishnah Berurah* 500:1; see also below, Mishnah 3:7):

אֵין נִמְנִין עַל הַבְּהֵמָה — *We may not be subscribed upon an animal,*[2] לְכַתְּחִלָּה בְּיוֹם טוֹב — if the subscription *initiates on a Yom Tov.*[3] אֲבָל נִמְנִין עָלֶיהָ מֵעֶרֶב יוֹם טוֹב — *But we may be subscribed upon it from the eve of Yom Tov.*[4] וְשׁוֹחֲטִין וּמְחַלְּקִין בֵּינֵיהֶן — *And* subscribers may *slaughter and apportion* an animal *among themselves.*[5] רַבִּי יְהוּדָה אוֹמֵר שׁוֹקֵל אָדָם בָּשָׂר כְּנֶגֶד הַכְּלִי אוֹ כְּנֶגֶד הַקּוֹפִיץ — *R' Yehudah says: A*

— NOTES —

1. In an alternative explanation, *Rashi* (loc. cit.) suggests that the prohibition against commerce on the Sabbath and on a Yom Tov was decreed by the Sages lest a person come to record his business transactions and perform the forbidden labor of *writing*.

2. I.e., join a group of people who are arranging for a butcher to slaughter an animal for their group. Our Mishnah teaches that such a group may not be formed on a Yom Tov. The Gemara (27b) qualifies that it is prohibited to form the group only if a price is specified — e.g., a group of two or three people may not say to the butcher, "We will take this animal; each of us will pay three *zuz*" (see *Rav; Rambam Commentary*).

3. I.e., one may not form such a group on a Yom Tov. The next clause in the Mishnah will consider the law if the group was formed prior to the onset of the Yom Tov.

4. I.e., if a group had been formed prior to the onset of the Yom Tov, they may admit additional members to their group on Yom Tov (*Yerushalmi;* cf. *Beur Halachah* 500:1). [*Tiferes Yisrael* suggests that if the group was formed — i.e., the prices had already been established — prior to the onset of the Yom Tov, then it is permitted to mention the money at the time of acquisition on Yom Tov, and even to calculate each person's share in the payments (cf. *Rashba*). In terms of actual practice, the question as to whether one may make mention of the price on the Sabbath or on a Yom Tov, if the price is already known and set, is the subject of disagreement among the authorities (see *Shulchan Aruch, Orach Chaim* 323:4).]

5. I.e., as long as no discussions are held concerning how to apportion the responsibility for payment, a subscription group may be initiated on Yom Tov, and they may divide up the animal in halves, in thirds, in quarters, etc. (*Rav*).

פרשת כי תשא
FRIDAY
PARASHAS KI SISA

person may weigh meat against a vessel or against a cleaver.[6] וַחֲכָמִים אוֹמְרִים אֵין מַשְׁגִּיחִין בְּכַף מֹאזְנַיִם כָּל עִקָּר — *But the Sages say: We do not look to a scale at all.*[7]

———————————— NOTES ————————————

6. One may not place standardized weights in one scale to weigh meat in the opposite scale against them on a Yom Tov, because this is considered a weekday activity. One may, however, use some other object whose weight is known in place of the standardized weights (*Rav; Rashi*).

7. I.e., one may not make any use of scales on a Yom Tov. Indeed, not only may one not use them for weighing — even in the unusual and indirect manner permitted by R' Yehudah — but if the scale is hanging from the ring that holds the scales in balance when weighing an item, it may not even be used to store and safeguard the meat from mice — as it would *appear* as if he wanted to weigh the meat, even though his actual intention may be just to safeguard it. [This restriction is derived from the phrase כָּל עִקָּר, *at all,* indicating that *any* use of scales is prohibited.] The Sages consider any use of scales as inconsistent with the sanctity of a Yom Tov (*Rav* from Gemara 28a).

GEMS FROM THE GEMARA

The Gemara (28a) cites two rulings of the Amora Rav Yehudah in the name of Shmuel in regard to the weighing of meat on a Yom Tov.

The first ruling is that, on a Yom Tov, a professional butcher is prohibited to weigh meat in his hand. [A skilled butcher would sometimes hold a weight in one hand and meat in the other, to determine the weight of the meat. Since this was his normal method of weighing meat during the week, it is prohibited on Yom Tov (*Rashi*).]

The second ruling is that, on a Yom Tov, a professional butcher is prohibited to weigh meat by placing it in water. [A container with markings on its side would be partially filled with water. The markings designated the various heights to which the water would rise when pieces of meat of various weights were immersed in the water. A skilled butcher could ascertain the weight of a piece of meat by seeing how high it would cause the water to rise. This is therefore prohibited on a Yom Tov (*Rashi*). Nevertheless, there is a certain degree of expertise that one must possess in order to employ this method. Therefore, only a professional butcher is prohibited to use this method, because only he can obtain an accurate weight from it (see *Rashash*).]

The Gemara then digresses to discuss other laws regarding meat on a Yom Tov. It cites Rav Chiya bar Ashi, who ruled that, on a Yom Tov, it is prohibited to make a "handle" in a piece of meat. [It was customary for a butcher to make a hole in the meat as a handle that would help his customer carry the meat home. The Rabbis prohibited doing so on a Yom Tov so as to demonstrate that commerce is prohibited on Yom Tov (*Rashi*).]

פרשת כי תשא
FRIDAY
PARASHAS KI SISA

Ravina, however, qualifies the prohibition, explaining that it is permitted to make a hole by hand. [I.e., it is permitted to make the hole in the meat with one's finger. This unusual method serves to distinguish it from the normal, prohibited manner of making the hole with a knife or other implement (*Rashi*).]

The Gemara then cites a similar ruling in the name of Rav Huna, who stated that it is permitted to make a mark in a piece of meat on a Yom Tov. [Because the Rabbis were concerned that nonkosher meat might be exchanged for kosher meat by an unscrupulous messenger, they required that meat be marked in a distinct way, so that the recipient could recognize that it had not been exchanged (see *Rashi*; see *Shulchan Aruch, Yoreh Deah* 63 and 118 for the specifications of this requirement). Rav Huna rules that this identifying mark may be made on a Yom Tov.]

The Gemara then gives an example of what this ruling entails, citing the practice of Rabbah bar Rav Huna who, whenever he sent meat home — whether it was on a Yom Tov or on a weekday — would cut the meat into triangular pieces. [His family knew that meat that came from him would come in the shape of a triangle, and would use the meat only if it came in this form (*Rashi*; see *Shach, Yoreh Deah* 118:15; see the Gemara's continuation for further consideration of the subject of weighing meat on a Yom Tov).]

A MUSSAR THOUGHT FOR THE DAY

Moshe Rabbeinu's overriding positive character trait was humility, as the verse states (*Bamidbar* 12:3): וְהָאִישׁ מֹשֶׁה עָנָו מְאֹד מִכֹּל הָאָדָם אֲשֶׁר עַל־פְּנֵי הָאֲדָמָה, *Now the man Moshe was exceedingly humble, more than any person on the face of the earth*. In *A Torah Thought for the Day* we discussed a number of reasons for Moshe Rabbeinu wearing a mask over his face; some commentators suggest that there was a link between the mask and Moshe's humility.

Kli Yakar explains Moshe's mask as motivated by his self-consciousness. Wherever Moshe passed, people would peer at him because of his radiant face. Since Moshe was so humble, he found this extremely embarrassing and uncomfortable, so he covered his

FRIDAY
PARASHAS KI SISA

face with a mask (which, presumably, was still less conspicuous). Why did Moshe remove the mask when he came before Hashem (*Shemos* 34:34)? Because he was coming to learn Torah, and the Mishnah (*Avos* 2:6) tells us: לֹא הַבַּיְשָׁן לָמֵד, *The bashful person cannot learn.* He therefore removed the mask, which was only there because of his embarrassment.

R' Akiva Eiger (quoted in *So'les LeMinchah* 3:16) has a different approach to this subject. He maintains that although Moshe was by nature an exceedingly humble person, he was still not always able to act humbly. A leader must often rule with strength, as we see from the Gemara (*Sanhedrin* 8a), which relates that Hashem advised Yehoshua to rule with a strong hand. In the context of leadership, then, Moshe's humility was a hindrance! His mask was an attempt to hide his humility, so that he would be able to be an effective leader. But when Moshe would stand before Hashem — before Whom one can have no secrets — he would remove his mask, so as to appear with his characteristic modesty.

Mesillas Yesharim (Chapter 23) has a long exposition on the methods of acquiring the elusive character trait of humility. He says that there are two areas in which a person has to be careful when working on this *middah*. The first is one's general conduct — one should slowly acclimate himself to acting humbly. For example, when sitting in a public area, one should endeavor to place himself in a section used by those who are less distinguished. When one is part of a group, he should try to position himself toward the rear. One should wear modest clothing — dignified, but not flashy. These actions will serve — slowly, a bit at a time — to instill humility in one's heart.

The other area on which one needs to concentrate in order to become truly humble is the realm of thought. *Mesillas Yesharim* suggests a number of ideas that — should one regularly remind himself of them — will help a person acquire humility. For example, when one remembers that he comes from an almost insignificant drop of matter, it is difficult to be haughty! Should a former keeper of swine manage to rise and become king, does he not become humble again every time he is reminded of his origins?

Every person is destined for death, when one's body becomes worthless — food for worms. Of what use is one's current glory, when one will inevitably end up of no account? And after one's death, one is judged by the Heavenly Court — headed by Hashem Himself! At that point one's honor and greatness will seem insignificant, not even worth mentioning. If a person visualizes this last point well, maintains *Mesillas Yesharim,* his haughtiness will permanently leave him!

Another point to keep in mind, he continues, is that one's position in life is uncertain. A person's situation can reverse itself overnight, whether through financial reversals, health problems, or other troubles. Someone who was always self-sufficient, honored, and respected, could suddenly find that he is impoverished, physically needy, and reliant on society's kindness! How can one remain haughty when these thoughts are in the forefront of his consciousness?

פרשת כי תשא

FRIDAY
PARASHAS KI SISA

The last thing to keep in mind, concludes *Mesillas Yesharim,* is one's deficiency in his service to Hashem (for no one, no matter how righteous, is perfect). After thinking about that, one will certainly be embarrassed and ashamed, rather than haughty and proud.

HALACHAH OF THE DAY

Once one has finished בָּרוּךְ שֶׁאָמַר and begun the recital of *Pesukei D'Zimrah,* he may answer Amen to any blessing, as well as to *Kaddish.* He may also utter the appropriate responses to *Borchu* and *Kedushah,* and he may recite *Modim D'Rabbanan.* Additionally, he should join the congregation in their recital of the first verse of the *Shema,* and he may recite the blessing of אֲשֶׁר יָצַר if he has the need to relieve himself in the middle of *Pesukei D'Zimrah.*

If one finds himself in the midst of *Pesukei D'Zimrah* when the congregation reaches the Torah reading, it is preferable that he not be called up to the Torah for an *aliyah.* However, if he is the only Kohen or Levi present, or the *gabbai* did call him to the Torah, he may ascend to the Torah, recite the blessings, and even read in the Torah along with the reader.

If, after beginning *Pesukei D'Zimrah,* one realizes that he has neglected to recite the *Birchos HaTorah,* he should pause to recite them, together with their accompanying verses. Likewise, if one sees that the proper time frame for the recital of *Krias Shema* is drawing to a close, he should interrupt his recital of *Pesukei D'Zimrah* and recite all three chapters of the *Shema.*

On days that the *Hallel* is recited in its abridged form (Rosh Chodesh and the last six days of Pesach), if one is reciting *Pesukei D'Zimrah* when the congregation begins *Hallel,* he should pause, recite the verses of *Hallel* together with the congregation — without reciting either the opening or the closing *berachos* of *Hallel —* and then return to the point of *Pesukei D'Zimrah* where he left off.

In all cases where responses are permitted during *Pesukei D'Zimrah,*

FRIDAY

PARASHAS KI SISA

it is preferable that the interruption be made between the various chapters that make up the *Pesukei D'Zimrah*, if at all possible. Thus, for example, if one realizes that the congregation is nearing its recital of *Kedushah*, he should not begin a new chapter; rather, he should finish the chapter he is in the middle of, and then wait until after the recital of *Kedushah* before beginning the next chapter.

This concludes our discussions of the laws of a person's morning routines, his preparations for *tefillah*, the donning of *tzitzis* and *tefillin*, and the recital of *Birchos HaShachar, Amen*, and *Pesukei D'Zimrah*.

One who follows the guidelines we have detailed herein will have begun his day in a most meritorious fashion. It is our hope that the One above will then bless him with much success throughout the rest of his day.

A CLOSER LOOK AT THE SIDDUR

In today's studies, we discussed Moshe's practice of wearing a mask, except while he was speaking with Hashem or teaching Torah to the nation. There are two practices that are related both to this topic and to prayer. The first is mentioned by R' Menachem Recanati in his commentary to the Torah. He says that there was a custom that when the elders of the congregation would return to their seats after reading from the Torah (in those times they would read themselves, rather than read along with a reader, a *baal korei*), they would cover their faces (and, as *Levush* notes, would then explain to those present the portion they had just read aloud). The reason for this practice is based on what we discussed earlier; the one who reads aloud from the Torah mirrors Moshe's role in transmitting the Torah to the Jewish people. Just as Moshe would cover his face after he finished teaching, the elder would cover his face after he finished reading from the Torah.

[Although this custom is not currently practiced, another custom — with roots in the same principle — is still performed: In many synagogues, someone will stand next to the *baal korei* when the *baal korei* himself is called to make the blessings and to read from the Torah for an *aliyah* of his own. This custom (from *Shulchan Aruch, Orach Chaim* 141:4) is based on the parallel between the *baal korei* and Moshe Rabbeinu — just as Moshe gave over the Torah to the nation, so does the *baal korei*. And just as the nation listened to Moshe, the *oleh* listens to the *baal korei*. Here, where the *oleh* is also the *baal korei*, another congregant stands in to represent the role of the nation, usually signified by

פרשת
כי תשא

FRIDAY
PARASHAS
KI SISA

the *oleh*. In fact, *Mishnah Berurah* (ad loc.) says (quoting *Levush*) that the reason a third person — the *gabbai* — stands next to the Torah during the Torah reading is to parallel Hashem's role at the giving of the Torah. Just as Hashem chose who would ascend the mountain to give the Torah to the nation, so does the *gabbai* decide who will ascend as the *oleh,* who represents the nation.]

The second practice is mentioned by *Maggid Meisharim*: "And when Moshe would speak with the nation, he would not wear the mask, so they could look at him and absorb the light from him while he spoke with them. After he stopped speaking with them he would replace the mask, because that radiance was the radiance of the *Shechinah,* the manifestation of Hashem's Presence. Just as it is forbidden to gaze at a rainbow or at the Kohanim while they raise their hands to bless the people, it is forbidden to gaze at that radiance. This is so even though it *was* permitted for them to look upon Moshe while he was speaking with them. This is similar to the *bigdei Kehunah,* holy vestments, for during the Temple service one may make use of them but at other times it is forbidden."

This excerpt, forbidding the nation to gaze at Moshe's face except when he was teaching them, also mentions the corresponding items forbidden by the Gemara (*Chagigah* 16a). The Gemara there says that one who gazes at a rainbow, the king, or the hands of the Kohanim during the priestly blessings, is punished by his eyes becoming weak. All these are forbidden because the *Shechinah* rests upon them, and one is forbidden to look at the *Shechinah*. [The verse in *Yechezkel* (1:28) compares the appearance of the glory of Hashem to that of a rainbow; in our discussions we have seen that Moshe — the ruler of Israel — was visited by the Divine Presence upon his face; and the *Shechinah* rested upon the hands of Kohanim when they blessed the people.] Although today we are unfortunately not at the level of holiness to deserve that the *Shechinah* rest upon the hands of the Kohanim when they bless us, *Mishnah Berurah* (128:89) explains that our custom is also to avoid looking at the hands of the Kohanim. This serves as a remembrance of the *Beis HaMikdash,* where the Divine Presence did rest upon the hands of the Kohanim.

QUESTION OF THE DAY:
What is another reason that Moshe did not wear the mask when teaching Torah to the Jews?

For the answer, see page 68.

פרשת כי תשא

A TORAH THOUGHT FOR THE DAY

SHABBOS
PARASHAS KI SISA

This week's *Haftarah* relates the story of Eliyahu on Mount Carmel. King Achav and Queen Izevel ruled with an iron fist, advancing idol worship throughout the kingdom. Eliyahu challenged Achav's hold on the people, staging a showdown on Mount Carmel between himself and the prophets of the Baal. In one of the more spectacular events recorded in the Scriptures, Eliyahu publicly refuted the false prophets and won back the hearts of the nation for Hashem.

The showdown between Eliyahu and the false prophets was really a confrontation between Eliyahu and Achav. In response to the evil deeds of Achav and Izevel, Eliyahu brought a terrible drought upon the land. Unfortunately, the royal couple remained unrepentant despite the devastating impact of the hunger. After three years, Hashem sent Eliyahu to bring the conflict to a head and end the drought. The Gemara in *Sanhedrin* lists Achav as one of four who lost their portion in עוֹלָם הַבָּא, the World to Come. Who was Achav, and why weren't the three years of drought enough to gain his repentance?

The verse states (*I Melachim* 16:34): בְּיָמָיו בָּנָה חִיאֵל בֵּית הָאֱלִי אֶת־יְרִיחֹה בַּאֲבִירָם בְּכֹרוֹ יִסְּדָהּ וּבִשְׂגוּב צְעִירוֹ הִצִּיב דְּלָתֶיהָ כִּדְבַר ה' אֲשֶׁר דִּבֶּר בְּיַד יְהוֹשֻׁעַ בִּן־נוּן, *In his days, Chiel the Beth-elite built up Yericho; with [the death of] Aviram his firstborn he laid its foundations; and with [the death of] Seguv, his youngest, he installed its doors; like the word of* Hashem *that He had spoken through the hand of Yehoshua son of Nun.*

The "word of Hashem" refers to the edict issued by Yehoshua, forbidding anyone to rebuild Yericho or name another city by that name, under penalty of all his children dying. *Radak* explains that Chiel named his city Yericho, and between laying the foundation and installing the city gates, his children died. The Gemara in *Sanhedrin* relates that Eliyahu and Achav arrived at the same time to pay a *shivah* visit after the death of Chiel's youngest child. During the visit, Achav and Eliyahu argued as to why Chiel's sons had died. Eliyahu said it was because of Yehoshua's oath, while Achav claimed it was mere coincidence. Achav pointed out that in the second passage of *Krias Shema,* Hashem promises to punish the Jews for worshiping *avodah zarah* by stopping the rains; yet, despite Achav filling the land with idols, Hashem had not done so! Eliyahu answered that the reason the rains had not stopped was because he, Eliyahu, prayed daily that Hashem should not do so; however, if he would stop davening for rain, Hashem would immediately bring a drought! The verse states (ibid. 17:1):

פרשת כי תשא

SHABBOS PARASHAS KI SISA

וַיֹּאמֶר אֵלִיָּהוּ הַתִּשְׁבִּי . . . אֶל־אַחְאָב חַי־ה' אֱלֹהֵי יִשְׂרָאֵל . . . אִם־יִהְיֶה הַשָּׁנִים הָאֵלֶּה טַל וּמָטָר כִּי אִם־לְפִי דְבָרִי, *Eliyahu HaTishbi said . . . to Achav, "As* HASHEM, *God of Israel, lives . . . I swear that there will not be dew nor rain during these years* **except by my word."** To prove his point, Eliyahu stopped praying for rain, and the land was plunged into a severe three-year drought and famine.

For further discussion of Achav, see *A Mussar Thought for the Day.*

MISHNAH OF THE DAY: BEITZAH 3:7

The beginning of the coming Mishnah digresses from the topic of the previous and following Mishnayos — viz., the purchase of meat — to consider the sharpening of knives with which to slaughter the animal and butcher its meat on a Yom Tov (see *Rashba*).

While the Mishnah focuses on butchers' knives (because butchers must sharpen their knives frequently), the law applies to all cutting instruments:

אֵין מַשְׁחִיזִין אֶת הַסַּכִּין בְּיוֹם טוֹב — *We may not sharpen the knife* on a whetstone or on a millstone **on a Yom Tov**,[1] אֲבָל מַשִּׁיאָהּ עַל גַּבֵּי חֲבֶרְתָּהּ — *but one may sharpen one* knife **against another** knife.[2]

──────── NOTES ────────

1. Sharpening a knife is categorized as an act that is מִיחֲזֵי כִּמְתַקֵּן, *appears to be fixing* — and fixing is, in turn, a subcategory of the forbidden labor of מַכֶּה בְּפַטִּישׁ, *striking the final blow.* [The actual fixing of a broken knife would be Scripturally prohibited, because the dispensation that permits one to perform on a Yom Tov labor that is forbidden on the Sabbath as long as it is in the course of food preparation (אֹכֶל נֶפֶשׁ, *food for a [living] soul*) applies only to forms of labor that are directly involved in preparing the actual food itself (e.g., slaughtering or cooking). Forms of labor that are themselves only preparatory to the preparation of the actual food (מַכְשִׁירֵי אֹכֶל נֶפֶשׁ, *preparations for [the preparation] of food for a [living] soul*) remain forbidden (see further in *Gems from the Gemara* to this Mishnah).] Since the process of sharpening a knife has the appearance of fixing it, the Rabbis forbade such sharpening on a Yom Tov as being too much of a "weekday" activity (*Rav; Rashi;* see *Meiri; Rosh Yosef; Pnei Yehoshua;* cf. *Pri Megadim, Orach Chaim, Mishbetzos Zahav* 323:8).

2. Since this form of sharpening employs a שִׁנּוּי, *change,* from the usual method that one would employ on a weekday, it does not have the appearance of a weekday activity, and is therefore permitted (*Rav; Rashi*). [However, there is a difference of opinion in the Gemara (28a) as to whether the Mishnah here in fact permits the actual sharpening of one knife against another knife. According to one view, he may only rub one knife against another knife to remove surface film (שַׁמְנוּנִית) from the former. According to this opinion, one is permitted only to *seemingly* sharpen

SHABBOS

PARASHAS KI SISA

The Mishnah returns to the parameters of purchasing meat on Yom Tov:

לֹא יֹאמַר אָדָם לְטַבָּח שְׁקֹל לִי בְדִינָר בָּשָׂר — *A person may not say to a butcher* on a Yom Tov, *"Weigh me out a dinar's worth of meat."*[3] אֲבָל שׁוֹחֵט וּמְחַלְּקִים בֵּינֵיהֶם — *But he may slaughter* an animal, *and they may* then *apportion* the meat *among themselves.*[4]

NOTES
---

one knife against another knife (see *Chasam Sofer, Chidushim* §1 and *Teshuvos, Yoreh Deah* §15; see also *Shulchan Aruch, Orach Chaim* 509:2).]

3. By specifying a *dinar's* worth, he is mentioning money; and as we saw in our commentary to the previous Mishnah, it is forbidden to make such mention in a transaction that takes place on a Yom Tov (*Rashi*). [Although the previous Mishnah also forbade the *weighing* of the meat, our Mishnah assumes that the butcher knows this and will estimate the weight of the meat (see *Rosh Yosef;* cf. *Ran;* see also *Meleches Shlomo; Shinuyei Nuschaos; Rambam, Hil. Yom Tov* 4:21).]

4. I.e., on a Yom Tov a butcher may provide his customers with meat only in the manner described in the previous Mishnah — viz., to deliver the slaughtered animal over to a group for them to apportion among themselves, without mentioning the costs.

GEMS FROM THE GEMARA

In the course of its discussion of our Mishnah, the Gemara (28b) digresses to discuss another knife-related Yom Tov issue: whether a slaughterer may show his knife to a sage on a Yom Tov.

[The cutting edge of the knife used for the ritual slaughter (*shechitah*) of an animal or fowl must be absolutely smooth, without nicks or imperfections. The Sages decreed that a slaughterer must take his knife to a sage for inspection before he begins slaughtering (see *Chullin* 17b). The Gemara now asks whether this inspection might be considered a weekday activity, because it appears as if he intends to sell the meat in the market (*Rashi;* see *Rashba,* who cites other reasons why this inspection might be forbidden on a Yom Tov).]

The Gemara replies that Rav Mari the son of Rav Bizna permitted it, but that other Rabbis prohibited it. The Gemara then cites Rav Yosef, who rules that on a Yom Tov a scholar should inspect his own knife in his home, and then lend it to others. [Since he is inspecting the knife in his own home, it will not became public knowledge and hence, does not appear like a weekday activity (see *Rashi*).]

Having cited a ruling made by Rav Yosef, the Gemara now returns to the issue of sharpening knives on a Yom Tov with a statement by Rav Yosef on the issue. Rav Yosef stated that if a knife became dull, it is permitted to sharpen it on Yom Tov — but this applies only when it is still sharp enough that it can cut when pressure is applied.

פרשת
כי תשא
SHABBOS
PARASHAS
KI SISA

[The Gemara had already noted that R' Yehudah disagrees with the ruling of our Mishnah and permits even *preparations for [the preparation] of food for a [living] soul* on a Yom Tov — if those preparations could not have been accomplished prior to the onset of the Yom Tov (אִי אֶפְשָׁר לַעֲשׂוֹתָן מֵעֶרֶב יוֹם טוֹב) — e.g., fixing a utensil that was damaged on Yom Tov. Accordingly, R' Yehudah would permit sharpening a knife that became dulled or chipped on Yom Tov (see *Shulchan Aruch, Orach Chaim* 509:1 with *Beur Halachah* s.v. אותו and וה״ה and 495:1, for a dispute concerning the final ruling). Thus, even according to R' Yehudah, if the knife developed a nick prior to the onset of a Yom Tov, it would certainly be prohibited to repair it on the Yom Tov, because the owner should have repaired it earlier. But if the knife became so dull that it cannot cut in the normal manner subsequent to the onset of the Yom Tov, then even though this problem might have been anticipated before the Yom Tov, it is nevertheless permitted to sharpen the knife on the Yom Tov, because it was not incumbent on the owner to realize beforehand that it would become so much duller on Yom Tov (*Rashi*). Thus, according to R' Yehudah — whose opinion Rav Yosef follows — one may sharpen the knife (see *Rashba*).]

A MUSSAR THOUGHT FOR THE DAY

In *A Torah Thought for the Day* we discussed the argument between Achav and Eliyahu about the death of Chiel's children. We may ask: What did Achav really think? The death of Chiel's children followed the exact pattern mentioned in Yehoshua's oath. Moreover, when negotiating the terms of his surrender to Ben-hadad king of Aram later in the *Navi* (*I Melachim* 20:3-9), Achav agreed to give up his wealth and family, but not the item that Ben-hadad demanded: מַחְמַד עֵינֶיךָ, *that which is precious in your eyes* (v. 6), which the Gemara says was "the Torah"! Who was this enigmatic Achav, and what did he truly believe? Achav was evil beyond redemption; the Gemara tells us that he lost his portion in the World to Come. On the other hand, he refused to give up the Torah to Ben-hadad of Aram while agreeing to surrender his vast wealth and family.

R' Isaac Sher explained that Achav truly loved and valued the Torah

SHABBOS

PARASHAS KI SISA

more than his family and wealth. However, it was the Written Torah that he loved, not the Oral Torah. As far as the Oral Torah was concerned, Achav believed that he and his "prophets" were more in tune with the needs of the generation and more capable of interpreting the Written Torah than Eliyahu and the Rabbis. For example, Achav filled the land with *avodah zarah*, rationalizing that the idol worship of Moshe's days was primitive, unsophisticated, and a negation of true monotheism. In contrast, he felt that the idols *he* had promulgated throughout Eretz Yisrael were not forbidden in the Torah, because they captured the true essence of Divine worship, and made God understandable and accessible to all!

Achav's argument with Eliyahu at the *shivah* house of Chiel, his support for the false prophets of the Baal, and his attempts at destroying the Torah leadership, were all predicated on his denial of the Oral Torah. The Gemara in *Sanhedrin*, discussing Yehoshua's oath against rebuilding Yericho, debates whether or not the oath applied to someone, like Chiel, who only named another city Yericho. The conclusion was that Yehoshua had included the naming in the prohibition; however, Achav did not agree. He argued that Yehoshua did not have the power to enact a binding oath. Only Hashem could do this, and Yehoshua's prohibition was not the word of God. Second, even if God had told Yehoshua to enact such an oath, Achav refused to accept that the oath included naming another city Yericho as well. Furthermore, Achav used the fact that Hashem had not stopped the rains as proof positive that his form of idol worship was not what the Written Torah had forbidden, and that it validated his philosophy of reinterpreting the Torah as demanded by the needs of each generation.

Responding to Achav, Eliyahu explained that the land would have been subject to drought and famine if not for his prayers, and that he would prove it by withdrawing his prayers (ibid. 17:1): חַי־ה׳ ... אִם־ יִהְיֶה הַשָּׁנִים הָאֵלֶּה טַל וּמָטָר כִּי אִם־לְפִי דְבָרִי, *I swear that there will not be dew nor rain during these years **except by my word***. In doing so, Eliyahu hoped to prove that Achav's modern brand of idol worship was the same *avodah zarah* prohibited in the Written Torah, and also to prove that his assumed right to reinterpret the Torah "as needed" was wrong.

Three years later, Achav had not changed his philosophy. The nation was suffering from drought and famine, and was still immersed in idol worship. Dispatched by Hashem to confront Achav, Eliyahu challenged him to a miraculous public refutation on Mount Carmel. After Eliyahu succeeded in showing the Jews that Achav's philosophy of *avodah*

פרשת כי תשא
SHABBOS
PARASHAS KI SISA

zarah was false, Achav and the nation proclaimed their belief in Hashem and the Oral Torah with the ringing declaration (that has been incorporated into the final moments of the Yom Kippur service): ה' הוּא הָאֱלֹהִים ה' הוּא הָאֱלֹהִים, HASHEM, He is the God! HASHEM, He is the God! (ibid. 18:39).

HALACHAH OF THE DAY

Having discussed many of the laws pertaining to a person's morning routines, we have become familiar with the manner in which an observant Jew begins his day. We will now turn our attention to a complex topic that we face many times throughout each and every day — the intricate and detailed laws of Kashrus (dietary laws).

Before we begin discussing the laws themselves, an introduction is in order.

Rambam (*Hilchos Me'ilah* 8:8) states: "It is appropriate that one meditate, according to his intellectual capacity, regarding the laws of the Torah, to understand their deeper meaning. Those laws for which he finds no reason and knows of no purpose should nevertheless not be treated lightly."

When the Bnei Yisrael accepted the Torah at Har Sinai, they made the famous and far-reaching declaration (*Shemos* 24:7): נַעֲשֶׂה וְנִשְׁמָע, *We will do and we will hear.* With these words, those present at the Revelation accepted upon themselves and all their future generations an unconditional commitment, to fulfill the word of Hashem irrespective of any understanding. נַעֲשֶׂה, *We will do,* precedes נִשְׁמָע, *we will hear.* As we see in the second half of the *Rambam's* words quoted above, our requirement to act is completely independent of our ability to understand.

Yet, *Rambam* does state that we should try to comprehend the underlying concepts and the rationale that lies behind each mitzvah. The question arises: Why? If we are required to act regardless of whether or not we understand, why embark on a seemingly purposeless intellectual pursuit?

The answer to this question is vital to our having a healthy approach to the fulfillment of Hashem's commandments. While our understanding, or lack thereof, of the mitzvos has no bearing on our responsibility to act, there is indeed great value in gaining an understanding of the deeper meaning of the mitzvos. The purpose of understanding a mitzvah is not to comprehend what is accomplished through its fulfillment, as that is certainly beyond human ability. The purpose is to perceive

פרשת כי תשא
SHABBOS PARASHAS KI SISA

and understand the lessons that we can draw from the mitzvah. Thus, an understanding of the rationale of a mitzvah elevates its performance from a mere physical act to an act that makes a spiritually significant impact on our lives.

To illustrate: Our Sages teach in the Mishnah (*Berachos* 5:3): "One who says [in referring to the mitzvah of *shiluach hakein* (the chasing away of the mother bird before taking her eggs or chicks)]: 'Even young birds merit your kindness!' is silenced." *Ramban* explains (Gemara 33b) that such a person "is silenced" because he implies that the reason for this mitzvah is Hashem's compassion for birds, whereas in truth Hashem gave us this mitzvah in order to instill in *us* the quality of mercy. He gave the mitzvos to the Jewish people so that they could mold their characters and shape themselves into true servants of Hashem through their observance. We see, therefore, that from the mitzvah of *shiluach hakein* we can learn to internalize feelings of compassion for other creatures. This is a valuable lesson that will elevate us in our service of Hashem.

It is with these ideas in mind that we will begin tomorrow to explore the topic of Kashrus.

A CLOSER LOOK AT THE SIDDUR

We continue our study of the Sabbath morning prayers.

Once a month, on the Sabbath that precedes Rosh Chodesh, special prayers are added to the morning services, between the reading of the *Haftarah* and *Mussaf,* after the prayers for the congregation that we have discussed in the last weeks. This group of prayers is referred to as *Bircas HaChodesh,* the Blessing of the New Month.

The purpose of this blessing is to inform the congregation of the date of Rosh Chodesh; it is recited on the Sabbath because that is when the greatest number of people would congregate in shul.

Most congregations begin the *Bircas HaChodesh* by reciting the יְהִי רָצוֹן prayer, which is similar to one that the Gemara (*Berachos* 16b) attributes to the Amora Rav, who would say it every day at the end of his *Shemoneh Esrei* prayer. Since it lists a full gamut of people's spiritual and physical needs, it was selected to serve as our supplication for a blessed new month. [It is for this reason that in some versions of the prayer, it ends with the words בִּזְכוּת תְּפִלַּת רַב אָמֵן סֶלָה. Other versions omit these words entirely, or substitute בִּזְכוּת תְּפִלַּת רַבִּים, *in the merit of the multitude's prayers . . .*]

**SHABBOS
PARASHAS
KI SISA**

It is interesting that *Abudraham* does not mention this יְהִי רָצוֹן prayer as the introductory prayer for the blessing of the new month; rather, in his view the יְהִי רָצוֹן prayers that we recite after the Torah readings on Mondays and Thursdays are said here. He explains why these prayers are apropos to the blessing of the new month. We state therein: יְהִי רָצוֹן ... לְקַיֵּם בָּנוּ חַכְמֵי יִשְׂרָאֵל הֵם וּנְשֵׁיהֶם וּבְנֵיהֶם וכו׳, *May it be the will . . . to preserve among us the Sages of Israel, them, their wives, their children*, etc. Because the Torah Sages are the ones who have the responsibility of declaring the new month, and they have the power to add a day to a month or subtract a day, therefore, at the time of this prayer we ask that they be given continued strength to carry out their responsibilities, so that we should once again merit the establishing of the new month based on קִדּוּשׁ בֵּית דִּין, the *beis din* declaring it holy.

[Our custom to say these יְהִי רָצוֹן prayers after the reading of the Torah also can be explained in like manner. As the Sages are the ones who uphold the learning and teachings of the Torah, after the Torah is read we say a prayer for those whose primary occupation is Torah and mitzvos. This is similar to the reason that we recite יְקוּם פֻּרְקָן after the Torah reading on Shabbos, as we discussed in earlier studies.]

Toward the conclusion of this prayer, we request that Hashem grant us: חַיִּים שֶׁיְּמַלֵּא ה׳ מִשְׁאֲלוֹת לִבֵּנוּ לְטוֹבָה אָמֵן, *a life in which Hashem fulfills the request of our hearts for the good*. This means that although a person thinks that he knows what is good for him, this is not always the case. It might very well be that the "good" he thinks will be beneficial to him, will actually cause him harm. Thus, we place ourselves in Hashem's hands, and ask Him to provide the fulfillment of only those requests that are *actually* good for us.

We will continue our study of *Bircas HaChodesh* next week.

QUESTION OF THE DAY:

Why did Ovadiah divide the 100 prophets he hid into two groups of 50?

For the answer, see page 68.

ANSWERS TO QUESTION OF THE DAY

Sunday:
One lesson this teaches is that no Jew is complete without his fellow Jew.

Monday:
The Gemara in *Berachos* says that a good leader is honored by being "announced" by Hashem.

Tuesday:
We learn that sometimes *for you* the Sabbath may be desecrated — when it is necessary to save a life (*Meshech Chochmah*).

Wednesday:
The Kohen Gadol backs away as he leaves the Holy of Holies on Yom Kippur.

Thursday:
Hashem was promising that He would reward even those who are undeserving with the gifts of life and health.

Friday:
He did not wear the mask so that there would be no barrier between the word of Hashem and the Jews.

Shabbos:
He learned this tactic from Yaakov Avinu, who divided his camp before meeting with his brother Eisav.

פרשת ויקהל
Parashas Vayakhel

פרשת ויקהל

A TORAH THOUGHT FOR THE DAY

SUNDAY
PARASHAS VAYAKHEL

וַיַּקְהֵל מֹשֶׁה אֶת־כָּל־עֲדַת בְּנֵי יִשְׂרָאֵל וַיֹּאמֶר אֲלֵהֶם
אֵלֶּה הַדְּבָרִים אֲשֶׁר־צִוָּה ה׳ לַעֲשֹׂת אֹתָם

Moshe assembled the entire assembly of the Children of Israel and said to them, "These are the things that Hashem *commanded to do them"* (Shemos 35:1).

R' Tzadok HaKohen explains that we ascribe significance to the names of the various Torah portions; we do not merely create a name from one of the first few words of the *parashah*. Even if the custom did develop in such a fashion, the very fact that the Jewish people collectively accepted these names for the weekly Torah portions has meaning.

In Jewish law and literature, we encounter a concept described as *"Minhag Yisrael Torah* — The customs of the Jewish nation are law." This means that the soul and spirit of the Jewish people is aware of the importance and holiness of certain practices, and will respond by accepting these practices as part of Judaism. So if we, as a nation, have accepted the names of the weekly Torah portions as they are, these names must have cosmic significance in helping us understand each particular *parashah*.

In addition, we find the following comment made by the *Shelah* (R' Yeshayah Horowitz): If someone is an ignoramus who tries to study Torah but fails to understand anything, he should recite, with all of his heart, the individual names of each of the Five Books of the Torah. Then, he should say the names of the individual *parshiyos*. He should proceed with reciting the names of all the books of the Prophets, the tractates of the Talmud, and the Midrashim. He will then merit to understand the entirety of the Torah in the World to Come. *Shelah* definitely accords great prominence and spiritual meaning to the names of the *parshiyos*.

The specific content within each weekly Torah portion has its source in *Zohar*, cited by *Magen Avraham* 282: "It is forbidden for the Torah reader to stop reading in the middle of a section, even by one word. Rather, he should stop reading where Moshe stopped. This prohibition includes arranging to read the portion of one Shabbos on another Shabbos." *Magen Avraham* explains that not only must we never stop reading within a passage (as demarcated by the blank spaces that must be left between passages in a *Sefer Torah*), but we must also make sure to read the weekly portions as they were arranged, and not create our own portions to be read.

**SUNDAY
PARASHAS
VAYAKHEL**

Not only is the name of each *parashah* significant, but from *Magen Avraham* we see that the entire *parashah* is designated to be read as one unit. *Maharitz* in *Siddur Eitz Chaim* suggests, based upon this *Zohar,* that all of the contents within each weekly *parashah* are thematically related.

The same concept is seen in *Tosafos* (*Megillah* 31b), who explain why the *parshiyos* of *Nitzavim/Vayeilech* are read separately during calendar years when there are two Shabbosos between Rosh Hashanah and Yom Kippur. It would seem more logical to separate the *parshiyos* of *Mattos/Masei* in such a year, since they total a combined 244 *pesukim,* whereas *Nitzavim/Vayeilech* together have only 70 *pesukim. Tosafos* answer that the theme of *Netzavim's* curses is most appropriate to be read before Rosh Hashanah, so that the year's curses will be exhausted and will not extend to the coming year. We see from *Tosafos* that the theme of each *parashah* determines when it is read, and that each one has a unifying theme.

For discussion of the theme of *Parashas Vayakhel,* see *A Mussar Thought for the Day.*

MISHNAH OF THE DAY: BEITZAH 3:8

After the previous Mishnahs that taught us the proper method of purchasing meat on a Yom Tov, the coming Mishnah teaches the proper manner of purchasing other food on a Yom Tov:

אוֹמֵר אָדָם לַחֲבֵרוֹ — *A person may say to his friend* on Yom Tov:[1] מַלֵּא לִי בְּלִי זֶה — *"Fill up this vessel for me,"*[2] אֲבָל לֹא בְּמִדָּה — *but not with a measure.*[3] רַבִּי יְהוּדָה אוֹמֵר אִם הָיָה בְּלִי שֶׁל מִדָּה לֹא יְמַלְאֶנּוּ — *R' Yehudah says: If it was a measuring vessel, he may not fill it.*[4]

--- NOTES ---

1. This "friend" is actually a grocer with whom the buyer has a relationship such that the grocer trusts that he will be paid after the Yom Tov even though no mention of money is made at the time of the transaction on the Yom Tov.

2. I.e., a vessel whose volume is known and which has been designated as a measure but not yet used in this capacity (*Rav,* in accordance with the view of Shmuel found in the Gemara 29a; cf. Rava's interpretation there).

3. I.e., he may not ask his friend to fill up a vessel that has already been used as a measure (*Rav*).

4. R' Yehudah disagrees and maintains that even *if it was* [only designated as] *a measuring vessel* and had not yet been used for this purpose, one may not ask to have it filled — even when no mention is made of the quantity desired (*Rav*).

פרשת ויקהל

SUNDAY

PARASHAS VAYAKHEL

מַעֲשֶׂה בְּאַבָּא שָׁאוּל בֶּן בָּטְנִית — *It occurred with* the Tanna *Abba Shaul ben Batnis,* שֶׁהָיָה מְמַלֵּא מִדּוֹתָיו מֵעֶרֶב יוֹם טוֹב וְנוֹתְנָן לַלָּקוֹחוֹת בְּיוֹם טוֹב — *that he would fill his measures from the eve of Yom Tov and would give them to his customers on Yom Tov.*[5] אַבָּא שָׁאוּל אוֹמֵר אַף בַּמּוֹעֵד עוֹשֶׂה כֵן — *Abba Shaul,* a different Tanna of the same name, *says: Even during Chol HaMoed he did so,*[6] מִפְּנֵי בֵּרוּרֵי הַמִּדּוֹת — *for the clarifications of the measures.*[7] וַחֲכָמִים אוֹמְרִים אַף בְּחֹל עוֹשֶׂה כֵן מִפְּנֵי מִצּוּי הַמִּדּוֹת — *And the Sages say: Even on weekdays he did so, for the draining of the measures.*[8]

The Mishnah concludes with another ruling that relates to the purchase of food on a Yom Tov:

─── NOTES ───

5. This anonymous Tanna understood that Abba Shaul ben Batnis conducted himself in this manner because it is prohibited to measure on a Yom Tov in *any* manner, since measuring gives the appearance of making a sale in a weekday manner (*Rashi*).

6. Abba Shaul maintains that Abba Shaul ben Batnis did not necessarily conduct himself in this manner because he was of the opinion that it is prohibited to measure on a Yom Tov. Indeed, notes Abba Shaul, Abba Shaul ben Batnis would even prefill his measures during Chol HaMoed, when there is certainly no prohibition on measuring. Rather, Abba Shaul ben Batnis poured the measure at night because during Chol HaMoed, when people did not work, many would come during the course of the day to Abba Shaul ben Batnis in the *beis midrash* (House of Study) to ask their Torah questions. Were he to spend as much time as was necessary to give what he held to be an honest measure during the daytime, he would have to curtail his time in the *beis midrash.* Hence, to insure the accuracy of his measures, and to maximize his availability in the *beis midrash,* he would fill his measures the night before (*Rav* from Gemara 29b).

7. When one pours from a large container into a measure, foam forms on top of the measure. In order to measure correctly, one must wait for the foam to be clarified — i.e., to subside — and then top off the measure with liquid. In order to ensure that there was ample time for the foam to subside and at the same time maximize his time in the *beis midrash,* Abba Shaul ben Batnis would fill his measures at night (*Rashi, Tos. Yom Tov* from Gemara 29b; see *Rashi,* however, who prefers omitting this clause from the text of the Mishnah; *Rav* evidently omits it as well; see *Tos. Yom Tov*).

8. The Sages maintain that Abba Shaul ben Batnis conducted himself in the manner that he did throughout the year. Thus, his reason must have had nothing to do with either the laws of Yom Tov or the exigencies of Chol HaMoed. Rather, when being poured from the measure into another vessel in which they will be sold, some liquids, such as oil, on account of their viscosity tend to cling to the walls of the measure. It was in order to give the most honest measure possible that Abba Shaul ben Batnis would suspend the measures above the vessels overnight *every* night, so as to be sure to drain the last drops from the measures (*Rav; Rashi*).

SUNDAY
PARASHAS VAYAKHEL

הוֹלֵךְ אָדָם אֵצֶל חֶנְוָנִי הָרָגִיל אֶצְלוֹ — *A person may go to a shopkeeper whom he frequents,*[9] וְאוֹמֵר לוֹ תֶּן לִי בֵּיצִים וֶאֱגוֹזִים בְּמִנְיָן — *and say to him* on Yom Tov, *"Give me a* specific *number of eggs or nuts."*[10] שֶׁכֵּן דֶּרֶךְ בַּעַל הַבַּיִת לִהְיוֹת מוֹנֶה בְּתוֹךְ בֵּיתוֹ — *For this is* also *the manner of a householder,* i.e., a private person, *to count* items *in his house.*[11]

--- NOTES ---

9. I.e., a storekeeper with whom the buyer has a relationship such that the storekeeper trusts that he will be paid after the Yom Tov, even though no mention of money was made at the time of the transaction on the Yom Tov (see above, note 1).

10. The Mishnah here teaches that it is permissible to specify a quantity — i.e., that this is not forbidden as too much of דֶּרֶךְ מִקָּח וּמִמְכָּר, *the usual manner of commerce.*

11. Since even a private person counts his items in his home, selling by count is not considered obviously commercial in character. By contrast, weighing or measuring food is a procedure that is associated with commerce, and (as we have seen in this and preceding Mishnayos) is therefore prohibited.

GEMS FROM THE GEMARA

The Gemara (29a) cites a related Baraisa that expands on the practices of Abba Shaul ben Batnis. The Baraisa relates:

Abba Shaul ben Batnis collected three hundred barrels of wine from the clarifications of the measures. [Abba Shaul ben Batnis calculated that he had retained this amount of wine by not allowing the foam to properly settle. Although the number three hundred is often used by the Talmud as an exaggeration, it may well be that he calculated the exact amount he had retained in the following manner. For example, if he had a large 100-*log* barrel of wine and sold one *log* to each of a hundred customers, the barrel should have been empty. However, some wine would remain because of unsettled foam. He collected the residue until he had amassed three hundred barrels of this leftover wine (see *Rashi*). *Tos. Rid* adds that, although we saw in the Mishnah that Abba Shaul ben Batnis took extraordinary precautions in regard to the accuracy of his measurements, sometimes so many customers would come on Chol HaMoed that the supply of pre-measured wine would not suffice. He would then have to pour more wine into containers on the spot. The customers would not want to wait for the foam to settle and would take the wine as is. It was from such transactions that Abba

SUNDAY

PARASHAS VAYAKHEL

Shaul ben Batnis accumulated the extra three hundred barrels of wine.]

The Baraisa continues:

And his colleagues collected three hundred barrels of oil from the draining of the measures. [They calculated that they had gained this amount of oil due to their not allowing it to completely drain from their measures into the vessels of the customers. Neither Abba Shaul ben Batnis nor his colleagues wished to retain such "ill-gotten gains" for themselves.]

The Baraisa continues:

They brought these barrels to the treasurers of the Holy Temple in Jerusalem. [They did not actually consecrate this wine and oil, as they did not regard it as their property. They merely brought it to the treasurers to let them use it for the Temple's needs, if they would so desire (*Rashi;* cf. *Maharsha*).]

The Baraisa continues:

The Rabbis said to them, "You are not obligated to do this." [People who purchase wine and oil are aware of the fact that if they do not wait for the foam of the wine to settle or for the measuring vessel of the oil to drain, they will not receive a complete amount. Still, it is usually not worth their time to wait and they willingly overlook and forgive that small amount of wine or oil. Since the sellers did not deliberately intend to cheat, they may keep this extra wine or oil (*Rashi*).] Abba Shaul ben Batnis and his colleagues replied to the Rabbis, "Nonetheless, we do not want to keep this" [i.e., they did not wish to benefit from other people's possessions (*Rashi*)]. The Rabbis said to them, "Since you have decided to act stringently in this matter, use them for public needs."

[The Rabbis explained that since this surplus wine and oil came from the public, it should be returned to the public by using it for communal needs, so that they may benefit from it. Donating it to the Temple would not accomplish this (*Rashi*).]

The Gemara explains this ruling on the basis of another Baraisa, that states:

One who stole, but does not know from whom he stole [for example, he stole from many people; he now is obligated to return the stolen items (or their value) but is unable to do so, yet he now wishes to repent (*Rashi*)], he should use the stolen money for public needs. [Providing for a public need is the best manner of returning funds to these individuals, because they too will benefit from this (*Rashi*).]

The Gemara, in the name of Rav Chisda, elaborates: What are examples of public needs? The construction or maintenance of water holes, ditches, and caves to serve as water reservoirs.

A MUSSAR THOUGHT FOR THE DAY

פרשת ויקהל

SUNDAY
PARASHAS VAYAKHEL

What does the name "*Vayakhel* — And he (Moshe) assembled" signify? R' Yaakov Weinberg explained this based upon the Gemara in *Berachos* (6a), which states:

From where do we derive that the Divine Presence is with a group of ten (a *minyan*) praying? Because the verse in *Tehillim* (82:1) states: אֱלֹהִים נִצָּב בַּעֲדַת־אֵל, *God stands with the Divine assembly*. From where do we derive that Hashem is with two people when they study Torah together? Because the verse in *Malachi* (3:16) states: אָז נִדְבְּרוּ יִרְאֵי ה׳ אִישׁ אֶת־רֵעֵהוּ וַיַּקְשֵׁב ה׳ וַיִּשְׁמָע, *Then the God-fearing men spoke, each one to his friend, and* HASHEM *listened and heard*. And from where do we derive that even when one person studies Torah, Hashem is with him? Because the verse in *Shemos* (20:21) states: בְּכָל־הַמָּקוֹם אֲשֶׁר אַזְכִּיר אֶת־שְׁמִי אָבוֹא אֵלֶיךָ וּבֵרַכְתִּיךָ, *In every place that My Name is mentioned, I will come to you and bless you*. Since we know that Hashem's Presence is with even one person who learns, why do we need to derive (from other verses) that Hashem is with two or ten people? The answer is that Hashem writes down in His Book of Remembrances a group of two, while an individual's study is not written there. Concerning a group of ten, the Gemara explains that Hashem actually comes to them even before they start praying.

Tosafos ask: How can we suggest that Hashem writes down only the Torah study of a group of two? Don't we pray on Rosh Hashanah for Hashem to inscribe us in His Book of Life, whether we are with a group or not? Besides, the Mishnah in *Pirkei Avos* (2:1) says: וְכָל מַעֲשֶׂיךָ בְּסֵפֶר נִכְתָּבִים, *All of your actions are recorded in a Book!*

Tosafos answer that the Gemara agrees that all our actions are written down in God's Book. But when we study with a partner, the action is recorded in its own separate book. *Tosafos* indicate that Hashem has separate books for mitzvos done by individuals and for mitzvos accomplished by groups.

R' Weinberg explains that we know that when the Talmud discusses "books" of Hashem, the reference is merely figurative. Hashem has no physical body, and there is no physical existence in Heaven. But the imagery of separate books does have meaning. The explanation is that when a group does a mitzvah together, it is quite a different spiritual reality than when an individual performs a holy deed. It is not simply a difference in the quantity, of more people being involved in the action. Rather, the action is qualitatively different in the eyes of Hashem when

SUNDAY

PARASHAS VAYAKHEL

a group is involved. Therefore, it warrants a separate book. It deserves a separate "writing," and cannot be "written" together with the actions of individuals.

R' Weinberg explains that this is why this *parashah* is called וַיַּקְהֵל, *And he (Moshe) assembled*. The key to the entire passage is to understand the importance of a congregation and the power of its communal actions. The Jewish people fulfilled their mission in bringing the Divine Presence into the world through the construction of the Mishkan, and they did it as a community. They understood the unique value of the actions of a group, especially those of an entire nation, and they appreciated every detail of their communal building of the Mishkan.

HALACHAH OF THE DAY

There have been attempts made to attribute the laws of Kashrus (at least in part) to reasons of health. These ideas were expressed by no less an authority than *Rambam* in his *Moreh Nevuchim* (Part III, Chapter 48). According to *Rambam's* writings, all foods forbidden by the Torah are unwholesome and unhealthy.

Most other traditional scholars have rejected this theory outright. *Abarbanel* argues that attributing the laws of Kashrus to medicinal reasons likens the Torah to a mere medical text. A similar argument is made in the *sefer Akeidas Yitzchak* (§60), which strongly criticizes *Rambam's* view. He reasons that if the laws of Kashrus were based on health concerns, the Torah would not distinguish between Jew and non-Jew, for as the Psalmist writes (*Tehillim* 145:9): וְרַחֲמָיו עַל־כָּל־מַעֲשָׂיו, *His mercies are on all His works*.

Indeed, it is highly implausible to attribute the Divine laws of Kashrus to medical and health reasons. The Torah is the word of Hashem, eternal and inviolable. To relegate the mitzvos to medical advice threatens to rob them of these qualities. Medical knowledge is an evolving science that is refutable, while the Torah's truth is objective and immutable. To attribute laws of the Torah to explanations that may be disproved is to define the eternal with the temporal, a rather stilted equation.

One of our most recurrent activities, and indeed an activity that has been imbued by the Torah with many a mitzvah responsibility, is the activity of eating. In Kabbalistic and chassidic thought, אֲכִילָה בִּקְדֻשָּׁה, *consecrated consumption,* plays an important role in the service of Hashem.

The first sin committed by man was done through an act of eating. When Adam and Chavah succumbed to the desire to eat from the

SUNDAY
PARASHAS VAYAKHEL
פרשת ויקהל

eitz hadaas, they brought into the human character the desire to eat that which is forbidden. It is our task to take this physical act, the one through which sin was first brought into the world, and elevate it to the level of *achilah b'kedushah.* But how is this to be accomplished?

The verse tells us (ibid. 115:16): הַשָּׁמַיִם שָׁמַיִם לַה׳ וְהָאָרֶץ נָתַן לִבְנֵי־אָדָם, *The heavens belong to HASHEM, and the earth was given to man.* The *Chidushei HaRim* explains that the earth was given to man so that he should turn it into a semblance of Heaven. It is man's task to raise the mundane to a level of spirituality, and to sublimate and transform the temporal into the sublime.

The act of eating may be seen as standing at the crossroads where the physical and the spiritual meet. The body requires sustenance in order to function. The body craves to indulge in the physicality of consumption. The soul, however, has the power to direct the energy derived from this sustenance and to use it in the pursuit of a higher goal. As the verse in *Mishlei* (13:25) states: צַדִּיק אֹכֵל לְשֹׂבַע נַפְשׁוֹ, *A righteous person eats to satisfy his soul.*

The Gemara in *Berachos* (8b) describes the halachic obligation to eat on Erev Yom Kippur: "He who eats on the ninth of Tishrei is considered to have fasted on the ninth and the tenth." The wording of the Sages implies that eating on Erev Yom Kippur is of greater value than fasting on Yom Kippur! After all, the fast itself is only one day, whereas eating on Erev Yom Kippur is said to have the value of a two-day fast. Why is this so? The answer may be given that while the abstinence of a fast is risk-free, eating is fraught with the danger of becoming too closely involved in raw physicality. Greater glory is given to Hashem when a person, while eating, ignores the physical component of the act and elevates it to a spiritual act, a mitzvah.

We now see that the consumption of food contains a spiritual element that needs to be fostered. If so, we can begin to see why the Torah has created a whole set of laws to address how and what we eat. Tomorrow we will see further the role that Kashrus plays in one's spiritual development.

QUESTION OF THE DAY:
Why are the laws of Shabbos written next to the discussion of Moshe's radiance?

For the answer, see page 134.

פרשת ויקהל

A CLOSER LOOK AT THE SIDDUR

SUNDAY
PARASHAS VAYAKHEL

In the *Nusach Sefard* version of the *Kedushah* that is recited during *Mussaf* on Shabbos, we focus on the concept of *achdus,* unity. We say: כֶּתֶר יִתְּנוּ לְךָ ה' אֱלֹהֵינוּ מַלְאָכִים הֲמוֹנֵי מַעְלָה עִם עַמְּךָ יִשְׂרָאֵל קְבוּצֵי מַטָּה. יַחַד כֻּלָּם קְדֻשָּׁה לְךָ יְשַׁלֵּשׁוּ, *A crown they give You, Hashem, our God — the group of angels on high with Your nation Yisrael, the group below. All of them **together** will recite "Holy" three times.*

What does it mean to have true unity with others? *Bilvavi Mishkan Evneh* explains what genuine harmony with others — אַחְדוּת — is. In the physical realm, we describe things as being together based on their proximity. When we take two wooden boxes and nail them together, we say that the two boxes are now one. If we were to separate the two boxes, we would then say that they are again disparate entities. By contrast, in the spiritual world proximity is not part of the equation of unity. Spiritual unity is based upon the inner core and nature of things. Separate items whose function is the same are called unified. Individual people whose goals and purposes are the same are considered as one.

Bilvavi Mishkan Evneh provides an example of this concept by analyzing Korach and his assembly who rebelled against Moshe. *Pirkei Avos* (5:20) mentions "Korach and his assembly" as the classic example of a dispute that was not for the sake of heaven. *Midrash Shmuel* asks: The parties involved in the dispute were Korach and *Moshe.* Why then does the Mishnah mention "Korach and his assembly," while failing to mention Moshe? He answers that, in truth, there was a dispute between Korach and the members of his assembly. Though externally they all rebelled against Moshe, individually, each one had a different motive and agenda. Each member of the assembly was disputing Moshe for his own purposes, for his own benefits. There was no real unity among Korach and his assembly.

When we say in the *Kedushah* that all the angels and the entire Jewish people together, יַחַד, say praise to Hashem, this is a true union of purpose. All of Hashem's creations were created for His glory, as the verse says (*Yeshayah* 43:7): כֹּל הַנִּקְרָא בִשְׁמִי וְלִכְבוֹדִי בְּרָאתִיו יְצַרְתִּיו אַף־ עֲשִׂיתִיו, *All who are called by My Name and whom I have created for My glory, I have formed him and I have made him.* The purpose of all creation is to bring forth the glory of Hashem; there is no other goal! As *Bilvavi Mishkan Evneh* describes, when each and every person aspires to fulfill the will of Hashem, then even if they are doing different things, the inner core and intention of all is for the honor of Hashem. This is genuine unity. When we, along with the angels, praise Hashem, then there are no longer disparate entities called angels and men — there is simply a oneness and togetherness.

Bilvavi Mishkan Evneh continues, explaining that this oneness of purpose between different entities or beings needs to be expressed within each individual person as well. Each of us has various competing components to our lives. We must gather them together and form a oneness. When we lack this oneness, our spiritual growth is slowed or even stunted. This is why *Chovos HaLevavos* writes that we should pray that Hashem save us from *pizur nefesh* — separation, a lack of oneness within ourselves.

פרשת ויקהל

MONDAY

PARASHAS VAYAKHEL

A TORAH THOUGHT FOR THE DAY

שֵׁשֶׁת יָמִים תֵּעָשֶׂה מְלָאכָה וּבַיּוֹם הַשְּׁבִיעִי יִהְיֶה לָכֶם
קֹדֶשׁ שַׁבַּת שַׁבָּתוֹן לַה׳ כָּל־הָעֹשֶׂה בוֹ מְלָאכָה יוּמָת
לֹא־תְבַעֲרוּ אֵשׁ בְּכֹל מֹשְׁבֹתֵיכֶם בְּיוֹם הַשַׁבָּת

On six days, work may be done, but the seventh day shall be holy for you, a day of complete rest for Hashem; whoever does work on it shall be put to death. You shall not kindle any fire in all of your dwellings on the Shabbos day (Shemos 35:2-3).

The *Chasam Sofer* offers a beautiful thought on these verses. The Torah says here that we are not allowed to burn any fires on Shabbos. This is, he explains, because we are supposed to be burning a passionate fire to serve Hashem throughout the week, so that by the time Shabbos comes, the flame rises by itself without our having to light it. It is forbidden to light this spiritual fire only on Shabbos. It cannot be that we are oblivious to the sanctity of Hashem the rest of the week, and suddenly wake up on Shabbos needing to address our spiritual side.

Another interpretation is suggested by *Nachalas Yaakov*. Zohar understands the verse here to mean that we are not permitted to get angry on Shabbos; that is, we are not allowed to ignite the fires of fury. If we get angry on Shabbos, we expel from within us the *neshamah yeseirah,* the additional soul Hashem grants each Jew on Shabbos. It is as if we reignite the fires of Gehinnom, which cease on Shabbos. This is because, as the Gemara (*Nedarim* 22a) states: When one gets angry, all the fires of Gehinnom rule over him.

Pri Megadim understands the statement — "the fires of Gehinnom cease on Shabbos" — to mean that the strength of evil, the power of the *yetzer hara,* is weakened on Shabbos. Thus, it requires more effort to transgress a Torah commandment. Naturally, then, it should be easier to refrain from sin on Shabbos, and if we still manage to go astray, we receive greater punishment for expending so much effort to commit a sin.

R' Avraham Pam writes about this idea as well. He bases his insights on a Midrash that says (see *Bereishis* 2:3) that after Adam HaRishon sinned, Shabbos came before Hashem and said: During the week, no one has ever been killed, and You are going to begin carrying out Adam's punishment, today, on Shabbos, my day? Is this my holiness? Is this my blessing? Adam was thus saved in the merit of Shabbos.

MONDAY
PARASHAS VAYAKHEL

R' Pam writes: During the week, it is a great sin to cause pain and aggravation to someone else, but on Shabbos especially, greater care is required to refrain from causing any ill will. This is because one who causes pain to someone on Shabbos is degrading the very holiness of the day. Shabbos will go before Hashem and cry: "Is this my holiness, is this my blessing?"

In addition, *Pri Megadim* writes that since we receive a *neshamah yeseirah* on Shabbos, we are expected to act with more holiness, due to the presence of this additional soul. If we do the opposite and commit sins, we defile not only our regular soul but our additional *neshamah* as well. This is a grave offense.

What is more, says *Pri Megadim,* sinning is caused in part by a lack in our belief in Hashem. If we truly knew and understood that Hashem is watching our every move and will visit serious consequences upon us for our sins, we would never sin. Shabbos is a day when we testify that Hashem created and continuously maintains the world; it is an expression of our *emunah.* One who sins on Shabbos not only denies the total mastery of Hashem over the world, but he is doing it on Shabbos, a day designated for expressing the Master of the World's control over the universe. For this reason, sinning on Shabbos is more reprehensible than sinning during the week.

MISHNAH OF THE DAY: BEITZAH 4:1

As we have seen at the end of the preceding chapter, the Sages were concerned that activities on Yom Tov not resemble the weekday manner of conducting commerce. The next Mishnah begins with two illustrations of actions that should not be performed in their usual manner on Yom Tov, in order to distinguish them from weekday activities (עוּבְדָא דְחוֹל):

הַמֵּבִיא כַּדֵּי יַיִן מִמָּקוֹם לְמָקוֹם — *One who brings pitchers of wine from place to place*[1] לֹא יְבִיאֵם בְּסַל וּבְקוּפָּה — *may not bring them in a basket or box;*[2] אֲבָל מֵבִיא הוּא עַל כְּתֵפוֹ — *but he may bring them on his shoulder,* אוֹ לְפָנָיו — *or in his hand, in front of himself.*[3]

---- NOTES ----

1. Within the 2,000-*amah techum* (*Rav*).

2. He may not place three or four pitchers in a box and carry them, because this resembles the weekday activity of carrying burdens (*Rav*).

3. He may carry one or two pitchers on his shoulder, because it is apparent that

פרשת ויקהל

MONDAY

PARASHAS VAYAKHEL

וְכֵן הַמּוֹלִיךְ אֶת הַתֶּבֶן — *Similarly, one who transports straw*,[4] לֹא יַפְשִׁיל אֶת הַקּוּפָּה לַאֲחוֹרָיו — *may not lower the box upon his back* and carry it in this manner,[5] אֲבָל מְבִיאָהּ הוּא בְּיָדוֹ — *but he may bring it in his hand.* וּמַתְחִילִין — *We may begin* בַּעֲרֵמַת הַתֶּבֶן — *using a stack of straw*,[6] אֲבָל לֹא בְּעֵצִים שֶׁבַּמּוּקְצֶה — *but not wood that is in a backyard*.[7]

—— NOTES ——

he needs them for Yom Tov (*Rav*). Similarly, carrying items by hand shows that they are needed for Yom Tov (*Tiferes Yisrael*).

The determining factor is the mode of carrying, not the amount of jars carried. Accordingly, one may not carry even one jar in a box, but he can carry as many as possible in his hands (*Tos. Yom Tov;* see also *Mishnah Berurah* 510:28; cf. *Shitah Mekubetzes*).

4. For animal feed or fuel (*Rashi*).

5. Because this would give the appearance of preparing to carry many loads or to carry this one for a long distance in the normal weekday manner. This would be demeaning to the sanctity of Yom Tov (*Rashi*).

6. Even though the owner of this stack of straw did not designate it for Yom Tov use, and he was not in the habit of using this straw as fuel (which would also remove its *muktzeh* status), he may nevertheless use it as fuel on Yom Tov. This ruling seems to indicate that the Tanna of the Mishnah rules leniently with regard to the laws of *muktzeh* (*Rashi*).

7. The infrequently used space behind houses was called a *muktzeh,* because it was set behind the houses and was seldom entered; it is therefore "set out" of one's mind. It was used as a long-term storage area for wood and other items not in current use (*Rashi*). This wood may not be used because it is considered מֻקְצֶה מֵחֲמַת חֶסְרוֹן כִּיס, *muktzeh due to monetary loss* (as lumber reserved for construction is generally too valuable to be used for other purposes). Though, as mentioned in the previous note, this Tanna is generally lenient regarding the laws of *muktzeh,* he agrees that items *muktzeh due to monetary loss* may not be moved (*Rav*).

GEMS FROM THE GEMARA

The Mishnah ruled that pitchers may be carried on Yom Tov only in a manner unusual for weekday activity. The Gemara cites a Baraisa that qualifies this ruling:

The Tanna taught: If it is not possible to deviate from the normal manner of transporting, it is permitted to carry the pitchers in the normal way. [For example, if one invited many guests and needs to carry a large quantity of wine in one trip, the Rabbis did not impose the requirement to transport in an unusual fashion (Rashi).]

MONDAY
PARASHAS VAYAKHEL

The guiding principle for permissible modes of deviation in transporting items is that the deviation should change the manner of carrying to one that is easier than the normative manner performed during the week; the derivation should not increase one's exertion (Rashi). The Gemara offers practical examples of how this can be accomplished:

Rava instituted in Mechuza: Something that they normally carry with exertion on the shoulder, let them carry with a pitchfork on Yom Tov. Rava decreed that a burden that a single person could carry on his shoulder with great effort, such as a keg or a sack of fruit, should be carried with a pitchfork, which lessens the effort required to carry it (Rashi).

[The "pitchfork" under discussion here is a piece of wood that is hollowed out on one end to allow a person to insert his head into the recess, with the two "tines" resting on his shoulder. Two loads can then be attached to the two "tines" so that the person can thereby carry a double load. The "handle" of the pitchfork is long enough to reach the ground when it is slanted downward. When one stops to rest, the "pitchfork" is supported on the ground (Rashi to Bava Metzia 83a, cited by Maharshal here; cf. Tosafos here).]

The Gemara continues quoting Rava's examples of permissible deviations:

Something that they normally carry with a pitchfork, let them carry with a pole resting on the shoulders of two people to lessen the effort required; something that they normally carry with a pole on the shoulders, let them carry on a hand-held pole. Although this deviation does not make it easier to carry the load, it also does not make it more difficult, and is therefore a valid deviation (Rashi).

The Gemara continues:

Something that they normally carry on a hand-held pole, let them spread a kerchief over it. This, too, does not affect the effort required since the weight of the kerchief is negligible, but it is a valid deviation in that the item being carried is now covered (Rashi).

The Gemara concludes Rava's statement regarding spreading a kerchief over the carried item:

And if it is not possible to do this, it is permitted to carry in the normal manner. For the master said in the aforementioned Baraisa: If it is not possible to deviate, it is permitted to carry in the normal manner.

A MUSSAR THOUGHT FOR THE DAY

פרשת ויקהל

MONDAY
PARASHAS VAYAKHEL

In *A Torah Thought for the Day* we focused on the concept that a transgression is more severe when it is committed on Shabbos. Let us now discuss the other side of the coin: the effect that Shabbos has upon our positive deeds.

Reishis Chochmah writes: One's prayers on Shabbos are more powerful than during the week, as is one's Torah study.

Ben Ish Chai states: Each member of Klal Yisrael has the ability to build an exalted and spiritual structure through his Torah study. This structure is one's portion in the World to Come. Therefore, since Shabbos is מֵעֵין עוֹלָם הַבָּא, *a semblance of the World to Come*, we must increase our Torah study on Shabbos. By learning on Shabbos, we increase the power of our spiritual building. This is why the Kabbalists have written that one's Torah study on Shabbos is one thousand times (!) more powerful than one's learning during the week.

Perhaps the most significant statement on this issue is attributed to the Chofetz Chaim. R' Elyah Lopian heard from the Chofetz Chaim that since *Chazal* say that Shabbos is equal to the entire Torah, any mitzvah performed on Shabbos is equal to all 613 mitzvos! Therefore, according to the explanation of the Vilna Gaon — that every letter of Torah study is a separate mitzvah — on Shabbos, one multiplies every letter by 613. The result is that when we learn on Shabbos, there is no end to the amount of mitzvos we can amass.

R' Yechezkel Levenstein writes similarly in the name of the *Alter of Kelm*: All mitzvos — every detail of the mitzvos — that are fulfilled on Shabbos have the power of Shabbos and are therefore equal to the entire Torah.

Noam Mitzvos puts it this way: If one learns the whole day (during his "free" time, when not involved in the other mitzvos of the day) on Shabbos, but during the week merely sets aside some minimal time to learn daily, nevertheless, it is considered by Hashem as if he learned Torah the entire week. Hashem sees what is in a person's heart. This person demonstrates (through his actions on Shabbos) that if he had the time during the week, he would spend it engaged in learning Torah.

In this light, *BeMaalos HaShabbos* suggests that we now understand the statement of the *Zohar* that the *neshamah yeseirah* is asked, when it returns to Heaven after Shabbos, what חִדּוּשׁ, *new insight*, was originated on Shabbos. This *chiddush* does not refer only to an insight within the realm and depth of Torah study, but also includes *any* improvement — strengthening of a character trait, enhancing one's *davening,* reciting *berachos* more intently, or resolving to deal in business strictly according to halachah, etc. — that occurred on Shabbos. There is no greater *chiddush* than acquiring a new laudable trait.

MONDAY
PARASHAS
VAYAKHEL

If mitzvos done on Shabbos are more powerful than those performed during the week, then Shabbos is certainly an ideal time to begin any new spiritual venture. The increased forces of holiness present on Shabbos will enable the new project to meet success. This is why the Holy One expects us to constantly think of ways to improve ourselves on Shabbos. Hence, our additional soul is asked every week what *chiddush,* what new spiritual pursuit, was advanced during that Shabbos.

HALACHAH OF THE DAY

The Gemara in *Yoma* (39a) states: "It was said by the students of R' Yishmael: Sin dulls the heart of man." The Gemara derives this from the verse that states (*Vayikra* 11:43): וְלֹא תְטַמְּאוּ בָּהֶם וְנִטְמֵתֶם בָּם, *do not make yourself tamei through them (prohibited species) lest you shall become contaminated through them.* The word used for *"you shall become contaminated"* is וְנִטְמֵתֶם. This word may also be read as וְנִטַמְתֶּם, which would mean, *you shall become dull-hearted.*

The food one eats has a profound impact upon one's nature. Modern medicine has only recently discovered that the DNA present in every cell controls the nature of that organism. Similarly, every cell possesses a spiritual nature that is carried through the food chain. One who eats any particular animal brings into himself the nature and characteristics of that species. The fact that this is not recognized by current scientific thought is of no moment. Science, despite its hubris, has only begun to scratch the surface of the mysteries of the human body, and knows nothing at all of the unquantifiable spirit. It requires no great leap of faith to speculate that in due time science will discover the immutable truths that we have accepted on faith alone for 3,000 years.

Hence, it is the laws of Kashrus that serve as the guardian of our souls. These laws determine what we may and may not use as the fuel with which we fire our spiritual engines. Pure fuel results in a pure soul. Tainted fuel will stop up the works that are so vital to our spiritual growth.

Vegetative matter has no character; it therefore cannot affect the

MONDAY

PARASHAS VAYAKHEL

soul in any way. Accordingly, it is no wonder that all vegetative species are permitted by Torah law. Furthermore, all of the animals permitted by the Torah are ruminators that subsist on vegetative matter alone. Thus, the kosher food chain is one of simple foods that cannot affect man in a negative way. The Torah does not permit the eating of carnivorous animals or fowl. Their cruel nature would inject into our souls something contrary to Torah values. While we cannot expect to understand why each and every particular species may be prohibited, we can certainly accept that Hashem, the Creator of all, understands their nature better than we, and prohibits those capable of having injurious effects upon our souls.

Thus, we see that the act of eating is one with great possibility for both good and evil. As the saying goes, one may choose to live to eat, to turn eating into a simple animalistic act of consumption. Or one may choose a higher road, to eat to live, to eat so that one may have the strength to serve his Creator. Such behavior elevates eating to mitzvah status. When combined with adherence to the laws of Kashrus that we will now begin to study, such eating produces energy capable of uplifting man to the greatest heights.

Let us close with the words of the *Mesillas Yesharim* (Ch. 1):

"If one looks more deeply into the matter one will see that the world was created for man's use. In truth, man is at the center of a great balance. For if he is drawn after the world and is distanced from his Creator, he becomes ruined and ruins the world with him. However, if he exercises self-control and cleaves to his Creator, using the world only as an aid in service of the Almighty, he is uplifted and uplifts the world with him . . . And if he shall be the warrior, victorious on all fronts, he will be the man of perfection meriting to cleave to his Creator, to leave the corridor and enter the palace to bask in the radiance of life."

A CLOSER LOOK AT THE SIDDUR

We say in the *Lecha Dodi* prayer in *Kabbalas Shabbos* on Friday night that Shabbos is the מְקוֹר הַבְּרָכָה, *the source of all blessing* in the world. *Reishis Chochmah* explains that all the days of the week derive their value, significance, and success from Shabbos, as they receive their sustenance from Shabbos. Thus, the sanctity of Shabbos is ever-present throughout the week. In this sense, Shabbos is really in the middle of the week, as it acts as the center and anchor of the week. This is why if one forgets to recite *Havdalah* or *Atah Chonantanu,* or if

פרשת ויקהל
MONDAY
PARASHAS VAYAKHEL

one falls behind in reviewing the weekly *parashah,* one has through Tuesday of the following week to fulfill these mitzvos. Each new week really begins on Wednesday.

Reishis Chochmah continues to elucidate by using the analogy of sunrise as a parallel to Shabbos. After sunrise, the sun gradually rises and increases the power of its rays of light. It does not appear suddenly in full force, so as not to blind us with the abrupt strength of its light. The same is true for the holiness of Shabbos. The rays of Shabbos are present during the week as well, and there is a gradual build-up to Shabbos.

If we are to properly access the *kedushah* and sanctity of Shabbos, we need to seriously prepare for it. We cannot expect to walk into Shabbos and easily feel its holiness. Attaining holiness on Shabbos must be a week-long endeavor. As *Reishis Chochmah* (*Shaar Kedushah,* Chapter 7) writes: One must act appropriately during the week so that on Shabbos one can accept its sanctity. When one prepares himself properly, Shabbos arrives and finds a receptacle capable of receiving its holiness . . . The *kedushah* of Shabbos is very exalted, and it is not possible to obtain it if one is clothed in the weekday attitude . . . Therefore, one should sanctify himself daily with *kedushas Shabbos* so that when Shabbos arrives, one will be able to accept its sacredness.

Reishis Chochmah states further that if we do not prepare, and at best give minimum thought to Shabbos during the week, we will be overwhelmed by the holy rays of light that will suddenly come upon us when Shabbos arrives. Thus, it will be impossible for us to feel the *neshamah yeseirah* and the sanctity of Shabbos. Consequently, we will become blinded by the Shabbos, not being able to feel or see the holiness, just as a sudden sunrise would blind us.

When should one's thoughts of Shabbos begin? One might suggest on Wednesday or Thursday, or at the very latest, on Friday, Erev Shabbos. Surprisingly, according to *Ramban* and *Kaf HaChaim,* preparations for Shabbos actually begin on the *previous Sunday morning!* *Ramban* (*Shemos* 20:8) writes: The verse: זָכוֹר אֶת־יוֹם הַשַּׁבָּת לְקַדְּשׁוֹ, *Remember the Shabbos to sanctify it* (ibid.), commands us to remember Shabbos every day, so that we should not forget it nor confuse it with other days. As R' Yitzchak says in the *Mechilta*: You should not count the days of the week like all others. Rather, when you count you should make reference to Shabbos. Other nations count the days of the week in a way that makes each day separate from another. This is why they call each day by an independent name. But the Jewish people refer to each day in connection with Shabbos. Sunday is "Yom Rishon BaShabbos," the first day on the path toward Shabbos, etc.

MONDAY

PARASHAS VAYAKHEL

Kaf HaChaim (132:26) writes: When the *Shir Shel Yom* (Song of the Day) is recited every morning, one should concentrate upon pulling the inspiration and light of Shabbos into the week. It is a mitzvah to count the days of the week by making reference to Shabbos. We do this by reciting the introductory sentence prefacing the *Shir Shel Yom*: הַיּוֹם יוֹם רִאשׁוֹן בַּשַּׁבָּת, *Today is the first day toward Shabbos*, etc.

Additionally, *Kaf HaChaim* explains that one of the reasons why it is so significant to count the days by referring to Shabbos is because we must recognize that all of the weekdays are dependent on Shabbos for their spiritual connection and existence. Without Shabbos, there would be no purpose to existence. The world would be devoid of holiness and true connection to Hashem. The rest of the week acts as a preparatory stage for our meeting with the Master of the world on Shabbos.

> **QUESTION OF THE DAY:**
> *Why does the Torah seem to say that for six days one "must" do work?*
>
> For the answer, see page 134.

A TORAH THOUGHT FOR THE DAY

פרשת ויקהל

TUESDAY
PARASHAS VAYAKHEL

קְחוּ מֵאִתְּכֶם תְּרוּמָה לַה' כֹּל נְדִיב לִבּוֹ
יְבִיאֶהָ אֵת תְּרוּמַת ה' זָהָב וָכֶסֶף וּנְחֹשֶׁת

Take from yourselves a portion for HASHEM, *everyone whose heart motivates him shall bring it, as the gift for* HASHEM: *gold, silver, copper* (Shemos 35:5).

When studying *Parashas Vayakhel*, one is struck by the fact that *Rashi's* commentary is sparse, especially for a Torah portion that is 122 verses long! *Rashi* to the verse cited above explains that he had already written previous expositions on the building of the Mishkan in the *parshiyos* of *Terumah* and *Tetzaveh*. This is why he refrains from extensive commentary here.

Naturally, after seeing such a *Rashi*, the question must be asked: Why, then, did the Torah itself repeat all of the complex details regarding the Mishkan's construction? Ostensibly, *Rashi* found few novel insights to teach in *Parashas Vayakhel* that he did not already explain in *Parashas Terumah* or *Tetzaveh*. If so, why does the Torah write it all again?

Rabbeinu Bachya points out that the building of the Mishkan is mentioned five times from the beginning of *Parashas Terumah* through *Parashas Pekudei*. The first time, in *Terumah*, Hashem tells Moshe all of its details; the second time, in *Parashas Ki Sisa* (31:1-11), it is mentioned more generally; the third time is here in *Vayakhel*, where Moshe commands the Jewish people regarding what he heard from Hashem; the fourth time is also in *Vayakhel*, when the Torah describes each detailed step, and the fact that the Jewish people did exactly as they were told for each component and vessel; and the fifth time (*Shemos* 39:33-43), the Torah describes the Bnei Yisrael bringing the completed Mishkan to Moshe. The reason why the Torah reiterates the building of the Mishkan again and again, and does not merely say in a verse or two that "the Jewish people fulfilled all that Hashem commanded," is to underscore the loving esteem in which Hashem held the Mishkan, and the enthusiastic manner with which the Bnei Yisrael responded to the command to erect it.

Rabbeinu Bachya notes that this is similar to when the Torah states the word יִשְׂרָאֵל five times in a verse (*Bamidbar* 8:19): וָאֶתְּנָה אֶת־הַלְוִיִּם נְתֻנִים לְאַהֲרֹן וּלְבָנָיו מִתּוֹךְ בְּנֵי יִשְׂרָאֵל לַעֲבֹד אֶת־עֲבֹדַת בְּנֵי־יִשְׂרָאֵל בְּאֹהֶל מוֹעֵד וּלְכַפֵּר עַל־בְּנֵי יִשְׂרָאֵל וְלֹא יִהְיֶה בִּבְנֵי יִשְׂרָאֵל נֶגֶף בְּגֶשֶׁת בְּנֵי־יִשְׂרָאֵל אֶל־הַקֹּדֶשׁ, *And I have given the Levites — they are given to Aharon and to his sons from among the Children of Israel, to do the service of the Children*

TUESDAY

PARASHAS VAYAKHEL

of Israel in the Tent of Meeting, and to atone for the Children of Israel, that there be no plague among the Children of Israel, through the Children of Israel coming into the Sanctuary. The Midrash comments: "This is similar to what happens when a king sends his son to school. When the child returns, the king asks, 'Did you eat, my son? Did you drink, my son? Did you rest, my son? Did you get off to school fine, my son? Did you return fine, my son?' " The king repeatedly says "my son" due to his love for him.

R' Shimshon Pincus, in his *sefer Tiferes Torah,* offers another insight, based on the Brisker Rav, as to why the Torah mentions the building of the Mishkan more than once. The first time, in *Parashas Terumah,* was when Moshe first received the prophecy and commandment to build the Mishkan. The second time, in *Vayakhel,* Moshe received another directive from Hashem as to how the Mishkan was to be built, and this communication itself was the vehicle for having the Mishkan erected. In other words, the verses themselves were the power and medium that gave the Jewish people the ability to erect the Mishkan. If so, the Torah isn't repeating itself; rather, without this second description, it would not have been possible for the Mishkan to have been built.

MISHNAH OF THE DAY: BEITZAH 4:2

The Mishnah continues to elaborate on the laws pertaining to the use of wood on Yom Tov:

אֵין נוֹטְלִין עֵצִים מִן הַסּוּכָּה — *We may not detach wood from a hut*[1] on Yom Tov, אֶלָּא מִן הַסָּמוּךְ לָהּ — *except from what adjoins it.*[2] מְבִיאִין עֵצִים מִן הַשָּׂדֶה — *We may bring detached wood from a field,* מִן הַמְכוּנָּס — *from that which had been gathered* into a pile before Yom Tov.[3] וּמִן הַקַּרְפַּף אֲפִילוּ מִן הַמְפוּזָּר — *But from an enclosure,*

---— NOTES ———

1. This refers to a person sitting in a hut that is not being used for mitzvah performance, e.g., during Pesach or Shavuos. Detaching wood from a structure is in violation of the *melachah* of סוֹתֵר, demolishing (*Rav*).

2. Since the wood is not attached to or interwoven with the walls of the hut, its removal is not deemed as an act of demolition (*Rav*).

3. By gathering the wood into a pile before Yom Tov, the owner has demonstrated his intention of using it, thereby removing its status of *muktzeh.* [The wood must be detached from the tree, and within the *techum* boundary before the start of Yom Tov.] Wood that is scattered over a field, however, is considered *muktzeh* and may not be used (*Rashi*).

**TUESDAY
PARASHAS
VAYAKHEL**

one may use *even from what is scattered.*[4] אֵיזֶהוּ
קַרְפֵּף — *What is* considered *an enclosure?* כָּל
שֶׁסָּמוּךְ לָעִיר — *Whichever is near to the city;*[5] דִּבְרֵי
רַבִּי יְהוּדָה — these are *the words of R' Yehudah.* רַבִּי
יוֹסֵי אוֹמֵר — *R' Yose says:* כָּל שֶׁנִּכְנָסִין לוֹ בְּפוֹתַחַת
Whichever they must *enter with a key,* וַאֲפִילוּ בְּתוֹךְ
תְּחוּם שַׁבָּת — *even if it is* anywhere *within the Sabbath techum* of two thousand *amos* from the city.

——— NOTES ———

4. An enclosure surrounded by a fence is considered a secure place; therefore, even wood that is scattered inside it is in a state of preparedness for use, and is not *muktzeh* (*Rashi*).

The Gemara (31a) states that the opinion expressed in the Mishnah is that of R' Shimon ben Elazar. The majority opinion, however, is that scattered wood is considered *muktzeh* in an enclosed area unless it is in a pile, and wood in an unenclosed area is always considered *muktzeh* (see *Rav*).

5. *Rashba* writes that as long as the enclosure is within 70 ⅔ *amos* of the city, it is considered *near*. *Rashi*, however, requires that the enclosure be immediately adjacent to the city.

R' Yehudah's requirement of close proximity applies even if one must enter the enclosure with a key (*Rav*).

GEMS FROM THE GEMARA

The Gemara quotes a Baraisa that prohibits taking wood from a *succah*, even during the intermediate days of Succos when there is no prohibition of demolishing. The Gemara cites a source for this prohibition:

Rav Sheishess said in the name of R' Akiva: From where do we know that wood of a *succah* is prohibited all seven days of Succos? For the verse states: חַג הַסֻּכֹּת שִׁבְעַת יָמִים לַה׳, *the festival of Succos, for seven days, unto* HASHEM (*Vayikra* 23:34), from which we can infer that for all seven days, the *succah* is sanctified for God's mitzvah and may not be used. And it was taught in a Baraisa: R' Yehudah ben Beseira says: How do we know that just as the sanctification of the Heavenly Name attaches itself upon a *chagigah* offering, so too, the Heavenly Name attaches itself upon a *succah*? For the verse states: חַג הַסֻּכֹּת שִׁבְעַת יָמִים לַה׳, *the festival of Succos, for seven days, unto* HASHEM; from the juxtaposition of the words חַג (signifying the *chagigah*) and הַסֻּכֹּת (signifying the *succah*), we can deduce that just as the *chagigah* is sanctified to Hashem, so too, the *succah* is sanctified to Hashem.

We see, then, that according to Biblical law a *succah* may not be

פרשת ויקהל

TUESDAY

PARASHAS VAYAKHEL

used during the entire festival of Succos. The implication is that this prohibition is final, and even a preceding stipulation that the *succah* may be used for other purposes aside from the mitzvah of *succah* is not valid. The Gemara now questions this from another Baraisa, which clearly states that a stipulation can remove the sanctification of the decorations of a *succah*:

But is a stipulation not effective for a hut used for the mitzvah of *succah*? Why, it was taught in a Baraisa: "If he covered the *succah* in accordance with the law, and he decorated it with colored cloth and embroidered linens, and hung in it nuts, almonds, peaches, pomegranates, clusters of grapes; glass bottles of wine, oil, and fine flour; or wreaths of grain, he is prohibited to use them until the night following the last day of the festival. But if he made a stipulation about them, everything follows his stipulation." Since the Baraisa first ruled that these decorations are prohibited to be used, they are obviously considered part of the *succah* and receive the same sanctification as the *succah*. Yet, we see that a stipulation is effective in removing their sanctification (*Rashi*). Why can it not do the same for the wood of the *succah*?

The Gemara answers:

Abaye and Rava both explained: The Baraisa refers to one who said, "I do not separate myself from the decorations for the entire twilight period at the beginning of the festival," so that sanctification never took effect upon them. But the wood of the *succah* itself, upon which sanctification does take effect, remains prohibited for all seven days.

Abaye and Rava answer that the stipulation referred to here is that the owner declares that he does not relinquish his right to use the items he placed in the *succah*. Therefore, when Yom Tov with its attendant sanctification begins, the decorations do not receive any sanctification [since the owner has stipulated that he does not want sanctification to take effect]. This type of stipulation, however, is not effective for the wood of the *succah,* because one is forced to refrain from using it at twilight because of the *melachah* of demolishing. As a result, the wood does become sanctified and remains prohibited for the entire festival (*Rashi*).

QUESTION OF THE DAY:
Why does the Torah describe the giving of donations as "taking"?

For the answer, see page 134.

A MUSSAR THOUGHT FOR THE DAY

פרשת
ויקהל

TUESDAY
PARASHAS
VAYAKHEL

Every year, when we read the *parshiyos* that detail the construction of the Mishkan, we seem to experience the same thoughts. We ask ourselves: Why did Hashem write out all of the intricacies and minutiae of the building of the Mishkan? This section can make us feel that we are in an architecture class rather than studying the Torah. At the very least, the detailed descriptions of the Mishkan and its vessels seem more appropriate for the Oral Law — the Mishnah and the Gemara. What are we to make of this seeming anomaly, and what can we learn from it?

R' Yaakov Yitzchak Ruderman's approach to this issue has much to teach us about our priorities in life. In *Sichos Levi,* R' Ruderman explains that it is fascinating that the Torah often teaches complicated laws and subjects from a single word and even a single letter (or a single *omitted* letter), leaving the rest for the Oral Law (Mishnah and Gemara) to flesh out and explain. Yet, the Torah writes an enormous amount of detail concerning the Mishkan in the *Chumash* itself!

This is, he explains, because every single detail of the Mishkan has enormous significance. When someone is excited and enthusiastic about something, he personally puts his time and energy into it. This is why Avraham woke up early and personally harnessed his donkey in preparation for the *Akeidah* (binding of Yitzchak). The Torah records every aspect of his journey and involvement in the episode, because every detail is precious when we are witnessing the dedication of Avraham's heart and soul to the fulfillment of Hashem's word.

Similarly, this is why Hashem tells Moshe (25:1-7) to collect donations from all Jews for the building materials of the Mishkan. He mentions the specific materials that they should bring, such as gold, silver, copper, and turquoise wool. It was not enough to donate money, and have a "Mishkan Building Committee" go and buy the materials, because the Mishkan was to be the combination of the efforts and the essence of all Jews.

Each possession we own is part and parcel of who we are. Hashem wanted each Jew to contribute of his/her essence to the Mishkan. In each bar of gold that was donated, in every piece of fabric that was given, there was a piece of that individual. The Jews invested part of their lives and energies to acquire these belongings and thus they, in many ways, were a representation of the donors' inner selves.

The Torah lists the various ways in which the items that the Jews

TUESDAY
PARASHAS VAYAKHEL

donated were used. Every single nuance, every architectural instruction is mentioned. Hashem wants to show us how He fashioned our possessions to form one whole collective structure that was a manifestation of all the Jews and all their substantive qualities. This explains why the Torah spends so many verses describing the Mishkan's construction.

Haven't we all had something we owned of which we were so enamored that we knew it like the back of our hands? Some of us may have had a car that we could describe in lengthy detail, down to its tailpipe. Others may have a home that they bought or are building that is so state-of-the-art that they fell in love with every nuance, from the beams to the drapes. They can describe every nook and cranny of the house.

R' Ruderman explains that Hashem feels similarly about His Mishkan. After all, it is His Home in the world. It is where He rests His Divine Presence among His special nation. It is no wonder that He is "fascinated" with every detail of the Tabernacle's construction and wants *us* to be as well. But most of all, Hashem focused upon the Mishkan's building and architecture because it is a representation of the collective soul of the Jewish people, constructed with the materials they lovingly donated from their personal possessions.

HALACHAH OF THE DAY

We now embark upon our exposition of the laws of Kashrus. It is important to note that these halachos are intricate and complex. They involve many principles that interact with and overlap each other. We will attempt to delve into these principles in as detailed a fashion as is compatible with the scope of this work. The desired outcome is that our readers will become sufficiently acquainted with the rules and principles of Kashrus to recognize a halachic question when faced with one, and to be able to pose the question to a competent halachic authority in an intelligent manner.

The first step in studying the laws of Kashrus is to identify the different types of *maachalos asuros,* forbidden foods, and the origins of their prohibitions. Only then can we begin to understand the myriad factors and components that form the very foundation of Hilchos Kashrus.

The prohibition of foods may be divided into three groups: (1) prohibitions of direct Biblical origin; (2) Rabbinic prohibitions predicated by concern lest one transgress a Biblical prohibition; and finally,

(3) prohibitions that are entirely of Rabbinic derivation.

We will begin with Biblically prohibited foods. The Torah forbids one to eat an animal designated as a בְּהֵמָה טְמֵאָה, *a nonkosher animal.*

פרשת ויקהל

TUESDAY
PARASHAS VAYAKHEL

The Torah forbids us to eat any land animal (or the milk of that animal) that does not have two distinctive *simanim,* signs or indicators, that attest to its kashrus. The animal must both chew its cud (ruminate) and have completely cloven hooves. Cows, goats, sheep, deer, bison, gazelle, antelope, ibex, and giraffes are all animals that have both of these characteristics and are, therefore, considered to be kosher animals. A pig does not chew its cud although it has split hooves. A camel chews its cud but does not have split hooves. Both of these animals — and certainly those animals that have neither of the two necessary indicators — are considered nonkosher animals.

It has been noted that to this day no species has been discovered that has split hooves but does not chew its cud other than the pig. Similarly, with the exception of the camel, the *shafan,* and the *arneves* (the latter two of which we no longer have a tradition identifying them — indeed, they may be extinct), no species has been discovered that chews its cud but does not have split hooves. These are precisely the species described by the Torah as having one kashrus indicator and not the other.

A CLOSER LOOK AT THE SIDDUR

We discuss serving Hashem with our possessions twice daily in *Krias Shema,* when we recite the verse *(Devarim* 6:5): וְאָהַבְתָּ אֵת ה׳ אֱלֹהֶיךָ בְּכָל-לְבָבְךָ וּבְכָל-נַפְשְׁךָ וּבְכָל מְאֹדֶךָ, *You shall love* HASHEM*, your God, with all your heart, with all your soul, and with all your resources.* The Gemara in *Yoma* (82a) comments: If the verse already states בְּכָל-נַפְשְׁךָ, *with all your soul,* why does it need to state בְּכָל מְאֹדֶךָ, *with all your possessions*? Because there are some people who value their possessions more than they value their souls. This Gemara reiterates the fact that we seem to care very deeply and passionately about our possessions, and some people would give their very lives to defend their possessions. But why is this so? Do we not intuitively understand that life itself is more important?

R' Tzadok HaKohen explains that a possession is often something much more than a simple object that we happen to own. What we own truly defines us and gives us power. When one acquires an object, he

פרשת ויקהל

TUESDAY

PARASHAS VAYAKHEL

gains power over that object. Even if he never uses it, the very fact that he is aware that he *could* use it if he so desires, gives him a tremendous feeling of power. Why else would people bid in auctions for antiques that will not and often cannot ever be put to use? It is the feeling of, "I own it. It is mine. It gives me a sense of control."

The Vilna Gaon explains that our fascination with possessions and power goes back to mankind's early existence. Chavah, after having been banished from Gan Eden as a result of sin, gave birth to her first child, and called him Kayin. She said (*Bereishis* 4:1): קָנִיתִי אִישׁ אֶת־ה׳, *I have acquired (kanisi) a man with* HASHEM. The child was her creation, her acquisition, but she acquired him with Hashem. Hence, the name Kayin really means possession. Why did Chavah feel it necessary to make this statement? And why would she make this the theme of her child's name, so she could remember it always?

We may explain that in Gan Eden individual possessions did not exist. There was no concept of jealousy or possessiveness, because there was an unlimited supply of everything for all. Immediately after leaving Gan Eden, Chavah realized that human beings would now need to possess things in order to function in the world. Their possessions would define who they were and what their focus in life would be. Chavah defined post-Eden existence as a world of possessions. The acquisition of possessions would be the drive of mankind. Chavah wanted to emphasize the point that Hashem is the One behind the acquisition of our possessions, so that she would not get too attached to them for the wrong reasons.

R' Tzadok suggests further that these concepts also explain an episode with Yaakov. Yaakov had just completed his preparations for battle against his brother Eisav. He had divided his family into two camps so as to provide an escape for at least one of the camps during battle. The two camps crossed over a body of water, and then, when Yaakov went back across the water, he found himself vulnerable and alone in the middle of the night. This is when he was attacked by and wrestled with the angel (see *Bereishis* 32:9,21-25). The question is: Why did Yaakov allow himself to be alone?

Rashi (32:25) provides the answer, based on the Gemara in *Chullin* (91a). Yaakov had crossed over the water with his family but realized that he had forgotten some small vessels, so he returned for them. He apparently did not want to disturb or inconvenience anyone else from his camp, and went back for his vessels alone.

But why would Yaakov endanger himself, just for a few petty vessels? Indeed, the Gemara (ibid.) derives from this incident that one should never walk alone at night in a dangerous neighborhood. So, what was Yaakov thinking?

פרשת ויקהל

**TUESDAY
PARASHAS VAYAKHEL**

R' Tzadok states that Yaakov, similar to all holy, righteous individuals, took great pride in his possessions because he sanctified all that he owned by using everything for the service of Hashem. Even small vessels are not to be wasted or discarded, because they have a use and serve a purpose in our sanctification of the world. Hence, Yaakov went back to retrieve his small vessels so as not to waste any spiritual potential that Hashem had granted him through those objects.

We all have possessions, and we all need to have possessions. But how do we use them? What is the reason for our drive to get them? Do we simply want to feel powerful through the ownership of materialistic things? Or do we use our possessions for spiritual purposes?

Whenever we acquire possessions, we must keep in mind the verse in *Krias Shema*. We must strive to serve Hashem with all of our possessions, just as Yaakov did.

פרשת ויקהל

A TORAH THOUGHT FOR THE DAY

WEDNESDAY
PARASHAS VAYAKHEL

וַיֹּאמֶר מֹשֶׁה אֶל־בְּנֵי יִשְׂרָאֵל רְאוּ קָרָא ה'
בְּשֵׁם בְּצַלְאֵל בֶּן־אוּרִי בֶן־חוּר לְמַטֵּה יְהוּדָה

Moshe said to the Children of Israel, "See, Hashem has proclaimed by name — Betzalel, son of Uri, son of Chur, from the tribe of Yehudah" (Shemos 35:30).

Betzalel was given the mantle of leadership for the construction of the Mishkan — a position of supreme prominence. Yet, from the *Chumash* itself, we know almost nothing about him. What's more, the Gemara in *Sanhedrin* (69b) reveals that when the Mishkan was built, Betzalel was a mere 13 years of age! What were the special attributes and accomplishments of Betzalel that were responsible for his selection to a position of such greatness?

Daas Zekeinim MiBaalei HaTosafos seems to cite Betzalel's lineage as the primary reason for his being chosen as chief architect of the Mishkan. As the above verse states, Betzalel was the grandson of Chur. Chur was killed by a mob when he tried to prevent the Jews from worshiping the Golden Calf. Thus, it was only appropriate that his grandson, Betzalel, should construct the Mishkan, the purpose of which was to atone for the sin of the Calf.

It would appear, asks R' Henoch Leibowitz, that this answer of the *Daas Zekeinim* simply creates more questions. How can we suggest that Betzalel was an appropriate choice to build an edifice that was to atone for the Golden Calf because he was Chur's grandson? If anything, we would think that he would be the last person to ask for atonement for that tragic sin. His grandfather was killed by those that now needed atonement. He descended from someone who not only did not commit the sin, but tried to prevent it! Betzalel certainly needs no atonement, so why was he chosen to represent those who do? Furthermore, how could he be suited to grant atonement to those who killed his grandfather? Would he not harbor some negative feelings toward those for whom he was now trying to help attain atonement?

R' Leibowitz explains that it is not the genealogy of Betzalel upon which the *Daas Zekeinim* means to focus. It is the reality of how righteous Betzalel made himself. The fact is that it should have been extremely difficult for Betzalel to deal with Chur's murder, and then enthusiastically embrace the construction of an edifice that would lead to the atonement of that transgression. Through superhuman spiritual strength, Bezalel managed to summon the resolve to build the Mishkan, which would provide atonement for those whom he had every right to despise and hate. He conquered a natural inclination for revenge, or at least, indifference, proving to the entire Jewish people what a genuinely righteous person is capable of doing.

**WEDNESDAY
PARASHAS
VAYAKHEL**

R' Chaim Shmulevitz points out that the overriding quality necessary for someone who would be involved with the construction of the Mishkan was that he possess a "generous heart" (*Shemos* 25:2), a yearning to be part of bringing Hashem's Presence into the world through the Mishkan. All those who had such a yearning were then given the necessary wisdom to build the structure, along with its treasured vessels. The individuals with this unquenchable pining to construct the Mishkan became true *"chachmei lev,"* and their hearts' craving for holiness became the definitive source of their subsequent knowledge.

In this light, explains R' Leibowitz, Betzalel was the person who possessed the most generous heart and powerful desire to build Hashem's Mishkan. Hashem did not choose someone whose ancestors actually committed Chur's murder or played a role in the sin of the Golden Calf, though one would think such a descendant would want nothing more than to bring atonement to his ancestors. Instead, Hashem chose Betzalel, because he overcame what appeared to be an intractable impediment from any involvement with the Mishkan. No one else experienced such an enormous obstacle and triumphed over it. Hence, no one else could have shown the Jewish people what it means to have the most powerful desire to build a Mishkan.

MISHNAH OF THE DAY: BEITZAH 4:3

The Mishnah continues its discussion of actions prohibited on Yom Tov:

אֵין מְבַקְּעִין עֵצִים לֹא מִן הַקּוֹרוֹת — *We may not chop wood, neither from beams,*[1] וְלֹא מִן הַקּוֹרָה שֶׁנִּשְׁבְּרָה בְּיוֹם טוֹב — *nor from a beam that broke on Yom Tov.*[2] וְאֵין מְבַקְּעִין לֹא בְקַרְדֹּם — *We may not chop*

--- NOTES ---

1. I.e., wood that has been stacked up to be used in construction (*Rav*), and is therefore *muktzeh* (*Tiferes Yisrael*).

2. Despite the fact that a broken beam can no longer be used for construction and its major use would now be for firewood, it is still considered *muktzeh* because at the onset of Yom Tov it had been *muktzeh* (*Rav*). This is in accordance with the

WEDNESDAY

PARASHAS VAYAKHEL

וְלֹא בְמַגָּל וְלֹא בִמְגֵרָה — nor wood, neither with an ax, with a saw, nor with a sickle;[3] אֶלָּא בְקוֹפִיץ — only with a butcher's cleaver.[4] בַּיִת שֶׁהוּא מָלֵא פֵּירוֹת — If a room filled with produce was sealed before Yom Tov, וְנִפְחַת — but on Yom Tov it became breached, נוֹטֵל מִמְּקוֹם הַפְּחָת — one may take produce from the place of the breach.[5] רַבִּי מֵאִיר אוֹמֵר — R' Meir says: אַף פּוֹחֵת לְכַתְּחִלָּה וְנוֹטֵל — One may even breach the wall initially and take the produce.[6]

――――― NOTES ―――――

rule: מִגּוֹ דְּאִתְקְצַאי לְבֵין הַשְּׁמָשׁוֹת אִתְקְצַאי לְכוּלֵּי יוֹמָא, since it was muktzeh during twilight [i.e., the beginning of the Sabbath or Yom Tov] it is muktzeh for the whole day, even though the conditions that had rendered the object muktzeh no longer exist.

3. These are artisans' utensils, and using them is the normative manner of cutting wood. The Rabbis prohibit their usage, since it was possible to chop the wood before Yom Tov (Rambam, Hil. Yom Tov 4:10).

4. This tool, designed for cutting meat, is not usually used by an artisan for cutting wood. The Rabbis did not want to totally prohibit chopping wood since that might prevent one from cooking necessary food, and therefore permitted chopping performed in an unusual manner (Rambam, Hil. Yom Tov ibid.).

The Gemara (31b) comments that the Mishnah here is חַסּוּרֵי מִחַסְּרָא, missing words. This sentence of the Mishnah should be understood as if it read: "One may chop beams that were broken before Yom Tov (since they are not muktzeh); however, when they are chopped they should not be chopped with an ax etc." (Rav).

Although chopping wood into small pieces constitutes the forbidden labor of grinding, the Mishnah speaks of splitting wood into larger pieces, which would not involve this prohibition (Rosh, Ohr Zarua 2:360 citing Ritva: cf. Ran).

5. The Mishnah refers to a room whose walls were made by merely stacking bricks one on top of the other without using mortar or any other bonding agent. The breaching of such a wall involves a Rabbinic but not a Biblical violation. As such, the produce contained in the room is not muktzeh, since even if one were to violate the Rabbinic prohibition and breach the wall, the produce would be permissible (Rav).

6. R' Meir's opinion is that there is not even a Rabbinic prohibition to breach the inferior wall discussed in our Mishnah (Rav).

QUESTION OF THE DAY:

Why does the Torah tell the Jewish people, רְאוּ, "see" the appointment of Betzalel?

For the answer, see page 134.

GEMS FROM THE GEMARA

פרשת
ויקהל

WEDNESDAY
PARASHAS VAYAKHEL

Our Mishnah stated that one may not chop wood with an ax. The Gemara explains:

Rav Chinana bar Shelemya said in the name of Rav: This prohibition refers only to using the wide edge of the ax blade, but using its narrow edge is permitted. [The ax had a different type of sharpened edge on each side. The Mishnah prohibits using only the wide blade that cuts wood, because this is similar to work of an artisan; it did not prohibit use of the narrow edge, which is used to chop wood (*Rashi*).]

The Gemara asks:

This is obvious! Our Mishnah taught that one may chop with a butcher's cleaver. Since a butcher's cleaver has only a narrow blade and is permitted to be used, why should the narrow blade of an ax be different?

The Gemara explains that Rav Chinana's statement is necessary, for you might have said that these words of the Mishnah's leniency apply only to a butcher's cleaver, which has no wide blade; but in the case of a single tool that has both an ax blade and a cleaver blade, I would say that since this side with the wide blade is prohibited, this other side with the narrow blade is also prohibited. Rav Chinana therefore informs us that this is not so; the narrow side of this tool is permitted.

The Gemara then presents another version of Rav Chinana's statement:

Some taught that this statement refers to the end of our Mishnah, which said: Only with a butcher's cleaver is it permissible to chop wood. Rav Chinana bar Shelemya said in the name of Rav: This leniency was taught only about using the narrow edge of the cleaver blade, but using its wide edge is prohibited.

The Gemara asks:

This is obvious! Our Mishnah taught: neither with an ax. Since an ax has only a wide blade (according to this version of the discussion) and is prohibited for use, why should the wide blade of a butcher's cleaver be different?

The Gemara explains that Rav Chinana's statement is necessary, for you might have said that these words of the Mishnah's stringency apply only to an ax, which has no narrow blade, but in the case of a single tool that has both a cleaver blade and an ax blade, I would say that since this narrow side is permitted, this wide side is also permitted. Rav Chinana therefore informs us that this is not so; the wide side of

WEDNESDAY

PARASHAS VAYAKHEL

this tool is prohibited. [I.e., one might have thought that the Mishnah prohibits an ax that has only wide edges and is not used to chop wood, since is used *only* as an artisan's tool. But a butcher's cleaver that has one narrow blade might be viewed as a tool designed for chopping and, consequently, either side may be used on Yom Tov to chop wood. Rav Chinana therefore informs us that it is nevertheless prohibited to use the wider blade for any purpose (*Rashi*).]

There is no practical difference between the two versions of Rav Chinana's statement. Both agree that the narrow blade of any tool with two blades is permitted to be used to chop wood, and the wide one is prohibited to be used. The difference between the two versions is due to the tools available in their area. In the first version's area, an ax had a wide and a narrow edge while a butcher's cleaver did not have a wide edge; in the second version's area, a butcher's cleaver was double edged while an ax did not have a narrow edge (*Sfas Emes* in explanation of *Rashi;* cf. *Tosafos Rid* and *Rosh*).

A MUSSAR THOUGHT FOR THE DAY

Betzalel's tremendous strength in marshaling the willpower to assist those who transgressed and worshiped the Golden Calf, despite what should have been a natural aversion to helping them achieve atonement, is a powerful instruction regarding the human ability to triumph against all odds. This power is within all of us. We need to access the power of *ratzon,* the force of resolve.

In a description of the raw might of willpower, though utilized in the context of sin, *Maharal* explains a passage in *Sanhedrin* (102b), which states that at times a person might "pick up the bottom of his garment" to chase after a transgression. There are, he explains, two levels of desire to sin. In one scenario, a person might have thoughts of sinning, but within his deep self he is aware of the intrinsic evil in his errant wishes, and he hopes that Hashem will place a hindrance in his path, prohibiting him from carrying out his intentions. If such a hurdle presents itself before him, he takes it as a sign from Hashem, and he is grateful for the reminder to stay away from sin.

There is, however, a stronger extent of desire. Sometimes, even when a person is confronted with an obstacle to sin, and even though he recognizes that it was probably sent from Hashem to assist him in resisting his desires, he resolves that he will overcome all that is placed

פרשת ויקהל
WEDNESDAY
PARASHAS VAYAKHEL

in his path to guarantee that his desires are fulfilled. He will not alter his path, and will even "pick up the bottom of his garment" to prevent himself from tripping on a rock that may cause him to stumble and become thwarted from committing his evil plans.

Maharal's thoughts apply to the opposite side of the coin as well. Someone could long for the performance of a given mitzvah, but if an obstacle should arise, if a challenge should present itself in his path, the desire to do good might ebb, as he is compelled to reconsider his original intentions. But then there is the person who displays an insatiable desire to carry out a good deed. Any rock placed before him, any challenge that comes his way, serves only to highlight that he will do whatever it takes to see his initial desires to fruition, as he picks up his garments to lift himself above any rock and surmounts all obstacles.

R' Shlomo Wolbe cites the famous saying of the Sages: אֵין לְךָ דָּבָר הָעוֹמֵד בִּפְנֵי הָרָצוֹן, *There is nothing that can stand in the way of willpower.* Desire, *ratzon,* is the deepest and most powerful of all human traits. R' Wolbe cites *Sefer HaYashar* (attributed to *Rabbeinu Tam*), which states that Hashem brought numerous entities into the world at the time of Creation. Above them all, he states, are "the soul, the intellect, and knowledge." But there is something even higher than these powers. The creation above all else in the world, that which is closest to Hashem Himself, is חֵפֶץ, the כֹּחַ הָרָצוֹן, *the might of willpower.* R' Wolbe concludes that no matter what we learn in the realm of *mussar* and service of Hashem, we must always be aware of the vital component of all spiritual growth: *ratzon.* We must work hard, every day, to increase our desire to get close to Hashem, and we must always pray for success in this area.

HALACHAH OF THE DAY

As we mentioned yesterday, the Torah tells us that the pig has split hooves but does not chew its cud, while there are three species that chew their cud but do not have split hooves. We will digress for a moment and make a point for which it is well worth digressing.

The Gemara comments about Moshe Rabbeinu's seemingly incredible knowledge of the animal kingdom. It (*Chullin* 60b) states: Was Moshe Rabbeinu a hunter or an archer? Obviously not, but Hashem taught him about the various species. This refutes those who claim the Torah is not of Divine origin. *Malbim* notes that the Torah put its

WEDNESDAY

PARASHAS VAYAKHEL

credibility on the line when listing the four animals that possess only one of the indicators of kashrus but not the other. He cites the conclusion of the Gemara that since the Torah lists only these species, apparently no others exist that have split hooves but do not ruminate or vice versa. As a matter of fact, the Gemara takes this line of reasoning a step further: The Gemara rules, as cited in *Shulchan Aruch,* that if one is in the desert and finds an animal with a mutilated mouth and he cannot discern whether it is a ruminator or not, he should examine the hooves to see if they are split. If the hooves are indeed split, and he is certain that the animal is not a pig, he may assume that the animal is indeed a kosher animal. Similarly, if one finds an animal with mutilated hooves, he may determine the kosher status of the animal by examining its mouth. If the animal is a ruminant and it is not one of the three species mentioned by the Torah as being a ruminant without split hooves, he may assume that the animal is kosher.

The Gemara explains: Hashem is the Master of the universe. He knows that no other non-ruminating beast exists with cloven hooves besides the pig, and no other ruminators with non-cloven hooves exist besides the *gamal, arneves,* and *shafan.* In addition, the Torah lists only ten species that have both *simanim* of kashrus. Naturalists have explored every far-flung corner of the globe and have discovered countless species that were unknown to the ancients. To date, they have not discovered any new species that ruminates and has cloven hooves, nor have they found one that possesses only one of these indicators. Does this not attest to the Divine nature of the Torah?

A CLOSER LOOK AT THE SIDDUR

We mention *ratzon* in our morning prayers in one of the first verses recited upon entering a shul. Beginning with מַה טֹבוּ, we say a collection of six verses that concludes with the verse in *Tehillim* (69:14): וַאֲנִי תְפִלָּתִי־לְךָ ה' עֵת רָצוֹן אֱלֹהִים בְּרָב־חַסְדֶּךָ עֲנֵנִי בֶּאֱמֶת יִשְׁעֶךָ, *But as for me, my prayer is to You,* Hashem, *at an opportune time* (eis ratzon); *God, with an abundance of Your kindness, answer me with the truth of Your salvation.*

What is meant by the reference to an עֵת רָצוֹן, *an opportune time?* Isn't Hashem available to hear our prayers at any time of day or night? *Rashi* explains that we are asking Hashem to ensure that it is an appropriate time for beseeching, so that the prayers we are about to recite

WEDNESDAY PARASHAS VAYAKHEL

are accepted. As *Devarim Rabbah* states, there are times when the gates of prayer in heaven are open, and there are times when they are closed. There are times when Hashem is relating to the world with מִדַּת הַדִּין, *strict justice,* as a result of the actions of the world's inhabitants; we therefore ask Hashem to create a place for our prayers, even if He is now relating to the world with anger.

We then attempt to receive the flow of *ratzon* that we ask Hashem to release into the world, and channel it to ourselves. We try to engender within ourselves a deep desire to come close to Hashem, which is the primary purpose of prayer. This is how we achieve proper awareness and concentration when we pray.

Radak explains David's intent in this verse to be that he is always praying for help and salvation because he doesn't want to miss the appropriate time at which his requests will be granted. The Gemara in *Berachos* (7b) interprets the phrase עֵת רָצוֹן to refer to any time when a congregation prays together.

Abudraham cites a Midrash that identifies at least one time period that is an opportune time for prayers. This is on Shabbos afternoon at the time of the *Minchah* prayer. The Midrash states that David tells Hashem: Contrast the Jewish people with the nations of the world. When gentiles celebrate, they eat and drink — at times becoming intoxicated — sing and make merry, without once mentioning Hashem's Name. But when the Jews rejoice on Shabbos, we don't forget You, Hashem. We take a break from our festivities, gather in the House of Hashem, and praise You for all the goodness You provide for us.

This is the reason for the custom to recite the above verse during *Minchah* on Shabbos before we remove the Torah from the *aron kodesh* for the Torah reading. Kabbalists describe these moments as *ravin d'ravin,* when the deepest of all innermost desires comes forth. It is a time of extreme closeness with Hashem, a time when our prayers are readily accepted.

Another reason why it is a time of extreme closeness with Hashem is suggested by *Chidushei HaRim*. He says that late Shabbos afternoon is a time when we convey to Hashem that we do not want our *neshamah yeseirah,* our additional soul, and the Shabbos Queen to leave us. We say: קָשָׁה עָלַי פְּרִידַתְכֶם, *It is difficult for us to see You depart.* We wish to access as much spiritual greatness as we can during these last few moments of Shabbos. Hashem sees our desire for closeness with Him and responds in kind.

פרשת ויקהל

A TORAH THOUGHT FOR THE DAY

THURSDAY
PARASHAS VAYAKHEL

וְהַמְּלָאכָה הָיְתָה דַיָּם לְכָל הַמְּלָאכָה לַעֲשׂוֹת אֹתָהּ וְהוֹתֵר
And the work had been enough for all the work; to do it — and there was extra (Shemos 36:7).

The Jewish people were very enthusiastic with respect to their contributions for the Mishkan. The Torah here indicates that they brought much more than was actually necessary to fund the construction. Though the word מְלָאכָה usually means *work*, it is used here to state that they had enough materials. *Ramban* explains that occasionally the Torah uses the word *melachah* to indicate money or objects (see there for several examples of this usage).

Midrash Rabbah (51:2) describes Moshe visiting Betzalel and seeing that there were extra materials that had been donated. He asked Hashem what should be done with the extra donations, and Hashem told him to make a מִשְׁכָּן לָעֵדוּת, *a Tabernacle for the testimony*. Moshe went and did so. The commentaries are bewildered by this Midrash: To what is this referring? What is this additional מִשְׁכָּן לָעֵדוּת that Moshe built?

Matnos Kehunah states simply that the allusion is to the *Kodesh HaKodashim*, the Holy of Holies, where the *Aron* was kept. The Holy of Holies is called a separate Mishkan to indicate its significance. The extra money was used for this part of the Mishkan. *Maharzav* rejects this approach because there would be no reason to refer to the Holy of Holies as a separate Mishkan when it was part and parcel of the general Mishkan. [Moreover, if the money was needed to build the Holy of Holies, then why was it considered "extra" in the first place? Surely the money that was collected was earmarked for construction of the Holy of Holies as well!]

Maharzav suggests a novel interpretation — that Moshe indeed built an entire structure, a second Mishkan. One Mishkan was where the sacrificial service was conducted, and another Mishkan was designated for עֵדוּת, *testimony*, where Moshe would communicate with Hashem. Thus, there was one Mishkan for *avodah*, and a second one for *dibur* with Hashem.

R' Shimon Schwab utilizes the approach of *Matnos Kehunah* and explains that the Mishkan itself is called *eidus*, to stress that the focus of the Mishkan's importance was the לֻחוֹת הָעֵדוּת, *the Tablets of Testimony*, the covenant of Torah that Hashem gave to the Jewish people. The holiness of the Mishkan was derived from the holiness of the Torah. Since the Torah has no limit and its insights and lessons are

פרשת ויקהל

THURSDAY
PARASHAS
VAYAKHEL

endless, therefore the final tally of the Mishkan materials revealed that there were extra donations. Just as it is not possible to completely plumb the depths of the Torah, so too the donations for the Mishkan seemed to be without limit — they were vast, and there was extra.

Hashem told Moshe to use the extra funds for the Mishkan HaEidus, since the focal point of the Mishkan is the Luchos, the Torah, which is limitless. R' Schwab suggests that, in fact, the extra donations themselves turned the Mishkan into a Mishkan HaEidus, with its foundation in the holiness of Torah. All of the sacrifices and service that took place in the Mishkan resulted from the sanctity of the Torah that was present there. This is because the word of Hashem to Moshe, all of the commandments, came forth from the keruvim, the angelic figures placed on top of the Aron Kodesh, the Holy Ark. The extra donations were stored in the treasury of the Mishkan, the otzar, as a symbol for all to see that the identity and purpose of the Mishkan is for the Torah, which has no limit, for there is always extra, there is always more.

MISHNAH OF THE DAY: BEITZAH 4:4

The Mishnah continues to list actions that are forbidden on Yom Tov: מִפְּנֵי שֶׁהוּא אֵין פּוֹחֲתִין אֶת הַנֵּר — *We may not hollow out a lamp,*[1] עוֹשֶׂה כְלִי — *because one thereby makes a vessel;*[2] וְאֵין עוֹשִׁין פֶּחָמִין בְּיוֹם טוֹב — *nor may we make charcoal on Yom Tov;*[3] וְאֵין חוֹתְכִין אֶת הַפְּתִילָה לִשְׁנַיִם — *nor may we cut a wick into two.*[4] רַבִּי יְהוּדָה אוֹמֵר — But *R' Yehudah says:* חוֹתְכָהּ בָּאוּר לִשְׁתֵּי נֵרוֹת — *One may cut it with a flame into two lamps.*[5]

——— NOTES ———

1. One may not take a clump of potter's clay and press his fist into it to form an oil lamp (Rav).

2. Making a vessel is prohibited on Yom Tov, due to being considered as either building or as striking the final blow (see Rashi and Tos. to Shabbos 74b).

3. This too is considered to be production of a vessel, due to the fact that goldsmiths use charcoal in the process of the purification of gold (Rashi; cf. Ran).

4. This is also considered making a utensil (Rav).

5. R' Yehudah draws a distinction between a wick that is cut with a knife and one cut with a flame. If one needs wicks for two lamps, he may place the two ends of a wick in the two lamps with the middle of the wick forming a bridge between them. He may then kindle the wick, thus effectively separating it into two wicks. Since he intends to use both of the lamps, his action does not have the appearance of creating an additional wick, but simply as an act of kindling the two lamps (Rav).

פרשת ויקהל

THURSDAY
PARASHAS VAYAKHEL

GEMS FROM THE GEMARA

Germane to the discussion regarding the Mishnah's prohibition of trimming of wicks, the Gemara quoted the opinion of Rav Nassan bar Abba. The Gemara then digressed to cite another statement of this Amora. This statement commences:

Rav Nassan bar Abba also said in the name of Rav: The wealthy of Babylonia will descend to Gehinnom, as can be shown by this incident involving Shabsai bar Mereinus: Shabsai visited Babylonia and he requested merchandise from the wealthy people who lived there, but they would not give it to him. [Shabsai wished to earn money by taking merchandise, selling it, and keeping half of the profit (*Rashi*).]

The narrative continues:

He then asked for food, but they also would not feed him. Shabsai said: These wealthy people must have descended from the *eirev rav* (literally, *the large mixture*), for it is written (*Devarim* 13:18): וְנָתַן־לְךָ רַחֲמִים וְרִחַמְךָ, *He will bestow upon you [the attribute of] compassion and show mercy to you*. From this we learn that any Jew who is compassionate with people is certainly a descendant of our forefather Avraham; and anyone who is not compassionate with people is certainly not a descendant of our forefather Avraham.

The *eirev rav* to whom Shabsai referred were idolaters that joined the Jewish people as converts when the Jews left Egypt. These converts were not entirely sincere, and caused difficulties for the Jews during their wanderings in the Wilderness (see *Shemos* 12:38, 32:7 with *Rashi*). Thus, referring to someone as being a descendant of the *eirev rav* is a disparaging comment. In contrast, any true descendant of Avraham, Yitzchak, and Yaakov is imbued with the attribute of compassion. Hence, Shabsai declared that those clearly lacking this attribute must not be descendants of Avraham and are descendants of the *eirev rav*.

The Gemara cites another statement of Rav Nassan bar Abba:

Rav Nassan bar Abba also said in the name of Rav: Anyone who must look to another's table for sustenance is considered as if the world facing him is dark, as the verse (*Iyov* 15:23) states: נֹדֵד הוּא לַלֶּחֶם אַיֵּה יָדַע כִּי־נָכוֹן בְּיָדוֹ יוֹם־חֹשֶׁךְ, *He wanders about for bread, [asking,] "Where is it?"; he knows that the day of darkness is ready, at hand*. It is as if a sheet of darkness were spread opposite him, causing everything to appear dark (*Rashi*).

The Gemara adds:

Rav Chisda said: Also, his life is not a life. He is considered as if he were dead. Rav Chisda understands the phrase "day of darkness" in *Iyov* as a metaphor for death (*Maharsha*).

The Gemara digresses further to cite a Baraisa related to Rav Chisda's previous statement:

פרשת ויקהל

THURSDAY
PARASHAS
VAYAKHEL

The Rabbis taught in a Baraisa: There are three types of people whose lives are not lives, and these are they: One who must look to another's table for sustenance, one whose wife rules over him, and one whose body is racked with pain. And some add: Also someone who has but one shirt (i.e., one set of clothing). Since he does not have other clothing, he is unable to remove these to wash them. Inevitably, his dirty clothing will cause him to contract lice, which will cause him great pain (*Rashi*).

The Gemara asks:

But the Tanna Kamma did not include in his list someone who has only one shirt. Why not? The Gemara answers that it is possible for him to check his clothes and remove the lice from them.

A MUSSAR THOUGHT FOR THE DAY

When contemplating the reality of the Torah's vastness, there is a practical method with which to express one aspect of this limitlessness. This method involves the fulfillment of a group of six mitzvos that are applicable at all times. One can fulfill these mitzvos an unlimited number of times.

Sefer HaChinuch, in its introduction, groups these six mitzvos into a category called מִצְוֹת תְּמִידִיּוֹת, *constant mitzvos*. This means that whenever, wherever, we contemplate these six mitzvos, we can fulfill six of Hashem's commandments. *Mishnah Berurah*, in the second *Beur Halachah*, quotes this citation from *Sefer HaChinuch*.

Rama begins his glosses to *Shulchan Aruch* with the famous cardinal rule of the verse in *Tehillim* (16:8): שִׁוִּיתִי ה׳ לְנֶגְדִּי תָמִיד, *I have set* HASHEM *before me always*. One should place the *Ribbono Shel Olam* before him at all times, reminding oneself constantly that Hashem is watching. Every move we make, every action we take, every thought we think, is seen by Hashem, and just as we would act differently and be on our best behavior if there were a human king watching us, so too we should live this way always, since the King of all kings is watching us.

Beur Halachah comments that if one wants to fulfill this concept

THURSDAY
PARASHAS VAYAKHEL

properly, he should always have in mind to fulfill the six constant mitzvos of the *Sefer HaChinuch*.

What are these six mitzvos?

(1) To believe that there is a God Who created all that there is in the world, and that all that existed, exists, and will exist is from His will. He took us out of Egypt, gave us His Torah, and directs all the events of the world with His *hashgachah*. This is the mitzvah of אָנֹכִי ה׳ אֱלֹהֶיךָ, *I am Hashem, your God* (*Shemos* 20:2).

(2) We may not believe in other gods nor believe that Hashem gave over any powers of running His world to other forces or angels. Believing such things is idol worship. No force or power has the ability to do anything against Hashem's will. This is the mitzvah of לֹא יִהְיֶה לְךָ אֱלֹהִים אֲחֵרִים, *You shall not recognize the gods of others* (ibid. v. 3).

(3) To believe that Hashem is completely One; there are no other *shituf* forces that "partner" with Him. This is the mitzvah of שְׁמַע יִשְׂרָאֵל ה׳ אֱלֹהֵינוּ ה׳ אֶחָד, *Hear, O Israel, Hashem is our God, Hashem is the One and Only* (*Devarim* 6:4).

(4) We must love Hashem by learning His Torah, seeing His greatness, and praising Him. Our love for our spouses, children, wealth, honor, etc., should pale in comparison to the love we feel toward Hashem. If we involve ourselves in material pleasures purely for the sake of our own desires, we nullify this mitzvah. This is the mitzvah of וְאָהַבְתָּ אֵת ה׳ אֱלֹהֶיךָ, *You shall love Hashem, your God* (ibid. v. 5).

(5) We must fear Hashem and thus avoid sin. When we face temptation for transgression, we should remind ourselves of the fact that Hashem is watching and desist. This is the mitzvah of אֶת־ה׳ אֱלֹהֶיךָ תִּירָא, *Hashem, your god, you shall fear* (ibid. 10:20).

(6) We must be careful not to allow our eyes or heart to tempt us with sins involving lusts or false philosophies and beliefs. We should not run after the pleasures of life unless we have the intent for our health and well-being. This is the mitzvah of וְלֹא־תָתוּרוּ אַחֲרֵי לְבַבְכֶם וְאַחֲרֵי עֵינֵיכֶם, *you shall not explore after your heart and after your eyes* (*Bamidbar* 15:39).

Whenever we think of these six things, we fulfill mitzvos. *Sefer HaChinuch* writes that we should not go a moment without these six mitzvos all the days of our lives. [For an in-depth treatment of the Six Constant Mitzvos, see the once-weekly selections in Series One of *A Daily Dose of Torah*, in Vols. 11-13.]

HALACHAH OF THE DAY

פרשת ויקהל

THURSDAY
PARASHAS VAYAKHEL

The Torah forbids one to eat an עוֹף טָמֵא, *nonkosher fowl.*

Just as the Torah differentiates between kosher and nonkosher animals, so too it differentiates between kosher and nonkosher fowl. However, unlike the Torah's approach in regard to animals, the Torah does not give *simanim* to distinguish between those birds that are kosher and those that are not. Instead, the Torah simply lists twenty-four types of birds that are forbidden; all others are assumed to be kosher.

While the Torah does not give *simanim,* Oral Tradition passed down from Sinai does provide us with indicators to identify kosher fowl. However, since it has been determined that we lack the experience to apply these guidelines, we are permitted to eat only those fowl traditionally accepted as being kosher.

All variations of the common chicken are accepted as kosher. Similarly, common domestic ducks, geese, and doves are considered kosher. Many Sephardic communities have a tradition that quail is kosher. With the appearance of turkeys, the authorities questioned whether or not a reliable tradition exists as to their kosher status. Common custom today accepts the turkey as a kosher fowl.

There exists no definitive tradition regarding the status of the pheasant, peacock, guinea hen, partridge, swan, or certain species of wild ducks, geese, pigeons, and doves; these therefore should not be eaten. The eggs of any nonkosher fowl may also not be eaten.

The *Shulchan Aruch* issues a very interesting ruling in regard to a case where two communities have conflicting rulings and a person travels from one to the other. In such a scenario, *Shulchan Aruch* rules that one who finds himself in a community that has a tradition of eating a particular species of fowl may eat of that species even though he plans to return to his own community that has no such tradition. This differs from the usual rule that one is bound to follow his own tradition. The reason for this seeming departure from halachic norms is because, in this case, the reasoning of his home community for not eating the fowl is not based on a tradition that the fowl is forbidden; it is simply due to lack of a definitive tradition identifying it as a kosher bird. He may therefore rely on the tradition of the locale that he is currently in, which identifies the bird as being kosher.

פרשת ויקהל

THURSDAY
PARASHAS VAYAKHEL

A CLOSER LOOK AT THE SIDDUR

A well-known *Zohar* states: יִשְׂרָאֵל וְאוֹרַיְתָא וְקוּדְשָׁא בְּרִיךְ הוּא חַד הוּא, *The Jewish people, the Torah, and the Holy One, Blessed is He, are One*. Just as Hashem is limitless in His control of the universe, so too is the Torah limitless. *Ramban* writes that the Torah comprises the "Names" and "thoughts" of Hashem — it contains His essence. Hence, by definition both are endless and limitless.

We refer to the unlimited powers of Hashem in the third blessing of the *Shemoneh Esrei,* the blessing of *Atah Kadosh. Sifsei Chaim* explains that when we refer to Hashem as *Kadosh,* we are proclaiming that He is removed and separate from all of creation, above and beyond anything we can conceive. When we focus on His limitless abilities, we are forced to nullify ourselves before Him. We say to Hashem: אַתָּה קָדוֹשׁ, *You are holy,* we cannot have any real concept or understanding of who You are, given Your exaltedness. We then continue, saying: שִׁמְךָ קָדוֹשׁ, *Your Name is holy* as well — even what we do know about You, what You have revealed to us so that we can relate to You, remains unclear and unknown to us. Your Name, the ways by which You have chosen to be identified to us, and the information You have taught us about Your fundamental nature, is also Holy — it is very profound, above and beyond anything we can comprehend.

As *Ramchal* writes: One must know that Hashem's true essence and being cannot be comprehended to any extent. There is no way to draw any parallel between Him and any of the aspects of the world He created or any of the conceptions produced by the human mind. There are no words or descriptions that are accurately appropriate and proper that can be used correctly in relation to Him. Whenever we describe Him in word form, we do so by using borrowed terms and with the help of metaphors. Because we have nothing accessible for this purpose other than words that define natural experiences and reveal the laws of the created universe, it is impossible to work with anything else but such words and expressions. This is a most important point we need to underscore in regard to all we study and mention regarding Him.

Rambam echoes this theme, but adds some significant points: If so, what does the Torah mean when it says things like: וְתַחַת רַגְלָיו, *under His feet* (24:10); כְּתֻבִים בְּאֶצְבַּע אֱלֹהִים, *written with the finger of God* (31:18); יַד־ה׳, *the hand of H*ASHEM (9:3); בְּעֵינֵי ה׳, *in the eyes of H*ASHEM (*Bereishis* 38:7); בְּאָזְנֵי ה׳, *in the ears of H*ASHEM (*Bamidbar* 11:1), etc.? These phrases are used in accordance with the level of understanding

**THURSDAY
PARASHAS
VAYAKHEL**

of people, who can only comprehend physical existence, and the Torah speaks in terms that we can understand. All examples of this nature are merely metaphorical. For example, it says (*Devarim* 32:41): אִם־שַׁנּוֹתִי בְּרַק חַרְבִּי, *If I sharpen My shining sword . . .;* does Hashem really have a sword, and does He really kill with one?! Such phrases are allegorical. Evidence for this is that one prophet saw Hashem as wearing garments as white as snow, whereas another prophet saw God as wearing red garments from Bozrah. Moshe Rabbeinu himself saw (at the time of the splitting of the Reed Sea) Hashem as a warrior, but at Sinai, as a prayer leader showing him the order of prayer. This indicates that Hashem has no form or shape (since He appears differently at distinct times). Hashem's "appearance" varies according to each prophetic vision and what it contains. It is beyond Man's intellect to examine or grasp God's existence, as it is written: (*Yeshayah* 40:13) מִי־תִכֵּן אֶת־רוּחַ ה׳, *Who can appraise the spirit of* HASHEM; and it is also written (ibid. v. 18): וְאֶל־מִי תְדַמְּיוּן אֵל וּמַה־דְּמוּת תַּעַרְכוּ־לוֹ, *To whom can you liken God, and what likeness can you attribute to Him?*

R' Chaim Friedlander remarks that when we focus on God's limitlessness and His all-encompassing powers and abilities, we are forced to nullify ourselves before Him, pray with sincerity, and strive to fulfill His will.

QUESTION OF THE DAY:

What miracle is hinted at in this verse **(36:7)?**

For the answer, see page 134.

פרשת ויקהל

A TORAH THOUGHT FOR THE DAY

FRIDAY
PARASHAS VAYAKHEL

וַיַּעַשׂ אֶת־מִזְבַּח הָעֹלָה עֲצֵי שִׁטִּים חָמֵשׁ אַמּוֹת אָרְכּוֹ וְחָמֵשׁ־אַמּוֹת רָחְבּוֹ רָבוּעַ וְשָׁלֹשׁ אַמּוֹת קֹמָתוֹ

He made the Altar for the burnt-offering of acacia wood; five cubits its length, and five cubits its width — square — and three cubits its height (Shemos 38:1).

In *Parashas Vayakhel,* the Torah describes how Betzalel and his crew of skilled artisans fashioned the Mishkan and its various implements. One of these was the מִזְבַּח הָעֹלָה, the Altar where the burnt-offering (or elevation-offering) was brought. This Altar was also known as the מִזְבַּח הַנְּחֹשֶׁת, *the Copper Altar,* for it was covered with a layer of copper. It was also termed the מִזְבַּח הַחִיצוֹן, *the Outer Altar,* for it was located in the Mishkan's Outer Courtyard, while the Golden Altar, on which the *ketores* (incense) was brought, was located within the Sanctuary.

The commentaries ask a question regarding the title מִזְבַּח הָעֹלָה: If this Altar was used for offering all the *korbanos* of the *Beis HaMikdash,* why was it termed the Altar of the *korban olah,* the burnt-offering, in which the entire animal would be burnt (and ascend to Heaven, or become *elevated* to Hashem)?

In answer to this question, *Ayeles HaShachar* suggests that the Altar was called by this name because *olah*-offerings were brought on a constant, twice-daily basis, once every morning and once every afternoon, whereas other offerings were brought only on a seasonal basis (such as the *korban pesach*) or when the need arose (such as a *korban chatas* [sin-offering] that was necessary only when someone sinned). Alternatively, *Roke'ach* explains that the word עוֹלָה in the Altar's name is not related to the type of *korbanos* that were offered on it, but instead refers to the fact that Kohanim would actually *ascend* the large Altar (by way of the כֶּבֶשׁ, *ramp*) to perform their service. In contrast, the services appropriate to the much smaller Golden Altar, such as burning *ketores* and sprinkling blood upon it, were performed by a Kohen who was standing *alongside* the structure.

Malbim (*Vayikra* 1:5) offers a third meaning for the name מִזְבַּח הָעֹלָה. The Gemara (*Menachos* 49a) tells us that the inauguration procedure that makes a new Altar fit for use is the offering of the עוֹלַת תָּמִיד שֶׁל שַׁחַר, *morning korban olah,* upon it. Thus, *Malbim* explains, the term מִזְבַּח הָעֹלָה reflects the Altar's unique connection and dependency on the offering of the *korban olah.*

פרשת ויקהל
FRIDAY
PARASHAS VAYAKHEL

We may gain better insight into *Malbim's* explanation of this name by studying his introduction to the Book of *Vayikra* (Chapter 40), where he defines and explains various words and terminology found in the Torah. He notes that there are several different terms used to describe the offering of a *korban*. These include הַקְרָבָה, *drawing near* (see *Vayikra* 3:7) [this is the root from which the term *korban* is taken], הַבָאָה, *bringing* (see ibid. 5:11) [from which the expresion "*bringing* a *korban*" is derived], עֲשִׂיָּה, *making* (ibid. 14:19), הַקְטָרָה, *burning* (ibid. 9:14), and הַעֲלָאָה, *causing to ascend* (*Shemos* 40:29). While the Torah uses the first four expressions when speaking of *korbanos* that were offered in the *Beis HaMikdash*, הַעֲלָאָה is employed only when speaking about a *korban* offered on a *bamah* (temporary Altar) [see, for example, *Shemos* 24:5 and *Bamidbar* 23:30], or when describing the initial *korban olah* that inaugurated the Altar. In explanation of this usage, *Malbim* writes that הַעֲלָאָה refers to the physical act of placing a *korban* upon an Altar and causing it to ascend to Heaven. Accordingly, this action is noteworthy when it is performed on an impermanent *bamah* or on a new Altar, which until this point has not been designated for *korbanos*. When speaking about such a *korban,* the Torah therefore highlights that the person offering it did something that was heretofore out of the ordinary for this altar, and *caused* the offering *to ascend*. The Altar in the *Beis HaMikdash,* however, was a place designated for *korbanos*. The Torah thus does not feel the need to tell us the obvious, that a person caused his *korban* "to ascend." [See also *Malbim's* comments to *Bereishis* 22:2 regarding Hashem's commandment to Avraham: וְהַעֲלֵהוּ שָׁם לְעֹלָה, *bring him up there as an offering,* in the narrative of *Akeidas Yitzchak*.]

MISHNAH OF THE DAY: BEITZAH 4:5

The Mishnah continues to list actions forbidden on Yom Tov:
אֵין שׁוֹבְרִין אֶת הַחֶרֶס וְאֵין חוֹתְכִין הַנְּיָיר — *We may neither break a shard nor cut a piece of paper,* לִצְלוֹת בּוֹ מָלִיחַ — *to roast a salted fish on it.*[1] וְאֵין גּוֹרְפִין תַּנּוּר וְכִירַיִם — *Nor may we shovel out an*

—— NOTES ——

1. When salted fish is roasted directly on a metal griddle, the metal gets so hot that the fish will burn. Therefore, people take a shard, a piece of paper, reeds or straw, soak them in water, and then place them between the fish and the grill (*Rashi*).

Making the earthenware or paper suitable for use violates the injunction against perfecting a utensil.

[There is a debate among the later commentators as to why cutting the paper is

FRIDAY

PARASHAS VAYAKHEL

oven or a double stove,[2] אֲבָל מְכַבְּשִׁין — but we may press down the ashes and dirt to level it.[3] וְאֵין מַקִּיפִין שְׁתֵּי חָבִיוֹת לִשְׁפּוֹת עֲלֵיהֶן אֶת הַקְּדֵרָה — We may not position two barrels near each other in order to set a pot upon them;[4] וְאֵין סוֹמְכִין אֶת הַקְּדֵרָה בִּבְקַעַת — nor may we support a pot with a piece of wood, וְכֵן בְּדֶלֶת — and similarly, a door may not be supported with a piece of wood.[5] וְאֵין מַנְהִיגִין אֶת הַבְּהֵמָה בְּמַקֵּל בְּיוֹם טוֹב — We may not drive an animal with a stick on Yom Tov.[6] וְרַבִּי אֶלְעָזָר בְּרַבִּי שִׁמְעוֹן מַתִּיר — But R' Elazar the son of R' Shimon permits this.

——— NOTES ———

not in violation of the forbidden labor of קוֹרֵעַ, tearing (see *Beur Halachah* to 340:13 and *Igros Moshe, Orach Chaim* 1:122:7).]

2. I.e., a stove with place for two pots. If plaster from the walls of the oven [or stove] fell onto its floor, it is prohibited to remove this debris, because it is considered repairing a utensil (*Rav*).

Our Mishnah follows the opinion of the Rabbis (28a-b), who prohibit מַכְשִׁירֵי אֹכֶל נֶפֶשׁ, labor for preliminaries to food preparation (*Rav*).

3. This is done to prevent the debris from touching the bread that was baking on the walls of the oven, causing it to burn (*Rashi*). [In Talmudic times, bread was baked by pasting the flat loaves of dough upon the walls of the oven.]

4. A fire would then be kindled between the two barrels as a makeshift stove. This is prohibited according to Rabbinic law because it is similar to the *melachah* of *building*, since it appears as if one is making a tent (*Rav*).

5. The Mishnah follows the opinion that wood is considered to be designated exclusively for use as firewood, and is *muktzeh* for any other purpose (*Rashi*).

6. Using a stick gives the appearance of driving the animal to the market to be sold (*Rav*). It is therefore prohibited even to use a stick that is not *muktzeh* (Gemara 33a).

GEMS FROM THE GEMARA

Our Mishnah stated that one may not shovel out an oven or double oven. The Gemara cites a dissenting opinion:

Rav Chiya bar Yosef taught a Baraisa in the presence of Rav Nachman: If he is unable to bake in the oven unless he shovels it out, it is permitted.

This Baraisa follows the opinion of R' Yehudah (see 28a), who permits labors that are preliminary to food preparation when they could not have been performed before Yom Tov. Our Mishnah, which does not record this leniency, follows the opinion of the Rabbis who disagree

פרשת ויקהל
FRIDAY
PARASHAS VAYAKHEL

with R' Yehudah and prohibit *melachah* for anything other than the direct preparation of food (*Rashi* as explained by *Rosh Yosef*).

The Gemara records a related incident:

Rav Chiya's wife had a half-brick fall off the oven wall into the oven on Yom Tov. Rav Chiya told her, "You realize that I prefer good bread." This was R' Chiya's way of telling her it was permitted to shovel out the oven on Yom Tov (*Rashi*).

The Gemara records yet another incident:

Rava told his attendant, "Roast a goose for me, and be careful of burning it."

It was common practice to roast geese in small ovens that had their opening on top. The food would be suspended from the opening, which would then be sealed until the food was roasted (*Rashi*). Rava was telling his attendant to shovel out the oven, so that there should not be a brick or stone that protrudes from the floor and touches the goose as it roasts. Since this stone would get very hot, it would burn the goose at the point of contact (*Rashi*). It would appear that Rava here and R' Chiya in the previous incident accept R' Yehudah's ruling (see *Chidushei HaMeiri, Korban Nesanel*).

The Gemara presents another ruling related to the use of ovens on Yom Tov:

Ravina said to Rav Ashi: Rav Acha of Hutzal told us that for the master (i.e., Rav Ashi) they spread mud over the mouth of his oven on Yom Tov to seal in the heat when meat is roasting inside. But this should be prohibited, since a labor must be performed to produce the mud. [Mixing earth and water to make mud involves a subcategory (תּוֹלָדָה) of the *melachah* of לָשׁ, *kneading* (*Rashi*; cf. *Ran*).]

[A difficulty raised by various commentators is that kneading is a *melachah* that is permitted on Yom Tov for the preparation of food. It should therefore be permissible to mix earth and water when this is needed to aid in the roasting process. To resolve this, *Pnei Yehoshua* writes that making mud to seal the oven door is only a form of מַכְשִׁירֵי אֹכֶל נֶפֶשׁ, *preliminaries to food preparation*, but is not part of the food preparation itself. Hence, since this mixing could be done before Yom Tov (or because it is possible to seal the door with material that does not require kneading), it is prohibited on Yom Tov.]

Rav Ashi replies:

Rav Ashi said to him: We rely on the banks of the Euphrates River to supply the mud, and consequently do not have to perform any prohibited labors to produce our own.

FRIDAY

PARASHAS VAYAKHEL

The Gemara qualifies this:

But these words of leniency are true only when he marked the mud off yesterday before Yom Tov. The mud that was to be used on Yom Tov was marked off and moved to another side (*Rashi*).

It must be marked off in order to designate it for Yom Tov use so it will not be *muktzeh;* and it must be moved to the side to avoid violation of the *melachah* involved in creating a hole by removing dirt on Yom Tov (*Mishnah Berurah* 507:38-40 from *Levush* and *Bach*).

A MUSSAR THOUGHT FOR THE DAY

The Gemara (*Zevachim* 62b) notes that the Torah describes the Altar's shape in several ways. In *Parashas Terumah* (27:1), as well as in the verse cited in *A Torah Thought for the Day,* the Torah tells us that the מִזְבֵּחַ must be רָבוּעַ, *square.* Additionally, when describing the process in which blood of the offerings was applied to the sides of the Altar, the Torah (see *Vayikra* 1:5 and 3:2) tells us that this blood is to be thrown עַל הַמִּזְבֵּחַ סָבִיב, *on the Altar, all around.* We may learn from this description, explains the Gemara, that the dimensions of the Altar are to be similar *all around,* or equilateral.

The Gemara explains that both of these descriptions are necessary, for had the Torah stated only that the dimensions of the Altar were to be identical *all around,* perhaps we would have understood that the Altar was to be round (the dimensions of a circle are identical at each point of its circumference). Thus, we are told explicitly that the Altar was to be רָבוּעַ, *square.* However, if this word would have been the only description of the Altar, we might have understood that רָבוּעַ (which shares the same root as the word אַרְבַּע, *four*) is teaching only that the Altar must have four sides; perhaps, however, the Altar could be built in the shape of a rectangle, diamond, or other quadrilateral. It is therefore only from the combination of רָבוּעַ and סָבִיב that we may conclude that the shape of the Altar had to be a square. Although the Torah states that the Altar was to be five *amos* (cubits) square, the Gemara (*Zevachim* 62a) tells us that these dimensions were not absolute, and, based on the amount of space needed to accommodate the number of *korbanos* that were generally offered, the Altar could be as long and as wide as 60 *amos* in each direction. [Indeed, for much of the *Beis HaMikdash* era, the Altar measured 32 *amos* by 32 *amos*.] However, no matter what size the Altar was, the other two specifications of רָבוּעַ,

square, and סָבִיב, *all around,* always had to be fulfilled; it was always a perfect square.

FRIDAY — PARASHAS VAYAKHEL

We may better understand the specific need for the Altar to be square by studying *Maharal's* explanation (in *Gur Aryeh* to *Bereishis* 2:7 and *Chidushei Aggados, Kesubos* 111a) of another aspect of the Altar. Commenting on the Torah verse stating that Hashem created Adam עָפָר מִן־הָאֲדָמָה, *dust from the earth* (*Bereishis* 2:7), the Midrash (*Bereishis Rabbah* 14:8) explains that the earth Hashem, as it were, used to create Adam was from the spot where the Altar in the Beis HaMikdash would one day stand. [See also *Rambam, Hilchos Beis HaBechirah* 2:2.] The Midrash states that Hashem created man in such a manner so that, should he sin, he would be able to use this Altar to attain forgiveness.

Maharal offers insight into the deeper message of the Midrash. The place where the Altar stands is the center of the world. Accordingly, this is the one spot that contains a perfectly equal balance of all the vast spiritual potentials that Hashem implanted in the surrounding world. It is for this reason that this location was selected to be the place where the lofty service of the *Beis HaMikdash* would be carried out, for a disproportionate amount of any characteristic will never allow for the perfection that is necessary in order to serve, and become closer to, Hashem.

In stating that Adam was created from this spot, the Torah is telling us that man as well was created with the perfect blend of qualities. Unlike an animal — whose physiological makeup is such that it is able to perform only a small number of basic tasks and its behavior can generally be predicted with relative accuracy — a person possesses a wide array of *middos*. At times he is exacting and at times generous, at times social and at times craving solitude. Moreover, it is within man's abilities to achieve perfection by teaching himself to use each *middah* at the proper time and in the proper measure. It is for this reason, explains *Maharal,* that the place of the Altar is where man can achieve atonement. When a person sins, or allows one of his traits to get out of hand so his balance of perfection is temporarily lost, he must go to the Altar and offer a *korban* to Hashem. This interaction between man and the spot that epitomizes spiritual perfection and total balance will restore his own perfection, until he once again becomes a person who lives his life with total appropriateness, performing the proper action in every situation that presents itself.

Perhaps this message is echoed in the need for the shape of the Altar to be specifically equilateral. The Altar's representation of balance

FRIDAY
PARASHAS VAYAKHEL

and perfection, as well as its place in the middle of the world, demands that its physical form should also epitomize total equilibrium, with equal exposure to, and thus interaction with, all the qualities inherent in all four sides of the earth. Any inequality would take away from the message of the Altar — that man must strive to live a life in which his drives and character traits are in the correct proportion, so that he will achieve spiritual perfection.

HALACHAH OF THE DAY

One may not eat נְבֵלָה, *carrion*.

Even a kosher animal or fowl may not be eaten unless it is slaughtered in the manner prescribed by the Torah. An animal that has been slaughtered improperly, or an animal that died in any manner other than kosher slaughtering (*shechitah*), is a *neveilah* and may not be eaten.

The laws of *shechitah* are complex and are discussed in *Shulchan Aruch* at great length. Among the many variables that affect the kashrus of the *shechitah* are the type of knife used and its sharpness, as well as the manner in which the slaughtering is performed. Any improper pause or undue pressure during the act of slaughtering, or the use of a knife with an imperfect cutting surface, may render the animal a *neveilah*. Due to the complexities of these laws and the severe transgression one incurs for eating *neveilah*, only a truly God-fearing *shochet* (ritual slaughterer) who has proven his knowledge of these halachos, as well as his practical ability to do *shechitah* properly, should be used. For this reason it is customary to require a prospective *shochet* to receive *kabbalah*, certification, from a recognized halachic authority attesting to his ability, knowledge, piety, and trustworthiness.

While the laws of *shechitah* are not within the scope of this work, we will take the opportunity to make note of an interesting issue surrounding the topic of *shechitah*.

The question has arisen over the years as to the permissibility of dulling the senses of an animal prior to performing *shechitah*. Those who have proposed taking such action speak of the necessity of treating the animal humanely, refraining from exposing it to undue suffering. It is our belief that the manner of slaughtering prescribed by the Torah is humane. Indeed, the concept of refraining from inflicting suffering on living creatures is derived from the Torah itself. It is thus peculiar that over the last hundred years many attempts, some successful and others not, have been made to outlaw *shechitah* on the grounds that it is inhumane. It is even more bizarre that many of these laws were instituted in countries that showed themselves to be quite indifferent to the spilling of Jewish (human) blood. Anti-Semitism wears many different masks.

פרשת ויקהל

FRIDAY
PARASHAS VAYAKHEL

In some countries where laws of this nature were instituted, *shechitah* was subsequently permitted provided that the animal was stunned beforehand. However, halachic authorities were unanimous in their refusal to permit *shechitah* performed under such circumstances. Several reasons were cited for this position. For one thing, to agree to a requirement that the animal first be stunned would seem to be a tacit admission that the act of ritual slaughtering is inhumane; such acknowledgment would constitute a grave *chillul Hashem*. Additionally, it was feared that stunning the animal may render it a *tereifah* (a mortally injured animal). In any case, we do not permit the stunning of an animal prior to its *shechitah*.

A CLOSER LOOK AT THE SIDDUR

In *A Mussar Thought for the Day* we learned that the Altar must be a perfect square. Many commentaries, such as that of R' Samson Raphael Hirsch, suggest that the background for this law is the *Yerushalmi* (*Maasros* 5:3 and *Nedarim* 3:2) that teaches that it is either extremely rare, and according to some opinions impossible, for a square organism to be found in the natural world. By observing the world around us, we become aware of this phenomenon on our own. For example, trees, most plants, and fruits are all naturally circular or rounded in shape. An oval-shaped falling raindrop splashes into a rounded puddle of water upon hitting the ground. Tossing a pebble into a pond of water will produce circular ripples. The sun, moon, and planets, as well as their set paths of orbit, are all either round or elliptical. The petals of flowers, as well as the bones and bodies of all living organisms, are curved.

In contrast, continues R' Hirsch, we find many, many instances where the Torah commands us to construct an object specifically in a square shape. One example of this is the Altar we have been discussing. However, the Altar is not the only item in the Mishkan subject to this requirement. The smaller Golden Altar used for offering *ketores* was also square (30:2), as was the *Choshen* (Breastplate) worn by the Kohen Gadol (27:16). Furthermore, many areas of the Mishkan that

פרשת ויקהל

FRIDAY

PARASHAS VAYAKHEL

were not equilateral were nevertheless commanded to be rectangular, with straight sides connected to each other at right angles. These items include the Kohen Gadol's *Me'il* (Robe), the Mishkan Courtyard, the *Aron* and the *Shulchan*. Furthermore, although breads are normally baked in a round or oval shape, the *lechem hapanim* were specifically baked in a square mold. Similarly, the stones of the *Choshen* were not round, but square or rectangular. The Jewish camp in the Wilderness was also arranged in a square shape (see *Parashas Bamidbar*). Of course, some mitzvah objects that we use on a daily basis are also specifically commanded to have four sides: *tzitzis* are affixed only to a garment with four corners, and *tefillin* are specifically to be — like the Altar — a perfect square. [See *A Taste of Lomdus* for further discussion of the squareness that is necessary for *tefillin*.]

R' Hirsch suggests a deeper insight between circles and squares, which may be appreciated simply by looking at these two shapes. [See also *Bircas Yaavetz*, Vol. 2, p. 194.] Looking at a square (or any four-sided figure with right angles, such as a rectangle) makes it clear that someone exactingly drew this figure; a line drawn with precise straightness suddenly turns, and goes in a totally different direction. Similarly, not every area of the square is the same; some lines run horizontally and some vertically, some places are straight and some are angled. It is clear that a decision was made to draw these lines in precisely this manner. A circle, on the other hand, whose entire perimeter is exactly the same, does not immediately suggest that any exacting plan was involved in drawing this figure, for a circle continues in its own pattern indefinitely. Once we understand the arc of even a small part of a circle's perimeter, we may easily predict the form and size of the rest of this shape.

Thus, explains R' Hirsch, we may understand that a circle symbolizes the unbridled potential of the natural world, which will continue endlessly in the direction in which its natural potential propels it. However, this potential does not accomplish anything beyond itself, and, like the round shape of a circle, remains raw and unfinished. A square, on the other hand, which a person painstakingly draws — and decides when to sharply angle one line into another one that heads in a different direction — speaks of the existence and power of *bechirah* (free choice), which says that man has the ability to create areas that are not present, and in fact not planned, in nature. By appropriately using his gift of *bechirah*, man may, instead of using one continuous motion to sketch a rough circle, instead draw the more refined shape of a square.

FRIDAY
PARASHAS VAYAKHEL

This added dimension of accomplishment is *ruchniyus* (spirituality), in which we are able to use Hashem's world to achieve something that is totally beyond it — a connection with Him. This goal is the purpose of mankind, the Jewish people, and, in its most elevated form, the *avodah* of the *Beis HaMikdash*. It is to demonstrate this objective of *avodas Hashem* that many mitzvah items, especially in the Mishkan, were specifically square or rectangular. It is this shape that best epitomizes the role of man: to take raw unbridled potential and, using his latent abilities and the *bechirah* he was given, turn it into a finished and refined product.

We may remember this lesson as we don our four-cornered *tallis* and *tefillin* every morning in preparation for davening; the purpose of these square objects is to remind us that we possess *bechirah,* and must use this ability to change the raw potential of creation into refined service of Hashem.

A TASTE OF LOMDUS

In *A Mussar Thought for the Day* we learned that the Altar must be square. The Gemara in *Chullin* (18a) discusses the degree of exactness that this requirement demands. Was an Altar in which part of one of the walls was slightly notched with a small hole, instead of being totally smooth, invalid? Similarly, was one of the right-angle corners acceptable if it was slightly chipped? What margin of error, or deviation from a totally perfect square with perfectly straight walls and corners, does the Torah allow?

In apparent answer to this question, the Gemara states that the range of damage that the Altar is allowed to sustain and nevertheless remain acceptable is a crack or chip that is smaller than the size of חֲגִירַת הַצִפּוֹרֶן, *stopping a fingernail,* i.e., the width necessary to stop a fingernail that is being passed over this surface. [In contemporary terms, this measurement is identified by halachic authorities as approximately one millimeter, or slightly less than 0.04 of an inch. A crack that is larger than this, the Gemara tells us, is unacceptable.]

However, the Gemara challenges this measurement by quoting a Baraisa that cites two opinions as to the size of a crack or chip that invalidates the Altar. R' Elazar ben Yaakov states that the size of damage that disqualifies the Altar is a crack the size of a *kezayis* (olive), and R' Shimon bar Yochai rules that this measurement is the larger size of a *tefach* (handbreadth). Both opinions agree, however, that an

FRIDAY
PARASHAS VAYAKHEL

imperfection of any smaller size — such as the one-millimeter חֲגִירַת הַצִּפֹּרֶן — does not invalidate the Altar. How, then, can the Gemara maintain that a crack of this size is unacceptable?

In response to this challenge, the Gemara states that in fact, these two measurements — a חֲגִירַת הַצִּפֹּרֶן and a *kezayis* or *tefach* — are both relevant, but they are speaking of two different degrees of perfection necessary in two different areas of the מִזְבֵּחַ. In *Parashas Ki Savo* (*Devarim* 27:6), the Torah tells us that the מִזְבֵּחַ must be constructed from אֲבָנִים שְׁלֵמוֹת, *whole stones*. Thus, when the Gemara originally stated that any crack or chip bigger than חֲגִירַת הַצִּפֹּרֶן invalidates the Altar, it was referring to such a crack on one of the Altar's *stones*; a blemish like this renders a stone incomplete, and disqualifies it from being used for the Altar's construction. However, in addition to the need for the individual stones that are used in the construction to be unblemished, we have learned that the Altar as a whole must be square (38:1). *Rambam* (*Hilchos Beis HaBechirah* 2:16) explains that this was achieved by fitting whole stones together and filling up the cracks between them with earthen cement-like material to form one unified structure. Finally, the entire Altar was coated with a covering of limestone. The Gemara explains that the two opinions recorded in the Baraisa are speaking of the requirement that the Altar be square, and is telling us that any crack in the lime covering the walls or corners that is smaller than a *kezayis* [or, according to R' Shimon bar Yochai (in accordance with whom the *Rambam* rules), a *tefach*], is considered inconsequential and thus does not invalidate the Altar's status of being square.

There is another mitzvah where the article used is also required to be square — the mitzvah of *tefillin*. [The Gemara in *Menachos* (35a) tells us that we know that *tefillin* must be square from a *Halachah LeMoshe MiSinai*, an oral tradition that was taught to Moshe at Sinai.] Just as the Gemara discusses the size of a crack on the walls of the מִזְבֵּחַ that deem it as no longer "square," many authorities discuss the same question in regard to *tefillin*; how big must a nick or chip be in order to invalidate *tefillin*?

In answer to this question, the Chofetz Chaim states in his *Beur Halachah* (32:39) that we may apply to the laws of *tefillin* the Gemara's discussion of the size of a crack that did not invalidate the מִזְבֵּחַ. Thus, explains the *Beur Halachah*, we may conclude that *tefillin* containing a chip the size of the one-millimeter measurement of חֲגִירַת הַצִּפֹּרֶן, or even slightly larger, remain acceptable for use.

FRIDAY
PARASHAS VAYAKHEL

Many commentaries, among them *Eretz Tzvi* (1:12:1), are perplexed by the *Beur Halachah's* application of חֲגִירַת הַצִּפּוֹרֶן concerning the Altar to the laws regarding the squareness of *tefillin*. Although the Gemara's initial supposition was that חֲגִירַת הַצִּפּוֹרֶן is the measurement that will disqualify the Altar's squareness, the Gemara concluded that this measurement is referring to something altogether different, namely, the size of a crack that renders a stone incomplete, and no longer acceptable for use in the Altar. What does the *Beur Halachah* see in this Gemara that enables it to be applied to *tefillin*?

[In an attempt to explain the *Beur Halachah*, *Hilchos HaGra U'Minhago* suggests that the Chofetz Chaim is telling us that studying the laws of the מִזְבֵּחַ teaches us that — relative to the square object that is being considered — a small crack does not disqualify the exactness of a much larger square. Thus, just as the Gemara tells us that a crack smaller than one *tefach* does not disqualify the large מִזְבֵּחַ, we may deduce that חֲגִירַת הַצִּפּוֹרֶן does not invalidate *tefillin*.]

Birur Halachah explains as follows: The Gemara's conclusion is that the measurement of חֲגִירַת הַצִּפּוֹרֶן is speaking of the size of the crack that causes the stones of the Altar to lose their title of *whole,* and the measurement of *kezayis* or *tefach* is referring to the perfection needed for the lime that covered the Altar. From this we may infer several laws. The first, and obvious, is that a crack the size of חֲגִירַת הַצִּפּוֹרֶן is the measurement that invalidates a stone for use in the Altar, but does not invalidate the squareness of the Altar. The second law is that the measurement of a *kezayis* or a *tefach does* indeed disqualify the squareness of the Altar.

Thus, explains *Birur Halachah,* the Chofetz Chaim understands that since the entire *bayis* (box) of the *tefillin* is smaller than a *tefach,* it is not possible that the Altar's acceptance of a crack smaller than a *tefach* should apply to *tefillin*. As such, it is possible that we in fact do not know the true measurement that invalidates the squareness of *tefillin*. However, we can appreciate that this measurement cannot be *smaller* than חֲגִירַת הַצִּפּוֹרֶן, for, in choosing to explain this measurement as speaking of the perfection needed for the Altar's whole stones, the Gemara is telling us that this small size crack is negligible. Accordingly, this measurement of acceptability may be applied to the squareness of *tefillin* as well, and the *Beur Halachah* thus concludes that *tefillin* that are slightly chipped by a חֲגִירַת הַצִּפּוֹרֶן measurement are still considered to be square, and thus remain acceptable for use.

FRIDAY

PARASHAS VAYAKHEL

[As a matter of practical halachah, the Chofetz Chaim rules (*Mishnah Berurah* 39:26) that it is appropriate to have one's *tefillin* inspected by a reliable *sofer* twice every seven years. However, if *tefillin* become chipped, they must be given to a *sofer* for inspection as soon as possible, in order to ensure that this damage did not invalidate them (see also *Mishnah Berurah* 32:181).]

QUESTION OF THE DAY:
What was the significance of the 5x5-amah size of the Altar?

For the answer, see page 134.

A TORAH THOUGHT FOR THE DAY

פרשת ויקהל

SHABBOS
PARASHAS VAYAKHEL

This week's *Haftarah* describes the fashioning of the ornaments and vessels of the first *Beis HaMikdash*. Shlomo HaMelech assembled the greatest artisans of his generation to create Hashem's home. Specifically, the *Haftarah* describes Hiram from Tyre as "a man filled with wisdom, insight, and knowledge to perform all work in copper." It was Hiram who fashioned the two great pillars named Yachin and Boaz, the Laver, and all the other copper utensils used in the *Beis HaMikdash*.

The Midrash (*Kallah Rabbasi* Ch. 3) states: Seven people entered Gan Eden . . . Hiram, king of Tyre. Why? Because he made a Mishkan just as Moshe had. Only seven people merited to enter Gan Eden without transitioning through death. The non-Jewish Hiram was one of them. Granted, he was a uniquely gifted artist and graciously gave of his talents to aid Shlomo in building the *Beis HaMikdash*; however, what was so special about his contributions that merited such a singular reward?

When Moshe built the Mishkan, all those who participated in its construction were focused on doing the work "for the sake of Hashem." In the verse (25:8): וְעָשׂוּ לִי מִקְדָּשׁ וְשָׁכַנְתִּי בְּתוֹכָם, *They shall make for Me a Sanctuary, so that I may dwell among them*, Rashi underscores the words *for Me* and explains that Hashem demanded that the Mishkan be built "exclusively for His Name." In the construction of the מִזְבֵּחַ, the verse states (20:21): מִזְבַּח אֲדָמָה תַּעֲשֶׂה־לִּי, *An Altar of earth shall you make for Me*. There too the words *for Me* are explained to mean "exclusively for God's Name."

Maadanei Shmuel points out that all mitzvos should be performed because Hashem commanded them; nevertheless, if they are done for an ulterior motive, they are still considered to have been fulfilled. However, if the Mishkan or the *Beis HaMikdash* are not built "for His Name," the construction is deemed unacceptable. The reason for this is apparent when contrasting the building of the Mishkan with, say, the giving of charity. Regardless of the motive, charity is accomplished because in the end the needy receive the needed funds. However, the Temple, which is built to represent and house Hashem's manifest Presence, will not do so if it is built for any reason other than His glory.

The above Midrash compares Hiram's constructing of the copper ornaments and vessels of Shlomo's *Beis HaMikdash* with Moshe's construction of the Mishkan. Just as Moshe's Mishkan was constructed solely for the sake of Hashem, so too, Hiram's artistic creations were

SHABBOS

PARASHAS VAYAKHEL

intended solely for the sake of Hashem. Moreover, we now understand the importance of Ḥiram being identified as a non-Jewish king. Granted that he was an excellent craftsman; however, he was primarily a monarch, and monarchs usually do not engage in such labor even if they are gifted artisans. However, when asked to participate and contribute to the construction of Hashem's Temple, Ḥiram embraced the opportunity with great humility and for the sole intention of honoring Hashem. In return, Hashem gifted Ḥiram by inviting him into Gan Eden.

MISHNAH OF THE DAY: BEITZAH 4:6

The Mishnah discusses the *muktzeh* status of various types of wood on Yom Tov:

רַבִּי אֱלִיעֶזֶר אוֹמֵר — *R' Eliezer says:* נוֹטֵל אָדָם קֵיסָם מִשֶּׁלְּפָנָיו — *A person may take a sliver* of wood *from that which is before him* in his house[1] לַחֲצוֹץ בּוֹ שִׁינָּיו — *with which to pick his teeth* on Yom Tov; וּמְגַבֵּב מִן הֶחָצֵר וּמַדְלִיק — *and one may gather* slivers of wood and hay *from the courtyard and* use them to *kindle* a fire on Yom Tov, שֶׁכָּל מַה שֶּׁבֶּחָצֵר מוּכָן הוּא — *because everything that is in the courtyard is considered prepared* and therefore not *muktzeh*. וַחֲכָמִים אוֹמְרִים — *But the Sages say:* מְגַבֵּב מִשֶּׁלְּפָנָיו וּמַדְלִיק — *One may gather* only *from that which is before him* in his house, *and* may *kindle* a fire on Yom Tov only with such wood.[2]

— NOTES —

1. R' Eliezer's opinion is that wood is permitted to be moved on Yom Tov even not for the purpose of kindling. Although this initial ruling implies a permit for wood specially taken from "before him" in his home, in truth R' Eliezer extends this permit to wood in one's courtyard as well (as is evident from R' Eliezer's next ruling). The Mishnah states his ruling in this way to emphasize that the Sages who disagree with him prohibit using even wood that is lying in the house for any purpose other than kindling on Yom Tov (*Rav*).

2. The Sages dispute R' Eliezer on two points: (1) They maintain that one may gather only from that which is before him, in the house, and not from the courtyard. Since hay and slivers of wood are small objects, gathering them requires an expenditure of effort, and they cannot be considered prepared when in the courtyard; therefore, they are classified as *muktzeh*. In the house, however, they are not *muktzeh*. (2) The Sages also hold that one may use these materials only for kindling and not for other purposes, such as cleaning teeth. This is because they hold that wood may be used only for kindling on Yom Tov, and not for any other purpose (*Rav*).

GEMS FROM THE GEMARA

פרשת
ויקהל

SHABBOS
PARASHAS
VAYAKHEL

The Mishnah discussed the use of a sliver of wood as a toothpick. The Gemara cites a ruling that permits wood to be splintered to slivers on Yom Tov for this use if the sliver may also be used as animal food:

Rav Yehudah said: If items are suitable to be used as food for an animal, the prohibition of perfecting a utensil does not apply to them. For example, it is permitted to trim hay or leaves of reeds on the Sabbath to use as a toothpick (*Rashi*). Since these materials are soft enough for an animal to eat, anything fabricated from them would not be a lasting item; hence, the prohibition of perfecting a utensil has not been violated (*Ran*).

The Gemara asks:

Rav Kahana challenged Rav Yehudah from the following Baraisa: We may handle fragrant woods on the Sabbath to smell them, or to wave them before a sick person who needs the air. And one may roll such a piece of wood between his fingers to stimulate the fragrance and smell it, but he may not clip it to smell it. [He may not clip it so that the place of the incision will be moist and contain a more fragrant aroma, because if he were permitted to do so, he might also unwittingly cut it to use as a utensil to pick his teeth. That would be in violation of the Biblical *melachah* of making a utensil (*Rashi*).]

The Baraisa continues:

However, if he did clip it, he is exempt from punishment, but it is prohibited. He may not clip it to pick his teeth; and if he did clip it for this purpose, he is liable to bring a *chatas*-offering.

Since some types of fragrant wood are suitable for use as animal food, this Baraisa, which prohiits clipping all sticks for use as a toothpick, contradicts Rav Yehudah, who permitted this!

The Gemara answers that the Baraisa discusses specifically wood that is *not* used for animal food:

Rav Yehudah said to Rav Kahana: Now, if you had found a Baraisa that said that clipping a stick suitable for animal food is exempt from Biblical liability, but is prohibited Rabbinically, it would be a difficulty for me, because I said that this is permitted. A Baraisa that states that one is liable for a *chatas*-offering should certainly present a difficulty! However, that Baraisa was taught with regard to hard wood, which is not suitable for use as animal food. Hence, this does not contradict Rav Yehudah's lenient ruling that was made regarding soft wood, which is suitable for animal food.

פרשת ויקהל

SHABBOS

PARASHAS VAYAKHEL

The Gemara objects to this answer, since this does not seem to be the intent of the Baraisa:

Can hard wood be rolled to stimulate fragrance? If the Baraisa is referring to hard wood, how could it be rolled between one's fingers for fragrance?

The Gemara answers:

It is as if the Baraisa were missing words of explanation, and this is what the Baraisa means to teach: One may roll it between his fingers and smell it. However, when were these words said? Only with regard to soft wood; but hard wood he may not clip. And, if he did clip it, he is exempt from punishment, but it is prohibited. He may not clip it to pick his teeth, and if he did clip it for this purpose, he is liable for a *chatas*-offering. Thus, the Baraisa's stringency not to clip wood for fragrance was limited to wood unfit for animal food, and therefore does not contradict the ruling of Rav Yehudah.

A MUSSAR THOUGHT FOR THE DAY

In *A Torah Thought for the Day* we cited the Midrash that says that King Hiram of Tyre was rewarded for his work in the *Beis HaMikdash* by transitioning into Gan Eden without the process of death. Why was this the particular reward for his artistry and devotion?

What exactly is Gan Eden, and why was it created? There are many opinions as to whether Gan Eden actually physically exists. The Torah in *Bereishis* seemingly presents it as such, and many accept that it does exist. The verse states (*Bereishis* 2:15): וַיִּקַּח ה' אֱלֹהִים אֶת־הָאָדָם וַיַּנִּחֵהוּ בְגַן־עֵדֶן לְעָבְדָהּ וּלְשָׁמְרָהּ, HASHEM God took the man and placed him in the Garden of Eden, to work it and to guard it. The Raavad explains that Adam's "work" in Gan Eden had nothing to do with caring for the trees and flowers. His "work" was to expose Hashem's manifest presence in the laws of nature. The verse states (ibid. 3:8): וַיִּשְׁמְעוּ אֶת־קוֹל ה' אֱלֹהִים מִתְהַלֵּךְ בַּגָּן לְרוּחַ הַיּוֹם, They heard the sound of HASHEM/God manifesting itself in the garden toward evening.

Gan Eden was the world as it should have been, and as it can be. Within its perfection lay the irrefutable proof of Hashem's existence, and His reasons for creating the universe. With all their needs cared for, Adam and Chavah had many lifetimes of years to freely explore and understand the extent of Hashem's love and majesty. Once understood, it was their responsibility to "guard" that knowledge by passing it on to the generations that would follow. Unfortunately, after Adam and Chavah sinned, Hashem withdrew the overt evidence of His presence

פרשת ויקהל

SHABBOS
PARASHAS VAYAKHEL

and hid Himself behind the veil of nature. Of course, humanity's "work" remains the same. Our "work" is still to expose Hashem's presence in the laws of nature; however, in a world of challenges, distractions, and limited time, our work is far more difficult.

As history unfolded, Hashem provided us with aids to help us recognize and understand Him: the *Avos*, the miracles of Egypt and the Wilderness, the Torah, the gift of Eretz Yisrael, and finally the *Beis HaMikdash*. Each of these landmarks of our development allowed us to see evidence of Hashem's mastery that otherwise remained hidden within nature. In fact, *Chazal* tell us that at Har Sinai the Jews had returned to the status of Adam and Chavah before sinning. This means that our awareness and acceptance of Hashem's mastery was on par with the experience of Adam and Chavah in Gan Eden.

Simply put, Gan Eden was knowing that we have no other purpose except recognizing and proclaiming Hashem's glory. The *Avos* and *Imahos* lived their lives with that awareness. Moshe and the Bnei Yisrael experienced that realization at the time of the Exodus, in the Wilderness, and at *Matan Torah;* and living in Eretz Yisrael at the time of the *Beis HaMikdash* was another opportunity to sense the presence of Hashem.

Hiram was the non-Jewish king of Tyre and a gifted master craftsman. As a monarch and an artist we could understand his feelings of personal ego and empowerment. However, with total humility Hiram embraced the opportunity of participating in building the *Beis HaMikdash* for the sole purpose of manifesting Hashem's glory in the world. What more appropriate reward could there be than inviting Hiram into Gan Eden to experience the unveiled presence of Hashem manifested in His physical universe!

HALACHAH OF THE DAY

One may not eat a *tereifah*, a mortally injured animal.

Any animal or fowl which, as a result of a birth defect, disease, or inflicted wound, suffers from a mortally defective organ or limb is considered a *tereifah* and may not be eaten.

While the literal meaning of the word טְרֵיפָה implies that we are speaking of an animal that was *torn,* i.e., it was assaulted by another animal and mortally injured, the *Rambam* tells us that the Torah does not differentiate between an animal whose injury is due to an assault and an animal whose injury is due to any other external or internal source.

SHABBOS PARASHAS VAYAKHEL

The defects that render an animal a *tereifah* are enumerated by the Sages based on Sinaitic tradition. A defect not mentioned by the Sages does not render an animal a *tereifah* even if contemporary medical knowledge indicates that the animal is certain to expire shortly. Conversely, a defect mentioned by the Sages confers *tereifah* status upon the animal despite the opinion of modern medicine that the animal will regain its health.

In accordance with the laws of *tereifah,* an animal that is suffering from fractures of certain bones, is lacking certain organs, or has certain organ walls perforated is considered a *tereifah* and may not be eaten. It is possible that even if one slaughters a seemingly kosher animal in the proper manner, it is in actuality a *tereifah* due to a latent *tereifah* condition of which one was unaware prior to the slaughtering. Although generally every animal and fowl is assumed to be free of any *tereifah* injuries, and therefore may be slaughtered and eaten without inspection, the lungs of an animal must be inspected after slaughtering in order to insure that the animal is not suffering from a condition that would render it a *tereifah*. This examination is known as *bedikah,* or *bedikas ha'rei'ah*. These halachos are discussed at great length in *Shulchan Aruch*.

While the rules of *tereifah* are of great relevance in the slaughterhouse, they rarely affect the home, since nowadays most kosher meat is purchased prepared and prepackaged. However, one must be aware of certain rules of *tereifah* in regard to the kashrus of fowl, since from time to time one may purchase a fowl and find a broken limb. One who does discover a broken wing or leg on a fowl, or a discoloration on the leg, should consult a competent halachic authority to determine the kashrus status of the fowl.

A CLOSER LOOK AT THE SIDDUR

Today, we will continue our study of the introductory prayer of *Yehi Ratzon* that we recite before *Bircas HaChodesh,* the Blessing of the New Month, that is recited before *Mussaf* on the Shabbos that precedes Rosh Chodesh: יְהִי רָצוֹן מִלְּפָנֶיךָ ה' אֱלֹהֵינוּ . . . וְתִתֶּן לָנוּ . . . חַיִּים שֶׁיֵּשׁ בָּהֶם יִרְאַת שָׁמַיִם וְיִרְאַת חֵטְא . . . חַיִּים שֶׁתְּהֵא בָנוּ אַהֲבַת תּוֹרָה וְיִרְאַת שָׁמַיִם, *May it be Your will, Hashem, our God . . . May You give us . . . a life in which there is fear of Heaven and fear of sin . . . a life in which we will have love of Torah and fear of Heaven.*

There seems to be a redundancy within this prayer, as we are apparently requesting the same thing several times. We may ask: What are

פרשת ויקהל
SHABBOS
PARASHAS VAYAKHEL

these two things — fear of Heaven and fear of sin — for which we are praying? Aren't fear of Heaven and fear of sin the same thing? And why do we again ask for a life in which we will have fear of Heaven, after we did so already earlier in the prayer?

R' Chaim Kanievsky, in his *Orchos Yosher,* explains the difference between these two requests. The most basic level of *yirah* is fear of Heaven, which means the fear of Hashem, Whose *Shechinah* is in Heaven and Who commanded us not to sin. But then there is another level of fear — a much more advanced one — a fear of the sin itself. This means that the prohibitions of the Torah have become so real to a person that he views a sin as some type of poison, which can instantly have a major impact on his spiritual health. This fear causes him to wish to avoid the sin itself because of its evil nature, not only because Hashem commanded him to do so.

R' Chaim explains that punishment for sinning is not something that is independent of the sin committed. Rather, Hashem created a natural effect, that the punishment is an outcome of the very sin. This makes the sin itself something that is to be feared.

When one's belief becomes so tangible and real that he views a sin as a burning fire that will destroy him if he transgresses, he can attain a much more exalted level of *yirah.* A story is told about the Vilna Gaon: in his early years prior to his bar mitzvah, he once accidentally touched *muktzeh* on Shabbos. Upon realizing that he had done so, he fainted. He viewed this transgression as severely as if he had accidentally cut off his hand — that is how real and dangerous the sin was in his eyes.

As to why we repeat our request for fear of Heaven later in the prayer, *Shiras David* explains that the second time, the request is paired with our request for אַהֲבַת תּוֹרָה, *love of Torah*. When one learns Torah with true *ahavah,* love of Hashem, his *yiras Shamayim* becomes magnified. As the Mishnah in *Avos* states (6:1): One who studies Torah לִשְׁמָהּ, *for its own sake,* becomes imbued with humility and fear. If a person succeeds in reaching such a level, he can pray for an ever higher level of fear of Heaven — one that is attained only after one has a love for Torah (see further in *Nefesh HaChaim, Shaar* §4).

QUESTION OF THE DAY:
What similarity do we find between the builders of the Mishkan and the builders of the Beis HaMikdash?

For the answer, see page 134.

ANSWERS TO QUESTION OF THE DAY

Sunday:
Shabbos, too, has a "shine" that makes it incomparable to the other weekdays (*Baal HaTurim*).

Monday:
This is an allusion to the 6,000 years that the world is to exist, during which we must do mitzvos (*Shelah*).

Tuesday:
When a prominent person accepts one's gift, it is as if the giver has received a gift (*Alshich*).

Wednesday:
We learn from this that one does not appoint a leader over the people without consulting them first (*Berachos* 55a).

Thursday:
The Torah says that there was both *enough* (דַּיָּם) and *extra* (וְהוֹתֵר). Why? Because although there was extra, Hashem made a miracle and all of it was used, so that no one's donation would be left out (*Ohr HaChaim*).

Friday:
This was an allusion to the *Luchos*, each of which had five of the Ten Commandments written upon it (*Daas Zekeinim*).

Shabbos:
Betzalel and Oholiav came from the tribes of Yehudah and Dan respectively; similarly, Shlomo was from Yehudah and Chiram (according to some opinions) was from Dan (see *Pesikta Rabbasi* 6:8).

פרשת פקודי
Parashas Pekudei

פרשת פקודי

SUNDAY

PARASHAS PEKUDEI

A TORAH THOUGHT FOR THE DAY

אֵלֶּה פְקוּדֵי הַמִּשְׁכָּן מִשְׁכַּן הָעֵדֻת אֲשֶׁר פֻּקַּד עַל־פִּי מֹשֶׁה עֲבֹדַת הַלְוִיִּם בְּיַד אִיתָמָר בֶּן־אַהֲרֹן הַכֹּהֵן

These are the reckonings of the Tabernacle, the Tabernacle of Testimony, which were reckoned at Moshe's bidding. The labor of the Leviim was under the authority of Issamar, son of Aharon the Kohen (Shemos 38:21).

Although the word פְקוּדֵי is often used to describe an *appointment* to a post or a task, *Rashi* renders its meaning here as an *accounting* of the weights of the metals that were contributed toward the construction of the Mishkan and all the vessels used in its service. As to why these are called עֲבֹדַת הַלְוִיִּם, *the labor of the Leviim, Rashi* explains that during the travels of the Jews in the Wilderness, it was the Leviim who carried the parts of the Mishkan from place to place. Furthermore, the Torah notes that the one who would be in charge (note that *Rashi* uses the term פָּקִיד to describe this) of assigning the tasks of moving to the various Levite families was Issamar, the son of Aharon.

There appear to be two glaring difficulties with this understanding. First, as part of the accounting of the materials used for the Mishkan in the *parashah,* the Torah includes (v. 24): כָּל־הַזָּהָב הֶעָשׂוּי לַמְּלָאכָה, *All the gold that was used for the work.* But this gold was used primarily for the vessels, such as the Menorah and *Shulchan*, rather than for the housing and Courtyard, and the one supervising the transportation of the vessels was Elazar, not Issamar. Second, we find that the Torah gives a detailed accounting of how all the silver and copper were used; why is there no such accounting for the gold?

We will answer the second question first. *Meshech Chochmah* explains that the verse could not give a full accounting of gold usage, because the holy vestments of the Kohen Gadol were not yet completed, and they required gold. This can be seen from the verse (39:3) regarding the אֵפֹד, *Apron:* וַיְרַקְּעוּ אֶת־פַּחֵי הַזָּהָב וְקִצֵּץ פְּתִילִם, *They hammered out the thin sheets of gold and cut threads.* Similarly, when describing the חֹשֶׁן, *Breastplate*, it says (ibid. v. 16): וַיַּעֲשׂוּ שְׁתֵּי מִשְׁבְּצֹת זָהָב וּשְׁתֵּי טַבְּעֹת זָהָב, *They made two gold settings and two gold rings.* Thus, when the verse speaks of a (full) accounting, it is referring only to the silver and copper, not to the gold. Likewise, when describing the work of the Leviim, the verse is not referring to the gold, for the care of the vestments was entirely in the hands of the Kohanim.

פרשת פקודי

SUNDAY

PARASHAS PEKUDEI

This explains why only Issamar was mentioned, for he supervised all movements of the silver and copper portions of the Mishkan that were transported by the Leviim.

Ramban also understands פְּקוּדֵי as an *accounting,* but interprets the verse as saying that all the material recorded later in the *parashah* (100 *kikar* of silver, etc.) was given first to Issamar with a precise weight and then given to the craftsmen to be used in the exact manner that is described. However, Issamar was in charge of only the items that would later be his responsibility during the transporting of the Mishkan, such as the אֲדָנִים, *sockets,* and וָוִים, *hooks.* The material for the major vessels, however, such as the Menorah, was given to Elazar, since he was to supervise their transport. Thus, they each had to be given gold: Elazar for the inner vessels, and Issamar for the "body" of the Mishkan. It should be noted that for the Menorah, gold was the sole component, whereas for some inner vessels that were made of wood, such as the *Aron* and the *Shulchan,* gold was used only as a covering. Similarly, gold was used as a covering for the קְרָשִׁים, *planks,* and בְּרִיחִים, *bars,* which were the responsibility of Issamar, and there was no way to determine how much gold was to be used for each item. Therefore, the Torah does not record that they were given the gold with an exact weight. Similarly, the appointment of Elazar is not recorded because the primary purpose of the *parashah* is to relate matters regarding the work of the Mishkan, and not those regarding its travels.

MISHNAH OF THE DAY: BEITZAH 4:7

The Mishnah discusses kindling fire on Yom Tov:

אֵין מוֹצִיאִין אֶת הָאוּר — *We may not produce fire,*[1] לֹא מִן הָעֵצִים — וְלֹא מִן הָאֲבָנִים — *neither from wood nor from stones,* וְלֹא מִן הֶעָפָר — *nor from earth,*[2] וְלֹא מִן הַמַּיִם — *nor from water.*[3] וְאֵין מְלַבְּנִין

— NOTES —

1. The Gemara (33b) explains that while one may ignite wood from a pre-existing fire, it is forbidden to start a new fire on Yom Tov. This Rabbinic prohibition is known as *molid,* which is an injunction against an act that creates something new (*Rav;* see *Rashi* on the Mishnah, 33a and 23a; cf. *Shitah Mekubetzes*).

2. Certain types of hardened earth, when dug, [may produce sparks] (*Rashi*).

3. Water in a clear glass dish, when placed under the bright sun, will act as a lens and focus the sun's rays. When combustible material such as straw is placed near the glass, it can ignite (*Rav*).

פרשת פקודי

SUNDAY
PARASHAS PEKUDEI

אֶת הָרְעָפִים לְצָלוֹת בָּהֶן — *And we may not heat tiles in order to roast upon them.*[4]

The Mishnah now discusses the preparations necessary to remove the *muktzeh* status from produce that is not totally edible:

וְעוֹד אָמַר רַבִּי אֱלִיעֶזֶר — *And R' Eliezer said yet another* leniency in addition to those mentioned in the previous Mishnah (4:6): עוֹמֵד אָדָם עַל הַמּוּקְצֶה — *A person may stand next to* foodstuffs that are *muktzeh*[5] עֶרֶב שַׁבָּת בַּשְּׁבִיעִית — *on Friday during the Seventh Year*[6] וְאוֹמֵר — *and declare:* מִכָּאן אֲנִי אוֹכֵל לְמָחָר — *From here I will eat tomorrow.*[7] וַחֲכָמִים אוֹמְרִים — *But the Sages say:* עַד שֶׁיִּרְשׁוֹם וְיֹאמַר — *Only if he marks off* the portion he plans to eat *and declares:* מִכָּאן וְעַד כָּאן — I will eat tomorrow *from here to here.*[8]

— NOTES —

4. The Mishnah refers to new tiles, which must be reheated to harden them and complete their manufacture. Heating the tiles in this manner is prohibited because this is considered making a utensil (*Rav*).

5. The term *muktzeh* here refers to figs and grapes that were set in the sun to dry. During the drying process they are inedible and therefore *muktzeh*. The fruits being discussed have already dried to the point that they are somewhat edible and some people would eat them, while others would allow them to dry longer. Therefore, their *muktzeh* status depends on their owner. If he declared his intention to eat them in their present state, they are designated and no longer *muktzeh* (see Gemara 26b; *Rashi*).

6. Produce that grows wild during the Sabbatical Year is exempt from the obligations of separating *terumah* and all other tithes. The issue addressed by our Mishnah — whether untithed produce is considered to be "prepared" so that it may be used on the Sabbath — is germane solely to the Sabbatical Year when the produce may be used without tithing (or during other years in the unlikely event that the owners tithed the produce before setting it out to dry). During other years this issue would not be relevant, since fruit set in the sun to dry is generally untithed (since the owners are not obligated to separate the tithes until the produce is completely processed). Untithed produce may not be tithed on the Sabbath and may therefore not be used (*Rav*).

7. Two points are made by R' Eliezer. (1) An oral designation is sufficient to remove the *muktzeh* status; and (2) it is not necessary to decide specifically which produce will be eaten; it is sufficient to state generally that one will eat "from here." This designation applies to whatever produce he will eventually eat, because of the principle of בְּרֵירָה [*bereirah*], *retroactive determination* [which allows one to institute a legal process and make its validation dependent upon events that have not yet occurred] (*Rav*).

8. The Sages disagree with both of R' Eliezer's points. They reject the principle of *bereirah*, and therefore require one to specifically designate the produce he plans to use by marking it (*Rav*).

GEMS FROM THE GEMARA

פרשת
פקודי

SUNDAY
PARASHAS
PEKUDEI

Our Mishnah ruled that one may not heat new tiles on Yom Tov, since this hardens and therefore completes the manufacturing process of the tiles (see note 4 on the Mishnah). The Gemara cites a Baraisa that will be shown to be related to the prohibition of heating tiles on Yom Tov:

It was taught in a Baraisa: If one brings the fire, and one brings the wood, and one places an empty pot into position, and one brings the water and places it into the pot, and one adds spices to it, and one stirs the pot with a ladle — all are liable for performing their act on the Sabbath.

Each individual violates a Biblical *melachah*. The one who brings the fire in the form of a coal is liable for מַבְעִיר, *kindling,* because the coal flames up when it is carried due to its motion in the air. The one who brings wood and adds it to the fire is also liable for מַבְעִיר. Those who place water or spices into the pot, as well as the one who stirs it, are liable for מְבַשֵּׁל, *cooking* (stirring a pot causes it to cook more quickly). The Gemara will soon explain what *melachah* the person who places an empty pot on the fire violates (*Rashi*).

The Gemara asks:

But it was taught in a Baraisa that rules on this case: The last individual is liable, but the others are exempt from punishment. This contradicts the previous Baraisa!

The Gemara answers:

This is not difficult: This Baraisa, which rules that they are all liable, discusses a case where the fire was brought first; and this Baraisa, which rules that only the last individual is liable, discusses a case where the fire was brought at the end. In the latter case, those placing the pot, wood, water, or spices violate no Biblical *melachah,* since the stove is still unlit (*Rashi*). The Baraisa, by using the term *exempt* rather than permissible, indicates that it is nevertheless prohibited Rabbinically to perform any of these acts before the fire is lit (see *Magen Avraham* to *Orach Chaim* 253:5 and *Shaar HaTziyun* 253:108 for a discussion of this prohibition).

The Gemara asks:

It is understandable how all (i.e., most of) those mentioned in the Baraisa are liable, because they perform an act that involves a Biblically forbidden labor. But the one who places the empty pot in position, what forbidden labor does he perform?

SUNDAY
PARASHAS PEKUDEI

The Gemara answers:

R' Shimon ben Lakish said: Here we are discussing one who places a new pot into position, and he is liable because of the same prohibition as heating tiles, concerning which our Mishnah teaches that it is prohibited. I.e., just as the initial heating hardens and therefore completes the manufacturing of the tiles, so does the initial heating of a pot complete its manufacturing process.

A MUSSAR THOUGHT FOR THE DAY

Rashi cites *Midrash Rabbah* (51:3), which says that the word מִשְׁכָּן is stated twice in our verse as an allusion to the *Beis HaMikdash*, which was twice taken away as collateral (from reading the word מִשְׁכָּן as מַשְׁכּוֹן) for the sins of Israel. The implication is that when the nation repents, the collateral can be redeemed, meaning that the *Beis HaMikdash* can be rebuilt. The Midrash states that this idea of the *Beis HaMikdash* being taken as collateral is alluded to in the verse (*Nechemiah* 1:7): חָבֹל חָבַלְנוּ לָךְ וְלֹא־שָׁמַרְנוּ אֶת־הַמִּצְוֹת וְאֶת־הַחֻקִּים וְאֶת־הַמִּשְׁפָּטִים אֲשֶׁר צִוִּיתָ אֶת־מֹשֶׁה עַבְדֶּךָ, *We have been destructive toward You; we have not observed the commandments, the precepts and the laws that You commanded Your servant Moshe*. The Midrash interprets the phrase חָבֹל חָבַלְנוּ as *We have been pledged to You*, as we find it used in the verse (*Devarim* 24:6): לֹא־יַחֲבֹל רֵחַיִם וָרָכֶב כִּי־נֶפֶשׁ הוּא חֹבֵל, *One shall not take a lower or upper millstone **as a pledge**, for he would be taking a life **as a pledge**.*

The *Dubno Maggid* is troubled by the order of the verse cited by the Midrash. The verse should have stated first the confession of the Jews that they had sinned, and then the result that the *Beis HaMikdash* was taken away as a pledge. Furthermore, the plain understanding of the Midrash as referring to both the first and second *Batei Mikdash* seems difficult, for the second *Beis HaMikdash* lacked the glory of the first, in that it was missing the *Luchos* and certain other implements. Moreover, for most of the existence of the second *Beis HaMikdash,* the Land of Israel was under the dominion of foreign powers and was not a truly independent monarchy. Indeed, the Sages tell us that the elders who remembered the first *Beis HaMikdash* wept when they saw the second because its glory was comparatively insignificant.

With his characteristic approach, the *Dubno Maggid* offers an allegory to explain the Midrash: Two people agreed to have their

SUNDAY
PARASHAS PEKUDEI

children marry. One was a craftsman of singular skill, who manufactured a unique product that could not be copied. The other was a storekeeper who was the only one who carried the tools needed by the craftsman. When they wrote the תְּנָאִים, the contract outlining their respective financial commitments toward the implementation of the marriage, which would call for some kind of security, the Rav ruled that it would be sufficient for the storekeeper to place the specialized tools in the hands of a trustworthy third party. By so doing, it would be assured that neither would back out: not the craftsman, because he needed the tools for his livelihood, nor the storekeeper, because the craftsman was his sole customer for these kinds of tools. Thus, through *one* pledge of collateral, *both* became indebted, and each had to uphold his side of the bargain. But after some time, the craftsman undertook a different career for which he no longer needed these tools, and the fear of losing their use no longer held any sway over him. The owner of the store, however, was still bound by the terms of the agreement, for if he would back out of his promise, the tools would be taken from him.

The arrangement at the time of the destruction of the *Beis HaMikdash* was of a similar nature. On the one hand, Hashem promised that He would eventually redeem us and restore the *Beis HaMikdash*. On the other hand, we could cause it to be redeemed only by repenting. Thus, both parties were bound by this taking of collateral: Hashem, for there is no other nation to serve Him there, and Israel, for there is no way for it to serve Hashem properly without the holy *avodah* afforded by the *Beis HaMikdash*. So here too, the single collateral was effective for both sides.

This mutual obligation holds true, however, only when we hold dear our task of serving Hashem, and work diligently toward that end. Only then does the absence of the "tools" of the *Beis HaMikdash* motivate us to *teshuvah*. But when we become indifferent toward serving Hashem and we disobey the Torah and mitzvos, the *Beis HaMikdash* and its key to closeness to Him become of little or no concern to us, and we feel no obligation to repent. Thus, it is only Hashem Who still carries the burden of His pledge. With this understanding, the Maggid explains that the verse in *Nechemiah* does not say חֲבֹל חָבַלְנוּ, *we have become pledged;* rather, חֲבֹל חָבַלְנוּ לָךְ, *we have made You the [only remaining side of the] pledge*. And how have we done this? וְלֹא־שָׁמַרְנוּ אֶת־הַמִּצְוֹת, for *we have not observed the commandments,* and the collateral is no longer of supreme importance to us.

פרשת פקודי

HALACHAH OF THE DAY

SUNDAY
PARASHAS PEKUDEI

One is forbidden to eat any שֶׁרֶץ, *swarming insect* or *rodent*.

The Torah prohibits us from eating any rodents, worms, amphibians or creeping, swimming, or flying insects. One who desires to eat a fruit or vegetable in which worms, ants, or mites are commonly found must first carefully examine the produce to ascertain that it is free from any such contamination. There is one type of insect, however, that is permitted — locusts. The Torah describes the features of certain species of locusts that are allowed to be eaten; these species are enumerated in *Shulchan Aruch*. Today, however, we lack a clear and definite tradition regarding which species are permissible and which are not. Accordingly, we do not eat locusts. There are certain Sephardic communities, however, that do have a tradition regarding the permitted species of locust.

One may not eat a דָּג טָמֵא, a *nonkosher fish*.

The Torah permits only those fish that have both fins and scales. Some species of fish have very tiny scales; still others have scales that fall off immediately upon their being removed from the water. These are nevertheless still permitted. Similarly, fish that presently have no scales, but will have scales at a more advanced point in their development may also be eaten. Regarding those that have tiny scales, the halachah requires that they be visible to the naked eye, albeit under optimal conditions, e.g., strong sunlight. If, however, the scales are so small that magnification is required to see them, the fish is not kosher.

It is a fact that any fish that has scales, also has fins. Therefore, if one finds a piece of a fish that has scales, he may conclude that it comes from a fish that also had fins, and it may thus be eaten.

Swimming creatures that are not fish (i.e., a sea horse or squid) are prohibited under the category of שֶׁרֶץ הַמַּיִם.

One may not eat (or drink) blood.

The Torah forbids eating the blood of even a kosher animal or fowl. For this reason, all meat that is to be cooked must be salted after the slaughtering in order to facilitate removal of the blood. Certain organs require the use of special procedures in order to rid them of their blood. The liver is so permeated with blood that it may be cleansed of the blood only through broiling.

All fish blood is permitted by Torah law. However, if one collects fish blood in a vessel, it is prohibited by dint of a Rabbinic decree lest it be confused with the blood of an animal. If it is readily recognizable as fish blood — for example if there are fish scales in the container together with the blood — it remains permissible.

פרשת
פקודי

SUNDAY
PARASHAS
PEKUDEI

A CLOSER LOOK AT THE SIDDUR

Each day we conclude the *Pesukei D'Zimrah* section of the *Shacharis* service with the prayer of יִשְׁתַּבַּח. This prayer serves as a rousing climax to the praises begun with בָּרוּךְ שֶׁאָמַר, and as a preamble to *Krias Shema* and its associated blessings, in which we affirm our commitment to accept the Kingship of Hashem and observe the mitzvos. The number fifteen plays a prominent role in this prayer. In the first half of the prayer, there are fifteen terms of praise: שִׁיר וּשְׁבָחָה הַלֵּל וְזִמְרָה עֹז וּמֶמְשָׁלָה נֶצַח גְּדֻלָּה וּגְבוּרָה תְּהִלָּה וְתִפְאֶרֶת קְדֻשָּׁה וּמַלְכוּת בְּרָכוֹת וְהוֹדָאוֹת, *song and praise, lauding and hymns, power and dominion, triumph, greatness and strength, praise and splendor, holiness and sovereignty, blessings and thanksgivings*. *Abudraham* explains that these praises correspond to the fifteen שִׁיר הַמַּעֲלוֹת that David HaMelech composed in *Tehillim* (Chs. 120-134), and the fifteen מַעֲלוֹת טוֹבוֹת, *great favors*, that we recite toward the end of מַגִּיד in the Haggadah of Pesach, in the song of דַּיֵּנוּ. Similarly, at the conclusion of the blessing (after בָּרוּךְ אַתָּה ה' in *Nusach Ashkenaz*) there are fifteen words: אֵל מֶלֶךְ גָּדוֹל בַּתִּשְׁבָּחוֹת אֵל הַהוֹדָאוֹת אֲדוֹן הַנִּפְלָאוֹת הַבּוֹחֵר בְּשִׁירֵי זִמְרָה מֶלֶךְ אֵל חֵי הָעוֹלָמִים, *God, King exalted through praises, God of thanksgivings, Master of wonders, Who chooses musical songs of praise — King, God, Life-giver of the world*, to symbolize the fifteen steps in the *Beis HaMikdash* upon which the Leviim stood when singing the *Shir Shel Yom* during the wine-libation of the *tamid*-offerings.

Nesiv Binah cites *Shelah*, who suggests that the number fifteen mirrors the number of words in the *Bircas Kohanim*, and states that there are two sets of fifteen praises in this prayer to allude that Hashem blesses us through the fifteen words in the Kohanic blessings.

Another interpretation of the source for the fifteen praises is based on the first verse of this week's *parashah*. In their second interpretation of the significance of the term מִשְׁכַּן הָעֵדֻת, *Mishkan of the Testimony*, *Daas Zekeinim* say that when the people suspected Moshe of stealing *shekalim* earmarked for the construction of the Mishkan, Moshe told them that the Mishkan itself would provide testimony of his honesty. Thereupon, they investigated and found that they had not counted

SUNDAY

PARASHAS PEKUDEI

the וָוִים לָעַמּוּדִים, *the hooks of the pillars,* which were made of silver. This realization was adduced from the verse וְהַמְלָאכָה הָיְתָה דַיָּם, *The work had been enough* (*Shemos* 36:7), whose first letters have a *gematria* of fifteen, matching the number of pillars. Immediately, Moshe sang fifteen praises of Hashem, which are those contained in the blessing of יִשְׁתַּבַּח.

Following the fifteen terms of praise, the prayer says: מֵעַתָּה וְעַד עוֹלָם, *from this time and forever.* R' Shimon Schwab explains (see similarly in *Iyun Tefillah*) that this expression refers back to the introductory phrase כִּי לְךָ נָאֶה, *Because for You it is fitting,* meaning to convey that "An immortal perpetuation of all these praises together befits You from now to eternity." Elaborating, he notes that when we praise something over and over, whether it is a beautiful view, or a piece of art, or even a natural wonder, we can become tired of it and it loses its appeal. This is not so in the case of Hashem, however, "Whose praises go on for eternity."

R' Schwab also addresses the custom that the *chazzan* leading the prayers begins to recite aloud from the expression בְּרָכוֹת וְהוֹדָאוֹת מֵעַתָּה וְעַד עוֹלָם. This is technically incorrect, he says, because all fifteen terms are to be thought of as one unit of praise. [This is a possible reason that the custom of Frankfurt was to begin with בָּרוּךְ אַתָּה on Rosh Hashanah and Yom Kippur.] Nevertheless, he notes that the prevailing custom is to begin with בְּרָכוֹת וְהוֹדָאוֹת. In a far more strident treatment of this issue, however, *Baruch SheAmar* maintains that this is completely incorrect, for it appears as though it is only the בְּרָכוֹת וְהוֹדָאוֹת that are מֵעַתָּה וְעַד עוֹלָם, and not the other praises enumerated. This is patently untrue, for each of them is to be understood as מֵעַתָּה וְעַד עוֹלָם, and to imply otherwise, he says, constitutes an insult to "the honor of Heaven." He therefore writes that the *chazzan* should begin his repetition from כִּי לְךָ נָאֶה, and that all the words from שִׁיר וּשְׁבָחָה through בְּרָכוֹת וְהוֹדָאוֹת should be recited together, as if in one breath. Wondering how this mistake came about, he points out that many *siddurim* have no punctuation marks (or only commas) in this series of words, but have a period after the expression קְדֻשָּׁה וּמַלְכוּת, incorrectly intimating that this is the end of the sentence. He concludes that one who is interested in this matter should alert the *chazzan* to this problem, and it will be a blessing for him.

QUESTION OF THE DAY:

For what was the Mishkan a testimony?

For the answer, see page 202.

A TORAH THOUGHT FOR THE DAY

פרשת פקודי

MONDAY
PARASHAS PEKUDEI

וּבְצַלְאֵל בֶּן־אוּרִי בֶן־חוּר לְמַטֵּה יְהוּדָה
עָשָׂה אֵת כָּל־אֲשֶׁר־צִוָּה ה' אֶת־מֹשֶׁה

Betzalel, son of Uri, son of Chur, of the tribe of Yehudah, did everything that Hashem commanded Moshe (Shemos 38:22).

Based on the Gemara in *Berachos* (55b), *Rashi* explains that the Torah's use of the expression אֲשֶׁר־צִוָּה ה' אֶת־מֹשֶׁה, rather than אֲשֶׁר צִוָּה, is used to teach that Betzalel understood aspects of Hashem's instructions that had been given to Moshe, but had not been relayed to him by Moshe. In particular, *Rashi* says that Moshe commanded Betzalel to construct the *Aron* and the other implements before the structure of the *Mishkan* itself (see *Parashas Terumah,* Chs. 25,26), whereas Moshe had been commanded to first build the structure and then to fashion the vessels (*Parashas Ki Sisa* 31:7-11). Nevertheless, Betzalel pointed out to Moshe that one must surely build the structure first, for if not, where was one to put the furnishings? Thereupon, Moshe conceded that Hashem's command was indeed as Betzalel surmised, and that his wisdom was of a quality that was worthy of his name בְּצַלְאֵל, implying that it was as if he were בְּצֵל אֵל, *in the shadow* (i.e., presence) *of God* when the original instructions were given.

In his comments to the Gemara, *Rashi* explains that the Gemara maintains that the original instructions follow the order outlined in *Parashas Ki Sisa* (ibid.), which lists אֹהֶל מוֹעֵד, *the Tent of Meeting,* before the utensils, whereas Moshe gave the command to build the utensils first. The difficulty with this, however, as many commentators note, is that the order presented in *Parashas Terumah* was also issued by Hashem! Although some say that Moshe deliberately changed the order (for a variety of reasons — see *Ritva* there), as the plain understanding of the Gemara suggests, others find this approach unacceptable, and reconcile the problem in other ways.

Among the latter group, *Pnei Yehoshua* offers an innovative solution. He points out that at the beginning of *Parashas Terumah,* the verse states (25:8): וְעָשׂוּ לִי מִקְדָּשׁ, *They shall make for Me a Sanctuary,* followed by: כְּכֹל אֲשֶׁר אֲנִי מַרְאֶה אוֹתְךָ אֵת תַּבְנִית הַמִּשְׁכָּן וְאֵת תַּבְנִית כָּל־כֵּלָיו וְכֵן תַּעֲשׂוּ, *like everything that I show you, the form of the Tabernacle and the form of all its vessels; and so shall you do* (v. 9). However, this verse is not a sufficient reason to determine that the

פרשת פקודי
MONDAY
PARASHAS PEKUDEI

Mishkan was to be constructed before the utensils, because it is natural to mention the general (Mishkan) before the specific (utensils). Therefore, since we have two *parshiyos* describing the command, there are two possible interpretations. The first is that the Torah is equating the importance of each by mentioning the Mishkan first in one place and the utensils in another, and there is no directive to build one before the other. [This is, in fact, what we adduce regarding the mitzvah of honoring one's parents, where one verse mentions the father first, while another mentions the mother first.] However, we might say that the Torah mentions the *Aron* and other utensils first to indicate that they are the more worthy portion of the Mishkan, for they are called קֹדֶשׁ קָדָשִׁים, *Holy of Holies,* and this is the reason that they had to be transported on the shoulders of the Leviim, rather than by wagon. Nevertheless, the order of the construction should be the Mishkan first, in keeping with the dictum מַעֲלִין בַּקֹּדֶשׁ וְאֵין מוֹרִידִין, *one should ascend in the level of holiness and not descend.*

As it was unclear to Moshe which was to be constructed first, it was left to Betzalel to determine this, since he had been invested with extraordinary wisdom in all matters pertaining to the Mishkan. What remains difficult, however, is that the Gemara says that Betzalel's argument was that it is customary to construct the housing before the furnishings. Betzalel did not mention the concept of מַעֲלִין בַּקֹּדֶשׁ וְאֵין מוֹרִידִין! *Pnei Yehoshua* answers that Betzalel did not suggest to Moshe that מַעֲלִין בַּקֹּדֶשׁ should dictate the order of construction, for that would imply that Moshe erred regarding (or was unaware of) a halachic principle that should have been employed to determine the order of construction. This would be dishonorable to Moshe, and would be similar to one who gives a halachic ruling in front of his teacher. Betzalel therefore used his wisdom to respectfully contend that even if there was no set order to the construction, it would be logical to build the Mishkan first, for if not, "Where will I put the utensils?"

Pnei Yehoshua fortifies this understanding by noting that, in fact, Betzalel could not have put the utensils into the Mishkan upon their completion in any event, because the Mishkan was not erected until Moshe did so on Rosh Chodesh Nissan, more than three months later! He adds that it is possible that from the very fact that Betzalel constructed the Mishkan first and then the utensils, Moshe learned the principle of מַעֲלִין בַּקֹּדֶשׁ, and when he erected the Mishkan he followed the same order.

MISHNAH OF THE DAY: BEITZAH 5:1

פרשת פקודי

**MONDAY
PARASHAS PEKUDEI**

The Mishnah discusses what may be done on Yom Tov to protect produce and other items from damage: מַשִּׁילִין פֵּירוֹת דֶּרֶךְ אֲרוּבָה בְּיוֹם טוֹב — *We may lower produce through a skylight on Yom Tov*,[1] אֲבָל לֹא בַּשַּׁבָּת — *but not on the Sabbath*.[2] וּמְכַסִּים פֵּירוֹת בְּכֵלִים מִפְּנֵי הַדֶּלֶף — *We may cover produce with cloths* to guard *against dripping rainwater*;[3] וְכֵן כַּדֵּי יַיִן וְכַדֵּי שֶׁמֶן — *and pitchers of wine and pitchers of oil also may be covered* to guard against dripping water. וְנוֹתְנִין כְּלִי תַּחַת הַדֶּלֶף בַּשַּׁבָּת — *And we may put a vessel under the dripping water on the Sabbath* to protect the house.

---- NOTES ----

1. If one had spread out fruit or grain on his roof to dry, and he fears that oncoming rains will ruin them, he may throw them on Yom Tov through a skylight into the house. However, it is Rabbinically prohibited for one to lift produce to pass it through a window, since this involves excessive exertion (*Rav*).

This Mishnah is referring to produce that is sufficiently dried to be edible. Otherwise, it would be *muktzeh,* and it would be prohibited to handle it even to avoid a financial loss (*Chidushei HaMeiri*).

2. On the Sabbath, the Sages were more stringent, and prohibited even this degree of exertion.

3. I.e., if produce is exposed to a ceiling leak, he may cover it to keep it dry. Although this activity is not needed for Yom Tov, it is nonetheless permitted because of the financial loss involved (*Rav*).

GEMS FROM THE GEMARA

The Mishnah stated that one is permitted to place a vessel under dripping water on the Sabbath. The Gemara cites a Baraisa that elaborates on this ruling:

A Baraisa taught: If the vessel became full, he may pour the water out and return the vessel to its place under the drip; and he need not refrain from repeating this procedure all day, if necessary.

The Gemara records an incident involving dripping water:

Water was dripping into the room where Abaye had his mill, and the millstones were in danger of becoming ruined. Abaye's millstones were cemented together with mud. If the water would dissolve the mud, the millstones would fall apart. The leak was so extensive that Abaye could not save the mill by putting utensils in place to catch the water (*Rashi*).

פרשת פקודי

MONDAY

PARASHAS PEKUDEI

The Gemara's narrative continues:

He (i.e., Abaye) came before Rabbah and told him of his problem. Rabbah said to him: Go and bring your bed up to the mill room so that the millstones will have the status of a vessel used for excrement, and then take them out.

Rabbah suggested that Abaye move his bed into the mill room, so that the wet millstones be rendered repulsive to Abaye by their presence near his bed. Abaye would then be permitted to remove the millstones under the special dispensation granted for a גְּרָף שֶׁל רְעִי, *vessel for excrement,* which allows removal of repulsive or foul-smelling *muktzeh* items from one's house or living quarters (*Rashi*).

Abaye analyzes Rabbah's response:

Abaye sat and had a difficulty with this ruling: But may we deliberately create a condition similar to a vessel for excrement? By bringing a bed into the mill room, the conditions of this leniency are being purposely created! The Gemara (21b) ruled that although a repulsive object may be removed if it happens to be in one's living quarters, one may nevertheless not cause it to be brought to the living quarters or go to the repulsive object, in order to become nauseated by it and be permitted to remove it (*Rashi ad loc.*). [Rabbah's opinion is that although this rule is valid, it does not apply here, since a financial loss is involved (*Tosafos*).]

The Gemara concludes the narrative:

In the meantime, Abaye's mill collapsed. Abaye said: This is coming to me, because I transgressed the master's directive.

Abaye felt that this happened as a Divine punishment for not immediately accepting his teacher's ruling, and he prayed that this be sufficient punishment to atone for his sin (*Rashi* as explained by *Maharshal*). Although one may accept stringencies on himself, it is not proper for a disciple to act more stringently than his teacher (*Tiferes Shmuel* §2).

A MUSSAR THOUGHT FOR THE DAY

In *A Torah Thought for the Day* we discussed the verse אֲשֶׁר־צִוָּה ה׳ אֶת־מֹשֶׁה, *as* HASHEM *commanded Moshe,* a phrase that appears several times in this *parashah*. One of the central points of this obedience is that one performs a mitzvah precisely as prescribed, neither adding to nor subtracting from its rules and guidance. Yet another is that one performs a mitzvah only because it is Hashem Who has so commanded him, and not because **he** has judged it to be appropriate or beneficial. In either sense, what is of paramount importance is that one not be swayed by any influences that hinder or deter him from performing a mitzvah to the best of his ability.

MONDAY
PARASHAS PEKUDEI

One of the classic lessons in this regard is presented by Yehudah ben Teima in *Pirkei Avos* (5:23). The Mishnah states: הֱוֵי עַז כַּנָּמֵר וְקַל כַּנֶּשֶׁר רָץ כַּצְּבִי וְגִבּוֹר כָּאֲרִי לַעֲשׂוֹת רְצוֹן אָבִיךָ שֶׁבַּשָּׁמַיִם, *Be bold as a leopard, light as an eagle, swift as a deer, and strong as a lion, to carry out the will of your Father in Heaven*. So valuable is this Mishnah, that the *Tur* saw fit to introduce his monumental work, the *Turim*, with it, and he interprets עַז כַּנָּמֵר in the following way: There are times when a person wishes to do a mitzvah, but he refrains from doing so because of those who snicker and jeer at him. Thus, the Mishnah warns that it is fitting that one be brazen against them, and not be restrained from doing the mitzvah. Similarly, one may feel embarrassed in front of people to a greater degree than before Hashem. The Tanna therefore directs that one should exhibit boldness against those who scoff, and not be ashamed. And this is what David HaMelech alluded to in the verse (*Tehillim* 119:46): וַאֲדַבְּרָה בְעֵדֹתֶיךָ נֶגֶד מְלָכִים וְלֹא אֵבוֹשׁ, *And I will speak of Your testimonies before kings, and I will not be ashamed*. Thus, despite his being pursued and forced to flee among idolaters, he was steadfast in his Torah adherence and study.

Expanding on the theme of בּוּשָׁה, *shame*, as a deterrent to proper behavior, *Orchos Tzaddikim* (*Shaar HaBushah* 38) notes that it takes many forms. Sometimes there is such a prevalent attitude of tolerating and even promoting unethical or immoral behavior, that one is made to feel very uncomfortable ("old-fashioned" or "prudish" are adjectives commonly used) in avoiding it. On the other hand, the performance of certain mitzvos is looked down upon and sneered at (portrayed as being mere rituals and medieval hocus-pocus), engendering shame and anxiety.

Nevertheless, one must persevere and be faithful to the mitzvos, both positive and prohibitional, for one thing is clear: the slave of a king does not abort the king's command no matter how much ridicule is heaped upon him, for the shame that he would suffer in doing so would be a thousand times more painful. Thus, if he is shamed into abandoning mitzvos, he has corrupted the proper use of this trait, and this is considered wicked. Furthermore, if one does not confess to the truth, admonish people who have sinned, or ask for help in understanding something because of fear of being laughed at, his "shame" is totally misdirected and inappropriate.

פרשת פקודי

MONDAY

PARASHAS PEKUDEI

Orchos Tzaddikim concludes by suggesting that the word חָסִיד, *a pious person,* is related to the word *white,* as indicated by the *Targum's* translation of the word חֲסִידָה as חַוָּרִיתָא (*Vayikra* 11:19), which means *white* (pale) as in the verse וְלֹא עַתָּה פָּנָיו יֶחֱוָרוּ, *and his face will not* **pale** *now* (*Yeshayah* 29:22). Also, the *Targum* defines the word חֶרְפָּה, *disgrace,* as חִסּוּדָא (*Bereishis* 34:14). This three-part relationship of piety, whiteness, and disgrace, he says, conveys the idea that the חָסִיד may suffer indignity and embarrassment in the pursuit of mitzvos, but he must remove the whiteness (embarrassment) caused by it. By doing so, he will not only be considered a חָסִיד, he will even rise to the lofty level of prophecy and true fear of Heaven.

HALACHAH OF THE DAY

One may not eat חֵלֶב, *forbidden fats.*

The fats on certain internal organs must be removed even from kosher slaughtered cattle, sheep, or goats before their meat may be eaten. This prohibition applies only to those animals to which the Torah refers as *beheimah,* common domestic animals, not to *chayos,* wild forest animals, such as deer and the like. Nor does it apply to fowl.

The removal of these fats involves a process known as *nikur.* It is a difficult task, and one that must be done by a skilled expert. Nowadays, the *nikur* is usually done in the slaughterhouse; however, there are those butchers who buy meat from which the fats have not yet been removed, and these butchers undertake the *nikur* on their own. Thus, it is not sufficient to merely obtain meat that comes from a kosher slaughterhouse; one must purchase meat from a butcher who is both knowledgeable and God-fearing, who will insure that all of the necessary steps have been taken in the proper manner to assure the kashrus of the end product.

The Torah forbids the eating of the גִּיד הַנָּשֶׁה, *the sciatic nerve.*

The Torah forbids the eating of the sciatic nerve of both hind thighs of any land animal — domestic or wild. The difficult task of removing the nerve together with its forbidden fats is also known as *nikur,* and must be done with great care by a God-fearing skilled expert.

Nowadays, it is the practice in most countries that the hind part of the animal is not eaten at all, thereby entirely avoiding the difficulties posed by this part of the *nikur* process.

One may not eat אֵבֶר מִן הַחַי, *a limb taken from a living creature.*

פרשת פקודי

MONDAY — PARASHAS PEKUDEI

One may not eat a limb of an animal or fowl that was removed while the animal was still alive. Although this prohibition does not apply to fish, one may not eat a part of a live fish due to the prohibition of בַּל תְּשַׁקְּצוּ, the prohibition against eating that which is considered disgusting (see *Yoreh Deah* 13:1).

It is interesting to note that the prohibition of *eiver min hachai* is the only law of Kashrus that applies to non-Jews as well as Jews. A ramification of this is that a Jew may not supply *eiver min hachai* meat to a non-Jew since, by doing so, he would be assisting him in the transgression of a Torah prohibition.

A CLOSER LOOK AT THE SIDDUR

After we conclude every *Shemoneh Esrei* and have taken three steps back, we recite the following prayer: יְהִי רָצוֹן מִלְּפָנֶיךָ ה' אֱלֹהֵינוּ וֵאלֹהֵי אֲבוֹתֵינוּ שֶׁיִּבָּנֶה בֵּית הַמִּקְדָּשׁ בִּמְהֵרָה בְיָמֵינוּ וְתֵן חֶלְקֵנוּ בְּתוֹרָתֶךָ. וְשָׁם נַעֲבָדְךָ בְּיִרְאָה כִּימֵי עוֹלָם וּכְשָׁנִים קַדְמוֹנִיּוֹת, *May it be Your will, Hashem our God and the God of our forefathers, that the Holy Temple be rebuilt, speedily in our days. Grant us our share in Your Torah, and may we serve You there with reverence, as in days of old and in former years.*

Rama (*Orach Chaim* 123:1) explains that *Shemoneh Esrei* is our substitute for the *avodah* done in the *Beis HaMikdash*. Nevertheless, we beseech Hashem to rebuild the *Beis HaMikdash*, so that we will be able to perform the actual *avodah* and bring *korbanos* (offerings). As to the request וְתֵן חֶלְקֵנוּ בְּתוֹרָתֶךָ, *Eitz Yosef* says that it means to convey that if we are not worthy of having our request granted, we ask that Hashem at least allow us to have a share in the Torah, for one who studies the laws of *korbanos* is considered as though he offered them. Interestingly, as *Iyun Tefillah* notes, the text of this prayer is taken directly from the Mishnah in *Avos* (5:23), and is the second half of the Mishnah that we discussed in *A Mussar Thought for the Day* (although some texts treat it as a separate Mishnah). The Mishnah states: עַז פָּנִים לְגֵיהִנֹּם וּבֹשֶׁת פָּנִים לְגַן עֵדֶן, *The brazen [person] goes to Gehinnom, but the shamefaced [person] goes to the Garden of Eden*, and is followed by the prayer of יְהִי רָצוֹן. Many of the commentators understand the Mishnah as a warning from Yehudah ben Teima that, although he advised that one be עַז כַּנָּמֵר, *bold as a leopard*, and employ the trait of brazenness and put aside any embarrassment that he might feel, brazenness is, in fact, a wicked trait that is to be used only "to carry out the will of your Father in Heaven." Thus, according to *Rambam*, עַזּוּת is appropriate

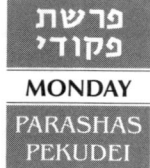

MONDAY
PARASHAS PEKUDEI

in admonishing scoffers of the Torah. But even then it must be used out of a genuine desire to rehabilitate the person. Similarly, according to *Tur,* it should be used only in the pursuit of mitzvos, but avoided at other times.

What remains noteworthy, however, is why the Mishnah concludes with a prayer, a feature that is not generally found in Mishnayos. The Vilna Gaon maintains that it was mistakenly inserted here rather than at the end of the chapter, while *Rav* interprets it as a separate request unrelated to the subject of our Mishnah. R' Akiva Eiger, however, links it directly, emphasizing that brazenness is a dangerous character trait that usually should be avoided, but was permitted in the pursuit of Torah, for without boldly asking questions, a student cannot learn. We therefore look forward to the future days of Mashiach, when מָלְאָה הָאָרֶץ דֵּעָה אֶת־ה', *The earth will be filled with knowledge of* Hashem (*Yeshayah* 11:9), and it will no longer be necessary to use עַזּוּת as a vehicle even for Torah. Thus, we are praying that the *Beis HaMikdash* should be rebuilt and עַזּוּת be eradicated.

Baruch She'amar points out that the Mishnah in *Sotah* says that at the end of the exile, before the arrival of Mashiach, חוּצְפָּא יַסְגֵּי, *brazenness will abound.* One might then assume that this trait has a measure of worthiness, for it portends the final redemption, and it should not be scorned. The Tanna therefore stresses עַז פָּנִים לְגֵיהִנֹּם, *The brazen [person] goes to Gehinnom;* although brazenness has a valuable aspect, it should not be used, for it is a terrible trait. As to it being a precursor of the redemption, we beseech Hashem that He rebuild the *Beis HaMikdash* בִּמְהֵרָה בְיָמֵינוּ, *speedily in our days,* and that He dispense with the need for any signs or omens.

QUESTION OF THE DAY:
Why doesn't the Torah say that Hashem commanded Betzalel to build the Mishkan?

For the answer, see page 202.

A TORAH THOUGHT FOR THE DAY

פרשת פקודי

TUESDAY
PARASHAS PEKUDEI

וַיַּעַשׂ אֶת־הָאֵפֹד זָהָב תְּכֵלֶת
וְאַרְגָּמָן וְתוֹלַעַת שָׁנִי וְשֵׁשׁ מָשְׁזָר
*He made the Ephod (Apron) of gold,
turquoise, purple, and scarlet wool,
and twisted linen* (Shemos 39:2).

Parashas Pekudei discusses how the *bigdei Kehunah* (priestly vestments), which the Kohanim were to wear when serving in the Mishkan and the *Beis HaMikdash,* were crafted. The Mishnah (*Yoma* 71b) points out that the eight *bigdei Kehunah* were divided into two sets; four vestments — the כְּתֹנֶת (Tunic), מִכְנָסַיִם (Breeches), אַבְנֵט (Sash), and מִגְבַּעַת (Headdress) — were worn by every Kohen. In addition to these, the Kohen Gadol wore an additional four articles of clothing: the חֹשֶׁן (Breastplate), מְעִיל (Robe), אֵפוֹד (an apron-like garment to which the חֹשֶׁן was attached, which was worn over the כְּתֹנֶת and מְעִיל), and צִיץ (the golden Head-plate that contained Hashem's Name). [Some of the Kohen Gadol's basic four vestments were slightly different than the similar items of clothing worn by an ordinary Kohen. Instead of the cone-shaped מִגְבַּעַת (Headdress), the Kohen Gadol wore a rounded מִצְנֶפֶת (Turban) on his head. Furthermore, some opinions (see *Yoma* 12b) maintain that the Kohen Gadol's אַבְנֵט (Sash) was made of different materials than the אַבְנֵט worn by an ordinary Kohen.] In this *parashah,* the Torah tells us how each vestment was made: which materials were to be used in its construction, and the manner — such as being woven or embroidered — in which these materials were to be crafted into a garment.

One of the materials that was used for several of the *bigdei Kehunah* was שֵׁשׁ, *sheish.* The Gemara (*Yoma* 71b) inquires as to the identity of this material. By studying the other areas in the Torah that speak about the vestments, we find that the Torah refers to this material also by another name — בַּד. [For example, when the Torah first speaks about the מִכְנָסַיִם (Breeches) in *Parashas Tetzaveh,* the verse states (28:42): וַעֲשֵׂה לָהֶם מִכְנְסֵי־בָד לְכַסּוֹת בְּשַׂר עֶרְוָה, *You shall make breeches of* בַּד *to cover the flesh of nakedness.* In *Parashas Pekudei,* the Torah in fact uses both בַּד and שֵׁשׁ together, and tells us that the breeches of בַּד were made of שֵׁשׁ מָשְׁזָר, twisted "*sheish*" (39:28). What, then, is בַּד? The Gemara explains that it is linen, for the word בַּד alludes to the manner in which the flax plant (from which linen is made) grows; instead of growing on a tree or bush with several branches coming from one central stem or

פרשת פקודי

TUESDAY
PARASHAS PEKUDEI

trunk, flax grows with each boll of seeds בַּד בְּבַד, *one by one*, on individual stalks. Thus, when the Torah tells us that a vestment is to include בַּד — and, by extension, שֵׁש — we are being told that the garment is to be made with linen.]

Mishmar HaLevi (*Zevachim* 47) is bothered by the fact that the Talmudic Sages seemingly did not know the simple translation of these two words used in the Torah, which is certainly an unusual phenomenon. The author of *Mishmar HaLevi* sent a letter asking this question to the Steipler Gaon. In his response, the Steipler explained (this letter is also printed in *Kisvei Kehillos Yaakov, Yoma* 10) that the reason why the Sages of the Gemara did not know that the translation of the word שֵׁש is linen, and instead had to deduce that שֵׁש is the same as בַּד, is because the words בַּד and שֵׁש are in fact not translations or synonyms of פִּשְׁתִּים, which is the word that the Torah uses for linen. [See, for example, *Vayikra* 13:47, *Devarim* 22:11, and, speaking specifically about the linen included in the *bigdei Kehunah, Yechezkel* 44:17-18.] When describing the *bigdei Kehunah,* explains the Steipler, the Torah generally does not name the material from which these garments were to be made. Rather, the Torah tells us the material's *color*. Just as the meaning of תְּכֵלֶת is *turquoise/blue*, אַרְגָּמָן is *purple*, and תּוֹלַעַת שָׁנִי is *scarlet*, the translation of the word שֵׁש is an *off-white* color that gives off an almost gleaming shine. Similarly, we find that שַׁיִשׁ is used in *lashon hakodesh* to refer to marble (*I Divrei HaYamim* 29:2 and *Megillas Esther* 1:6), for this stone has the same color and property as שֵׁש. The Sages of the Gemara indeed understood the meaning of this word, as they did every word in the Torah. However, they asked: What is the material to which the Torah is referring, which must be a gleaming off-white?

The Gemara answers this question by showing that this material also has another property, that of בַּד, which the Steipler explains is related to the words לְבַד, *alone*, and בּוֹדֵד, *lonely*. This quality of being unconnected to things that surround it, reasons the Gemara, implies that it is a material that grows בַּד בְּבַד, *one by one*, instead of on branches that come from a central stem or trunk. The material that grows in this manner, the Gemara concludes, is the flax plant, from which linen is taken. Accordingly, when the Torah commands us to use a material that is the color of שֵׁש, this description is referring to linen (and not to a different gleaming off-white material).

[The Steipler mentioned that תְּכֵלֶת, אַרְגָּמָן, and תּוֹלַעַת שָׁנִי are also the names of colors, and not of materials. Thus, we may ask: How do we know that the *bigdei Kehunah* must be made specifically with these

פרשת פקודי

TUESDAY

PARASHAS PEKUDEI

color *wools,* and not of other materials? *Rashash* points out that *Rashi* (*Yevamos* 4b ד״ה ותכלת עמרא) answers this question; he explains that the two primary materials of which the Torah speaks (and the verses in *Yechezkel* [44:17-18] tell us are included in the *bigdei Kehunah*) are wool and linen. Thus, after the Gemara establishes that *sheish* is linen, we may understand that the other three colors of תְּכֵלֶת, אַרְגָּמָן, and תּוֹלַעַת שָׁנִי are specifically dyed *wool.*]

MISHNAH OF THE DAY: BEITZAH 5:2

The Mishnah teaches that the following three categories of activities that the Sages prohibited on the Sabbath are also prohibited on Yom Tov:

כָּל שֶׁחַיָּבִין עָלָיו מִשּׁוּם שְׁבוּת — Any activity *from which one is obligated* to abstain *because of a Rabbinic injunction*[1] — מִשּׁוּם רְשׁוּת מִצְוָה בַּשַּׁבָּת — even *if it is a non-mandatory* mitzvah,[2] or *an* outright mitzvah — *on the Sabbath,* חַיָּבִין עָלָיו בְּיוֹם טוֹב — *one is* also *obligated* to abstain from it *on Yom Tov.*

The Mishnah now lists examples for each of the categories of activities that are prohibited Rabbinically on the Sabbath and Yom Tov:

וְאֵלּוּ הֵן מִשּׁוּם שְׁבוּת — *These are* prohibited *because of a Rabbinic injunction:* לֹא עוֹלִין בָּאִילָן — *We may not ascend a tree;*[3] וְלֹא רוֹכְבִין עַל גַּבֵּי בְהֵמָה — *nor ride upon an animal;*[4] וְלֹא שָׁטִין עַל פְּנֵי הַמַּיִם — *nor swim on the water;*[5] וְלֹא מְטַפְּחִין וְלֹא מְסַפְּקִין וְלֹא מְרַקְּדִין

— NOTES —

1. The first category, that of non-mitzvah acts, is called שְׁבוּת in our Mishnah, because this is the term generally used for Rabbinic injunctions. These acts, which contain no element of mitzvah observance, are obvious subjects of Rabbinic decrees, since there is no compelling reason to exempt them from any injunction (*Rav*).

2. The word רְשׁוּת usually refers to a purely voluntary act not related to mitzvah performance. In our Mishnah, however, an act that has some element of mitzvah observance, but is not mandatory, is referred to as רְשׁוּת. This is in contrast to the third category, מִצְוָה, which refers to an outright mitzvah (*Rav*).

3. Lest one tear off a branch, which would be a violation of the *melachah* of reaping (*Rav*).

4. Lest one cut a branch to use as a whip (*Rav*).

5. Out of concern that one might construct a swimmer's tube (*Rav*). This is a utensil made of woven reeds and shaped like a long barrel, which was used as an aid in learning to swim (*Rashi*). Constructing such a barrel violates both the labor of אוֹרֵג, *weaving,* and מְתַקֵּן מָנָא, *perfecting a utensil* (see *Shabbos* 74b with *Rashi*).

פרשת פקודי
TUESDAY
PARASHAS PEKUDEI

וְאֵלּוּ — *nor clap hands, nor slap thighs, nor dance.*[6] הֵן מִשּׁוּם רְשׁוּת — *And these are activities that are non-mandatory mitzvos, but were prohibited by the Sages:* לֹא דָנִין — *We may not adjudicate;*[7] וְלֹא מְקַדְּשִׁין — *nor betroth;*[8] וְלֹא חוֹלְצִין וְלֹא מְיַבְּמִין — *nor perform chalitzah nor perform yibum.*[9] וְאֵלּוּ הֵן מִשּׁוּם מִצְוָה — *And these are activities that are outright mitzvos but were nonetheless prohibited by the Sages:* לֹא מַקְדִּישִׁין — *We may not consecrate an animal or other item to the Temple;*[10] וְלֹא מַעֲרִיכִין — *nor make assessment vows;*[11] וְלֹא מַחֲרִימִין — *nor make*

---— NOTES ---—

6. Out of concern that one might repair musical instruments. This would be a violation of the Biblical labor of מְתַקֵּן מָנָא, *perfecting a utensil* (Rashi). [*Tosafos* to 30a discuss the reason that this prohibition is widely disregarded nowadays.]

7. Although related to a mitzvah, adjudicating is included in the category of רְשׁוּת because it is not an absolute obligation. There are times when a judge should forgo ruling on a case in order to allow someone more qualified to adjudicate. Adjudicating was banned on Yom Tov because it might lead to recording the verdict (*Rav*).

8. This refers to the act of a man consecrating his wife to himself, commonly by giving her any object of monetary value or a document (שְׁטָר). [The second phase of marriage is called נִשּׂוּאִין, *marriage,* and is effected by the *chupah* ceremony, which marks the completion of the marriage, after which the bride and groom begin life together.] Betrothal was prohibited because a document might be written to effect the marriage. Albeit betrothal can be considered an outright mitzvah, our Mishnah refers to an individual who is already married with children, and it is therefore categorized as a non-mandatory mitzvah (*Rav*).

9. As outlined in *Devarim* (25:5-11), if a married man dies without children, his brother must either marry the widow in what is known as יִבּוּם, *levirate marriage,* or free her to marry someone else through the rite of חֲלִיצָה, *chalitzah.* The Mishnah teaches that neither act may be performed on the Sabbath or Yom Tov. *Chalitzah* was prohibited because of the concern that a document might be written to record that the procedure took place. *Yibum* was prohibited because it might lead to the writing of a *kesubah* (*Rashi*). These are not considered to be outright mitzvos, since the Mishnah refers to a case in which there is an older brother who has priority in performing *yibum* and *chalitzah* (*Rav;* see *Yevamos* 24b and *Even HaEzer* 161:6).

10. The reason for prohibiting these next three activities is that they resemble מֶקָח וּמִמְכָּר, *buying and selling,* because the ownership of an object is transferred from the individual to the Temple treasury (*Rav*).

11. The Torah (*Vayikra* 27:1-8) states that if a person pledges the value of a certain person (עֶרְכְּךָ עָלַי) [or the value of his own assessment (עֶרְכִּי עָלַי)], he must donate to the Temple treasury the amount established by the Torah as the assessment of a person of that particular age [and gender] (*Rashi*).

פרשת
פקודי

TUESDAY
PARASHAS
PEKUDEI

a *cherem*;[12] וְלֹא מַגְבִּיהִין תְּרוּמָה וּמַעֲשֵׂר — nor separate *terumah* or *tithes*.[13]

The Mishnah concludes: כָּל אֵלּוּ בְּיוֹם טוֹב אָמְרוּ — All these prohibitions were promulgated for Yom Tov; קַל וָחֹמֶר בַּשַּׁבָּת — surely they apply to the Sabbath. אֵין בֵּין יוֹם טוֹב לַשַּׁבָּת אֶלָּא אוֹכֶל נֶפֶשׁ בִּלְבַד — There is no difference between Yom Tov and the Sabbath except in matters pertaining to *food preparation*.[14]

--- NOTES ---

12. A person may pronounce an object that he owns as *cherem* (set aside for priestly or Temple use). When he does not specify the exact nature of the *cherem*, it becomes the property of the Temple treasury (*Rav*).

13. Since the produce may not be eaten prior to separating *terumah* and tithes, the separation is forbidden on the Sabbath because it is considered מְתַקֵּן, *making usable*. [This injunction applies even if the *terumah* is to be given to a Kohen on Yom Tov, albeit it would appear that one is providing food for the Kohen's holiday needs (*Rav*).]

14. The Gemara (37a) comments that this section of the Mishnah is in accordance with the view of Beis Shammai (Mishnah 1:5). According to Beis Hillel, even labor not related to food preparation may be permitted in certain instances (*Rav*).

GEMS FROM THE GEMARA

From the previous Mishnah, the Gemara challenges the Mishnah's statement that there is no difference between the Sabbath and Yom Tov except for matters pertaining to food preparation. The Mishnah earlier (5:1) had stated that one may lower produce through a skylight on Yom Tov because of the financial loss that might be incurred if rain would fall on the produce, although this would be prohibited on the Sabbath. There, the Rabbinic prohibition applies to the Sabbath but not to Yom Tov. This contradicts our Mishnah, which states categorically that except for matters pertaining to food preparation, there is no difference between the Sabbath and Yom Tov.

After suggesting and rejecting a possible resolution, the Gemara advances another resolution to this contradiction:

Rather, Rav Pappa said: This is not difficult. This Mishnah, which applies all the Sabbath Rabbinic prohibitions to Yom Tov, follows Beis Shammai, while this previous Mishnah, which permits lowering produce through a skylight on Yom Tov, follows Beis Hillel. For we learned

TUESDAY
PARASHAS PEKUDEI

in a Mishnah (1:5): Beis Shammai say: We may carry neither a child nor a *lulav* nor a Torah scroll out to the public domain [on Yom Tov]. But Beis Hillel permit this. Beis Shammai permit carrying objects on Yom Tov into the public domain only for food-related needs, but not for other Yom Tov purposes. They would similarly forbid the moving of produce that is not being used for Yom Tov consumption, even if a financial loss were involved. Beis Hillel, however, permit objects to be carried out even for non-food-related purposes. Accordingly, they would be of the opinion that it is permitted to move the produce (*Rashi*; see *Rashi* above, 12a). Our Mishnah reflects the opinion of Beis Shammai, while the previous Mishnah reflects the opinion of Beis Hillel.

The Gemara challenges this comparison:

Perhaps it is not so. Possibly, Beis Shammai ruled stringently only there (in Mishnah 1:5), to safeguard against a violation of the Biblical *melachah* of carrying out to the public domain, but regarding moving produce within the private domain, which is merely a Rabbinic prohibition, they would not rule stringently, but would be lenient in this case in order to avoid a financial loss.

The Gemara rebuffs this challenge. It refutes the distinction that the Gemara had offered to distinguish between the enactment of a Rabbinic prohibition regarding moving items from a private to public domain and an enactment regarding moving items within a private domain:

Is moving an object in a private domain not necessary for carrying out to a public domain? I.e., every act of carrying out to a public domain begins with and includes an act of moving an object from within a private domain. Therefore, it stands to reason that prohibitions that apply to acts of moving within a private domain be governed by the stringencies that were enacted as a precaution against carrying out to a public domain. [Thus, moving of *muktzeh* objects in a private domain was prohibited out of concern that they should not be carried out to a public domain. Therefore, no distinction may be made that would imply a greater concern for carrying out to a public domain than for carrying within a private domain (see *Rashi*).]

QUESTION OF THE DAY:
Why does the verse describe the hammering of the gold before speaking of the construction of the Ephod itself?
For the answer, see page 202.

A MUSSAR THOUGHT FOR THE DAY

פרשת פקודי

**TUESDAY
PARASHAS
PEKUDEI**

We learned in *A Torah Thought for the Day* that several of the *bigdei Kehunah* contained linen. Further study of the Torah passages that detail the *bigdei Kehunah* reveals a surprising point: many of the vestments that were made with linen — specifically, the אֵפוֹד (39:2), חֹשֶׁן (39:8), and אַבְנֵט worn by the Kohen Gadol (39:29) — were to contain wool as well. The mixture of wool and linen together in one garment is a combination that is specifically forbidden by the Torah, and is termed *kilayim* (forbidden combinations) or *shaatnez*. The *bigdei Kehunah* may be worn despite the *shaatnez* they contain, for the same Torah that forbade *kilayim* to be worn is the one that specifically commanded this mixture to be present in the *bigdei Kehunah*. We similarly find the permission to wear otherwise forbidden *kilayim* when wearing *techeiles* in a four-cornered *tzitzis* garment. The Gemara (*Yevamos* 4a) derives this permit from the Scriptural juxtaposition of the prohibition of *kilayim*: לֹא תִלְבַּשׁ שַׁעַטְנֵז צֶמֶר וּפִשְׁתִּים יַחְדָּו, *you shall not wear combined fibers, wool and linen together* (*Devarim* 22:11) — and the commandment of *tzitzis*: גְּדִלִים תַּעֲשֶׂה־לָּךְ עַל־אַרְבַּע כַּנְפוֹת כְּסוּתְךָ אֲשֶׁר תְּכַסֶּה־בָּהּ, *you shall make for yourselves twisted threads on the four corners of your garment with which you cover yourself* (ibid. v. 12). [We will discuss the criteria for when *kilayim* is permitted in a *tzitzis* garment in *A Taste of Lomdus*.] What message may we glean from the fact that the "mitzvah garments" of *bigdei Kehunah* and *tzitzis* specifically include materials in combinations that are ordinarily forbidden?

Panim Yafos (*Devarim* 13:1) answers this question. A person naturally contains two drives that motivate him to action. One motivation is termed אַהֲבָה, *love,* which is the aspiration that a person has to affect and improve areas that are ostensibly beyond him, and, by interacting with them, bring himself closer to them and thus make him and the area into one. The other motivation is יִרְאָה, *awe* or *fear,* where a person has no desire for any type of relationship with that which he fears. On the contrary, awe and fear inspire that a distance be kept between oneself and this literally overwhelming other person or area. However, the simple awareness that the results of this separation will be unpleasant compels a person to perform the will of this person or reality.

These two emotions are inherent opposites, for אַהֲבָה is based on the desire to extend oneself to include others as well, or build beyond oneself, and יִרְאָה is the feeling that one's own wishes are irrelevant when faced with the open recognition of the strength or sheer greatness of

TUESDAY

PARASHAS PEKUDEI

the other. *Panim Yafos* explains that to a great degree, the varying personalities of different people determine which approach affords the motivation to succeed.

The ultimate level of *avodas Hashem,* however, is a step beyond this. Although it is necessary to employ one's natural inclinations in the service of Hashem, a person who uses both of these traits — אַהֲבָה and יִרְאָה — will achieve a higher level of service. Each of these two approaches to *avodas Hashem* has its own benefits and drawbacks. Although a person who lives his life based on אַהֲבָה will be driven to do whatever he can for the object of his love or desire, he will not be moved to do something in an area that does not particularly interest him. Conversely, a person motivated by יִרְאָה will never fail to satisfactorily perform. His performance, however, is missing the passionate zeal of someone whose actions come from within. The only way for a person to perfect his service of Hashem is to internalize both of these drives, and inspire himself using each one in its proper time.

It would appear, comments *Panim Yafos,* that doing so is a contradiction, for how is it possible for one person to feel these two diametrically opposite emotions? The answer is that such a person is in fact someone who developed himself until his motivation is *neither* אַהֲבָה nor יִרְאָה. His motivation is a third area — the more altruistic desire to serve Hashem. A person who, instead of being motivated by his natural inclinations, is driven to fulfill Hashem's word under all circumstances, will naturally use any approach that is possible in order to best fulfill his mission in life. [R' Dessler (*Michtav MeiEliyahu* Vol. 4, p. 175) suggests that a way in which אַהֲבָה and יִרְאָה may work together is that a person will concentrate on the יִרְאָה that is appropriate in order to realize the sheer necessity of performing a mitzvah, and, once he has this feeling, focus on his אַהֲבָה of Hashem, for thinking about having a wonderful relationship with Him will naturally motivate a person to perform the mitzvah in the best possible manner. We will see another example of this idea in *A Closer Look at the Siddur.*]

This, explains *Panim Yafos,* is the reason the Torah instructed that *kilayim* be used in the mitzvah garments of *tzitzis* and *bigdei Kehunah.* In prohibiting the combination of these materials, the Torah has told us that these two materials are inherent opposites, for they epitomize two wholly different approaches to life [we will further discuss this point in *A Closer Look at the Siddur*], and as such cannot co-exist. However, when each of these two approaches is seen only as a means of serving Hashem, which is the ultimate goal of both of them, no contradiction exists. The forum of *avodas Hashem* that a mitzvah garment epitomizes unifies these two very different approaches, for, instead of each being a means unto itself, each one becomes a method to achieve a common goal, and is applied as necessary. It is thus specifically within the greater context of the *Beis HaMikdash* [or, explains *Even Yekarah,* within *tzitzis* that remind us that the array of 613 mitzvos are in truth one all-encompassing unit] that both of these traits may co-exist and be united to create a greater perfection.

TUESDAY
PARASHAS
PEKUDEI

HALACHAH OF THE DAY

One may not eat טֶבֶל, *untithed produce.*
Produce grown in Eretz Yisrael is subject to the obligations of *terumos* and *maasros*. These requirements remain in effect today. Accordingly, one may not eat produce from Eretz Yisrael unless the required *terumos and maasros* have been set aside.

It has become common that fresh fruits and vegetables are imported from Eretz Yisrael, and thus make their way onto produce shelves the world over. [Indeed, they are often the most tempting produce on the shelves!] One must take care not to eat from these items without properly setting aside the necessary tithes beforehand. One should consult a competent halachic authority for proper instruction on the procedure of separating the tithes.

One may not eat עָרְלָה, *orlah,* the fruits of the first three years.

One who plants a fruit tree — whether inside or outside of Eretz Yisrael — may not eat any of the fruit produced during the first three years of the tree's growth. The laws of *orlah* have complexities that are beyond the scope of this work. One should consult a competent halachic authority to determine when the three years are seen as having elapsed; additionally, one should inquire as to the particular *orlah* laws that pertain to the growing of grapevines. There are times when one who replants an existing tree may have to wait three years from the time of the replanting. Once again, one who is faced with such a scenario should make inquiries of a competent halachic authority.

One may not eat חָדָשׁ, *chadash,* new grain.

The Torah prohibits eating any of the five types of grain — wheat, barley, oats, spelt, or rye — that took root from after the 16th day of Nissan until the 16th of Nissan of the following year.

There is a difference of opinion whether or not this Torah prohibition applies to grains that have been grown outside of Eretz Yisrael.

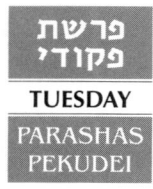

TUESDAY

PARASHAS PEKUDEI

There is therefore considerable controversy surrounding the question of whether one must refrain from eating *chadash* grain products outside of Eretz Yisrael. As different contemporary authorities have opposing views on this matter, it is not within the scope of this work to render a decision on this issue. One should consult his halachic authority regarding how he should conduct himself in this matter.

One may not make use of יֵין נֶסֶךְ, *wine of libation*.

One may not drink or derive any benefit at all from wine that has been poured in a sacrificial manner to *avodah zarah,* idolatry. The same prohibition applies to any item that has been served to a deity in a sacrificial manner. Other wines that have been handled by an idolater are forbidden through Rabbinic injunction, and will be discussed further at a later date.

A CLOSER LOOK AT THE SIDDUR

We continue our discussion of the Torah's commandment that the *bigdei Kehunah* specifically contain *shaatnez*. We learned that the *Panim Yafos* explains this command as teaching that one must utilize all forces available to serve Hashem fully.

The *Panim Yafos* gives another illustration of this idea, one that relates to the area of Torah study. The Torah is, of course, the cornerstone of our lives as Jews, and Torah study provides the basis of our relationship with Hashem, in our quest to better understand our mission in life. The laws and guidelines found in the Torah provide direction and meaning for every second of our day, and every occasion that we encounter over the course of our lives. Since any, even inadvertent, error that is made in studying, understanding, and applying the Torah's lessons to practical life is spiritually detrimental, a person with a tendency toward יִרְאָה would suppose that it is best to keep to the basic understanding of the text in front of him, and refrain from applying the Torah's teaching to any area that it does not specifically discuss. Such a person's energies in Torah study will be spent ceaselessly reviewing the text, to ensure that he will never fail to remember what the Torah clearly states. An אַהֲבָה personality inherently takes an opposite approach; since the Torah is clearly meant to guide us in our lives, he endeavors to apply his understanding of the Torah's teachings to each situation that he encounters. Furthermore, the sheer joy of Torah study allows him to suggest his own understandings of the texts, and apply one law to another, in areas that he had assumed to be unconnected, until he demonstrates that they are indeed one idea.

TUESDAY
PARASHAS PEKUDEI

Whose approach is correct? The *Panim Yafos* explains that, as we learned in *A Mussar Thought for the Day,* both approaches are indeed necessary to become a true Torah scholar. Although the full gamut of texts must be continuously reviewed in order that it be faultlessly and totally remembered, the beauty of Torah study and necessity of applying these lessons to our lives require that a person passionately and excitedly involve himself and his own intellect in the lessons being studied, in a manner that transcends the dry text. A true *talmid chacham* is one who approaches the Torah with both of these attitudes: the combination of יִרְאָה — engendered by his clear awareness of the Torah's greatness and importance — and the feeling of אַהֲבָה, which comes from making the Torah a living part of his life, for he realizes that the Torah's greatness is something that transcends the normal inclination of human emotion.

This lesson is in fact stated in *Eishes Chayil,* which many people recite on Friday night before *Kiddush.* Although the plain meaning of these verses is that they speak of the valor and virtues of the Jewish wife, *Midrash Mishlei* explains that they may also be allegorically understood as a parable for the greatness of the Torah. One praise we recite is: דָּרְשָׁה צֶמֶר וּפִשְׁתִּים, which literally means *she seeks wool and linen* [in order to sew garments for her household] (*Mishlei* 31:13). On an allegorical level, the *Panim Yafos* explains that this statement is about the Torah study that we have been discussing. Shlomo HaMelech is telling us that the Torah scholar studies and lives in the manner of צֶמֶר יִפְשְׁתִּים, *wool and linen,* which is the otherwise forbidden combination that was present in the *bigdei Kehunah.* Like the *bigdei Kehunah,* where opposites were channeled into the service of *kedushah,* this person is able to apply both virtues — the usually contradictory human emotions of אַהֲבָה and יִרְאָה — in his lifelong goal of better uncovering the Torah's greatness.

This lesson is learned not only from the fact that the *bigdei Kehunah* require a combination of materials that otherwise may never be joined, but by understanding the inherent qualities of the two materials themselves. As we suggested, the difference between אַהֲבָה and יִרְאָה is whether a person is motivated to grow by creating a relationship with the areas around him, or whether he serves Hashem by simply reacting to the demands placed on him by the objective and often detached reality that exists. These two perspectives are in fact epitomized

TUESDAY
PARASHAS PEKUDEI

in the materials wool and linen themselves. Wool, the Gemara tells us, grows in units on the back of an animal — symbolizing a life of relationship, or אַהֲבָה, in which areas come together to achieve greatness. Linen grows בַּד בְּבַד, or as a detached and objective independent reality unconnected to the areas that surround it, which characterizes יִרְאָה. Thus, the Torah tells us to use a material that alludes to the quality of יִרְאָה and to combine it with the strands of dyed wool that allude to אַהֲבָה. We now understand how the message of the *Panim Yafos* — the necessity of combining אַהֲבָה and יִרְאָה in areas of *kedushah* — is seen from the very makeup of the *bigdei Kehunah* themselves.

A TASTE OF LOMDUS

We have learned that several of the *bigdei Kehunah* contained *kilayim* mixtures of wool and linen, and that these otherwise forbidden vestments were worn by the Kohanim in their service in the *Beis HaMikdash*. In one approach cited in *Tosafos* (*Menachos* 40b-41a תד״ה תכלת), *Rabbeinu Tam* states that the Kohanim were permitted to wear the vestments that contained *shaatnez* only during the actual time that they were performing the *avodah* (Temple service), and had to remove them after serving. [It should be noted that the other opinions disagree with this ruling of *Rabbeinu Tam,* and maintain that the Torah's commandment to fashion the *bigdei Kehunah* from wool and linen permits these vestments to be worn in the *Beis HaMikdash* at all times. We discussed *Shaagas Aryeh's* treatment of this dissenting position in Series Two, *Parashas Tetzaveh,* Tuesday, *A Taste of Lomdus*.]

We learned in *A Mussar Thought for the Day* that another article of clothing that is permitted to be worn despite the *kilayim* that it contains is *tzitzis*. [To explain further: The Torah (*Bamidbar* 15:38) states that a four-cornered garment is to have two types of *tzitzis* strings attached to its corners: a *techeiles* (turquoise/blue) thread, which must specifically be made from wool, and white threads that may be made either of wool, of linen, or of the same material from which the garment is made. Thus, in commanding that we make a *techeiles* thread of wool immediately after prohibiting *kilayim* to be worn, the Torah is telling us that the *kilayim* prohibition is overridden by the command of *tzitzis,* and woolen strings may be attached to a linen four-cornered garment. In our times, we are unaware of the precise identification of the proper *techeiles* dye for *tzitzis,* which the Gemara (*Menachos* 44a;

see *Rambam, Hilchos Tzitzis* 2:2) states must specifically come from the blood of the *chilazon*. Thus, in our *tzitzis*, we fulfill only the mitzvah of affixing white strings to our four-cornered garments. Since the mitzvah of *techeiles* remains unfulfilled, we do not include *kilayim* in our *tzitzis* garments, and would only use linen *tzitzis* on a linen garment or woolen *tzitzis* on a woolen garment (see, however, *Mishnah Berurah* 9:17-19).]

פרשת
פקודי

TUESDAY
PARASHAS
PEKUDEI

The Gemara (*Menachos* 43a) states that from the fact that the Torah tells us (*Bamidbar* 15:39) that *tzitzis* are to be *seen* [וּרְאִיתֶם אֹתוֹ], we derive that *tzitzis* is a mitzvah that applies only during the daytime. Even so, rules *Rabbeinu Tam,* a person with *kilayim* strings on his *tzitzis* garment is permitted to continue to wear this garment at night, and does not transgress the prohibition of *kilayim* by doing so. We may ask: According to *Rabbeinu Tam*, what is the difference between the *kilayim* of the *bigdei Kehunah,* which he says may be worn only during the time of the *avodah,* and the *kilayim* of a *tzitzis* garment, which may be worn even at a time when no mitzvah is being fulfilled?

Rabbeinu Tam himself answers this question, and tells us that the basis for this distinction lies in the reason why *kilayim* is in fact permitted at the time of fulfillment of each of these mitzvos.

We may better understand *Rabbeinu Tam's* distinction by first studying a question that several commentaries (see *Teshuvos Chasam Sofer, Yoreh Deah* 69) raise with respect to the Torah's permit to include *kilayim* in the *bigdei Kehunah* and in *tzitzis*. The Torah's prohibition of *kilayim* specifically states (*Devarim* 22:11): לֹא תִלְבַּשׁ שַׁעַטְנֵז, **you shall not wear** combined fibers. The Gemara (*Yevamos* 4b) understands from this choice of words that the only *kilayim* the Torah is prohibiting is that which is being *worn* in the manner, and for the purpose, that clothing are normally worn. It is for this reason that the Mishnah (*Kilayim* 9:5) tells us that a salesman is permitted to don a *kilayim* garment in order to show it to a customer, because this is not the normal use of clothing. [Obviously, the potential buyer is either a non-Jew permitted to wear this garment, or a Jew who intends to remove either the wool or the linen before he wears it.] Similarly, *Tur* (*Yoreh Deah* 301; see also *Rama* 301:6) writes that a person who dons a *kilayim* garment to avoid paying taxes on it when crossing a border [for he wishes to conceal it under his clothing, or so it will appear that this item is his personal clothing and not merchandise that he is transporting for sale] does not violate the prohibition against wearing *kilayim*, as the item is not being "worn" for pleasure or comfort or protection from the elements, in the manner of a regular garment.

TUESDAY

PARASHAS PEKUDEI

With this background, the commentators ask: What is so singular about the permit for a Kohen to wear *bigdei Kehunah* when performing the *avodah*? These vestments are being worn in the fulfillment of a different purpose — that of a mitzvah — and not for personal pleasure, which is the usual purpose of a garment.

Rabbeinu Tam is also bothered by this question. And in answer, he states that there is really no reason why *kilayim* should be forbidden in *bigdei Kehunah,* since these vestments are not being worn for personal pleasure, but for the mitzvah of serving in the *Beis HaMikdash*. Indeed, unlike the permit to wear *kilayim* with *tzitzis*, which is derived from a clear Scriptural juxtaposition [see *A Mussar Thought for the Day*], we in fact do not find a specific exegesis expounded to permit *kilayim* to be worn when performing the *avodah*. Rather, similar to a clothing salesman who dons a *kilayim* garment to show it to a customer, the donning of the *bigdei Kehunah* simply is not included within the guidelines of the Torah prohibition against wearing *kilayim*.

This answers our previous question as well. These vestments are not permitted to be worn at a time when the *avodah* is not being performed, for at such a time, no mitzvah exists to wear them. They are being worn at this time in the manner of usual clothing, and are thus prohibited because they contain *kilayim*. On the other hand, *Rabbeinu Tam* says that when the Torah teaches us that despite the usual prohibition of לֹא תִלְבַּשׁ שַׁעַטְנֵז, *you shall not wear combined fibers*, גְּדִלִים תַּעֲשֶׂה־לָּךְ עַל־אַרְבַּע כַּנְפוֹת כְּסוּתְךָ, *you shall make for yourselves twisted threads on the four corners of your garment,* the Torah is telling us that we are to make *tzitzis* on the corners of our garments that we wear for our personal use; and, despite the presence of *kilayim*, we may wear the garment. Since the Torah clearly states that an otherwise forbidden *tzitzis* garment is permitted to be worn despite the fact that it contains *kilayim*, it is clear that the wearing of this garment is objectively being permitted. Thus, the Torah ordained that this garment is, as it were, inherently exempt from the prohibition against wearing *kilayim*. Accordingly, such a garment may be worn even at a time when no mitzvah is being fulfilled.

A TORAH THOUGHT FOR THE DAY

פרשת פקודי

WEDNESDAY
PARASHAS PEKUDEI

וְהָאֲבָנִים עַל־שְׁמֹת בְּנֵי־יִשְׂרָאֵל הֵנָּה
שְׁתֵּים עֶשְׂרֵה עַל־שְׁמֹתָם פִּתּוּחֵי חֹתָם
אִישׁ עַל־שְׁמוֹ לִשְׁנֵים עָשָׂר שָׁבֶט

The stones were according to the names of the sons of Israel, twelve according to their names, like the engraving of a signet ring, each man according to his name, for the twelve tribes (Shemos 39:14).

In *Parashas Tetzaveh* (28:21), *Rashi* explains that the verse repeats the seemingly superfluous phrase אִישׁ עַל־שְׁמוֹ to teach that the order of the tribes followed the order of תּוֹלְדֹתָם, *their birth,* as did the order of the stones enumerated earlier (ibid. vs. 17-20). Thus, Reuven's stone was *odem,* Shimon's was *pitedah* and so on (see Series Two, *Parashas Tetzaveh, A Torah Thought for the Day,* Wednesday, for a discussion of differing opinions on the subject of תּוֹלְדֹתָם). These stones played an important role in providing guidance in important matters of national interest, through the power of אוּרִים (from the word אוֹר, *light*) and תֻּמִּים (from the word תָּמִים, *completeness*). *Ramban* explains that these two words allude to the two-stage process through which an answer to a question posed to the אוּרִים וְתֻמִּים would come forth. First, through the Divine power of אוּרִים, individual letters of the stones on the *Choshen* would light up, hinting to the answer. Then, through תֻּמִּים, the Kohen Gadol was able to discern the precise answer from the jumble of letters, through a Divine spirit.

There is a difficulty, however, in that the letters ח,ט,צ,ק are not represented in the names of the tribes, and answers requiring those letters would not be available. Therefore, the Gemara (*Yoma* 73b) states that there were additional words on the stones, which were also of symbolic significance: namely, אַבְרָהָם יִצְחָק יַעֲקֹב — the names of the *Avos,* and the words שִׁבְטֵי יְשֻׁרוּן, *the tribes of Yeshurun.* With these additional words, all the letters were represented. As to where these words were placed, *Shemos Rabbah* (38:10) says that the names of the *Avos* were put on the *odem* stone before the name of Reuven, while שִׁבְטֵי יְשֻׁרוּן was engraved on the *yashfei,* following the name Binyamin. *Rambam* (*Hilchos Klei HaMikdash* 9:7) follows basically the same approach, but differs in two respects: He says (1) Aside from the *Avos,* the words שִׁבְטֵי יָ־הּ (not שִׁבְטֵי יְשֻׁרוּן) were used (see *Kesef Mishneh,* as to why Rambam does not follow the Gemara). (2) The names of the *Avos* were engraved above that of Reuven, while שִׁבְטֵי יָ־הּ was placed under

פרשת פקודי
WEDNESDAY
PARASHAS PEKUDEI

the name of Binyamin. In either case, the names of the *Avos* and the reference to the tribes were the beginning and ending of the names on the stones, enveloping the individual names of the tribes.

Rabbeinu Bachya, however, has an entirely different interpretation, maintaining that parts of these additional names were added to **all** of the names of the tribes except for Binyamin, so that upon each stone six letters would be engraved, symbolizing the six days of Creation. Thus, on the stone of רְאוּבֵן, which has five letters, the א of אַבְרָהָם was added to the side. Similarly, to שִׁמְעוֹן the ב of אַבְרָהָם was added, while the stone of לֵוִי, consisting of only three letters, had the remainder — רהם — of the name of אַבְרָהָם etched next to it. This procedure was followed until the additional words — אַבְרָהָם יִצְחָק יַעֲקֹב שִׁבְטֵי יְשֻׁרוּן — were spread throughout all the stones, ending with the letters ון added to the name of יוֹסֵף; only the name of בִּנְיָמִין stood alone, for it already consisted of six letters. [*Shach* notes that this system alludes to the fact that the additional names served as protection to the tribes for their having sold Yosef, an act in which Binyamin did not participate. As to why Yosef needed protection, it may be because they were punished because of him.]

Rabbeinu Bachya explains that each stone had six letters to signify that the six days of Creation were dependent on the twelve tribes. Furthermore, the total number of letters in the *Choshen* was seventy-two (12x6), symbolizing the exalted Kabbalistic Name of Hashem that consists of seventy-two letters. This conveys the message that the world, which was created in seventy-two hours (the twelve daytime hours of six days), continues to exist only because of the merit of the tribes that have seventy-two letters contained in their *Choshen* names. In conclusion, he notes that this idea is alluded to in the verse: עוֹלָם חֶסֶד יִבָּנֶה, *Forever will Your kindness be built* (*Tehillim* 89:3). The word חֶסֶד has a *gematria* of seventy-two, thus implying that the compassion through which Hashem administers the world rests on the merit of the שִׁבְטֵי יָ-הּ represented by the seventy-two letters engraved on the stones of the *Choshen*.

QUESTION OF THE DAY:
Why does the verse in Tetzaveh (28:11) state that the stones should be on (עַל) the names of the tribes?

For the answer, see page 202.

MISHNAH OF THE DAY: BEITZAH 5:3

פרשת
פקודי

WEDNESDAY
PARASHAS
PEKUDEI

The law of Sabbath and Yom Tov that governs and limits the distance that a person may walk is called תְּחוּם, *techum* [lit., *border*] (see *Shemos* 16:29; see also *Eruvin*, Chs. 4 and 5). The law of *techum* restricts one from walking to an area more than 2,000 cubits from his home or city in any direction. Placement of an *eruv-techumin* (a designated quantity of food) before the Sabbath or Yom Tov shifts the *center* of one's *techum* area from his actual location to the location of the *eruv*. (It does not add to the total distance one may walk; it merely realigns it. Whatever is gained in one direction is lost in the opposite direction.) Just as a person is restricted by considerations of his *techum,* so too a person's possessions become subject to his *techum*.

Since a person's *techum* is determined by his location at the onset of the Sabbath or Yom Tov, two people spending the day at different locations will have different *techumin*. Occasionally, these *techumin* will overlap. (For example, if two cities are separated by 3,000 *amos,* the residents of each are limited to the area within 2,000 *amos* of their city's border. Although neither can reach the other's city, there is an area of 1,000 *amos* in which the residents of both cities may mingle.)

The following Mishnah begins the discussion of the law of *techum* as it applies to the transport of one's possessions on Yom Tov:

הַבְּהֵמָה וְהַכֵּלִים כְּרַגְלֵי הַבְּעָלִים — *Livestock and utensils are* accorded a *techum* boundary *like* that of *the feet of their owners,* i.e., they may be moved only within the 2,000-*amah* boundary that surrounds the owner's Sabbath residence. הַמּוֹסֵר בְּהֶמְתּוֹ לִבְנוֹ אוֹ לְרוֹעֶה — *If one entrusts his animal to his son or to a shepherd* on Yom Tov, הֲרֵי אֵלּוּ כְּרַגְלֵי הַבְּעָלִים — *these* animals *are* accorded a *techum like* that of *the feet of their owners,* and not the *techum* of the son or shepherd.[1] כֵּלִים הַמְיוּחָדִין לְאֶחָד מִן הָאַחִין שֶׁבַּבַּיִת — *Utensils designated for* use by

---- NOTES ----

1. The Mishnah speaks of a case where there is more than one shepherd [or son] in the town who regularly cares for people's flocks. Since the owner has a choice of shepherds, neither of them can be assumed with certainty before the onset of Yom Tov to be the shepherd to whom the cattle will be entrusted. The animals therefore do not follow the shepherd's *techum*. If, however, there is only one shepherd to whom people regularly assign their animals, and it can be assumed that the animal will be entrusted to this shepherd, then the animal would follow that shepherd's *techum,* even if at the onset of Yom Tov the animal was still in the possession of the owner (*Rav*).

WEDNESDAY

PARASHAS PEKUDEI

one of the brothers of a house,[2] הֲרֵי אֵלּוּ בְּרַגְלָיו — *these are* accorded a *techum like* that of *his feet,* i.e., they are subject to his *techum* alone; וְשֶׁאֵין מְיוּחָדִין — *but those that are not designated* for any one brother, but are used by all members of the household, הֲרֵי אֵלּוּ בִּמְקוֹם שֶׁהוֹלְכִין — *these are* restricted to *the place where they* all *may go.* Thus, if they have different *techumin,* the utensils may be carried only within the area common to all of them.[3]

———————— NOTES ————————

2. This case involves brothers who inherited their father's house and its contents, but have not yet divided the estate. Thus, they still live together in the house and share the use of many of its utensils.

3. The utensils assume the *techum* restrictions of all the brothers [since they are partners in it], and they are therefore restricted to the area common to all of them. Thus, for example, if one brother placed an *eruvei techumin* 2,000 *amos* to the north of their residence, and the others did not join in the *eruv,* the object may be moved only in the area between the residence and the *eruv* (*Rav*). It may also not be moved north of the *eruv,* because the other brothers may not go there.

GEMS FROM THE GEMARA

The Gemara cites a Baraisa regarding an article being shared by two people with different *techumin:*

The Rabbis taught in a Baraisa: Two people borrowed a single garment jointly before Yom Tov, with the intention that this one would wear it to go to the study hall on the morning of Yom Tov, and this other one would wear it to attend a banquet on the evening of Yom Tov. However, these two destinations were both outside the *techum,* and in opposite directions. Thus: This one placed an *eruv* for it to the north, to enable him to reach his destination, while this one placed an *eruv* for it to the south.

[I.e., the *eruv* was placed for the garment, so that he may wear it and go to his destination (*Rashi*). Clearly, the *eruv* is for the person, not the garment. The Baraisa, however, is concerned with the impact of the two *eruvs* on the garment, and thus speaks of the *eruv* in terms of the garment rather than the person.]

The Baraisa continues:

Since each of the borrowers has a different *techum,* the garment is restricted to the *techum* area common to both of them. Therefore: The one who placed an *eruv* for it to the north may go to the north with this

> garment only as far as the feet of the one who placed an *eruv* for it to the south may travel; and the one who placed an *eruv* for it to the south may go to the south with this garment only as far as the feet of the one who placed an *eruv* for it to the north may travel.

פרשת פקודי

**WEDNESDAY
PARASHAS
PEKUDEI**

The garment must stay in the area common to both individuals. For example, one party placed his *eruv* 1,000 *amos* north of their house and the other placed his *eruv* 1,000 *amos* to the south of it. The one who placed his *eruv* 1,000 *amos* to the south gained 1,000 *amos* in that direction, but lost a corresponding 1,000 *amos* in the opposite direction, so that he may now travel 3,000 *amos* to the south but only 1,000 to the north.

Similarly, the one who placed his *eruv* 1,000 *amos* to the north may now travel 3,000 *amos* in that direction but only 1,000 to the south. Since they are both partners in the garment, they limit its range to just 1,000 *amos* in either direction of their home (*Rashi*).

The Baraisa concludes:

> And if they established their respective *techum* boundaries at the center point between them, with no overlap, one may not move it from its place. I.e., if each placed his *eruv* 2,000 *amos* away from the house, one to the north and one to the south, the result is that one of them has a *techum* of 4,000 *amos* to the north but nothing to the south, while the reverse is true of the other one. Since the garment may be taken only in the *techum* boundary common to both, in this case the garment may not be moved at all, because their *techumin* do not overlap (*Rashi*).

A MUSSAR THOUGHT FOR THE DAY

When describing the *Choshen,* the verse states simply: וַיַּעַשׂ אֶת־הַחֹשֶׁן מַעֲשֵׂה חֹשֵׁב, *He made the Breastplate of a weaver's craft* (39:8). However, in the command to fashion the *Choshen* in *Parashas Tetzaveh,* it is referred to as חֹשֶׁן מִשְׁפָּט, *Choshen of Justice* (28:15). Rashi, in his first interpretation, cites the Gemara (*Zevachim* 88b), which says that the word מִשְׁפָּט teaches us that the חֹשֶׁן atoned for קִלְקוּל הַדִּין, *miscarriages of justice.*

Akeidas Yitzchak notes that if we examine the details of the fashioning of the חֹשֶׁן, we can highlight four areas that correspond to flaws that can cause mistakes in verdicts or corrupt the legal system, and which are expressly forbidden by the Torah (*Devarim* 1:17). The first is a show of favoritism to one of the litigants, about which the verse states: לֹא־תַכִּירוּ פָנִים בַּמִּשְׁפָּט, *You shall not show favoritism in*

WEDNESDAY
PARASHAS PEKUDEI

judgment. As this behavior generally is spawned because that litigant is a distinguished member of the community, either because of wealth, scholarship, or some other notable feature, the order of the tribes written on the חֹשֶׁן is כְּתוֹלְדֹתָם, *in the order of their birth*. This symbolizes that in court, one's standing should be equivalent to what it was at the time of his birth, when there was nothing that distinguished him from the other litigant. [The fact that he may have been born earlier is generally not a reason to show favoritism.]

The second error stems from a judge who treats a case lightly, thinking of it as insignificant. The Torah alerts us to this danger in the phrase (ibid.): כַּקָּטֹן כַּגָּדֹל תִּשְׁמָעוּן, *small and great alike shall you hear*, teaching us that adjudication of a dispute involving a פְּרוּטָה, the smallest coin, requires the same examination and gravity as that involving a large sum, for to do less jeopardizes not only the specific case, but the entire judicial system. To reflect the importance of this concept, some of the twelve stones encased in the חֹשֶׁן are of relatively low value, such as the *leshem, shevo,* and *yashfei*, while others are extremely precious, such as the *odem, pitedah,* and *barekes*. Nevertheless, they all were equally important in the construction of the *Choshen*.

The third danger lies in a miscarriage of justice resulting from a judge's fear of one of the litigants. Here too, the Torah addresses this possibility, and warns the judge (ibid.): לֹא תָגוּרוּ מִפְּנֵי־אִישׁ כִּי הַמִּשְׁפָּט לֵאלֹהִים הוּא, *You shall not tremble before any man, for the judgment is God's*. *Ramban* explains that it is Hashem's will that there be justice among mankind, and He therefore directed that there be judges as his agents to ensure justice. Thus, one who corrupts his mission has sinned against Hashem. As a reminder that their role is as agents of Hashem, His Ineffable Name was written on parchment and placed in the fold of the *Choshen*. Furthermore, this alleviated anxiety over the fear that they may have had, for who can injure or damage one who is administering Hashem's justice?

Finally, and perhaps the most difficult, is the danger in not rendering a correct decision because of faulty logic or judgment. This danger is referred to in the verse (ibid.): וְהַדָּבָר אֲשֶׁר יִקְשֶׁה מִכֶּם תַּקְרִבוּן אֵלַי וּשְׁמַעְתִּיו, *any matter that is too difficult for you, you shall bring to me and I shall hear it*. Thus, the Torah warns that a judge who is unsure of how to decide must not be embarrassed if a case is too difficult for him, nor may he be so arrogant as to think that his post guarantees that his verdicts will always be correct. This idea is mirrored in the אוּרִים וְתֻמִּים, through which a particular course of action was Divinely prescribed, regardless of the arguments for or against it. That is the only sure-proof guarantee of a correct decision.

Thus, concludes *Akeidas Yitzchak,* the Gemara's statement that the *Choshen* brings atonement for miscarriages of justice is not so much a promise of atonement as a prescription and a symbolic *mussar* lesson on how to avoid sinning in the administration of justice. Undoubtedly, this is the loftiest form of atonement, for by internalizing these lessons, one learns how to judge fairly and to repent when one has erred.

WEDNESDAY
PARASHAS
PEKUDEI

HALACHAH OF THE DAY

Over the past several days, we have discussed those categories of foods that are Biblically forbidden. We will now turn to two prohibitions that involve Biblically forbidden food combinations:

One may not eat בָּשָׂר בְּחָלָב, *combinations of meat and milk.*

While the meat and the milk of kosher animals is permitted, a *cooked combination* of the meat and milk is forbidden by Torah law. Indeed, one may not even derive any benefit from such a combination. We will discuss the ramifications of this prohibition in detail at a future time.

One may not plant כִּלְאַיִם, a mixture of different species that will be grown together. One may not plant vegetables or grains near one another. This prohibition is known as *kil'ei zeraim.* One also may not plant any vegetable or grain near a grapevine. This is known as *kil'ei hakerem.*

There are two distinctions between these two different *kilayim* prohibitions. *Kil'ei zeraim* is forbidden only in Eretz Yisrael. Additionally, if one plants vegetables or grains in violation of the dictates of *kil'ei zeraim,* the produce is not prohibited. However, *kil'ei hakerem* is forbidden even outside of Eretz Yisrael, and produce of *kil'ei hakerem* is forbidden both for consumption as well as for the derivation of any benefit.

We will now turn to types of food that are forbidden by dint of Rabbinic injunction.

As we stated previously, the Sages prohibited the consumption of various foods for different reasons. There are certain Rabbinic injunctions that were made based on existing Torah law; there are others that were enacted in order to address issues and concerns perceived by the wisdom of our Sages.

The Rabbinic injunctions that are based on existing Torah law may be divided into two categories: (1) those that are extensions of existing

WEDNESDAY

PARASHAS PEKUDEI

Torah law and (2) those decrees issued by the Sages creating new prohibitions in order to protect against possible violation of Torah law.

First, we will discuss foods forbidden by the Sages as extensions of existing Torah law.

As we taught above, the Torah forbids the eating of the *gid hanasheh,* the sciatic nerve. The Sages broadened the Torah prohibition of *gid hanasheh* to include not only the sciatic nerve itself, but also additional parts of the nerve as well as the fats that surround it, which are not included in the Torah prohibition.

The Torah prohibition of *basar b'chalav,* cooked combinations of milk and meat, includes only mixtures of milk and meat that come from a *beheimah tehorah,* a kosher domestic animal such as a cow, sheep, or goat. It does not include the meat or milk of a *chayah,* a wild animal. [The terms "domestic" and "wild" are used here to define the species, not to describe the individual animal's characteristics. Thus, a trained domestic pet deer is still considered a *chayah,* not a *beheimah.*] The Sages, however, extended the Torah prohibition to include the meat and milk of *chayos* and fowl as well.

The Torah prohibition of *kil'ei hakerem* applies only to the produce of Eretz Yisrael. The Sages extended this prohibition to other lands as well.

A CLOSER LOOK AT THE SIDDUR

The first sentence of the middle blessing of the Shabbos *Minchah Shemoneh Esrei* is: אַתָּה אֶחָד וְשִׁמְךָ אֶחָד וּמִי כְּעַמְּךָ יִשְׂרָאֵל גּוֹי אֶחָד בָּאָרֶץ, *You are One and Your Name is One; and who is like Your people Israel, one nation on earth.* Abudraham explains that in the *Shacharis* service we say: יִשְׂמַח מֹשֶׁה בְּמַתְּנַת חֶלְקוֹ, *Moshe rejoiced in the gift of his portion,* to commemorate the giving of the Torah on Shabbos. Having demonstrated our acceptance of Hashem as the One and Only God, we now focus on the fact that it was only Israel from among the nations that accepted and observes the Torah.

As part of a beautiful exposition on the symbolism of the vestments, *Malbim* relates this prayer to the *Choshen* and *Ephod*: The *Ephod*, he notes, atones for the sin of *avodah zarah,* because a similar garment was used for idolatry, and to counteract that usage, the *Ephod* had to display symbols of faith. Thus, there were twenty-five letters on each of its shoulder straps. on which the names of the tribes were engraved, to signify the twenty-five letters that make up the verse: שְׁמַע יִשְׂרָאֵל

פרשת פקודי
WEDNESDAY
PARASHAS PEKUDEI

ה׳ אֱלֹהֵינוּ ה׳ אֶחָד, as well as the statement that follows it: בָּרוּךְ שֵׁם כְּבוֹד מַלְכוּתוֹ לְעוֹלָם וָעֶד. These two prayers represent the complete and unwavering acceptance of Hashem's Oneness which, according to the Midrash (*Bereishis Rabbah* 98:3), was affirmed at the time of Yaakov's passing. Yaakov gathered his sons around him to reveal the "end of days," but the *Shechinah* left him and he was unable to do so. Nevertheless, he asked them if they had any dispute or misgivings regarding their allegiance to Hashem, to which they responded: שְׁמַע יִשְׂרָאֵל ה׳ אֱלֹהֵינוּ ה׳ אֶחָד, *Hear, O Israel*, HASHEM *is our God,* HASHEM, *the One and Only.* He then said: שֵׁם בָּרוּךְ כְּבוֹד מַלְכוּתוֹ לְעוֹלָם וָעֶד, *Blessed is the Name of His glorious Kingdom for all eternity.*

The difference between these two declarations of faith is that שְׁמַע יִשְׂרָאֵל declares a belief in the absolute and inherent Oneness of Hashem and the fact that there is none other besides Him. בָּרוּךְ שֵׁם, on the other hand, declares the Oneness of Hashem, which spreads across all worlds, so that He is recognized as the King of all. This level, however, cannot be attained in the world at present, and will be achieved only in the future, when: וְהָיָה ה׳ לְמֶלֶךְ עַל־כָּל־הָאָרֶץ בַּיּוֹם הַהוּא יִהְיֶה ה׳ אֶחָד וּשְׁמוֹ אֶחָד, HASHEM *will be the King over all the land; on that day* HASHEM *will be One and His Name will be One* (Zechariah 14:9). Therefore בָּרוּךְ שֵׁם is said silently. Thus, in the Shabbos *Minchah Shemoneh Esrei,* the words אַתָּה אֶחָד refer to the Oneness of Hashem, symbolized by שְׁמַע יִשְׂרָאֵל, while וְשִׁמְךָ אֶחָד is symbolized by בָּרוּךְ שֵׁם. As an added feature to this analysis, *Malbim* notes that each of the straps of the *Ephod* were to have six names of the tribes upon them. This alludes to the six words that form שְׁמַע יִשְׂרָאֵל and בָּרוּךְ שֵׁם.

Having discussed both aspects of the Oneness of Hashem and their role in atoning for idolatry, *Malbim* addresses another form of oneness, the unity of the nation itself. This, he explains, was signified by the fact that Aharon wore the *Choshen* of Justice, for it was his task to unite the nation. It is the Kohen Gadol, in his role as chief justice and the head of the *Sanhedrin,* who must adjudicate the disputes and rifts that divide and separate the members of the nation. And it was Aharon's trait of: אוֹהֵב שָׁלוֹם וְרוֹדֵף שָׁלוֹם, *loving and pursuing peace* (*Avos* 1:12), that reconciled the differences and healed the wounds caused by quarrels and factionalism. It is he who embodied the verse: אֵלֶּה הַדְּבָרִים אֲשֶׁר תַּעֲשׂוּ דַּבְּרוּ אֱמֶת אִישׁ אֶת־רֵעֵהוּ אֱמֶת וּמִשְׁפַּט שָׁלוֹם שִׁפְטוּ בְּשַׁעֲרֵיכֶם, *These are the things that you should do: Speak the truth with one another; and in your gates judge with truth, justice and peace* (Zechariah 8:16). Thus, by wearing the *Choshen,* inscribed with

WEDNESDAY

PARASHAS PEKUDEI

the names of the tribes, עַל לִבּוֹ, *upon his heart,* he exhibited the unity of the nation. This concept is manifested in the third expression of the *Shemoneh Esrei* prayer as: וּמִי כְּעַמְּךָ יִשְׂרָאֵל גּוֹי אֶחָד בָּאָרֶץ, *and who is like Your people Israel, one nation on earth.* Malbim concludes by emphasizing that the *Choshen* and *Ephod* had to be attached, to signify that the unity of the nation must be connected to the Oneness of Hashem.

A TORAH THOUGHT FOR THE DAY

פרשת
פקודי

THURSDAY
PARASHAS PEKUDEI

כְּכֹל אֲשֶׁר־צִוָּה ה׳ אֶת־מֹשֶׁה כֵּן עָשׂוּ בְּנֵי יִשְׂרָאֵל אֵת כָּל־הָעֲבֹדָה. וַיַּרְא מֹשֶׁה אֶת־כָּל־הַמְּלָאכָה וְהִנֵּה עָשׂוּ אֹתָהּ כַּאֲשֶׁר צִוָּה ה׳ כֵּן עָשׂוּ וַיְבָרֶךְ אֹתָם מֹשֶׁה

Like everything Hashem *commanded Moshe, so did the Children of Israel perform all the labor. Moshe saw the entire work, and behold! — they had done it — as* Hashem *had commanded, so had they done! And Moshe blessed them* (Shemos 39:42-43).

Many commentators are puzzled as to why the Torah uses the seemingly redundant expression כֵּן עָשׂוּ, and indeed, struggle to explain why it is necessary to have two separate verses attesting to the fact that all the work was done in compliance with Hashem's command to Moshe. Among the answers is that of *Sforno,* who explains that the verse is telling us that the order in which Moshe was instructed to erect the Mishkan in the next chapter was itself the order followed by the craftsmen who fashioned the various parts of the Mishkan, and by those who brought the Mishkan to Moshe. The Torah is thus not repeating itself, but attesting to different stages of the work.

Kli Yakar also addresses this problem, noting that both verses appear to be redundant, since an earlier verse (39:32) had already established that Bnei Yisrael completed the work in accordance with Hashem's instructions to Moshe. Furthermore, he asks, why does the first verse use the term עֲבֹדָה to describe the work, while the second uses the word מְלָאכָה? He therefore presents an interpretation based on the Midrashic teaching that all aspects of the Mishkan reflected some aspect of Creation (see *Rabbeinu Bachya,* who discusses this Midrash at length). In this light, he says, we can distinguish between עֲבֹדָה and מְלָאכָה. It is appropriate to refer to the construction of the Mishkan as עֲבֹדָה, for in doing so they were obeying the decree of Hashem, much as a slave (עֶבֶד) obeys the will of his master. מְלָאכָה, however, connotes work performed by a worker for himself, as used in the verse: וַיְכַל אֱלֹהִים בַּיּוֹם הַשְּׁבִיעִי מְלַאכְתּוֹ אֲשֶׁר עָשָׂה וַיִּשְׁבֹּת בַּיּוֹם הַשְּׁבִיעִי מִכָּל־מְלַאכְתּוֹ אֲשֶׁר עָשָׂה, *By the seventh day God completed* **His work** *that He had done, and He abstained on the seventh day from all* **His work** *that He had done* (Bereishis 2:2). Nevertheless, we find that during creation there were two assessments as to the "quality" of the מְלָאכָה. At each stage (day) of creation, the Torah tells us: וַיַּרְא אֱלֹהִים כִּי־טוֹב, *God saw that it was good,* yet when it was completed, the verse states:

פרשת פקודי
THURSDAY
PARASHAS PEKUDEI

וַיַּרְא אֱלֹהִים אֶת־כָּל־אֲשֶׁר עָשָׂה וְהִנֵּה־טוֹב מְאֹד, *And God saw all that He had made, and behold it was very good* (ibid. 1:31). The reason for this, he explains, is that one must first determine if individual parts of a whole have been properly created in keeping with their design, function, etc. However, even perfectly produced items may be imperfect and even detrimental to the overall plan when they are mixed with, or have to co-exist with, other items. Therefore, when all was finished, Hashem testified that not only were the specific creations "good," but as a whole they were harmonious and "very good."

In like manner, regarding the building of the Mishkan, the Torah tells us that when they completed fabricating all of the individual parts of the Mishkan, their workmanship was judged to be precisely as Hashem had commanded Moshe. However, it was not yet clear that all the items would be placed in their proper location to ensure the general success and harmony of the Mishkan. Thus, after they brought the different components to Moshe, the Torah reiterates that the order and arrangements of all the varying parts were done in the manner that Hashem had directed.

Nevertheless, the Torah wished to express that all they had done was in keeping with the idea that the Mishkan was to mirror the creation of the world. Thus, the verse states that Moshe saw before him כָּל־הַמְּלָאכָה, a reference to the work of creation, and testified that they had replicated a model of creation that was indeed like that great מְלָאכָה itself. It was then that וַיְבָרֶךְ אֹתָם מֹשֶׁה, *Moshe blessed them.*

MISHNAH OF THE DAY: BEITZAH 5:4

The Mishnah continues to discuss the *techum* restrictions upon one's possessions:

הַשּׁוֹאֵל כְּלִי מֵחֲבֵירוֹ — If *one borrows a utensil from his friend:* מֵעֶרֶב יוֹם טוֹב — If he borrowed it *before Yom Tov,* כְּרַגְלֵי הַשּׁוֹאֵל — *it is* accorded a *techum like* that of *the feet of the borrower.*[1] בְּיוֹם טוֹב — However, if he borrowed it *on Yom Tov,* כְּרַגְלֵי הַמַּשְׁאִיל — *it is*

---NOTES---

1. Even if the lender merely promised the object to the borrower before *bein hashemashos* (twilight) of Erev Yom Tov, and the borrower first took the object home on Yom Tov, it is still considered governed by the *techum* of the borrower (Gemara 38a; see *Rav*).

accorded a *techum like* that of *the feet of the lender.*[2]
וְכֵן הָאִשָּׁה שֶׁשָּׁאֲלָה מֵחֲבֶרְתָּהּ תְּבָלִין וּמַיִם וּמֶלַח לְעִיסָתָהּ — And so too, a woman who borrowed from her friend, on Yom Tov, **condiments** for cooking food, **or water and salt for her dough,** **הֲרֵי אֵלּוּ כְּרַגְלֵי שְׁתֵּיהֶן** — these [the cooked foods and dough] **are** accorded a *techum like* that of **the feet of both of them,** and they may carry them only within their common *techum* area.[3] **רַבִּי יְהוּדָה פּוֹטֵר בַּמַּיִם מִפְּנֵי שֶׁאֵין בָּהֶם מַמָּשׁ** — *R' Yehudah exempts water* from this rule, *because it has no* noticeable *existence in* the pot or dough.[4]

——— NOTES ———

2. Since *techum* boundaries are determined at the onset of the Sabbath or Yom Tov for that entire day, when articles are lent *on* the Sabbath, they retain the *techum* of the lender. This ruling applies even where the borrower is accustomed to borrowing these items from the lender (*Rav*).

3. Since the condiments, salt, or water were borrowed on Yom Tov, they became subject to their owner's *techum* at the onset of Yom Tov. The food or dough to which they were added, however, belonged to someone else and are thus subject to their owner's *techum*. Therefore, the final product is restricted to the *techum* area common to both (*Rav*).

4. The water added to the food or dough becomes absorbed by it and is no longer recognizable in the final product (*R' Chananel* to Gemara 39a). R' Yehudah therefore does not consider it significant enough to retain its own *techum* designation against that of the food or dough.

Although this is generally true of salt as well, R' Yehudah refers to a thick salt that does not dissolve and remains noticeable (*Rav*).

GEMS FROM THE GEMARA

Our Mishnah stated: A woman who borrowed from her friend, on Yom Tov, condiments for cooking food, or water and salt for her dough, these are accorded a *techum* like that of the feet of both of them. The Gemara relates a discussion that took place regarding this ruling:

When R' Abba went up from Babylonia to Eretz Yisrael, he prayed: May it be the will of God that I say something that will be accepted by the scholars there. When he came up to Eretz Yisrael, he found R' Yochanan, R' Chanina bar Pappi, and R' Zeira having a discussion, and others say that it was R' Abahu, R' Shimon ben Pazi, and R' Yitzchak Nafcha that he encountered; and they were sitting and saying regarding the ruling of our Mishnah: Why should the dough be restricted to the *techum* common to both of them? Let the water and salt become

פרשת פקודי / THURSDAY / PARASHAS PEKUDEI

nullified in the dough, so that only the *techum* of the flour will apply?

R' Abba proposed an answer to their question:

R' Abba said to them: If a *kav* of one's wheat became mixed with ten *kabin* of his friend's wheat, may that person eat the entire mixture and rejoice at having gained an extra *kav*? Obviously not, for the principle of nullification applies only to matters of observance, and not to monetary matters. By the same token, the *techum* of the water does not become nullified in the dough, because the *techum* is based on ownership and ownership does not become nullified.

R' Abba's response was roundly rejected:

They (the other scholars) laughed at him for this explanation. R' Abba said to them: Have I taken your tunics, that you laugh at me? They laughed at him again.

The Gemara goes on at length to explain the reason the Rabbis rejected R' Abba's argument out of hand, and offers arguments to support his thesis. R' Abba's prayer that he would offer an insight that would be well received by the Sages of Eretz Yisrael, however, was clearly not accepted.

The *Chasam Sofer* (*Teshuvos Orach Chaim* 208) addresses this, and also notes the apparent difficulty of why the Gemara includes the seemingly belittling circumstance of how R' Abba's thesis was rejected. The *Chasam Sofer* explains that it is meant to teach a valuable lesson. R' Abba had prayed that he be granted the ability to say something on his arrival that would be accepted by the Sages of Eretz Yisrael. Not only was his prayer not granted, but the opposite occurred. This is because his prayer was inappropriate. A person's concern in scholarly debate should be only that his arguments receive a serious hearing, so that the truth of the matter be established, not that his position should be accepted.

A MUSSAR THOUGHT FOR THE DAY

The Mishnah in *Avos* (1:2) states: עַל שְׁלֹשָׁה דְבָרִים הָעוֹלָם עוֹמֵד עַל הַתּוֹרָה וְעַל הָעֲבוֹדָה וְעַל גְּמִילוּת חֲסָדִים, *The world stands on three things: Torah study, Avodah (the service of God), and kind deeds.* *Rabbeinu Yonah* understands this dictum to be saying that Hashem created the world for these things, meaning that one who engages in these activities is following Hashem's will and causing Him satisfaction. To underscore the importance of *Avodah,* which refers to the sacrificial offerings brought in the *Beis HaMikdash*, he maintains that Hashem chose Israel from among the nations, Eretz Yisrael from among all the lands, Yerushalayim from among its cities, Zion from among its other locales, and finally, the *Beis HaMikdash* as the choicest of places, just so that Israel could perform the service, which the verse describes as: לִרְצֹנוֹ לִפְנֵי ה׳, *it shall be pleasing before* HASHEM (*Vayikra* 1:3). With the destruction of the *Beis HaMikdash*, however, the opportunity to perform this service came to an end, and *Avodah* is now fulfilled by prayer.

THURSDAY
PARASHAS
PEKUDEI

The concept that prayer is a fitting substitute for *Avodah* is borne out from the Gemara (*Taanis* 2a) which, commenting on the verse: וּלְעָבְדוֹ בְּכָל־לְבַבְכֶם, *to serve Him with all your heart* (*Devarim* 11:13), states, "What is service of the heart? It is prayer."

As the source for the Mishnah's statement that Torah and *Avodah* represent two of the three things on which the world stands, many commentators cite the verse (*Yirmiyah* 33:25): כֹּה אָמַר ה׳ אִם־לֹא בְרִיתִי יוֹמָם וָלָיְלָה חֻקּוֹת שָׁמַיִם וָאָרֶץ לֹא־שָׂמְתִּי, *Thus said* HASHEM: *If My covenant with the night and with the day would not be; had I not set up the laws of heaven and earth*. *Rashi* explains the simple understanding of the verse to be conveying that just as the covenant that was established with day and night to come at set times cannot be altered and the laws of nature cannot be annulled, so too, the promise to David to have his dynasty re-established and to Yaakov to have his children redeemed will be kept. However, the Gemara (*Megillah* 31b) interprets the verse in a different way: "If not for the covenant established at the בְּרִית בֵּין הַבְּתָרִים with Avraham, promising to forgive his descendants for their sins by their bringing offerings, Hashem would not have created night and day nor any other part of creation." The Gemara in *Pesachim* (68b) makes a similar statement regarding Torah study.

Noting that this source implies a close relationship between Torah and *Avodah*, R' Chaim of Volozhin explains that the Torah is the source of holiness and bounty that is showered down upon the world from the "heavens." In a reciprocal manner, man offers up from the blessings of the "earth" offerings in recognition and appreciation of Hashem. This dual process is the metaphysical vehicle by which the heaven and earth (which are separate entities) are united, and this is so pleasing to Hashem that His blessings bestowed upon the earth become even greater. In this light, the verse in *Yirmiyah* is conveying the idea that if not for Torah and *Avodah* together, the connection between heaven and earth could not be forged, and the world could not exist.

In a *mussar* approach to this duality, R' Aharon Kotler notes that the

פרשת פקודי

THURSDAY

PARASHAS PEKUDEI

Vilna Gaon interprets the Mishnah as stressing the importance of these three things to man's attaining שְׁלֵמוּת, *completeness*. Thus, the Torah from above provides the wisdom by which one becomes spiritually elevated, motivating him to perform mitzvos and avoid sins, while the bringing of offerings and reciting of prayers display one's subjugation of the physical world to the service of Hashem, and the insignificance of his powers compared to the "One Above."

To highlight the interdependence of Torah and prayer, R' Aharon cites the verse (*Mishlei* 28:9): מֵסִיר אָזְנוֹ מִשְּׁמֹעַ תּוֹרָה גַּם תְּפִלָּתוֹ תּוֹעֵבָה, *If one turns aside his ear from hearing the Torah, his prayer, too, will be [considered] an abomination.* He explains that prayer is intended to be pleasing and bring satisfaction to Hashem in that it is indicative of man heeding Hashem's Will, in the same manner as offerings. By disregarding the Torah, not only is one's prayer not considered pleasing, it is actually reversed and considered תּוֹעֵבָה, *an abomination,* a word generally reserved for severe sins. The underlying reason for this is that the cornerstone of prayer is the sense of servitude and subjugation that one must feel when standing before Hashem and conversing with Him. Undoubtedly, one standing before a king or even a highly respected sage will feel humble and reverent, subjugating his ego and sense of self-importance. How much more so must one's feeling of awe and nothingness be when he stands before Hashem, with Whom one is not only conversing, but is beseeching Him to fulfill all of his needs, both physical and spiritual. Thus, one who "turns aside his ear from hearing the Torah" is not only unworthy of being answered, he has perverted the whole process of prayer through his עַזּוּת, *insolence* and *brazenness,* and lack of understanding.

R' Aharon concludes that there is a message here, particularly important for those engrossed in Torah, who may be lax in their diligence regarding fulfilling the Torah. They risk not only a lessening of their Torah knowledge and scholarship, but because they may be considered as being disrespectful to Torah, their prayers will be deemed an abomination rather than pleasing to Hashem.

QUESTION OF THE DAY:

Why is the building of the Mishkan referred to as avodah?

For the answer, see page 202.

HALACHAH OF THE DAY

פרשת
פקודי

THURSDAY
PARASHAS
PEKUDEI

Today, we will discuss foods the Sages forbade in order to protect one from transgressing a Torah prohibition.

According to Torah law, one may not eat a food if the likelihood exists that one will thereby come to transgress a Torah prohibition. If, however, that likelihood is not apparent or seems very far-fetched, the food may be permitted by Torah law. The Sages, however, in their wisdom, prohibited certain foods out of concern that eating them may cause one, even in a remote instance, to violate Torah law. Thus, while according to Torah law these foods are permissible, they are forbidden by decree of the Sages. Some examples of these foods are:

(1) *Chalav Akum,* non-Jewish milk. When an animal is milked and there is no Jewish person present, the milk is forbidden by Rabbinic decree. The Sages were concerned that a non-Jew may have mixed nonkosher milk (i.e., milk from a nonkosher animal) into the milk.

(2) *Gevinas Akum,* non-Jewish cheese. The Sages prohibited the eating of non-Jewish cheese out of fear that the cheese was, in all likelihood, produced using nonkosher rennet.

(3) Wine touched by an idolater: The Sages prohibited the derivation of any benefit from wine that an idolater may have touched. As we have seen previously, the Torah prohibits the use of wine that has been poured in a sacrificial manner to *avodah zarah.* The Sages were concerned that any wine that may have been touched by an idolater may have been used by him in the service of *avodah zarah.* They therefore forbade the use of any such wine. The laws that govern this prohibition are complex and beyond the scope of this work.

We will now turn to foods that the Sages have prohibited independent of any Torah law.

Certain foods were prohibited by the Sages not because they posed a threat to a particular Torah law, but rather because the Sages felt that the eating of these foods may prove to be spiritually harmful in other, less direct, ways. Among these foods are: *Bishul Akum,* foods cooked by an idolater: One may not eat food that has been cooked by an idolater. The Sages felt that the permissibility of eating food cooked by idolaters might precipitate an inappropriately close relationship between Jews and idolaters. Such a relationship would of course be fraught with the danger of spiritual harm to the Jewish individual involved.

פרשת פקודי

THURSDAY

PARASHAS PEKUDEI

For the same reason, the Sages instituted the two following Rabbinic injunctions: They forbade one to partake of either *pas akum*, bread baked by an idolater, or *stam yeinam*, wine of an idolater, even if it is known that the wine has not been used in the service of *avodah zarah*.

Finally, there are certain foods the Sages prohibited out of their concern for the safety of the Bnei Yisrael. Indeed, the Sages were more stringent regarding foods that pose a physical threat than they were regarding prohibitive issues. As the Gemara (*Chullin* 10a) states: חֲמִירָא סַכַּנְתָּא מֵאִסּוּרָא, *a danger to life is more severe than a prohibition*. Among these prohibitions is that of eating fish with meat.

A CLOSER LOOK AT THE SIDDUR

One of the many places in the *siddur* that *Avodah* is mentioned is in the prayer of מִזְמוֹר לְתוֹדָה that we recite each morning, in the *Pesukei D'Zimrah* section of *Shacharis*. As we have pointed out in earlier discussions of this prayer, it was a psalm sung in conjunction with the thanksgiving-offering that was brought by an individual who survived a life-threatening situation. The *Ri ben Yakar* suggests an allusion to this idea, noting that this psalm has forty words, symbolizing the forty breads (ten each of four varieties) brought with the offering, which are called לַחְמֵי תּוֹדָה, *breads of the todah*. As only communal offerings are brought on Shabbos and festivals, no תּוֹדָה was brought on these days, and therefore we, too, do not recite the prayer on these days. Interestingly, the *Tur* (*Orach Chaim* 281) notes that this custom was followed in Germany, but that it has no basis. *Beis Yosef* explains that the *Tur's* objection is based on his understanding that תּוֹדָה is a general expression of thanksgiving and not related to the offering. Nevertheless, he writes that the custom is not to recite it on Shabbos and festivals, based on *Shibbolei HaLeket* citing *Rashi*.

The phrase in the psalm relating to *Avodah* is: עִבְדוּ אֶת־ה׳ בְּשִׂמְחָה, *Serve* Hashem *with gladness* (*Tehillim* 100:2), and many commentators understand this expression as referring to prayer. Among them is *Mesillas Yesharim*, who states that when one stands to pray, his heart should be joyous, for true joy is that which one experiences in the knowledge that he has merited to serve his Master, and to engross himself in His Torah and mitzvos, which represent true, precious, and eternal שְׁלֵמוּת, *completeness*. In this sense, it is a most appropriate psalm to recite as part of *Pesukei D'Zimrah*, which introduces the

THURSDAY — PARASHAS PEKUDEI

Krias Shema and *Shemoneh Esrei* sections of the service.

There are interpretations, however, that view the verse as relating to *Avodah* in general, such as the performance of mitzvos. *Siach Yitzchak* explains that שִׂמְחָה, *joy,* is fundamental to the performance of a mitzvah. Thus, when a person is about to do a mitzvah, he should approach it as an opportunity to partake of a present that Hashem has sent him and be filled with joy. To emphasize this point, he notes that the Gemara (*Succah* 49b), when discussing the importance of the mitzvah of *tzedakah* and *chesed,* says: Lest one think that opportunities to perform charity and kindness will come effortlessly, Scripture states: מַה־יָּקָר חַסְדְּךָ אֱלֹהִים, *How* **precious** (in the sense of scarce) *is kindness that is [worthy] of [being before] You, O God* (*Tehillim* 36:8); that is, one must devote himself with great effort to perform *tzedakah* and *chesed,* and rejoice at the opportunity to do so.

Furthermore, *Siach Yitzchak* maintains that the greater the joy one feels when doing a mitzvah, the greater the reward for its performance. Accordingly, he notes that the *Arizal* revealed that the heights of understanding he merited to achieve "in the gates of wisdom" and "Divine spirit" was a reward for the exceptional joy with which he performed each mitzvah. He concludes by citing *Arizal's* interpretation of the verse (*Devarim* 28:47) in which Israel was warned that tragic happenings would occur: תַּחַת אֲשֶׁר לֹא־עָבַדְתָּ אֶת־ה׳ אֱלֹהֶיךָ בְּשִׂמְחָה וּבְטוּב לֵבָב מֵרֹב כֹּל, *because you did not serve* HASHEM, *your God, amid gladness and goodness of heart, when everything was abundant.* The sin was not that they did not exhibit joy in mitzvos, but that the joy was not greater than רֹב כֹּל, the joy they took in all the other pleasures and delights of the world, such as gold, pearls, and precious stones.

פרשת פקודי

A TORAH THOUGHT FOR THE DAY

FRIDAY
PARASHAS PEKUDEI

וּמָשַׁחְתָּ אֶת־מִזְבַּח הָעֹלָה וְאֶת־כָּל־כֵּלָיו וְקִדַּשְׁתָּ
אֶת־הַמִּזְבֵּחַ וְהָיָה הַמִּזְבֵּחַ קֹדֶשׁ קָדָשִׁים
You shall anoint the Burnt-offering Altar and all its utensils; you shall sanctify the Altar, and the Altar shall become Holy of Holies (Shemos 40:10).

Ramban is troubled by the description of the Altar as קֹדֶשׁ קָדָשִׁים, *Holy of Holies*, since that title is usually reserved for the area of the *Aron*, which is separated from the other part of the Mishkan by the פָּרוֹכֶת, *partition* (see *Shemos* 26:33). Since even the other interior part of the Mishkan, containing the Menorah, *Shulchan*, and the Golden Altar, is referred to only as קֹדֶשׁ, *Holy* (40:9), surely the Outer Altar (i.e., Burnt-offering Altar), located in the Courtyard, should not be called *holy of holies!*

He therefore suggests that this phrase is used to highlight that the Altar was used even for the **holiest** of offerings (such as עוֹלוֹת, *burnt*-offerings, and חַטָּאוֹת, *sin*-offerings, as opposed to the less holy שְׁלָמִים). In this sense, קֹדֶשׁ קָדָשִׁים is a description of the Altar's function, rather than the level of its holiness. Alternatively, *Ramban* says that the phrase is referring to the Altar's ability to consecrate other things, as indicated in the verse: כָּל־הַנֹּגֵעַ בַּמִּזְבֵּחַ יִקְדָּשׁ, *whatever touches the Altar shall become sanctified* (29:37). This verse teaches that even a disqualified offering that should not have been placed on the Altar can remain there and be burned once placed there, for it has touched the Altar and become sanctified.

Netziv (*Haamek Davar*) is perplexed by *Ramban's* second interpretation, because the Outer Altar is capable of sanctifying only an offering that is רָאוּי לוֹ, *fit for it,* whereas other vessels of the Mishkan sanctify even things that are not fit for them, endowing them with a holiness. [This does not include items that can never be put on the Altar, such as honey, or animals such as deer that are prohibited from becoming offerings.] For example, a *kometz* that had not been previously sanctified in a sanctifying vessel that is mistakenly placed on the Inner Altar may remain there, but if left on the Outer Altar, it must be removed. It would seem, then, that the expression קֹדֶשׁ קָדָשִׁים would be more appropriate to describe vessels other than the Outer Altar.

Netziv therefore maintains that all the utensils and implements were not sanctified at all until the eighth day of the מִלּוּאִים, the *Inauguration* of the Mishkan, and only after they were anointed on that day did they become sanctified. Thus, the verse stating וְהָיוּ קֹדֶשׁ means to indicate that it was **only then** that they became invested with holiness. Furthermore, the *ketores* (incense) was not offered, nor the Menorah lit, until that day. Necessarily, however, the Outer Altar was consecrated through anointing and the sprinkling of blood from the first day, because offerings were brought on all the previous days of the inauguration ceremonies. What then was the point of anointing it again on the eighth day? The Torah therefore uses the expression קֹדֶשׁ קָדָשִׁים to teach us that until that day the Altar had the holiness status only of a בָּמַת יָחִיד, *an individual's altar,* but now it had attained the full consecration of a communal Altar.

פרשת פקודי

FRIDAY
PARASHAS
PEKUDEI

MISHNAH OF THE DAY: BEITZAH 5:5

The Mishnah continues its discussion of *techum* laws as they apply to objects, and draws a distinction between a burning coal and its flame. The Mishnah then digresses briefly to two other instances where such a distinction has legal ramifications:

הַגַּחֶלֶת כְּרַגְלֵי הַבְּעָלִים — *A burning coal is* accorded a *techum* **like** that of *the feet of its owner* and is restricted to his *techum;* וְשַׁלְהֶבֶת בְּכָל מָקוֹם — *but a flame* can be transported **anywhere,** because it is not a tangible object.[1]

A related ruling:

גַּחֶלֶת שֶׁל הֶקְדֵּשׁ מוֹעֲלִין בָּהּ — As for *a burning coal belonging to hekdesh,*[2] *one commits me'ilah*[3] in it by using it for private purposes; וְשַׁלְהֶבֶת לֹא נֶהֱנִין וְלֹא מוֹעֲלִין — *but* as for *a flame* belonging to *hekdesh,* although *one may not derive benefit* from it, **one does not commit** *me'ilah* if one does derive benefit from it.[4]

NOTES
---

1. If someone lit his candle from another person's flame on Yom Tov, he may take the burning candle throughout his own *techum,* and is not restricted to the other's *techum* boundary (*Rav*).

2. *Hekdesh* — literally: *the holy estate;* anything consecrated to the Temple treasury or as an offering.

3. *Me'ilah* — misuse of *hekdesh* for private purposes. One who unintentionally uses *hekdesh* property must atone for his sin by bringing an *asham* (guilt)-offering (see *Vayikra* 5:14-16).

4. That is, if one lights a candle from a flame belonging to *hekdesh,* he has not committed *me'ilah* on the Biblical level, because the flame is not a tangible object.

פרשת פקודי

FRIDAY

PARASHAS PEKUDEI

Yet a third application of this distinction: הַמּוֹצִיא גַחֶלֶת לִרְשׁוּת הָרַבִּים חַיָּיב — **One who carries out a burning coal** on the Sabbath from a private domain **to a public domain**[5] **is liable** for having desecrated the Sabbath, וְשַׁלְהֶבֶת פָּטוּר — **but** if one carries out **a flame**[6] **he is exempt,** because it is not a tangible object.

The Mishnah continues its discussion of *techum* laws as they relate to objects: בּוֹר שֶׁל יָחִיד כְּרַגְלֵי הַיָּחִיד — **Water** drawn from **a water hole belonging to an individual is** accorded a *techum* **like** that of **the feet of the individual** who owns it. וְשֶׁל אַנְשֵׁי הָעִיר כְּרַגְלֵי אַנְשֵׁי אוֹתָהּ הָעִיר — **And** water drawn from a water hole **belonging** jointly **to the people of that city is** accorded a *techum* **like** that of **the feet of the residents of that city.**[7] וְשֶׁל עוֹלֵי בָבֶל — **And** water drawn from the water holes **of those going up from Babylonia** to Eretz Yisrael[8] כְּרַגְלֵי הַמְמַלֵּא — **are** accorded a *techum* **like** that of **the feet of the person who draws the water on Yom Tov.**[9] This water is considered ownerless at the start of Yom Tov, and does not have a *techum* of its own. It therefore assumes the *techum* of whoever acquires it first.

――――― NOTES ―――――

Therefore, he has not incurred the *asham* obligation. Nevertheless, it is forbidden by Rabbinic law to derive benefit from a flame belonging to *hekdesh* (*Rav*).

5. *Reshus hayachid* — a private domain; an area enclosed by walls or partitions. *Reshus harabim* — a public domain; a public thoroughfare. Carrying an object from a private to public domain, or vice versa, is one of the thirty-nine prohibited forms of labor on the Sabbath. One who transgresses this is liable for a *chatas* (sin)-offering to atone for an inadvertent transgression, and for the death penalty for a willful transgression.

6. If he threw the flame into the public domain (*Rav*).

7. I.e., it is restricted to an area 2,000 *amos* around the city (*Rav*).

8. These were established by Jews of the Diaspora, so those making the pilgrimage to Eretz Yisrael would have sufficient water (*Rav*).

9. This Mishnah is in dispute with R' Yochanan ben Nuri, who is of the opinion that ownerless property acquires its own *techum*. According to the Tanna of our Mishnah, ownerless property does not acquire any *techum* until it is legally acquired by someone. The water in this case is legally acquired by the person who draws it through the *kinyan* (act of acquisition) of הַגְבָּהָה, *lifting* (*Rav*).

The Mishnah attributes to the water the *techum* of the person who first draws it (כְּרַגְלֵי הַמְמַלֵּא), and does not render the more liberal ruling of כְּרַגְלֵי כָּל אָדָם, *like anyone's feet* (which would imply that it has no *techum* and may be carried anywhere), since the Mishnah subscribes to the concept of *bereirah*, retroactive determination. Therefore, once the person acquires the water, it assumes his *techum* retroactive to the beginning of Yom Tov (*Rav*).

GEMS FROM THE GEMARA

פרשת
פקודי

FRIDAY
PARASHAS
PEKUDEI

Our Mishnah had stated three differences between laws applicable to a burning coal and to a flame. The Gemara quotes a Baraisa that cites these three and an additional two differences:

The Rabbis taught in a Baraisa: The burning coal of an idol is prohibited for benefit; that is, a coal from an idol that has been burned (*Yoreh Deah* 242:1). The Torah prohibits deriving any benefit from an idol, as it says (*Devarim* 13:18): וְלֹא־יִדְבַּק בְּיָדְךָ מְאוּמָה מִן־הַחֵרֶם, *And no part of the condemned matter shall cling to your hand* (*Rashi*).

The Baraisa continues:

But a flame from the burned idol is permitted for benefit. I.e., one is allowed to light a candle from this flame (*Maharshal* here and *Yam Shel Shlomo* 5:14). [According to other opinions, only once the flame ignited something else, may one light from that second flame (*Pri Megadim* 298; *Mishnah Berurah* 298:19).]

The Baraisa concludes:

One who has foresworn benefit from his fellow is forbidden to benefit from his burning coal, but is permitted to benefit from his flame.

The Gemara compares two rulings regarding a flame, and questions the difference between them:

What is the difference between the flame of a burning idol, from which it is permitted to derive benefit, and a flame of *hekdesh,* from which it is prohibited to derive benefit? The Torah prohibits benefit from both *hekdesh* and an idol. In both cases, use of an intangible flame is not considered to be a violation of this Biblical prohibition. Why then did the Rabbis see fit to prohibit use of a *hekdesh* flame but not that of an idol?

The Gemara answers:

For an idol, which is repugnant [to Jews, and from which people tend to distance themselves in any case], the Rabbis did not see a need to decree against using its flame. In regard to *hekdesh,* however, which is not repugnant, and from which people do not distance themselves as they do from an idol, the Rabbis decreed against using its flame.

Certainly, people distance themselves from *hekdesh* more so than from non-holy items. They do so, however, not out of any feelings of repugnance, but because of the prohibition against deriving benefit from it. They therefore do not distance themselves to the same extent that they distance themselves from idols (*Rashi*).

The Gemara addresses another ruling of our Mishnah:

Rava posed the following contradiction to Rav Nachman. We learned

FRIDAY
PARASHAS PEKUDEI

in our Mishnah: Water drawn from a water hole belonging to an individual is accorded a *techum* like that of the feet of the individual who owns it. But this is contradicted by the following Baraisa: Water from flowing streams and gushing springs, these are accorded a *techum* like that of the feet of any person who has them.

Water from a flowing stream or spring, due to the fact that the waters were moving at the onset of the Sabbath or Yom Tov, did not acquire a residence. They therefore do not acquire their own *techum*, nor do they acquire the *techum* of their owner [if it is a private stream (*Rosh*)], nor of the person who draws the water (*Rashi*). We see, then, that waters are not limited to the *techum* of their owner, which would apparently contradict the ruling of our Mishnah.

The Gemara answers:

Rava said: What kind of water are we dealing with here in our Mishnah? With collected water, i.e., a water hole containing still water rather than running water. Since the water was stationary at the onset of Yom Tov, it acquired the *techum* of its owner. Running water, however, acquires no *techum* at all.

A MUSSAR THOUGHT FOR THE DAY

In *A Torah Thought for the Day* we cited several interpretations of the verse: וּמָשַׁחְתָּ אֶת־מִזְבַּח הָעֹלָה וְאֶת־כָּל־כֵּלָיו וְקִדַּשְׁתָּ אֶת־הַמִּזְבֵּחַ וְהָיָה הַמִּזְבֵּחַ קֹדֶשׁ קָדָשִׁים, *You shall anoint the Burnt-offering Altar and all its utensils; you shall sanctify the Altar, and the Altar shall become Holy of Holies* (40:10). In his remarks to the same verse in *Parashas Tetzaveh*, R' Samson Raphael Hirsch offers additional observations with valuable lessons. Similar to *Ramban's* second understanding of the term קֹדֶשׁ קָדָשִׁים, he maintains that it means a holy place from which other places receive their holiness. Thus, he notes that there are two areas where a distinction is drawn between קֹדֶשׁ קָדָשִׁים and קֹדֶשׁ. The first concerns location, with the area that contains the *Aron* called קֹדֶשׁ קָדָשִׁים, while the area containing the Menorah and *Shulchan* is called קֹדֶשׁ. Similarly, there are *korbanos* that are called קֹדֶשׁ קָדָשִׁים, such as the *olah-* and *chatas-* offerings, whereas others of lesser holiness, including *shelamim, pesach, maaser* and *bechor,* are called קָדָשִׁים קַלִּים. If we compare the relationship between the two groupings, whether in locale or offerings, the קֹדֶשׁ קָדָשִׁים relate to man's activities, to the Torah, and to his relation with it, whereas the קֹדֶשׁ "have as their direct object, man's possessions, his fate, the fortune he receives from Hashem's hand."

פרשת פקודי

**FRIDAY
PARASHAS PEKUDEI**

If we understand that the Altar is meant as a vehicle for man to offer himself and all his activities to sanctification, then it is clear that "being ready to actually carry out the precepts of the Divine Torah is the very first קֹדֶשׁ קָדָשִׁים, the most essential fundamental condition that forms the basis of the Mishkan, and on which the sanctification of all other relations rests ... It is the קֹדֶשׁ קָדָשִׁים that is the base and source of the sanctification of all other holy things in his life. The sanctification ... of that which he receives from Hashem is of value only if beforehand, before he has received it, he has placed himself, with every phase of his life, ready to carry out the will of Hashem."

Accordingly, he says, it is understandable that all *korbanos* must be brought after the morning עוֹלַת תָּמִיד, *the daily communal olah,* and none may be brought after the afternoon עוֹלַת תָּמִיד, so that all the *korbanos* are sandwiched between the two עוֹלוֹת תָּמִיד. This implies that the dedication of "all one's acts to ever progressive and ever higher perfection *has to form the basis and the goal of all offerings.*" Furthermore, the location and name of the Altar show that "nothing stands more in the service of sanctifying the actions of man than the Altar. It stands directly in front of the entrance to the Mishkan, opposite the *Aron* in the קֹדֶשׁ קָדָשִׁים. It is the real center of the space in front of and round about the Mishkan and represents — by the אֵשׁ דָּת flaming on its summit — giving oneself up to Hashem's Torah as the *condition* for entry into the Mishkan. That is why the Outer Altar is also called מִזְבַּח הָעֹלָה, *the Olah Altar,* for it is entirely based upon the sanctifying of actions, and it is thus קֹדֶשׁ קָדָשִׁים."

This powerful message is certainly well worth noting when we read the *parshiyos* of the Mishkan and of *korbanos,* whether in Torah readings or in prayers. As R' Hirsch sums up, "All Jewish ideas of Sanctuary are ideas of *sanctifying.* Something is not made holy so that holiness should be concentrated in it, with all other things left to non-holiness. Rather, *everything becomes holy so that it makes other things holy.*"

HALACHAH OF THE DAY

Before we continue our exploration of the laws of Kashrus, it would be prudent to take a moment to recap that which we have covered so far.

We have seen that prohibited foods may be divided into two groups: those whose prohibition is of Torah origin, and those whose prohibition is by Rabbinic injunction.

FRIDAY
PARASHAS PEKUDEI

The prohibitions of Torah origin may be sub-divided into two groups:

Primary prohibitions: These include nonkosher animals, fowl, and fish; *neveilah* (carrion), *tereifah* (mortally injured animal or fowl), *sheretz* (swarming insects and rodents), blood, *cheilev* (certain prohibited fats), *gid hanasheh* (the sciatic nerve), *eiver min hachai* (a limb from a living creature), *tevel* (untithed produce), *orlah* (fruits of the first three years), *chadash* (new grain), and *yayin nesech* (wine poured to *avodah zarah*).

Prohibited combinations: This includes *basar b'chalav* (prohibited combinations of meat and milk) and *kilayim* (different species grown together).

The foods prohibited by Rabbinic injunction may also be sub-divided into two groups:

Rabbinic injunctions based on existing Torah law: These include prohibitions such as the Rabbinic extensions to the prohibitions of *basar b'chalav, gid hanasheh, kilayim,* and *yayin nesech,* as well as the Rabbinic prohibitions of *chalav akum* and *gevinas akum*.

Rabbinic injunctions without a Torah-law basis: This includes the Rabbinic prohibitions of *bishul* and *pas akum, stam yeinam,* and those foods considered by the Sages to be dangerous.

Now that we have explored and reviewed the various categories of forbidden foods, we can turn our attention to the details of the prohibition of eating these foods.

According to Torah law, one who eats nonkosher food is liable for punishment or the need for sacrificial atonement only if the following criteria are met:

First, one must eat the minimal amount seen by the Torah as constituting *achilah*, an act of eating. The Torah views one as having accomplished an *achilah* only if he has eaten at least a *kezayis*. *Kezayis* translates literally as "similar to an olive." Practically, this is an amount equal to half an egg's volume. Contemporary authorities have determined this amount to be approximately one fluid ounce. In the case of liquids, one would be required to drink a *revi'is,* somewhat more than three fluid ounces. Since the *kezayis* is measured exclusive of what may remain between the teeth, one who eats exactly this amount would not be liable for punishment.

Tomorrow we will discuss the time span within which the eating must be completed, as well as the manner in which the food must be consumed in order for one to have transgressed a Kashrus prohibition.

A CLOSER LOOK AT THE SIDDUR

פרשת פקודי

**FRIDAY
PARASHAS PEKUDEI**

Commenting on the verse regarding the construction of the Outer Altar, in which the Torah says: וְצִפִּיתָ אֹתוֹ נְחֹשֶׁת, *and you shall cover it in* **copper** (27:2), Rashi says that this is meant לְכַפֵּר עַל עַזּוּת מֵצַח, *to atone for brazenness,* as it says, וּמִצְחֲךָ נְחוּשָׁה, *and your forehead is* **brazen** (*Yeshayah* 48:4). This loathsome trait is familiar from the *Viduy* section of the Yom Kippur services, in which we ask forgiveness: וְעַל חֵטְא שֶׁחָטָאנוּ לְפָנֶיךָ בְּעַזּוּת מֵצַח, *for the sin that we have sinned before you with brazenness. Radak* explains that the key element of brazenness is the lack of shame, which manifests itself with one's forehead and face boldly held high in defiance of the one who is admonishing him. It represents a toughness that evokes the message that the sinner will neither be subjugated nor made to feel remorse or embarrassment for what he has done.

Aside from the similarity in the words נְחֹשֶׁת and נְחוּשָׁה, *Maharil Diskin* wonders how the copper covering symbolizes the trait of עַזּוּת מֵצַח. He notes that when discussing the verse relating to the *Aron*: מִבַּיִת וּמִחוּץ תְּצַפֶּנּוּ, *from within and from without you shall cover it* (25:11), the Gemara states (*Yoma* 72b): "Any scholar whose inside is not like his outside is not truly a scholar." He explains that a scholar's *yiras Shamayim,* fear of Heaven, as exemplified by his behavior, should be drawn from the wisdom of Torah and its teachings, based on the intrinsic superiority of good deeds and mitzvos and the lowliness of poor character traits and sinfulness. Thus, the "gold" with which he has been imbued should be reflected in a "golden" exterior. However, for an ordinary person the Torah is less stringent in this regard, for a large measure of what keeps him observant is the בּוּשָׁה, *shame,* that he might feel (to parents, teachers, friends) when acting in an unseemly or wayward way. [It is this idea that R' Yochanan ben Zakkai expressed to his students shortly before his demise: יְהִי רָצוֹן שֶׁתְּהֵא מוֹרָא שָׁמַיִם עֲלֵיכֶם כְּמוֹרָא בָּשָׂר וָדָם, *May it be the will* (of God) *that the fear of Heaven should be upon you like the fear of flesh and blood,* for that would prevent you from sinning (*Berachos* 28b).] Thus, such a person is symbolized by the other utensils of the Mishkan, such as the *Shulchan,* which is constructed of עֲצֵי שִׁטִּים, *acacia wood,* and covered with the more precious gold, signifying an exemplary exterior that is engendered by an inferior motivation.

The Altar, however, has the reverse feature, in that its covering, copper, is *less* valuable than its base material, acacia wood, a feature

FRIDAY
PARASHAS PEKUDEI

that is not found in any other utensil. This signifies the character of the brazen individual, whose insolence is such that even the paltry level of *yiras Shamayim* that he has attained is hidden by his disrespectful and shameless behavior, and is viewed as ugly. It is thus the covering of the Altar that hints to the flaw of brazenness, and for which it atones.

In his comments to this עַל חֵטְא, *Iyun Tefillah* points out that it is particularly difficult to understand, because we are taught: הֱוֵי עַז כַּנָּמֵר, *Be bold as a leopard* (*Avos* 5:23). He understands this dictum in the sense that the *Tur* does. *Tur* writes that one must be obstinate in the face of those who scorn and laugh at one's pursuit of mitzvos, and not allow their scorn to deter or hinder him (see Monday's *Mussar Thought for the Day*). Rather than employing this trait for the beneficial use outlined by the Sages, we too often use it to be insolent toward Rabbis and scholars, and, even worse, toward Hashem. And for this behavior, the rains are withheld and the *Beis HaMikdash* remains destroyed.

QUESTION OF THE DAY:
When was the Outer Altar referred to as the "Olah Altar," and when was it called the "Copper Altar"?

For the answer, see page 202.

A TORAH THOUGHT FOR THE DAY

פרשת פקודי

SHABBOS
PARASHAS PEKUDEI

This week's *Haftarah* describes the inauguration of the First *Beis HaMikdash,* which took place on Succos of the year 2938. Shlomo invited the elders of the nation to witness the placement of the *Aron Ha-Kodesh* in the Holy of Holies. Reminiscent of the inauguration of the Mishkan, the presence of Hashem filled the "House" in the form of a cloud indicating Hashem's satisfaction. Shlomo delivered his blessing to the assembled nation and they celebrated for fourteen days, seven days before Succos and the seven days of Succos.

The *Haftarah* states (*I Melachim* 8:1): . . . . אָז יַקְהֵל שְׁלֹמֹה אֶת־זִקְנֵי יִשְׂרָאֵל לְהַעֲלוֹת אֶת־אֲרוֹן בְּרִית־ה', *Then Shlomo gathered together the elders of Israel . . . to bring up the Ark of the Covenant of* HASHEM. The very next verse states: וַיִּקָּהֲלוּ אֶל־הַמֶּלֶךְ שְׁלֹמֹה כָּל־אִישׁ יִשְׂרָאֵל, *All the men of Israel gathered to King Shlomo.* As we see in verse 8:1, Shlomo invited only the leadership of Israel to attend the historic inauguration of the *Beis HaMikdash;* he did not extend the same invitation to the rest of the nation. Yet, the *navi* records that *"all the men"* came for the momentous occasion. Why did Shlomo invite only the leadership, and why did the rest of the uninvited nation come to the celebration without invitation? He invited the leaders of the nation (elders, tribal heads, judges, etc.) in order to accord honor to the *Aron,* which was now being brought to the *Beis HaMikdash.* The *Abarbanel* writes that even though the rest of the nation were not invited, they came of their own volition, for they too wished to honor the *Aron.*

The Gemara in *Moed Katan* (9a) records that on Yom Kippur of the year of the inauguration, the Bnei Yisrael did not fast. The inaugural celebration ran from the 8th of Tishrei through the 21st of Tishrei, and Yom Kippur was on the 10th of Tishrei! They based the decision not to fast on a precedent set 486 years earlier at the inauguration of the Mishkan. That inauguration lasted 12 days, with each of the twelve *Nesiim,* tribal leaders, offering a personal *korban* — one per day. Although personal *korbanos* are usually forbidden on Shabbos, the *Nasi* whose turn fell on Shabbos was permitted to offer his *korban* on Shabbos! The Rabbis concluded that if the Torah allowed the more serious transgression of Shabbos to honor the inauguration of the Mishkan, it would certainly permit the relatively lesser transgression of eating on Yom Kippur to honor the inauguration of the *Beis Ha-Mikdash.* However, after the people were excused from fasting, the Torah leadership questioned whether or not they had ruled properly;

פרשת פקודי

SHABBOS

PARASHAS PEKUDEI

a Heavenly voice reassured them, "You (all those who celebrated and did not fast) are invited into the World To Come!"

What an amazing halachic story! Is it possible that the Sanhedrin of that generation permitted eating on Yom Kippur before making absolutely sure that they were not making a mistake?

Chasam Sofer explains that the Sanhedrin were not second-guessing eating on that Yom Kippur. However, their decision was predicated on the certainty that the intentions of the original invitees to the inauguration, all great scholars and *tzaddikim*, were 100 percent for the sake of Hashem's honor and glorification — just as were the intentions of the *Nesiim* at the time of the Mishkan. Their later questioning concerned those uninvited attendees, whom Shlomo had not invited because he could not be sure of the sincerity of their intentions; they had also eaten and not fasted, and the Sanhedrin feared that their intentions had not been solely for the glorification of Hashem's Name. Regarding them, too, the voice from Heaven confirmed, "You are invited into the World To Come!"

MISHNAH OF THE DAY: BEITZAH 5:6

The previous Mishnayos taught that property may not be taken beyond its owner's *techum* on the Sabbath or Yom Tov. Our Mishnah offers different applications of this rule:

מִי שֶׁהָיוּ פֵירוֹתָיו בְּעִיר אַחֶרֶת — **If one's produce was in another town** outside of his *techum* at the onset of Yom Tov, וְעֵרְבוּ בְּנֵי אוֹתָהּ הָעִיר לְהָבִיא אֶצְלוֹ מִפֵּירוֹתָיו — **and the people of that town placed an eruv** *techumin* in order **to bring some of his produce to him,** לֹא יָבִיאוּ לוֹ — **they may not bring** the produce **to him.**[1] וְאִם עֵרַב הוּא — **But if he placed an eruv** that extends his *techum* to that town, פֵּירוֹתָיו כָּמוֹהוּ — **his produce is treated as himself,** i.e., it is accorded his *techum*.[2]

---- NOTES ----

1. Since the owner did not extend his *techum* by placing an *eruv* before Yom Tov, they may not bring him his produce. The reason for this is, as mentioned earlier, that produce follows the *techum* of its owner (*Rav*).

2. The produce is thus within its own *techum*, and he may therefore retrieve it (*Rashi*). Similarly, the people of the town who placed an *eruv* extending their *techum* in his direction may deliver their produce to him (*Tiferes Yisrael*).

GEMS FROM THE GEMARA

פרשת פקודי

**SHABBOS
PARASHAS
PEKUDEI**

The Gemara presents a dispute regarding whose *techum* deposited items are associated with:

It was said: If one deposits produce with a friend for safekeeping, Rav says that the *techum* of the deposit is like that of the feet of the one to whom it was entrusted for safekeeping, even though he is not the actual owner; but Shmuel says that its *techum* is like that of the feet of the depositor, who is the actual owner.

The Gemara now records an incident that involves this issue:

Rav Chana bar Chanilai hung meat on the door bolt of his lodging before the onset of Yom Tov. [He had visited a nearby town on Erev Yom Tov, where local butchers had given him meat. Although he was lodging at an inn outside the *techum* of his hometown, he had also placed an *eruv* that enabled him to return to his hometown on Yom Tov (*Rashi*).] Rav Chana returned to the inn after the onset of Yom Tov, and wished to take his meat back with him to his town via his *eruvei techumin* (*Meiri*).

He (Rav Chana bar Chanilai) came before Rav Huna, to ask whether he was permitted to take the meat home on Yom Tov. Rav Huna told him: If you hung it on the door bolt of your inn, go take it home, but if your hosts hung it for you, do not take it home.

The Gemara questions Rav Huna's ruling:

Now, if Rav Chana bar Chanilai had hung it, would he have been permitted to take it home according to Rav Huna? But Rav Huna was a disciple of Rav, and Rav said that property is accorded a *techum* like that of the feet of the one to whom it was entrusted.

Since Rav Chana bar Chanilai's hosts where he was lodging presumably intended to accept responsibility for the meat when they advised him to hang it on the door bolt, they became its legal guardians and it should have been accorded their *techum* according to Rav (*Chidushei Meiri*). How could Rav Huna, Rav's disciple, reject his mentor's ruling?

The Gemara responds that Rav's ruling did not apply in this case:

This case, where Rav Chana bar Chanilai hung the meat on a door bolt, is different, for it is as if the innkeeper assigned him a specific corner.

I.e., when Rav Chana bar Chanilai hung the meat on his host's door bolt, the host did not accept responsibility for its safekeeping, but was simply designating a location for Rav Chana to hang the meat (*Rashi*). Hence Rav Huna's ruling is not germane to that of Rav.

פרשת פקודי
A MUSSAR THOUGHT FOR THE DAY

SHABBOS
PARASHAS PEKUDEI

Rav Dessler's opening essays in *Michtav MeiEliyahu* challenge us to question our true motives in serving or not serving Hashem. He approaches this issue from the perspective of happiness, questioning why people are or are not happy. In his analysis, he states that many people believe that wealth makes for happiness, and that if they were wealthy, they would also be happy. He quickly challenges this notion, and proves at some length that spirituality can be the only true source of happiness.

Chazal tell us that at the inauguration of the first *Beis HaMikdash*, Shlomo already knew that it would eventually be destroyed; yet, the occasion was celebrated with complete joy and conviction, without the slightest shadow of sadness. So much so, that Shlomo and the nation did not fast on that Yom Kippur, because they were so immersed in celebrating Hashem's presence within their midst.

The Gemara in *Kesubos* (104a) explains that the highest level of קְדֻשָּׁה, *holiness,* is the one that manifests sanctity from within the physical world. It was why R' Yehudah HaNasi, the wealthiest man of his generation, earned the title of "Rabbeinu HaKadosh," Our Holy Teacher. Despite his astounding wealth, he was able to testify at the end of his life that he had not derived any personal pleasure from his wealth. The commentaries explain that Rabbeinu HaKadosh certainly enjoyed his great wealth; however, it was not personal enjoyment, but rather it was solely for the sanctification of Hashem's Name — a pleasure that caused the inherent *kedushah* existing in the physical world to be manifest.

We would imagine that if we devoted years to constructing a building that was intended to manifest Hashem's glory and presence in the world, and we knew that it would eventually be destroyed, our pleasure in our monumental accomplishment would be somewhat compromised. Moreover, if the building had been the single greatest desire of our father, who had dedicated every living moment to the realization of this edifice, how much more so would the joy have been compromised. Yet, as we see in this *Haftarah,* Shlomo celebrated the inauguration of the *Beis HaMikdash* in a manner that proclaimed his absolute dedication to the glory of Hashem without expression of any personal emotions. Shlomo knew that David's sole unfulfilled request was "to dwell in the House of Hashem," and was aware that David had even requested to die a day earlier than intended (see *Shabbos* 30a) so that the *Beis HaMikdash* could be built a day sooner! Yet, Shlomo also

פרשת פקודי
SHABBOS
PARASHAS PEKUDEI

knew that Hashem had refused David's offer because: טוֹב לִי יוֹם אֶחָד שֶׁאַתָּה יוֹשֵׁב וְעוֹסֵק בַּתּוֹרָה מֵאֶלֶף עוֹלוֹת שֶׁעָתִיד שְׁלֹמֹה בִּנְךָ לְהַקְרִיב לְפָנַי, *I prefer one day of your Torah learning over the thousand olah-offerings that your son Shlomo will offer before Me.*

Happiness is the consequence of a life lived dedicated to the will of Hashem and the sanctification of His Name. It is not fine clothing, fancy meals, expensive cars, or beautiful buildings. It is not even the majesty of the *Beis HaMikdash* and the bringing of the *korbanos*. Those are merely the trappings that challenge us to see within and beyond to the essence of who we are and why we were created. By doing so, we come to the realization that every moment spent serving Hashem is worthy of an eternity of celebration.

HALACHAH OF THE DAY

As we noted yesterday, in the eyes of halachah one has performed an act of eating only if his actions fill certain criteria. We have seen that there is a minimal amount that must be consumed in order for consumption to be viewed as an act of eating. Halachah also requires that this minimum amount of food be consumed within a specific time span.

Obviously, one who eats half of the required minimal amount one day and the other half on a second day cannot be said to have performed one unified act of eating. It is easily understood that the required *kezayis* must be eaten within a time span that allows for the action to be seen as one single act. Sinaitic tradition has defined this time span as the amount of time necessary for one to eat a volume of wheat bread equal to three (or four) eggs while sitting in a comfortable manner. In the words of the Talmud, this time span is known as *k'dei achilas pras,* which translates literally as, "the amount of time necessary to eat half a loaf." Halachic authorities define this in contemporary terms, and the differing opinions as to the length of *k'dei achilas pras* range from approximately three to as much as nine minutes.

Similarly, regarding the drinking of prohibited liquids, the minimum amount of fluid considered to be a drink — a *revi'is* — must be consumed within the amount of time considered typical for one to drink a *revi'is*. There is disagreement among the *poskim* as to whether the time span for drinking a *revi'is* is uniform with respect to all drinks, or whether it varies according to the accustomed method of drinking each individual type of drink. For example, where one may sip wine, one generally does not sip soda.

פרשת פקודי
SHABBOS
PARASHAS PEKUDEI

One who does not conclude an act of prohibited eating or drinking within the prescribed time, while he is in violation of Torah law, is not liable to punishment or the requirement of sacrificial atonement.

Even if one consumes the prescribed minimum amount of a prohibited item within the prescribed minimal time span, he is liable for punishment only if he consumes the prohibited item in a manner consistent with the Torah's understanding of an act of eating. Let us explain:

One of the axiomatic principles of the Torah states that whenever the Torah speaks of one committing a particular act, it refers only to instances where that act is performed in the normal way. Thus, an action performed in an unnatural or unusual manner has no halachic validity. Accordingly, one who ingests a prohibited item in such a way has not transgressed Torah law.

Tomorrow, we will discuss some possible applications of this law.

A CLOSER LOOK AT THE SIDDUR

Today, we continue to discuss the prayers that we recite during *Bircas HaChodesh*, the Blessing of the New Moon, before *Mussaf* of the Shabbos preceding each Rosh Chodesh. After reciting the *Yehi Ratzon* prayer that we have studied earlier, we recite another paragraph, which begins with the words: מִי שֶׁעָשָׂה נִסִּים לַאֲבוֹתֵינוּ וְגָאַל אוֹתָם מֵעַבְדוּת לְחֵרוּת הוּא יִגְאַל אוֹתָנוּ בְּקָרוֹב..., *The One Who performed miracles for our forefathers and redeemed them from slavery to freedom . . . may He redeem us soon . . .* We may ask: Why are we mentioning our redemption from Egypt and a prayer for our ultimate redemption at the time of the blessing for the new month?

The simple explanation would be that we are asking for Hashem to redeem us in the coming month (R' Chaim Kanievski). *Levush* explains that since the mitzvah of Rosh Chodesh was the first one given to Klal Yisrael, when they were still in Egypt, just prior to the redemption, we again ask for redemption every time we establish the new month.

We may also add that the message of the renewal of the moon that establishes the new month is a sign for Klal Yisrael that they should not despair in the long dark exile. We reassure ourselves that just as the moon gets smaller and smaller, yet finally renews itself, so too, Klal Yisrael will renew itself to its original glory and even greater.

Shemuas Tefillasi cites the *Ramban*, who writes that it is a mitzvah to count every month from the first month of *Yetzias Mitzrayim,* so there

SHABBOS PARASHAS PEKUDEI

is a constant reminder of our redemption from Egypt. Therefore, he says, in the Torah no names were given to the Jewish months, as they are always referred to as the first from *Yetzias Mitzrayim,* the second from *Yetzias Mitrayim,* etc. The names Nissan, Iyar, Sivan, etc. were given later in Bavel. So, although when we bless the new month we do mention the Babylonian names and we do not say the third month from *Yetzias Mitzrayim* (interestingly, the *Binyan Shlomo* (22) strongly objects to this), we at least make a point to emphasize the redemption from Egypt while establishing the new month, to make reference to this reminder.

Finally, *Derech Pikudecha* explains that we are praying for redemption so that we will once again be able to establish the moon with witnesses and *beis din* as was done originally — and the first time this was done was at the time of *Yetzias Mitzrayim.*

QUESTION OF THE DAY:

Why did Shlomo bring the items sanctified by his father to the Beis HaMikdash only after it had been built?

For the answer, see page 202.

ANSWERS TO QUESTIONS OF THE DAY

Sunday:
The Mishkan was a testimony that Hashem had forgiven the Jews for the sin of the Golden Calf (*Sfas Emes*).

Monday:
Kli Yakar states that Betzalel, through *ruach hakodesh*, divined what Hashem had commanded Moshe, and fulfilled the commands.

Tuesday:
The Torah wanted to make clear that the gold was interwoven into the thread together with the other materials.

Wednesday:
This teaches that the names were engraved from the underside of the stones (*Maharil Diskin*).

Thursday:
Rabbeinu Bachya states that they approached the work of building as if it were the *avodah* performed in the Mishkan.

Friday:
Netziv writes that from the eighth day of the inauguration and on, it was known as the *Olah* Altar; it was called the Copper Altar only up to that point.

Shabbos:
Metzudas David states that Shlomo used his own funds to build the entire *Beis HaMikdash* and all of its vessels.

פרשת ויקרא
Parashas Vayikra

פרשת ויקרא

A TORAH THOUGHT FOR THE DAY

SUNDAY
PARASHAS VAYIKRA

אִם־עֹלָה קָרְבָּנוֹ מִן־הַבָּקָר זָכָר תָּמִים יַקְרִיבֶנּוּ
אֶל־פֶּתַח אֹהֶל מוֹעֵד יַקְרִיב אֹתוֹ לִרְצֹנוֹ לִפְנֵי ה'.
וְסָמַךְ יָדוֹ עַל רֹאשׁ הָעֹלָה וְנִרְצָה לוֹ לְכַפֵּר עָלָיו

If one's offering is a burnt-offering from the cattle, he shall offer an unblemished male; he shall bring it to the entrance of the Tent of Meeting, voluntarily, before HASHEM. *He shall lean his hands upon the head of the burnt-offering; and it shall become acceptable for him, to atone for him (Vayikra 1:3-4).*

The Midrash (*Vayikra Rabbah* 7:3) observes that the burnt-offering, or *korban olah,* was brought to atone for one's sinful thoughts. As *Ramban* (to verse 4) explains, this is why it is totally consumed by the flames of the Altar. It is designated completely for Hashem because only He, Who knows man's thoughts, knows the sin for which one brings this offering.

The translation of the word לִרְצֹנוֹ, *voluntarily* (verse 3), follows *Rashi's* citation of the Gemara (*Rosh Hashanah* 6a) that derives from this word that a sacrifice may not be offered without its owner's consent. But more literally, the word means *for his acceptance,* denoting that the offering causes him to be accepted *before* HASHEM. Based on this literal translation, *Chasam Sofer* is troubled with the Torah's repetition of the same idea in verse 4, using the word וְנִרְצָה, *it shall become acceptable.* Additionally, he notes that *Rashi* in verse 3 cites *Toras Kohanim* (3:13), which states that one should not hand his offering to a Kohen, telling him to bring it to the *Beis HaMikdash* (or the Mishkan) for him; rather, he should exert himself to bring the animal to the place where it will be sacrificed. Why, asks *Chasam Sofer,* does the Torah tell us this specifically here? There is already (in *Kiddushin* 41a) a general rule pertaining to mitzvah performance: "A mitzvah is greater when performed by oneself than when performed by one's messenger." Surely that rule applies here — why the need to specifically single out the act of bringing an offering to the *Beis HaMikdash?*

To answer these questions, *Chasam Sofer* points out that there is a complication facing one who wishes to bring an *olah*-offering. Satan, who wishes to trap each Jew in sin, cannot read one's thoughts, and has no way of knowing whether one had sinful thoughts. But should one bring an *olah,* Satan will know that the person is faced with this particular challenge. Now Satan will focus all his energies on trying to challenge the person with sinful thoughts!

**SUNDAY
PARASHAS
VAYIKRA**

Yet there is another reason, aside from atonement for sinful thoughts, for which one brings a *korban olah*: one can offer an *olah* if he wishes to come before Hashem, to come closer and please Him with a gift. The verse therefore stresses that one should bring the *olah*-offering himself — not with a messenger — so that Satan will not know if he is bringing the offering for atonement or for coming closer to Hashem's presence. Hashem, Who reads each person's mind, knows his intent, and will grant his atonement.

Thus, concludes *Chasam Sofer*, the verses should be read as follows: אִם־עֹלָה קָרְבָּנוֹ מִן־הַבָּקָר זָכָר תָּמִים יַקְרִיבֶנּוּ, *If one's offering is an olah-offering from the cattle, he shall offer an unblemished male;* אֶל־פֶּתַח אֹהֶל מוֹעֵד יַקְרִיב אֹתוֹ, *he, himself, shall bring it to the entrance of the Tent of Meeting,* not through a messenger, as if his intent is to appear before Hashem with a gift of an offering לִרְצֹנוֹ לִפְנֵי ה׳, *for his acceptance before Hashem.* Yet, when וְסָמַךְ יָדוֹ עַל רֹאשׁ הָעֹלָה, *he shall lean his hands upon the head of the olah-offering,* which he is really bringing to atone for his sinful thoughts, then וְנִרְצָה לוֹ לְכַפֵּר עָלָיו, *it shall become acceptable for him, to atone for him.*

MISHNAH OF THE DAY: BEITZAH 5:7

The final Mishnah of the tractate deals with laws that apply to guests, and laws regarding animals on Yom Tov:

מִי שֶׁזִּמֵּן אֶצְלוֹ אוֹרְחִים — *If one invited guests from out of town to come to him* on Yom Tov,[1] לֹא יוֹלִיכוּ בְיָדָם מָנוֹת — *they may not take portions* of their host's food back *with them* when they return home after the meal,[2] אֶלָּא אִם כֵּן זִכָּה לָהֶם מְנוֹתֵיהֶם מֵעֶרֶב יוֹם טוֹב — *unless he had transferred ownership of their portions to them before Yom Tov.*[3]

———————— NOTES ————————

1. These guests live in a town beyond their host's *techum,* but have made an *eruvei techumin* that allows them to travel to him on Yom Tov (*Rav*).

2. The food became subject to the host's *techum* at the onset of Yom Tov, and this remains the food's *techum* for the remainder of the day, even after the food is transferred to the guests. Therefore, since the owner has not made an *eruvei techumin* that would allow him to reach the home of his guests, his food may not be taken there either (*Rashi*).

3. That is, before Yom Tov, he legally transferred ownership of his guest's portions to them. Although the guests were not present then, the host could accomplish this by handing the portions over to a third party, so the third party should acquire them on behalf of the guests. This transfer of ownership is effective even without

SUNDAY
PARASHAS VAYIKRA

אֵין מַשְׁקִין וְשׁוֹחֲטִין אֶת הַמִּדְבָּרִיּוֹת — **We may not water**[4] **and slaughter range animals,**[5] אֲבָל מַשְׁקִין וְשׁוֹחֲטִין אֶת הַבַּיָּיתוֹת — **but we may water and slaughter domestic animals.** אֵלוּ הֵן בַּיָּיתוֹת — **These are** considered **domestic animals:** הַלָּנוֹת בָּעִיר — **those that pass the night in the town.** מִדְבָּרִיּוֹת הַלָּנוֹת בָּאֲפָר — **Range animals** are *those that pass the night in the pasture.*

— NOTES —

the consent or foreknowledge of the guests, because of the principle that a beneficial act can be performed on behalf of a person even without his knowledge [זָכִין לְאָדָם שֶׁלֹּא בְּפָנָיו]. Since the guests are then the legal owners of these portions at the onset of Yom Tov, the portions are subject to their *techum,* and may be taken back to their homes or anywhere else within their *techum* limits (*Rav*).

4. The Gemara notes that in truth watering *alone* is permissible, since the owner bears responsibility to provide for his animals (*Ran*). The reason our Mishnah mentions watering is to teach that it is advisable for one to first water his animal and then slaughter it, since at times it will enable the hide of the animal to be removed with less difficulty.

5. I.e., animals that pasture freely and are not seen for an extended period of time. Since they are not always accessible to their owner at the onset of Yom Tov, they are considered *muktzeh,* and thus may not be slaughtered on Yom Tov (*Rashi*).

GEMS FROM THE GEMARA

The Gemara cites a Baraisa that elaborates on the distinction between domestic animals and range animals mentioned in our Mishnah:

The Rabbis taught in a Baraisa: These are the range animals, and these others are the domestic animals: Range animals are any that go out during the Pesach season and graze in the pasture, and then return to a settlement during the first rains. This rainy season begins during the month of Cheshvan (*Rashi*).

The Baraisa continues:

And these are the domestic animals: Any that go out and pasture beyond the *techum* of a settled area, but come back to spend the night within the *techum.* Rebbi says: Both of these are domestic animals. Rather, these are the range animals: Any that go out and graze in the pasture, and do not return to a settlement either in the summer or in the winter.

The difference between range animals and domestic animals is that *muktzeh* laws forbid the slaughter of range animals but not of domestic animals. Since the Baraisa quotes a definition for range animals in Rebbi's name, we may conclude that Rebbi agrees that they are *muktzeh.* The Gemara questions this assumption:

But does Rebbi subscribe to a broad application of *muktzeh* law? R' Shimon bar Rebbi inquired of Rebbi: What is the law concerning eating unripe dates on Yom Tov according to R' Shimon? Rebbi answered him: *Muktzeh* law does not apply according to R' Shimon except in the case of dried figs and raisins while they are drying. Although fresh figs and grapes are edible fruits that are fit for use on the Sabbath, they nevertheless become inedible while they are drying out. By putting them out to dry before the Sabbath, one has intentionally set them aside, and even R' Shimon agrees that they then become *muktzeh*. In the case of unripe dates, however, no one intentionally made these dates unfit for use; in fact, some people actually eat them in their unripe state. Therefore, R' Shimon does not ascribe the *muktzeh* laws to them (*Rashi*). Since Rebbi cited R' Shimon's application of *muktzeh* law, he presumably agrees with it. Why then does he consider range animals *muktzeh*?

SUNDAY
PARASHAS VAYIKRA

The Gemara offers a possible answer:

If you prefer, say: These (the range animals) are also like dried figs and raisins, inasmuch as they were fit to use, and he sent them away. Therefore, even R' Shimon concedes that they are *muktzeh*.

The Gemara then offers a second possible answer:

And if you prefer, say: Rebbi said this to explain the opinion of R' Shimon, but he himself does not subscribe to this (the narrow application of *muktzeh* law). He therefore rules that range animals are *muktzeh*.

The Gemara concludes and offers a third possible answer:

And if you prefer, say: Rebbi said his definition of range animals according to the opinion of the Rabbis. He meant as follows: As for me, my opinion is that there is no broad application of *muktzeh* law; but even you, who subscribe to a broad application of *muktzeh* law, should at least concede to me that whichever animals go out and graze in the pasture at Pesach time and then return at the first rains, they are domestic animals and are therefore not *muktzeh*. But the Rabbis answered Rebbi: No! They are considered range animals and are therefore *muktzeh*.

QUESTION OF THE DAY:
What segulos are attained by bringing the olah and shelamim offerings?

For the answer, see page 268.

פרשת ויקרא
A MUSSAR THOUGHT FOR THE DAY

SUNDAY
PARASHAS VAYIKRA

As we discussed in *A Torah Thought for the Day,* one reason the *korban olah* was brought was to atone for one's sinful thoughts. Indeed, explains *Rabbeinu Bachya,* it is because of this that the very first offering the Torah discusses is the *olah.* One's thoughts perforce precede any sinful endeavor, making it appropriate that the *olah* be discussed before the other offerings.

In a similar vein, he explains, the Torah lists the various types of *olah*-offerings in order. In verse 3 the Torah discusses the *olah*-offering brought from cattle. Cattle are expensive, and are brought as offerings by wealthy individuals. This is appropriate, says *Rabbeinu Bachya,* because the rich are the most likely to have arrogant thoughts, being prideful of their money and power. The average person, who is less likely to be arrogant, brings a sheep or goat for an *olah,* as described in verse 10. The poorest people sin the least in this regard; for them, bringing a turtledove or young dove suffices, as explicated in verse 14.

Chazal tell us (*Yoma* 29a): "Sinful thoughts are worse than sins." This statement seems strange — a thought does not harm anyone, nor does it have any physical manifestation. Why is a sinful thought worse than a palpable physical sin? *Rambam* (*Moreh Nevuchim* 3:8) explains by means of an analogy: One might harm two people in the same way, he says, yet the sin of one who affronts a righteous and respected person is certainly qualitatively worse than one who affronts a lowly slave. Similarly, when one sins with his body, his actions are influenced by the physicality of the world, causing his animalistic tendencies to overtake him. This is certainly bad, but not nearly as bad as one who sins with his mind! The mind is the most treasured aspect of man, meant to be unencumbered by physicality and materialism, and to provide a conduit through which one can connect with Heaven. It certainly should not be used for something for which it is not intended. With his sinful thought, one takes his mind from the greatest heights and causes it to sink to the lowest levels. This is much more of a wrongdoing than a physical act of sin.

We see that sinful thoughts are not, as one might think, harmless, and therefore one must actively avoid having them. However, because of their nature, they are particularly difficult to control. How does one banish sinful thoughts? *Avos D'Rabbi Nassan* (20:1) provides a solution: "R' Chanina S'gan HaKohanim says: If one places words of Torah on his mind, then thoughts of bloodshed, thoughts of famine,

פרשת ויקרא

SUNDAY
PARASHAS VAYIKRA

foolish thoughts, immoral thoughts, thoughts of the Evil Inclination, adulterous thoughts, idle thoughts, and thoughts of being obligated to others are removed from him. For we find this in *Sefer Tehillim* (19:9), written by David, King of Israel: פִּקּוּדֵי ה׳ יְשָׁרִים מְשַׂמְּחֵי־לֵב מִצְוַת ה׳ בָּרָה מְאִירַת עֵינָיִם, *The orders of HASHEM are upright, gladdening the heart; the command of HASHEM is clear, enlightening the eyes.*" [The heart signifies the cognitive abilities; when one places פִּקּוּדֵי ה׳, *the orders of HASHEM* — the Torah — on his *heart,* in his thoughts, they are *gladdened,* and not disturbed by the thoughts of negativity enumerated above.]

The converse, concludes the Baraisa, is also true: Should one not place words of Torah on his mind, than he will be encumbered with these eight types of negative thoughts. We see from this how important Torah study can be in dealing with sinful thoughts.

HALACHAH OF THE DAY

As we saw yesterday, halachah does not consider eating accomplished in an unnatural or unusual manner to be an act of eating. We will discuss some applications of this principle.

Gluttonous eating (*achilah gasah*) is not considered a natural act of eating. Therefore, one who has overeaten to the extent that he now feels a revulsion toward food does not violate Torah law if he now ingests nonkosher food. If, however, he is merely satiated by having eaten a meal, but feels no *revulsion* toward food, any subsequent eating is considered natural, and would render him liable for punishment.

Swallowing food whole without chewing is generally considered within the realm of normal eating. However, one who swallows food that is scalding hot is not liable for an act of eating.

Authorities disagree as to whether the consumption of raw meat constitutes a natural act of eating.

Consumption of foods into which repugnant matter has been introduced, thereby causing the food to be inedible, is not considered an act of eating.

There is an important exception to the above guidelines regarding unnatural eating. These rules apply only to those prohibitions in regard to which the Torah uses any form of the word *achilah,* eating. In regard to prohibitions where the Torah does not use such phraseology, one is liable even for eating done in an unnatural way. Thus, *basar b'chalav* (forbidden mixtures of milk and meat) and *kil'ei hakerem* (forbidden

SUNDAY

PARASHAS VAYIKRA

mixtures of the vineyard), where the verse does not use such terminology, are Biblically prohibited even when eaten in an unnatural manner.

Although one who eats nonkosher foods is liable for punishment only if all the previously noted requirements (i.e., minimum amounts, time considerations, etc.) are met, he may still be in violation of Torah law even when those conditions are not met. We will now see examples of this phenomenon.

As we have seen, one is Biblically liable for punishment only if he eats a specific amount of a prohibited food within a specific time span. The Talmud cites a dispute as to whether one remains in violation of Torah law if he eats less than the specified amount of food. The halachic ruling follows the stringent view. (This Talmudic concept is known as *chatzi shiur asur min haTorah*.) Thus, even one who eats less than the minimum *shiur* of nonkosher food transgresses Torah law, even though he is not liable for punishment. Similarly, one who does not conclude eating the nonkosher food within the prescribed time span is also in violation of Torah law.

A CLOSER LOOK AT THE SIDDUR

In *A Mussar Thought for the Day* we quoted a verse from *Tehillim* Chapter 19. This *mizmor* is recited in the *Pesukei D'Zimrah* of *Shacharis* on Shabbos morning. *Yalkut Shimoni* (673) to its third verse — יוֹם לְיוֹם יַבִּיעַ אֹמֶר וְלַיְלָה לְלַיְלָה יְחַוֶּה־דָּעַת, *Day following day utters speech, and night following night declares knowledge* — brings a fascinating Midrash. The Torah tells us that Moshe was in Heaven for forty days and nights (*Shemos* 34:28): וַיְהִי־שָׁם עִם ה' אַרְבָּעִים יוֹם וְאַרְבָּעִים לָיְלָה, *He remained there with* HASHEM *for forty days and forty nights*. But the Midrash is troubled: How did Moshe know when it was day and when it was night? There are no days and nights in Heaven! For it is written: גַּם־חֹשֶׁךְ לֹא־יַחְשִׁיךְ מִמֶּךָ וְלַיְלָה כַּיּוֹם יָאִיר כַּחֲשֵׁיכָה כָּאוֹרָה, *Even darkness obscures not from You; and night shines like the day; darkness and light are the same* (*Tehillim* 139:12); וּנְהוֹרָא עִמֵּהּ שְׁרֵא, *and light dwells with Him* (*Daniel* 2:22).

The Midrash suggests a few methods Moshe may have used to count the passing days and nights; one well-known method is attributed to R' Avdimi. He says that when Hashem taught Moshe verses of the Torah, Moshe knew it was day, and when they focused on sections of Mishnah he knew it was nighttime. [Some — based on this Midrash — have the custom of not studying *Chumash* during the period from nightfall to midnight. See *Shaar HaTziyun* 238:1.]

**SUNDAY
PARASHAS
VAYIKRA**

The *Midrash* mentions another difference between day and night even in Heaven, one that bears directly on our study of the *siddur*. When Moshe saw the *Shemoneh Esrei* precede the recitation of the *Shema,* he knew it was evening; when he saw the *Shema* precede the *Shemoneh Esrei,* he knew it was daytime.

This puzzling *Midrash* is better understood by referencing a *Gemara* (*Berachos* 4b) that records a dispute regarding the order of the *Shacharis* and *Maariv* services. R' Yochanan is of the opinion that both in the morning and evening, the *Shema* precedes the *Shemoneh Esrei,* so that Hashem's redemption of the Jewish people is mentioned before one approaches Him in prayer. But R' Yehoshua ben Levi disagrees: At the *Maariv* service, he says, one should recite the *Shema* only after the *Shemoneh Esrei* prayer.

We now understand the *Midrash,* which seems to be in consonance with R' Yehoshua ben Levi's opinion. Thus, when Moshe saw the recitation of the *Shemoneh Esrei* precede the *Shema,* he knew it was nighttime. However, this is troubling, as the halachah follows R' Yochanan's opinion! How can we reconcile this? *Beur HaRe'eim* (*Shocher Tov* 19:28) answers the question by explaining why R' Yochanan requires that the גְּאֻלָּה, *redemption,* mentioned in the blessings of the *Shema* be immediately followed by *Shemoneh Esrei.* He quotes *Rashi,* who in turn cites *Yerushalmi:* "One who does not place the גְּאֻלָּה before the *Shemoneh Esrei* can be compared to the king's friend. When he came and knocked on the king's door, the king approached, only to find that his friend had already left." In a similar vein, one who praises Hashem for His great kindnesses to the Jewish nation brings Hashem close to him; that is the most appropriate time for asking that Hashem fulfill one's requests.

Moshe Rabbeinu was in Heaven, says *Beur HaRe'eim,* and in Heaven one cannot be considered as leaving Hashem's presence! In Heaven it is therefore perfectly proper to recall Hashem's praise (in the גְּאֻלָּה section of the blessings of *Shema*) without following it immediately with prayer. But on earth the halachah follows R' Yochanan's opinion, and the גְּאֻלָּה praises always precede the *Shemoneh Esrei.*

[For more on the subject of סְמִיכַת גְּאֻלָּה לִתְפִלָּה, see Series One, Friday of *Parashas Shemos, A Closer Look at the Siddur.*]

פרשת ויקרא
A TORAH THOUGHT FOR THE DAY

MONDAY
PARASHAS VAYIKRA

וְשָׁחַט אֶת־בֶּן הַבָּקָר לִפְנֵי ה' וְהִקְרִיבוּ בְּנֵי אַהֲרֹן הַכֹּהֲנִים אֶת־הַדָּם וְזָרְקוּ אֶת־הַדָּם עַל־הַמִּזְבֵּחַ סָבִיב אֲשֶׁר־פֶּתַח אֹהֶל מוֹעֵד

He shall slaughter the bull before HASHEM; the sons of Aharon, the Kohanim, shall bring the blood and throw the blood on the Altar, all around — which is at the entrance of the Tent of Meeting (Vayikra 1:5).

The book of *Vayikra* discusses many of the *korbanos* that were offered in the *Beis HaMikdash*. Ramban (*Sefer HaMitzvos, Shoresh* 12, see also *Sefer HaChinuch* 138) tells us that in stating: לְכָל־דְּבַר הַמִּזְבֵּחַ וּלְמִבֵּית לַפָּרֹכֶת וַעֲבַדְתֶּם עֲבֹדַת מַתָּנָה אֶתֵּן אֶת־כְּהֻנַּתְכֶם, *regarding every matter of the Altar and within the Curtain, you shall serve; I have presented your priesthood as a service that is a gift* (*Bamidbar* 18:7), the Torah tells us that the Kohanim were the ones who were charged with carrying out the many aspects of the *avodah* in the *Beis HaMikdash*, which included preparing and actually offering the *korbanos* on the Altar.

However, although only a Kohen was permitted to perform the majority of the sacrificial *avodos,* the Gemara (*Zevachim* 32a) states that the first step of the *korban* process, which was *shechitah* (slaughter) of the animal, was allowed to be carried out by a *zar* (a non-Kohen). This principle — termed שְׁחִיטָה כְּשֵׁרָה בְּזָר, *slaughter (of an offering) is acceptable when performed by a non-Kohen* — is understood from a close reading of our Torah passage that discusses the offering of the *korban olah* (elevation-offering): וְשָׁחַט אֶת־בֶּן הַבָּקָר לִפְנֵי ה' וְהִקְרִיבוּ בְּנֵי אַהֲרֹן הַכֹּהֲנִים אֶת־הַדָּם וְזָרְקוּ אֶת־הַדָּם עַל־הַמִּזְבֵּחַ סָבִיב, *He shall slaughter the bull before HASHEM; the sons of Aharon, the Kohanim, shall bring the blood and throw the blood on the Altar, all around.* Since the Torah mentions slaughtering an animal in preparation for its use as a *korban* before introducing the Kohen's role in *korbanos,* we may derive that, in contrast to all other *avodos,* a Kohen does not have to be the one who slaughters an animal used for a *korban;* his role begins only with קַבָּלָה, *receiving* the blood in a vessel to bring it to the Altar upon which it is thrown.

Moreover, not only is a non-Kohen *allowed* to slaughter his *korban* on his own, he is actually *commanded* to do so. Rashi (*Pesachim* 7b ד"ה פסח וקדשים; see also the *Vilna Gaon's Eliyahu Rabbah* to *Keilim* 1:8) explains that the commandment of: וְשָׁחַט אֶת־בֶּן הַבָּקָר לִפְנֵי ה', *He*

MONDAY
PARASHAS VAYIKRA

shall slaughter the bull before H<small>ASHEM</small>, is a continuation of the previous verses (2-4), which state: אָדָם כִּי־יַקְרִיב מִכֶּם קָרְבָּן ... וְסָמַךְ יָדוֹ עַל רֹאשׁ הָעֹלָה, *When a man among you brings an offering ... he shall lean his hand upon the head of the olah-offering.* Just as the commandment of *he shall lean his hand upon the head of the olah-offering* [termed סְמִיכָה, *leaning*] is speaking to the owner of, or the person who dedicated, the animal to be used as a *korban*, the commandment of slaughtering a *korban* is a duty that is also incumbent on the owner of the *korban*. In the event that a person was unable to slaughter his *korban* on his own — as is in fact the case with most people — he was permitted to appoint a שָׁלִיחַ, *agent,* to act as his representative and do so on his behalf. Alternatively, one of the Kohanim would slaughter the animal. [See *A Taste of Lomdus* for discussion of the Kohanim's role in slaughtering *korbanos*.]

Tosafos (*Yoma* 32b ד"ה אם כן) explain that the Torah permits a *zar* (non-Kohen) to slaughter a *korban* because *shechitah* is not on the same level of *avodah* as are the other *avodos,* such as throwing the animal's blood on the Altar or burning its fats. We may understand this difference, explain *Tosafos,* by observing that in contrast to these other actions that are performed only in the setting of the Mishkan or *Beis HaMikdash, shechitah* is used for non-sacrificial purposes as well. Thus, the *shechitah* process is not something specific to the *Beis HaMikdash,* and is unlike the other *avodos* that are performed only when offering *korbanos.*

R' Zalman of Volozhin (see also *Torah Temimah* to *Vayikra* 1:42) notes that the Midrash (*Yalkut Shimoni, Parashas Acharei Mos* 579) appears to take issue with the Gemara's principle that *shechitah* is allowed to be performed by a non-Kohen. The Midrash states that R' Yishmael teaches that during the entire period of the Wilderness, the Bnei Yisrael were not permitted to slaughter animals for their own personal benefit. Therefore, states the Midrash, when a Jew wished to consume meat, he would bring his animal to a Kohen, who would slaughter it and perform the other *avodos* necessary for offering it as a *korban.* It appears, R' Zalman of Volozhin notes, that this Midrash — which stresses that a Jew would bring the animal specifically to a *Kohen* to slaughter — argues with the Gemara's principle of שְׁחִיטָה בְּשֵׁרָה בְּזָר, *slaughter (of an offering) is acceptable when performed by a non-Kohen.*

We may answer this contradiction, says R' Zalman of Volozhin, based on the explanation of *Tosafos* that we cited above. We learned that the reason why a non-Kohen may slaughter an animal for use as a *korban* is because *shechitah* is performed also for reasons other than

פרשת ויקרא
MONDAY
PARASHAS VAYIKRA

the *avodah* of *korbanos*. *Shechitah*, Tosafos tell us, is not a process that is unique to the *Mishkan* or *Beis HaMikdash*. Accordingly, a non-Kohen's permission to slaughter a *korban* animal is based on his license to slaughter an animal for food. However, in the Wilderness, personal meat — the meat of non-sacrificial animals — was forbidden to be eaten. As such, no opportunity for *shechitah* existed outside of the Mishkan, and, since *shechitah* at this time was something that was performed only in order to offer a *korban,* the Midrash tells us that, during the period that the Jews were in the Wilderness, this service — like all *avodos* unique to *korbanos* — was allowed to be performed only by a Kohen.

MISHNAH OF THE DAY: ROSH HASHANAH 1:1

In many areas of halachah, it is necessary to distinguish between one year and the next. However, the date that determines when one year ends and the next begins is not the same in every context. This Mishnah lists various dates that mark the beginning of a year, and the halachic purposes that each one serves:

בְּאֶחָד בְּנִיסָן רֹאשׁ — *There are four New Years:* אַרְבָּעָה רָאשֵׁי שָׁנִים הֵם — *On the first of Nissan is the New Year for* reckoning *the* year of a Jewish *king's* reign;[1] וְלָרְגָלִים — *and* Pesach, which occurs in Nissan, is the new year *for the festivals,* regarding the prohibition against delaying the bringing of a vowed offering.[2]

———— NOTES ————

1. This rule is relevant to legal documents. It was customary to date documents by the current year of the monarch's reign ("In such-and-such year of King So-and-so . . ."). This custom was adopted for the sake of peaceful relations with the monarchy (see *Gittin* 80a). The Rabbis derived from Scriptural sources that the reckoning of a Jewish king's reign begins on the first of Nissan. Thus, even if a king ascended the throne shortly before Nissan, e.g., in Shevat or Adar, his first year ends when Nissan arrives, and from that day on we start counting his second year (*Rav*).

2. The designation of Pesach as the first festival is relevant for the prohibition against delaying the fulfillment of vows (בַּל תְּאַחֵר). The Torah states: כִּי תִדֹּר נֶדֶר לַה׳ אֱלֹהֶיךָ לֹא תְאַחֵר לְשַׁלְּמוֹ, *If you make a vow to* HASHEM, *your God, do not delay in fulfilling it* (*Devarim* 23:22). When a person vows to bring an *offering,* the verse requires him to bring it within a certain time limit, otherwise he transgresses the negative commandment. The duration beyond which one may not delay is the passage of three festivals from the date of the vow. Our Mishnah tells us that these festivals must be in sequence from Nissan: Pesach, Shavuos, Succos. Thus, if he made his vow between Pesach and Shavuos, his time limit would not end until five festivals had

פרשת ויקרא

**MONDAY
PARASHAS VAYIKRA**

בְּאֶחָד בֶּאֱלוּל רֹאשׁ הַשָּׁנָה לְמַעְשַׂר בְּהֵמָה — *On the first of Elul is the New Year for the maaser of animals.*[3] רַבִּי אֶלְעָזָר וְרַבִּי שִׁמְעוֹן אוֹמְרִים — *However, R' Elazar and R' Shimon say:* בְּאֶחָד בְּתִשְׁרֵי — *It is on the first of Tishrei.*[4] בְּאֶחָד בְּתִשְׁרֵי רֹאשׁ הַשָּׁנָה לַשָּׁנִים — *On the first of Tishrei is the New Year for* reckoning *the years* of a non-Jewish king's reign,[5] וְלַשְּׁמִטִּין וְלַיּוֹבְלוֹת — *for the* commencing of the *shemittah and Yovel years,*[6] לַנְּטִיעָה וְלַיְרָקוֹת — *for* determining *the*

───── NOTES ─────

passed (i.e., Shavuos, Succos, Pesach, Shavuos, and Succos). The designation of Pesach as the starting point in this calculation is derived from *Devarim* 16:16 (*Rav*).

The Gemara notes that our Mishnah follows the view of R' Shimon. Other Tannaim dispute this view, and maintain that the three festivals need not be in any particular order (*Rav*).

3. It is a Biblical obligation (see *Vayikra* 27:32) to separate a tenth of the cattle, sheep, and goats born to one's herds and flocks each year to be brought as offerings. This is known as *maasar beheimah,* the animal tithe.

One may not designate animals born in one year as *maaser* for animals born in another year. Rather, all the animals from which one takes *maaser* (i.e., all the animals in the pen from which one in ten will be taken) must have been born in the same year. The Gemara derives this from a verse in *Devarim* (14:22) that states this law regarding the *maaser* of grain, and is understood, based on a seeming superficiality, to apply also to the *maaser* of animals (see *Rav*).

The Tanna Kamma's opinion is that in this context the year begins on the first of Elul. Thus, animals born before the first of Elul are counted with the animals of the previous year, while those born on that date or later are counted with the animals of the next year. He also derives this from the aforementioned comparison in *Devarim* 14:22 between the *maaser* of grain and the *maaser* of animals. The Tanna Kamma understands this parallel to mean that just as the new year for *maaser* of grain begins upon its completion (ripening), so does the new year for *maaser* of animals follow their completion (birth). Since many domestic animals give birth in the month of Av, the new year for *maaser* of animals is the first of Elul (*Rav*).

4. In their opinion, the comparison between the *maaser* of animals and the *maaser* of grain teaches that just as the New Year for *maaser* of grain is on the first of Tishrei (as noted later in the Mishnah), so is the new year for *maaser* of animals on the first of Tishrei (*Rav*).

5. The meaning of this phrase parallels that in the opening of the Mishnah (see note 1), only there the reference was to Jewish kings, while here it is to non-Jewish kings (*Rav*).

6. Every seventh year (שְׁמִיטָה, *shemittah*) it is forbidden to cultivate the land of Eretz Yisrael. This restriction applies also every fiftieth year (יוֹבֵל, *Yovel*), which is the year that immediately follows seven *shemittah* cycles. The Mishnah teaches that from the beginning of Tishrei it is forbidden under Biblical law to sow or plow (*Rav*).

MONDAY

PARASHAS VAYIKRA

halachic age of a young *tree*,[7] *and for the* tithing of vegetables.[8] בְּאֶחָד בִּשְׁבָט רֹאשׁ הַשָּׁנָה לָאִילָן — *On the first of Shevat is the New Year for the tree*,[9] כְּדִבְרֵי בֵּית שַׁמַּאי — *according to the opinion of Beis Shammai.* בֵּית הִלֵּל אוֹמְרִים — *However, Beis Hillel say:* בַּחֲמִשָּׁה עָשָׂר בּוֹ — *It is on the fifteenth of* Shevat.

--- NOTES ---

7. Fruit that grows on a tree during its first three years is forbidden for consumption or any other benefit (עָרְלָה, *orlah*). In regard to this law, the new year starts on the first of Tishrei. Hence, for example, if a tree was planted in the month of Av, its first year concludes at the end of Elul [and the second year begins on the first of Tishrei] (*Rashi*).

8. Produce of one year may not be designated as the *terumah* or *maaser* for produce of another year. The Mishnah teaches that the new year for vegetables begins on the first of Tishrei (*Rav*).

9. The produce of each year must be treated separately with respect to *terumah* and *maaser*, as explained in the previous note. The new year for a tree and its fruit begins, according to Beis Shammai, on the first of Shevat. Hence, one may not designate fruit that emerged on the tree before the "New Year for the tree" as the *terumah* or *maaser* of fruit that emerged afterwards [or vice versa] (*Rav*). Unlike vegetables [and grain], which are subject to *maaser* upon their ripening, fruit is classified by the year in which it begins to emerge, i.e., the point where the flower falls off and the fruit begins to emerge in its place (*Rashi* to *Bamidbar* 17:23; cf. *Rambam, Hil. Shemittah VeYovel* 4:9).

Another legal consequence of this New Year relates to the laws governing the *shemittah* cycle. On the first, second, fourth and fifth years of the cycle, the owner takes the second tithe to Jerusalem and eats it there, or he exchanges it for money, which hetakes to Jerusalem and uses to buy food to eat there (מַעֲשֵׂר שֵׁנִי, *maaser sheni*). In the third and sixth years of the cycle, however, he distributes the second tithing to the poor (מַעֲשֵׂר עָנִי, *maasar ani*). The New Year for the tree also determines whether *maaser sheni* or *maaser ani* must be separated from fruit (*Rambam Commentary; Rav*).

GEMS FROM THE GEMARA

The Mishnah stated that the first of Tishrei is the New Year for *Yovel* years. The Gemara questions this:

The New Year for *Yovel* years — it is on the 10th of Tishrei (i.e., Yom Kippur)! For it is written regarding the onset of the *Yovel* year: בְּיוֹם הַכִּפֻּרִים תַּעֲבִירוּ שׁוֹפָר בְּכָל־אַרְצְכֶם, *on Yom Kippur you shall sound the shofar throughout your land* (*Vayikra* 25:9).

The Gemara answers:

Who is the Tanna of this Mishnah? It is R' Yishmael the son of R'

פרשת ויקרא

MONDAY
PARASHAS VAYIKRA

Yochanan ben Beroka, whose opinion is that the *Yovel* year begins on the first of Tishrei. For it has been taught in a Baraisa: When the verse states: וְקִדַּשְׁתֶּם אֵת שְׁנַת הַחֲמִשִּׁים *You shall sanctify the fiftieth year* (ibid. v. 10), what is it teaching? Do we not already know that *Yovel* is in the fiftieth year? The answer is that since in the previous verse it is stated: בְּיוֹם הַכִּפֻּרִים תַּעֲבִירוּ שׁוֹפָר בְּכָל־אַרְצְכֶם, *on Yom Kippur you shall sound the shofar throughout your land,* it could be thought that the year is sanctified only from Yom Kippur and on. The Torah therefore states: וְקִדַּשְׁתֶּם אֵת שְׁנַת הַחֲמִשִּׁים, *You shall sanctify the fiftieth year.* This teaches that the year becomes sanctified from its beginning, i.e., from the first of Tishrei, Rosh Hashanah. Thus, from the first of Tishrei one is forbidden to work the land, and on the first of Tishrei one must free his Jewish slaves (see *Rashi* to the Mishnah).

The Baraisa continues to elaborate on this opinion:

From here R' Yishmael the son of R' Yochanan ben Beroka said: From Rosh Hashanah until Yom Kippur, slaves would neither become free to return to their homes, nor did they remain enslaved to their masters. Rather, they would eat, drink, and rejoice, with crowns on their heads. [The crowns were optional; they were manifestations of their freedom (*Rashi*).] During the interim period from Rosh Hashanah until Yom Kippur, they were not free to return to their homes because the verse first states (v. 9): וְהַעֲבַרְתָּ שׁוֹפַר תְּרוּעָה ... בְּיוֹם הַכִּפֻּרִים, *And you shall sound a broken blast upon the shofar . . . on Yom Kippur,* and only afterwards states (v. 10): וּקְרָאתֶם דְּרוֹר בָּאָרֶץ, *and you shall proclaim liberty in the land.* This implies that until Yom Kippur liberty is not proclaimed. They were not enslaved to their masters, because of the verse (v. 10): וְקִדַּשְׁתֶּם אֵת שְׁנַת הַחֲמִשִּׁים, *You shall sanctify the fiftieth year,* which teaches that *Yovel* begins on Rosh Hashanah; it follows that the slaves go free at the beginning of the year (*Rashi*). From the dissonance between these verses, R' Yishmael the son of R' Yochanan ben Beroka deduces that while the slaves' freedom *begins* on Rosh Hashanah, it is not complete until Yom Kippur (see *Rashba,* end of 7b).

The Baraisa concludes:

When Yom Kippur would arrive, *Beis Din* would sound the *shofar,* slaves would become free to return to their homes, and fields would return to their ancestral owners.

QUESTION OF THE DAY:
If a corner falls off the Altar, what is the law?
For the answer, see page 268.

A MUSSAR THOUGHT FOR THE DAY

פרשת ויקרא

MONDAY
PARASHAS VAYIKRA

We continue with our discussion of the rule that שְׁחִיטָה כְּשֵׁרָה בְּזָר, *slaughter (of an offering) is acceptable when performed by a non-Kohen*. The Torah states that when a person wished to offer an animal as a *korban*, he would bring it to the *Beis HaMikdash* and *lean his hands upon the head* of the animal. This service is termed סְמִיכָה, *leaning*. Next, the animal was slaughtered (שְׁחִיטָה), and then the animal's blood was *received* (קַבָּלָה) in a vessel and *brought* (הוֹלָכָה) to the Altar, upon which it would be *thrown* (זְרִיקָה). Additionally, specified parts of the animal would be burned on the Altar's fires. [When offering a *korban olah*, the entire animal was burned.] We learned that the first two steps of the *korban* process — סְמִיכָה, *leaning*, and שְׁחִיטָה, *slaughter* — were specifically performed by the owner of the *korban*, and the remaining stages — the services of receiving, bringing, and throwing the blood, as well as burning the animal on the Altar — were performed only by Kohanim. If, as we learned, the Kohanim were the ones charged with carrying out the *Beis HaMikdash avodah*, why does the Torah command that the *korban's* owner [or, in the case of שְׁחִיטָה, a representative acting on his behalf] perform סְמִיכָה and שְׁחִיטָה?

We began to answer this question in *A Torah Thought for the Day*; *Tosafos* explain that since *shechitah* is a process that applies also to areas outside the *Beis HaMikdash*, we may understand that *shechitah* is not on the same level as the other processes performed specifically in the *Beis HaMikdash*. Thus, *shechitah* is not relegated specifically to Kohanim.

R' Samson Raphael Hirsch offers a deeper look at the distinction between *shechitah* and the other *avodos* performed on a *korban*, and explains why the Torah specifically commanded the owner of the *korban* [or a representative acting on his behalf] to slaughter his *korban* animal. As we learned, the blood of the *korban* was received in a Temple vessel, brought to the Altar, and thrown onto designated places on the Altar. Although the Kabbalistic explanations of the ultimate effects and spiritually elevated meanings of *korbanos* is beyond our comprehension, R' Hirsch explains that on a basic level, we can understand that a *korban* animal is standing in the place of the person who is offering it. This person is elevating himself by passionately dedicating his blood — or life-force and vitality — to Hashem, by having the animal's blood used in a sanctified forum epitomized by

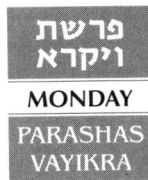

**MONDAY
PARASHAS
VAYIKRA**

its being placed in a Temple vessel and brought to the Altar. Once it arrives at this holy place that exemplifies the transformation of the physical into the spiritual, it is used in a service in which it becomes, as it were, elevated Heavenward. Thus, the latter three *avodos* of קַבָּלָה, *receiving,* הוֹלָכָה, *bringing,* and זְרִיקָה, *throwing,* are the ones by which the substance representing a person's direction and vitality becomes sanctified to Hashem. *Shechitah,* however, is not a service in and of itself. It is merely the tool through which the potential of the blood that will soon be used in *avodas Hashem* is unlocked from the limiting boundaries of the physical body, which often do not allow this inner vitality and drive to be used for *kedushah.* The message of *shechitah* is that before a person is able to use his unique personality and latent potentials to become closer to Hashem in areas of *kedushah,* he must first free, as it were, these abilities from being limited by his physical inclinations. Even a person with a tremendous desire to study Torah or perform acts of *chesed,* for example, will not do so at a time when he is too lazy to leave his comfortable home.

It is for this reason that specifically the owner of the *korban* — and not the Kohanim who perform the other aspects of the *avodah* — is the one who is commanded to slaughter the *korban.* The first step of becoming closer to Hashem — which is a person's allowing himself to look beyond his physical desires and restrictions in the eventual goal of achieving spirituality — can come only from the person himself. Although outside influences are undoubtedly able to help a person become closer to Hashem, these external factors are unable to *begin* the process of inner spiritual growth. The only person who is able to slaughter his *korban* animal — or unlock the vitality of the personality within himself that he wishes to elevate — is the owner of the *korban.*

It is for this reason that specifically the owner of the *korban* must also be the one who performs סְמִיכָה, *leaning.* By fully leaning on the animal with his two hands and his full force and declaring the purpose for which this *korban* is being offered, the person demonstrates that he is totally giving himself over to the process that this animal is about to undergo. In סְמִיכָה, a person states that he wishes that the *korban* represent him in his aim of becoming closer to Hashem. Although other people are able to assist him in this *korban* process, it is essential that the person himself realize what it is that he is doing, and resolve that he indeed wishes to change and grow.

פרשת ויקרא

HALACHAH OF THE DAY

MONDAY
PARASHAS VAYIKRA

It is possible for one to be in violation of Torah law even though the food he ate is not, in and of itself, prohibited. Let us explain:

There is a Talmudic principle that dictates that *taam k'ikar* — the *taam*, the taste of an item, is akin to the essence of the item. We shall see that this principle has very far-reaching ramifications in questions of Kashrus. Simply put, one who does not partake of an actual nonkosher food substance, but instead eats a food — even one that is itself kosher — into which a noticeable nonkosher taste has been absorbed, is in violation of the Torah law prohibiting the consumption of the forbidden food represented by that taste. This is because the principle of *taam k'ikar* mandates that whenever nonkosher taste is absorbed into permitted food to the extent that the taste is noticeable, the kosher food assumes the nonkosher characteristics of the nonkosher food.

The principle of *taam k'ikar* and the means by which *taam* is transmitted (known as *nosein taam*) will be discussed at length at a future time.

While one who eats a kosher food imbued with nonkosher taste is in violation of Torah law, he is not liable for punishment.

To summarize the information we have covered the last few days:

One who eats nonkosher food is liable for punishment only under the following conditions:

(1) He eats a *kezayis* of nonkosher food or drinks a *revi'is* of a nonkosher liquid.

(2) He eats the *kezayis* within a time span of four minutes or drinks the *revi'is* within the typical amount of time necessary for its consumption.

(3) He eats the food or drinks the liquid in a natural manner.

If one eats less than the required amount, or consumes it in a longer time period, he is in violation of Torah law due to the principle of *chatzi shiur*. He is not, however, liable for punishment.

If one eats food that has become imbued with a noticeable taste of nonkosher food, he is in violation of Torah law due to the principle of *taam k'ikar*.

Tomorrow we will begin to discuss the complex rules of *bitul*, the nullification of prohibited foods.

A CLOSER LOOK AT THE SIDDUR

פרשת
ויקרא

**MONDAY
PARASHAS
VAYIKRA**

As we learned, *Parashas Vayikra* discusses the procedures for offering many of the *korbanos* in the *Beis HaMikdash*. Although, in our times, we are unfortunately not privileged to enjoy — or even, to a large degree, understand — the close spiritual relationship between Hashem and the Jewish people that the *avodas hakorbanos* achieved, the Gemara in *Menachos* (110a) states that we may nevertheless realize some of the merit of the *korbanos* by studying the Torah passages that speak of them. In this manner, it is considered as if the actual *korban* about which a person has studied has been offered. It is for this reason, explains the *Mishnah Berurah* (1:13), that many people are accustomed to read the Torah passages that discuss the *korbanos* every day, before reciting *Pesukei D'Zimrah*. By doing so, one can achieve the merit of the *korbanos* even in our times.

Although we do not recite the Torah passage that speaks of a *korban olah* as part of *Shacharis*, we read the fifth chapter of Mishnah *Zevachim*, beginning אֵיזֶהוּ מְקוֹמָן שֶׁל זְבָחִים, which details the laws of the *olah* and various other *korbanos*. Moreover, we recite the passage describing the offering of the *korban tamid*, which includes the commandment: וְשָׁחַט אֹתוֹ עַל יֶרֶךְ הַמִּזְבֵּחַ צָפֹנָה לִפְנֵי ה׳, *he shall slaughter it on the north side of the Altar before* HASHEM (*Vayikra* 1:11).

Rabbeinu Bachya (*Vayikra* 7:37) offers a deeper insight into why we read the passages and laws of the *korbanos*, and the merit that results from our doing so. Dry and mindless reading of the text does not count for us as if we have offered a *korban*. Rather, we must focus on, and internalize, the messages of the *korbanos* in order to motivate ourselves to better serve Hashem. Thus, the benefits of studying the laws of the *korbanos* are similar to those of actually offering a *korban* in the sense that both of these approaches will assist a person to become better focused and more devoted to Hashem.

With this perspective in mind, let us study a message that R' Hirsch sees in the laws of *shechitah*. As we learned in *A Mussar Thought for the Day*, R' Hirsch understands that it is the owner of a *korban* who should slaughter his animal, because slaughtering an animal to be used as a *korban* is not, strictly speaking, a stage of the *Beis HaMikdash avodah*. Rather, it is a necessary preparatory step that must be taken before the actual *korban* services, which involve the animal's blood, may be performed.

R' Hirsch notes that this perspective in the law of *shechitah* teaches

MONDAY
PARASHAS VAYIKRA

us an important principle to keep in mind when planning our lifelong service of Hashem. As we learned in *A Mussar Thought for the Day, shechitah* — which releases the animal's blood from its body — epitomizes the process in which the vitality of human potential and personality is freed from its physical limitations, or from situations that do not allow it to achieve greatness or closeness with Hashem. Although this preparatory step is necessary, it is not governed by the usual guidelines of *avodah,* from which we may learn that the act of realizing what our impediments are and doing what we must to allow us to overcome them is not, in itself, our objective in life. Not by "slaughter" and by "self-destruction," R' Hirsch stresses, is Hashem served. The role of *shechitah* — i.e., the realization of what it is that restricts us in life, and an assessment of measures that must be taken to overcome these obstacles and unlock our potential — is as a preparation for the other, actual, stages of *avodah,* which is the actual bringing of the blood to the Altar to be elevated, or, in more practical terms, the actual living of our lives on a higher and holier stage of existence.

How can we internalize this lesson and apply it to our lives? When we are motivated to better serve Hashem and feel the need to improve ourselves by changing a character trait or habit that is preventing us from realizing who it is that we can truly become, we must keep in mind that our greater goal goes beyond overcoming this trait: The ultimate goal of *shechitah* is to bring one's newly unlocked abilities to the Altar, to be used in the service of Hashem.

A TASTE OF LOMDUS

We learned in *A Torah Thought for the Day* that the Gemara (*Zevachim* 32a) teaches that שְׁחִיטָה כְּשֵׁרָה בְּזָר, *slaughter (of an offering) is acceptable when performed by a non-Kohen.* Rashash (*Yevamos* 33b) and *Shaar HaMelech* (*Hilchos Bi'as HaMikdash* 6:10) explain that Rashi (*Yevamos* 33b ד"ה שחיטה בזר כשירה) tells us that although a *zar* (non-Kohen) is permitted to slaughter an animal for use as a *korban,* he may not do so on Shabbos, and, in the event that he does, he is liable for desecrating the Shabbos for he has violated the Torah prohibition of נְטִילַת נְשָׁמָה, *taking a life* (cf. *Chazon Ish* to *Yevamos* ibid., who understands Rashi differently).

Many commentaries ask: Why is this so? We know that the *avodah* in the *Beis HaMikdash,* which included performing otherwise forbidden

**MONDAY
PARASHAS
VAYIKRA**

melachos [such as *slaughtering,* and *burning* offerings and incense], was permitted to be done on Shabbos. If *shechitah* is an area of *avodah* that is permitted to be performed by a *zar,* why is he not allowed to do so on Shabbos? Why does *Rashi* understand that his *shechitah* on Shabbos violates Torah law?

Toras Michael (45) answers this question by explaining that although a *zar* is allowed to slaughter a *korban,* this permission does not mean that, in the specific *avodah* of slaughtering *korbanos,* he is considered similar to a Kohen. Rather, while a non-Kohen is *allowed* to slaughter any form of offering, the only time that he is specifically *commanded* to slaughter a *korban* is when he is the one bringing it. In contrast, by stating: לְכָל־דְּבַר הַמִּזְבֵּחַ וּלְמִבֵּית לַפָּרֹכֶת וַעֲבַדְתֶּם עֲבֹדַת מַתָּנָה אֶתֵּן אֶת־כְּהֻנַּתְכֶם, *regarding every matter of the Altar and within the Curtain, you shall serve; I have presented your priesthood as a service that is a gift* (*Bamidbar* 18:7), the Torah is informing us that the Kohanim are the ones who are *charged* with ensuring that the totality of the *avodah,* which includes *shechitah,* is performed.

The Gemara (*Menachos* 72b) explains that the permission to offer a *korban* on Shabbos is understood from the need to offer a particular *korban* בְּמוֹעֲדוֹ, *in its set time,* even when this happens to be Shabbos. Thus, only a קָרְבַּן צִבּוּר, *communal offering,* such as the daily *tamid*-offering or the *mussaf*-offering appropriate to Shabbos or Yom Tov, may be offered on Shabbos, for these *korbanos* have a particular time, or day, during which they must be offered. In contrast, since a personal *korban* may be offered on a weekday, the license of bringing a *korban* בְּמוֹעֲדוֹ, *in its set time,* does not apply, and therefore a personal *korban* may not be offered on Shabbos.

With this background, *Toras Michael* explains that when the Torah states that certain types of *korbanos* are to be offered on Shabbos, this statement is not to be understood as the *permission* to bring these offerings. Rather, the specification of offering a *korban* בְּמוֹעֲדוֹ, *in its set time,* states that although it is Shabbos and the actions of slaughtering an animal and burning its fats are otherwise forbidden, a קָרְבַּן צִבּוּר, *communal offering,* is to nevertheless be slaughtered and offered on the Altar. Since the Kohanim were the only ones to whom the overall commandment of offering *korbanos* was directed, it follows that this commandment of offering a קָרְבַּן צִבּוּר *in its appropriate time* is speaking specifically to a Kohen. Although it is true that a *zar* is *allowed* to slaughter a קָרְבַּן צִבּוּר, he is not the person who is being commanded to do so; hence, he is not allowed to do anything that is in contradiction

פרשת ויקרא
MONDAY
PARASHAS VAYIKRA

to Shabbos. Thus, although it is true that his wrongly slaughtering a *korban* would not invalidate its use, for *shechitah* is acceptable when performed by a *zar*, Rashi tells us that a person who slaughters an animal on Shabbos without being specifically *commanded* to do so is desecrating the Shabbos.

Mas'as HaMelech (*He'aros* 57) notes that this approach, which states that the *avodah* in the *Beis HaMikdash* is permitted to be performed on Shabbos only when a specific commandment charges that this action be taken, and is not dependent on the inherent achievement of an acceptable *korban*, allows us to answer a contradiction posed by R' Elchanan Wasserman (*Kovetz Shiurim* I, *Pesachim* 193) between two ostensibly similar areas. On Yom Tov, when cooking is permitted only if this food will be enjoyed on Yom Tov itself, the Gemara (*Pesachim* 46b) discusses whether a person is permitted, for example, to cook a larger pot of soup than is necessary, with the justification that this food may possibly be used on Yom Tov, in the event that unanticipated guests should visit.

Commenting on this Gemara, the *Meiri* states that even the one who maintains that it is forbidden to cook a larger amount than is needed for Yom Tov agrees that in the event this food is ultimately consumed on Yom Tov — for example, if guests indeed do arrive — no violation of Yom Tov has been committed. This ruling appears to contradict a Gemara (*Menachos* 64a) that tells us that a Kohen who wrongly slaughters two animals — instead of one — to use as a *korban tamid* on Shabbos morning, is fully liable for the desecration of Shabbos for this unnecessary act of slaughter. Furthermore, the Gemara clearly tells us that he is liable even in the event that the first animal is invalidated (such as if its blood spills onto the floor instead of properly being received in a Temple vessel), and the second animal is the one that is ultimately used. Based on this ruling — that the ultimate use of the item (in this case, the slaughtered animal) does not retroactively justify its preparation — R' Elchanan asks: How can the *Meiri* maintain that the ultimate use of the extra food for Yom Tov retroactively determines that the original act of cooking was permitted?

Mas'as HaMelech answers this question based on the principle we have been discussing. The reason why otherwise forbidden actions may be performed in the *Beis HaMikdash* on Shabbos is not because a *korban* is achieved by doing so, but because the Torah specifically commanded that this action be taken. Thus, since the slaughter of the

MONDAY

PARASHAS VAYIKRA

second, unnecessary, animal was an act the slaughterer did on his own, without the Torah's directive to do so, the ultimate use of this *korban* does not retroactively justify this act of uncommanded Shabbos desecration. In contrast, cooking on Yom Tov is permitted for the purpose of enjoying Yom Tov. Since this food was ultimately eaten on Yom Tov, the *Meiri* reasons that this enjoyment retroactively justifies the cooking and therefore Yom Tov was not violated.

פרשת ויקרא

A TORAH THOUGHT FOR THE DAY

TUESDAY
PARASHAS VAYIKRA

וְשִׁסַּע אֹתוֹ בִכְנָפָיו לֹא יַבְדִּיל וְהִקְטִיר אֹתוֹ הַכֹּהֵן הַמִּזְבֵּחָה
עַל־הָעֵצִים אֲשֶׁר עַל־הָאֵשׁ עֹלָה הוּא אִשֵּׁה רֵיחַ נִיחֹחַ לַה׳

And he shall split it with its feathers — he need not sever it; the Kohen shall cause it to go up in smoke on the Altar, on the wood that is on the fire — it is a burnt-offering, a fire-offering, a satisfying aroma to HASHEM *(Vayikra 1:17).*

As *Rashi* here notes, the last Mishnah in Tractate *Menachos* observes that the Torah uses the same term a few times in this passage. Earlier, regarding the *olah*-offering from cattle, the Torah describes it as אִשֵּׁה רֵיחַ־נִיחֹחַ, *a fire-offering, a satisfying aroma* (1:9). The Torah then uses the same phrase in this verse, regarding the *olah* that comes from fowl. Later, discussing the *minchah* (meal-offering), the Torah uses the same phrase again (2:2). This, says the Mishnah, teaches us an important lesson: Whether one does more (such as bringing an expensive offering of cattle) or does less (offering a meager *minchah*), it is considered equivalent — as long as his intent is for the sake of Heaven.

Ohr HaChaim explains that there is an unspoken question hinted at in this Mishnah, and a powerful message in its answer. One might ask: Wouldn't the Torah have been able to teach us this rule — that the pauper's and the wealthy man's offerings are equivalent — even more simply, without needing to repeat itself? Let the Torah have used the phrase אִשֵּׁה רֵיחַ־נִיחֹחַ, *a fire-offering, a satisfying aroma,* for the least expensive of these offerings, the *olah* from fowl (see Series One, Tuesday of *Parashas Vayikra, A Torah Thought for the Day*). We could then reason to ourselves: If Hashem considers this scanty offering as *a fire-offering, a satisfying aroma* before Him, then certainly the more expensive *minchah* and the *olah* from cattle should be considered such! Why did the Torah need to repeat this phrase a few times?

The answer, explains *Ohr HaChaim,* is that had the Torah written this phrase only once, one would argue that the value of the *olah* brought from fowl is due solely to Hashem's mercy on the poverty-stricken — that He considers the pauper's offering more valuable than it actually is! And, one would assume that the affluent person, with his *olah* from cattle, is actually bringing a more important offering. [Indeed, it must be that the *olah* from fowl is of lesser value at some level, because if it is truly equivalent to the other offerings, then we lose the logical construct that enables us to infer that the other, more

פרשת ויקרא
TUESDAY
PARASHAS VAYIKRA

expensive, offerings are also considered אִשֵּׁה רֵיחַ־נִיחֹחַ.]

But this is not true. The Torah here — by repeating the phrase three times — teaches us that the offering of the pauper is *exactly* equivalent to that of the rich man! So much so, that the Torah needed to repeat the phrase a number of times; had the Torah not repeated the phrase אִשֵּׁה רֵיחַ נִיחֹחַ in the context of the *olah*-offering from cattle or the *minchah,* we would not have been able to extrapolate from the verse about the *olah* from fowl to teach us that those are also considered *a fire-offering, a satisfying aroma.*

Torah Temimah (86) says that common sense would indicate that the statement of *Chazal* equating the *olah* from fowl and the *olah* from cattle would apply only in the appropriate contexts. If a wealthy person would bring an *olah* from fowl when he could well afford to bring an *olah* from cattle, or if a pauper would economize and do without for decades so as to bring an *olah* from cattle, then *Chazal's* statement would presumably not apply. Although this would seem to be a logical argument, *Torah Temimah* cites *Tosafos* (*Shevuos* 15a), who say that as long as one's intent is for the sake of Heaven, then one's mitzvah is the same, whether he brings a more- or less-expensive offering (see also *A Closer Look at the Siddur*).

MISHNAH OF THE DAY: ROSH HASHANAH 1:2

At four specific times during the year, God judges the deeds of mankind, and, based on those deeds, makes decisions regarding certain matters. These judgments are enumerated and explained in the coming Mishnah:

בְּאַרְבָּעָה פְּרָקִים הָעוֹלָם נִידּוֹן — *At four junctures* during the year *the world is judged:* בְּפֶסַח עַל הַתְּבוּאָה — *on Pesach for the grain;*[1] בַּעֲצֶרֶת עַל פֵּירוֹת הָאִילָן — *on Shavuos for the fruit of the tree;*[2]

───── NOTES ─────

1. Since Pesach is the time when the grain (specifically, barley) begins to ripen, God chose this time to decide whether the grain harvest of the coming year will be plentiful or meager (*Meiri; Rambam Commentary*). The Gemara (16a), citing a Baraisa, states that Hashem commanded Bnei Yisrael to bring the *omer,* a barley offering, on Pesach (*Vayikra* 23:10), so that this judgment would be favorable. This is the Scriptural indication that the judgment for grain is on Pesach (*Rav*).

2. The judgment during Shavuos corresponds to the time when fruits begin to ripen (*Meiri*). The Gemara again quotes the Baraisa cited above (see note 1) that states that the offering of the Two Loaves of wheat was brought on Shavuos (ibid. v. 17)

TUESDAY
PARASHAS VAYIKRA

בְּרֹאשׁ הַשָּׁנָה כָּל בָּאֵי עוֹלָם עוֹבְרִין לְפָנָיו כִּבְנֵי מָרוֹן — on Rosh Hashanah all who come to the world [i.e., all men] pass before Him like young sheep,[3] שֶׁנֶּאֱמַר ״הַיֹּצֵר יַחַד לִבָּם הַמֵּבִין אֶל־כָּל־מַעֲשֵׂיהֶם״ — as it is stated: "Who fashions their hearts together, Who understands all their deeds";[4] וּבֶחָג נִידּוֹנִין עַל הַמַּיִם — and on the festival, i.e., Succos, they are judged for the water.[5]

───────── NOTES ─────────

in order to invoke Hashem's blessing on the fruit harvest. This is the Scriptural indication that the judgment for trees takes place on Shavuos (Rav).

This Baraisa is in accord with the Tanna whose opinion is that the Tree of Knowledge, from which Adam ate, was actually wheat (Sanhedrin 70b). Since wheat is referred to by the Torah as a tree, the offering of a wheat sacrifice incurs blessing on the fruits of the trees (Rav).

3. I.e., all human beings pass individually before the Creator to be judged like young sheep who pass through a small opening in their pen for the purpose of tithing (Rav). In an alternative translation, the Gemara (18a) renders כִּבְנֵי מָרוֹן as: "like soldiers who pass in file before a king." That this judgment takes place on Rosh Hashanah is derived by the Gemara (8a) from Devarim 11:12: מֵרֵשִׁית הַשָּׁנָה וְעַד אַחֲרִית שָׁנָה, from the beginning of the year until the end of the year — viz., on the first of Tishrei ("the beginning of the year") humans are judged as to what will happen to them until the end of the coming year (Ran).

4. Tehillim 33:15. This is understood to mean: On the day on which He fashioned their hearts, i.e., created them, which is the first of Tishrei, He understands, i.e., analyzes and judges, all their deeds (see Ritva).

[The question arises: If man is judged on Rosh Hashanah, presumably his judgment encompasses all matters relating to him, including the amount of rain that will fall on his field and the size of the grain and fruit crop that his land will yield. What, then, is the purpose of the judgments of the other three festivals? Ran answers that on the three festivals the world as a whole is judged as to how much rain will fall and how much produce will grow. On Rosh Hashanah, however, God decides what share of these gifts each individual will receive (cf. Turei Even סוף ד״ה ר׳ יוסי אומר).]

5. Since Succos is the start of the rainy season in the Holy Land, it is an appropriate time for the world to be judged with respect to the amount of rain that will fall throughout the coming year (Meiri).

The mitzvah of נִסּוּךְ הַמַּיִם, water libation, was performed during Succos (see Rambam, Hil. Temidin U'Mussafim 10:6) so as to invoke Hashem's blessing on the year's rainfall; this indicates that the judgment for rainfall takes place on Succos (Rav from Gemara 16a).

QUESTION OF THE DAY:
Why is the bird korban not divided in half?

For the answer, see page 268.

GEMS FROM THE GEMARA

פרשת ויקרא

**TUESDAY
PARASHAS
VAYIKRA**

The Gemara quotes various teachings of R' Yitzchak that present insights into how one may merit a favorable judgment during the Days of Judgment:

And R' Yitzchak said: Any year that is poor in its beginning [i.e., that Israel behaves on Rosh Hashanah as a pauper, praying and beseeching God as a poor man pleading for bread (*Rashi*)] becomes prosperous at its end, as it is stated: מֵרֵשִׁית הַשָּׁנָה וְעַד אַחֲרִית שָׁנָה, *from the beginning of the year until the end of the year* (*Devarim* 11:12). This derivation is expounded based on the fact that the term *from the beginning* (מֵרֵשִׁית) is written without an *aleph,* so that it can be read as meaning "from the poverty." To this the verse concludes: וְעַד אַחֲרִית שָׁנָה, *until the end of the year,* indicating that its end will be that it will have a future. [The word אַחֲרִית is sometimes used in Scripture to indicate a condition of prosperity, as in *Yirmiyah* 29:11: לָתֵת לָכֶם אַחֲרִית וְתִקְוָה, *to give you a future and a hope.*]

The Gemara relates another teaching of R' Yitzchak:

And R' Yitzchak said: A person is judged only for his actions of that moment [i.e., even though Hashem knows that he will act wickedly in the future, He judges him as per his actions at the present time], as it is stated regarding Yishmael (*Bereishis* 21:17): כִּי־שָׁמַע אֱלֹהִים אֶל־קוֹל הַנַּעַר בַּאֲשֶׁר הוּא־שָׁם, *For God has heeded the cry of the youth as he is, there.* Yishmael had been sent out of Avraham's house and was dying of thirst in the desert. In response to his mother Hagar's weeping, Hashem sent an angel to inform her that He had heard the boy's outcry and would spare him. The Midrash (*Bereishis Rabbah* 53:14) relates that the angels pleaded with Hashem to let Yishmael die, since in the future his descendants would kill many Jews. Hashem asked the angels whether, at the present moment, Yishmael was righteous or wicked. When the angels responded that Yishmael was presently righteous, Hashem replied that He judges the world as of that moment [*as he is, there*], and Yishmael was therefore spared (*Rashi*).

Similarly, Hashem judges us on Rosh Hashanah according to our state on that day. Even though He knows that we will slip somewhat during the year, He judges us according to whatever level we have reached on Rosh Hashanah (*Aruch LaNer*).

A final quote from R' Yitzchak:

And R' Yitzchak said: Four things cause the unfavorable decree against a person to be torn up. These are: charity, crying out, change of name, and change of action.

פרשת ויקרא

TUESDAY

PARASHAS VAYIKRA

The Gemara then cites the sources for these four things having the capability to cancel a bad decree: Charity, for it is written (*Mishlei* 11:4): וּצְדָקָה תַּצִּיל מִמָּוֶת, *and charity will rescue from death.* Crying out, for it is written (*Tehillim* 107:28): וַיִּצְעֲקוּ אֶל־ה׳ בַּצַּר לָהֶם וּמִמְּצֻקוֹתֵיהֶם יוֹצִיאֵם, *Then they cried out to* Hashem *in their distress, and He would take them out from their straits.* Change of name, for it is written (*Bereishis* 17:15): שָׂרַי אִשְׁתְּךָ לֹא־תִקְרָא אֶת־שְׁמָהּ שָׂרָי כִּי שָׂרָה שְׁמָהּ, *Sarai your wife, you shall not call her name Sarai, for Sarah is her name,* and it is written in [the very next verse]: וּבֵרַכְתִּי אֹתָהּ וְגַם נָתַתִּי מִמֶּנָּה לְךָ בֵּן, *I will bless her; indeed, I will give you a son through her.* Change of action, for it is written regarding the wicked city of Nineveh (*Yonah* 3:10): וַיַּרְא הָאֱלֹהִים אֶת־מַעֲשֵׂיהֶם כִּי־שָׁבוּ מִדַּרְכָּם הָרָעָה, *God saw their deeds, that they repented from their evil way,* and it is written [immediately thereafter]: וַיִּנָּחֶם הָאֱלֹהִים עַל־הָרָעָה אֲשֶׁר־דִּבֶּר לַעֲשׂוֹת־לָהֶם וְלֹא עָשָׂה, *God relented concerning the evil He had said He would bring upon them, and He did not do it.*

A MUSSAR THOUGHT FOR THE DAY

The verse (quoted in *A Torah Thought for the Day*) makes it clear that the *olah* from fowl is placed on the Altar whole, with its feathers. [Verse 16, earlier, says: וְהֵסִיר אֶת־מֻרְאָתוֹ בְּנֹצָתָהּ, *He shall remove its crop with its feathers.* But as *Rashi* explains, that is referring only to the feathers that are directly above the crop — the rest of the feathers remain on the bird.] The Midrash (*Vayikra Rabbah* 3:5, also cited by *Rashi*) observes that the smell of burning feathers is unpleasant and disgusts the person smelling it. This is troubling, as *Eitz Yosef* explains, for one does not generally present an offering to Hashem that he would not give to another person. As the prophet Malachi puts it (*Malachi* 1:8): הַקְרִיבֵהוּ נָא לְפֶחָתֶךָ הֲיִרְצְךָ אוֹ הֲיִשָּׂא פָנֶיךָ, *Present it, if you please, to your governor: Would he be pleased with you or show you favor?*

But here the Torah tells us to disregard the unpleasant smell, and to put the bird — feathers and all — on the Altar. Why? The Midrash says that it is done so the offering should look bigger; plucked, the bird looks even smaller than it already is! Hashem favors the pauper's offering, and as the *Imrei Yosher* puts it, "To Hashem, it is an aroma as satisfying as the scent of the incense used in the *Beis HaMikdash*."

Although we do not have the ability today to bring offerings in the *Beis HaMikdash*, R' Yerucham Levovitz says that there is a practical lesson to learn from this verse. Human nature is such that people appreciate and enjoy being around other people who are respectable and are meticulous about their personal hygiene. Such people wear elegant clothing, have a pleasant body odor, and are a pleasure to socialize with.

פרשת ויקרא

TUESDAY
PARASHAS VAYIKRA

But at times one encounters someone who occupies an unfortunate station in life — perhaps he has had one downturn too many, perhaps he has a troubled soul. His clothing is torn, worn-out, and dirty. His body emits an unpleasant stench, and it is difficult to remain near him. One's instinctual response in such a situation is to immediately leave. A person with more generous feelings might even tell this indigent, "I will do what you wish — I can fulfill your request; but why don't you dress in cleaner, nicer clothing?"

But we, says R' Yerucham, are commanded (*Devarim* 13:5), אַחֲרֵי ה׳ אֱלֹהֵיכֶם תֵּלֵכוּ, *Hashem, Your God, you shall follow*! We must follow Hashem's example, and here the Torah teaches us the proper behavior in such a situation. The pauper's offering — its offensive smell notwithstanding — is a satisfying aroma to Hashem, and Hashem favors the pauper! Similarly, one should favor this unfortunate person, try to bring him close, and not only disregard his stench, but — as Hashem does — find it satisfying. By complaining to the troubled about their hygienic or sartorial lapses even while fulfilling their requests, one can negate the good that he is doing.

Indeed, concludes R' Yerucham, the very *Shechinah,* the manifestation of Hashem's presence on earth, is with the downtrodden: מָרוֹם וְקָדוֹשׁ אֶשְׁכּוֹן וְאֶת־דַּכָּא וּשְׁפַל־רוּחַ, *I abide in exaltedness and holiness, but I am with the despondent and lowly of spirit* (*Yeshayah* 57:15). Therefore, one should bring this person close; when one honors the downtrodden, he honors Hashem, Who accompanies such a person. But should he look down at the impoverished and unfortunate, let him be aware that he is being repelled by one whose aroma is sweet enough to be emanating from the very Altar of the *Beis HaMikdash*.

HALACHAH OF THE DAY

One of the fundamental issues that often arises when discussing questions of Kashrus is that of בִּטּוּל, the *nullification* of prohibited foods. *Bitul* refers to the halachic principle through which an amount of prohibited food that has become mixed into permissible foodstuffs may be seen as becoming בָּטֵל, *nullified,* and thus no longer halachically

פרשת ויקרא

TUESDAY

PARASHAS VAYIKRA

significant. (In our discussions, we will use the word *bitul* when speaking of the principle of nullification, and the word *bateil* when speaking of that which has become nullified.)

We will discuss two different forms of *bitul*: *bitul b'rov,* nullification of a smaller amount of an item that has become mixed into a larger amount (*rov*) of another item; and *bitul b'shishim,* nullification of a prohibited substance or taste in a ratio of 60:1. These two forms of *bitul* apply to two different forms of mixtures. *Bitul b'rov* is the ordinary means through which a minority becomes *bateil* in the majority. According to Torah law, a food mixture bears the halachic characteristics of its majority. In accordance with this principle, a food mixture of which the majority is permissible may be eaten. However, this principle may be employed only when there is no taste of the nonkosher food discernible in the mixture.

When the taste of a nonkosher food is noticeable in a food mixture, we have seen that the principle of *taam k'ikar* dictates that the entire mixture takes on the characteristics of the nonkosher food that has imbued the mixture with its taste. This being the case, the permissible majority of the food mixture cannot nullify the prohibited minority, because even the permissible majority is now viewed as nonkosher, on account of the nonkosher taste that it carries.

It is in this type of case, where a nonkosher food had imbued a food mixture with its taste, that *bitul b'shishim,* nullification in a ratio of 60:1, is required in order to nullify not only the prohibited item itself, but even its prohibited taste.

Generally speaking, when two combined foods are similar-tasting, or, using the terminology of halachah, when it is a mixture of מִין בְּמִינוֹ, *a kind in its own kind,* we may apply simple *bitul b'rov*. When the mixture is מִין בְּשֶׁאֵינוֹ מִינוֹ, *a kind in another kind,* so that the two items when cooked together impart their different tastes to each other, *bitul b'shishim* is required in order to nullify the prohibited taste.

As we shall see, these laws are quite complex, and the above is merely a very simplified general statement given for the purpose of introduction.

One very important note on the topic of *bitul*:

It is the opinion of most *poskim* that once a prohibited substance becomes *bateil,* the mixture in which it is contained may be eaten even by the most scrupulous of individuals. Indeed, there are those authorities who soundly censure one who hesitates to eat such a mixture, as this shows a reservation about the efficacy of *bitul,* an attitude these authorities regard as being heretical.

A CLOSER LOOK AT THE SIDDUR

פרשת ויקרא

**TUESDAY
PARASHAS
VAYIKRA**

In *A Torah Thought for the Day* we cited the words of our Sages: "Whether one does more or does less, it is considered equivalent — as long as his intent is for the sake of Heaven." As we explained there, the Sages were referring to, respectively, the offerings of the rich and the poor. And — as we have discussed many times — in the absence of the *Beis HaMikdash*, our prayers take the place of offerings. Indeed, we find that this adage is applied to prayer, as well. *Tur* (*Orach Chaim* 1) writes (in the context of the importance of praying that the Jewish people's exile be reversed and that the *Beis HaMikdash* be rebuilt): "He should let his prayers fall before Hashem, whether one prays more or less, as long as his intent in his prayers is for the sake of Heaven. For a little prayer with intent is better than much prayer without."

Shulchan Aruch (*Orach Chaim* 1:4), continuing in the same vein, applies this concept to all prayer. As *Magen Avraham* (1:6) explains, if someone is not capable of praying more but still prays as much as he can with proper concentration, his prayers are as favored by Hashem as those of a person who prays much with the appropriate intent. Of course, says *Mishnah Berurah* (1:12), if one does have the choice, it is certainly better to pray more and still have the proper concentration on the prayers' meaning! [The concept that the quality of *avodas Hashem* is more important than its quantity is also applied by the commentaries to such areas as Torah learning, reciting *Tehillim,* etc. See *Mekor Chaim* 1:4, *Aruch HaShulchan* 1:21.]

The *Ben Ish Chai* (in his *Sefer Benayahu, Menachos* 110a) explains *Chazal's* statement about doing more or less as directly pertaining to prayer, based on this story: One Friday night, a *tzaddik* dreamed that he saw an otherworldly elder. In the dream, the *tzaddik* asked, "Of the people in the two synagogues in my town, who prays most properly?" The elder answered by identifying two locations — one in each synagogue. "The prayers of the two people in those spots are accepted and more pleasing than those of any person in their respective synagogues!"

That morning, the *tzaddik* made sure to pray the *Shacharis* of the Shabbos service next to the first location mentioned in the dream. But the person praying beside him was obviously not praying from a *siddur* with Kabbalistic or mystical intentions — he was staring at the *siddur,* reading word by word. When it was time to rise for the *Shemoneh Esrei,* the *tzaddik,* peering into the other man's *siddur,* saw

TUESDAY

PARASHAS VAYIKRA

that he was actually reciting the weekday *Shemoneh Esrei*! Not wishing to interrupt his neighbor's prayer, the *tzaddik* waited until after he finished his own *Shemoneh Esrei*, and told him, "You must have forgotten — today is Shabbos; now you will need to recite the Shabbos *Shemoneh Esrei*." The other Jew answered, "I know it is Shabbos, but I always say the weekday *Shemoneh Esrei* anyway. You ask why? Shabbos is the most important day of the week, how can I dishonor it by praying a shorter *Shemoneh Esrei*?"

The next morning, Sunday, the *tzaddik* went to the other synagogue, and found the same sort of situation as the day before. Here, though, the person identified in the dream prayed the *Shemoneh Esrei* of Shabbos! When he finished, the *tzaddik* approached him, too, and suggested that he needed to repeat the *Shemoneh Esrei*, this time using the weekday version. "I know that today is a weekday," the other answered, "but I say the Shabbos *Shemoneh Esrei* all week. Shabbos is the most important of all days, so it follows that its prayers are more exalted than the weekday prayers. Since the Shabbos prayers are so lofty, I recite them every single day so as to bring the best prayers before Hashem!"

The *Ben Ish Chai* concludes: *Whether one does more* — like the simple Jew who recited the longer weekday *Shemoneh Esrei* on Shabbos — *or does less* — like the other simpleton who recited the shorter Shabbos *Shemoneh Esrei* each weekday — *it is considered equivalent* — even though their actions were polar opposites — *as long as his intent is for the sake of Heaven* — their prayers, coming from pure and good-hearted (albeit misguided) intentions, were accepted by Hashem above all others.

[Note: Obviously, when praying, one must follow halachic guidelines.]

A TORAH THOUGHT FOR THE DAY

פרשת ויקרא

WEDNESDAY
PARASHAS VAYIKRA

וְנֶפֶשׁ כִּי־תַקְרִיב קָרְבַּן מִנְחָה לַה' סֹלֶת יִהְיֶה קָרְבָּנוֹ וְיָצַק עָלֶיהָ שֶׁמֶן וְנָתַן עָלֶיהָ לְבֹנָה

When a person offers a meal-offering to HASHEM, his offering shall be of fine flour; he shall pour oil upon it and place frankincense upon it (Vayikra 2:1).

Animal offerings are intended, says *Ramban* (*Vayikra* 1:9), to help us understand that we have sinned to Hashem both with our bodies and our souls, and that if not for Hashem's beneficence, *we* would be taking the place of the animal being brought to the *Beis HaMikdash's* Altar (see Series One, Monday of *Parashas Vayikra*, *A Torah Thought for the Day*): "The offering atones such that its blood replaces his blood, its soul replaces his soul, its limbs replace his limbs." How, then, do we understand the significance of the *korban minchah*, the meal-offering? It does not have blood or limbs or a soul, and does not seem to parallel the human body.

Indeed, *Sefer HaChinuch* (116) explains that the *korban minchah* — not being alive — influences a person less than do the animal-offerings. But it does also come to sensitize one to his actions, in that a person sees that because of his sins he is required to burn and destroy his money, his possessions.

Yet, on a different level, there is a parallel between one who brings a *korban minchah* and one who brings an animal-offering. The Gemara (*Menachos* 104b, cited by *Rashi* here) takes note of the language used in this verse to introduce the concept of the meal-offering. The Torah here uses the word נֶפֶשׁ, *a person* (rather than אָדָם, *a man,* as it does earlier, 1:2), to describe the one bringing the *minchah*. But the word נֶפֶשׁ has another connotation — it means "soul." Based on this change from the language used by the animal-offerings, the Gemara explains that the message of the verse is that Hashem tells the person bringing this offering: "One bringing a *korban minchah* is generally a pauper — I consider his offering as if he has sacrificed his very soul to Me!" Thus, by the *minchah* too, Hashem considers one's offering as if he sacrificed his own soul, although bringing a non-live offering does not engender the feeling of self-sacrifice in the person bringing the offering as does an animal-offering.

Why is the *korban minchah* different from all other offerings in this regard? The Chofetz Chaim, in his *sefer Machaneh Yisrael* (§5), addresses Jewish soldiers who did not always have the ability to obtain

WEDNESDAY
PARASHAS VAYIKRA

kosher food. He tells them that whenever they pass through a village with Jewish inhabitants, they should approach the locals for kosher food, although it may be difficult and — should they meet with a negative response — even embarrassing and demeaning. He says that should they be discouraged by the difficulty of the task, they should remember that each mitzvah is rewarded based on the difficulties sustained in trying to fulfill it.

This, says the Chofetz Chaim, is demonstrated by our verse: וְנֶפֶשׁ כִּי־תַקְרִיב קָרְבַּן מִנְחָה לַה׳, *When a person offers a meal-offering to* HASHEM. As we explained, this verse is understood by the Sages to refer to the pauper's offering being accepted as if he brought his own soul to be offered on the Altar. Hashem looks at the way the mitzvah was performed: Was it easy? Was there pressure one had to overcome — perhaps ignoring other people's jeers, perhaps poverty or infirmity — to properly perform the mitzvah? The reward one will eventually receive for the mitzvah is commensurate to the pain he endured in order to fulfill it: הַזֹּרְעִים בְּדִמְעָה בְּרִנָּה יִקְצֹרוּ, *Those who tearfully sow will reap in glad song* (*Tehillim* 126:5).

The poverty-stricken person who manages — with great effort — to bring a *korban minchah* receives enormous reward for his efforts. This, says the Chofetz Chaim to his audience of Jewish soldiers, should encourage them to perform the mitzvah of keeping kosher in a difficult and even hostile environment! (See also *A Mussar Thought for the Day*.)

MISHNAH OF THE DAY: ROSH HASHANAH 1:3

Although the first two Mishnahs of our chapter dealt with Rosh Hashanah and related issues, the bulk of the Mishnahs in our tractate deal with *Kiddush HaChodesh,* the sanctification of Rosh Chodesh. The Jewish calendar is in large part based on the orbit of the moon around the earth. The lunar cycle is about 29½ days and there are approximately twelve lunar cycles for every solar cycle, or in calendric terms, twelve months in a year. While the calendar is based on precise astronomical computations, there is also a mitzvah to sanctify each new month based on the sighting of the new moon (*Shemos* 12:2; *Rambam, Hil. Kiddush HaChodesh* 1:7). Our Mishnah discusses *Beis Din's* notification to far-flung communities of the particular day sanctified as Rosh Chodesh:

עַל שִׁשָּׁה חֳדָשִׁים הַשְּׁלוּחִין יוֹצְאִין — *At* the beginning of each of *six* specific *months, the messengers go forth* to inform distant Jewish communities as to which day has been declared to be Rosh Chodesh:[1] עַל נִיסָן מִפְּנֵי הַפֶּסַח — They would go forth *at* the beginning of *Nissan on account of Pesach*;[2] עַל אָב מִפְּנֵי הַתַּעֲנִית — *at* the beginning of *Av on account of the Fast* on the ninth day of Av; עַל אֱלוּל מִפְּנֵי רֹאשׁ הַשָּׁנָה — *at* the beginning of *Elul on account of Rosh Hashanah*;[3] עַל תִּשְׁרֵי מִפְּנֵי תַקָּנַת הַמּוֹעֲדוֹת — *at* the beginning of *Tishrei on account of the correct determination of the festivals*;[4] עַל כִּסְלֵיו מִפְּנֵי חֲנוּכָּה — *at* the beginning of *Kislev on account of Chanukah*; וְעַל אֲדָר מִפְּנֵי הַפּוּרִים — and *at* the beginning of *Adar on account of Purim*. וּכְשֶׁהָיָה בֵּית הַמִּקְדָּשׁ קַיָּים — And when the Holy Temple was still *in existence*, יוֹצְאִין אַף עַל אִיָּיר — *they went forth at* the beginning of *Iyar* מִפְּנֵי פֶּסַח קָטָן — *on account of the minor Pesach*, i.e., Pesach Sheni.[5]

WEDNESDAY
PARASHAS
VAYIKRA

NOTES

1. For the six months listed here, the court would dispatch messengers to the Diaspora to inform the people about which of the two possible days had been declared Rosh Chodesh (*Rashi*).

[We will learn in a later Mishnah (2:2) that this was not the original method of disseminating the knowledge of when Rosh Chodesh had been proclaimed.]

2. Pesach begins on the 15th of Nissan. The messengers had to inform the people when the first day of Nissan was established so they would know when the 15th was to be (*Rashi*).

3. Elul was virtually always a month of 29 days. Thus, the people had to be informed when the first day of Elul had been declared in order to celebrate the 30th day as Rosh Hashanah. Although it was possible that the court would decide that Elul should be a full 30 days, making the 31st day Rosh Hashanah, the people were halachically justified in observing only the 30th day because in most years Rosh Hashanah did occur on the 30th and one may rely on a majority in cases of doubt (*Rav*; cf. *Tosafos*).

4. The messengers departed the day after Rosh Hashanah and traveled as far as they could until Succos. Although, as noted earlier, Rosh Hashanah was normally celebrated on the 30th day after Rosh Chodesh Elul, the possibility did exist that Elul would be made into a 30-day month and the first of Tishrei would be pushed off a day. It was therefore necessary to inform the people of the court's decision regarding the first of Tishrei in order that they not be nervous about the dates observed for Yom Kippur and Succos (*Rav*).

5. Those who could not bring the *pesach*-offering on the 14th of Nissan, because they were *tamei* or some distance away from the Temple Courtyard at the time, were required to bring an offering one month later, on the 14th of Iyar (*Rashi*). Notably, the Mishnah does not mention that messengers went forth at the beginning of Sivan on account of the festival of Shavuos. *Yerushalmi* (1:4) explains that unlike the other festivals, Shavuos is not tied to a specific date in a month. Rather, it is observed on the 50th day of the *Omer* counting (with the count beginning on the second day of Pesach).

פרשת ויקרא

GEMS FROM THE GEMARA

WEDNESDAY
PARASHAS VAYIKRA

The Mishnah stated that messengers would be sent to inform the Diaspora of the sanctification of the new month at the beginning of Av, on account of the Fast on the 9th day of Av. The Gemara questions why there was no similar concern for the fast days of Shivah Asar B'Tammuz, Tzom Gedaliah, and Asarah B'Teves:

But let them go out also for Tammuz and Teves, so the people would know when to fast in these months. For Rav Chana bar Bizna said in the name of R' Shimon Chasida: What is the meaning of that which is written (*Zechariah* 8:19): כֹּה־אָמַר ה׳ צְבָאוֹת צוֹם הָרְבִיעִי וְצוֹם הַחֲמִישִׁי וְצוֹם הַשְּׁבִיעִי וְצוֹם הָעֲשִׂירִי יִהְיֶה לְבֵית־יְהוּדָה לְשָׂשׂוֹן וּלְשִׂמְחָה, *Thus said* HASHEM, *Master of Legions: The fast of the fourth* [i.e., the fourth month from Nissan, which is the month of Tammuz], *the fast of the fifth* [the month of Av], *the fast of the seventh* [the month of Tishrei], *and the fast of the tenth* [the month of Teves] *will be to the House of Yehudah for joy and for happiness.* The verse calls them צוֹם, *a fast,* but then calls them days of שָׂשׂוֹן וְשִׂמְחָה, *joy and happiness!* The explanation for this is that at a time when there is peace [i.e., the Temple is standing], they will be for joy and for happiness. But when there is no peace [i.e., when the Temple is destroyed], they will remain fast days. The prophets did not rescind the fast days permanently, because they knew that the Second Temple would also be destroyed eventually. The spiritual disrepair that led to the destruction of the First Temple would not be remedied sufficiently to warrant final abrogation of those fast days (*Ritva*). We thus see that according to Rav Chana bar Bizna all of these fast days are in force nowadays, since the Temple still lies in ruins. Why, then, were no messengers sent forth for the months of Tammuz and Teves to notify the people of the fasts in those months?

The Gemara answers by offering a modified interpretation of the verse:

Rav Pappa said: This is what the verse means: At a time when there is peace, the former fast days will be for joy and for happiness; but at a time when there is a governmental decree to persecute the Jews, they are obligatory fast days as in the past. And if there is neither a governmental decree nor peace, then if the people want to fast, they fast, and if they want to omit fasting, they do not fast. Since these fasts are not obligatory, we do not trouble messengers to journey out at the beginning of Tammuz or Teves.

The Gemara asks:

If it is so that the four fasts are optional, then Tishah B'Av, which is one of the four fasts mentioned in the verse, should be optional as well. Consequently, the Mishnah should not say that messengers went out at the beginning of Av.

Rav Pappa defends his answer:

Rav Pappa said: Tishah B'Av is different, since tragedies were repeated on it. For the master said: On Tishah B'Av, the Temple was destroyed for the first time and the second time, the city of Betar was conquered, and the city of Jerusalem was plowed under. Therefore, even though messengers were not sent out for the months of Tammuz and Teves, they were sent out for the month of Av.

[During the Tannaic period in which this Mishnah was first taught, the acceptance of these fasts was not widespread. Now, however, these fasts have been accepted by the nation and neither a community nor an individual has the right to disregard them (*Ritva*). See also *Shulchan Aruch, Orach Chaim* 550:1.]

פרשת ויקרא
WEDNESDAY
PARASHAS VAYIKRA

A MUSSAR THOUGHT FOR THE DAY

In *A Torah Thought for the Day* we quoted the Gemara that infers from the Torah's use of the word נֶפֶשׁ, *soul*, in relation to the *korban minchah* that Hashem accepts the meal-offering of the impoverished as if they had brought their very soul as an offering before Him. R' Eliyahu Lopian (in his *Lev Eliyahu* to *Parashas Vayikra*) explains the Gemara, and also sees in it a lesson applicable even nowadays, when we cannot, unfortunately, ourselves bring a *korban minchah*.

A wealthy person, he explains, might bring an expensive animal — a bull — for an *olah*-offering. Even someone who is less affluent can afford to bring a sheep or a goat. These people certainly do not deplete all their assets, nor do they endure extreme hardship, by bringing these offerings! Still, when they bring the animal — with the proper intentions and following the proper laws — as an offering on the *Beis HaMikdash's* Altar, it is accepted with favor by Hashem: עֹלָה אִשֵּׁה רֵיחַ־נִיחֹחַ לַה׳, *an olah-offering, a fire-offering, a satisfying aroma to* HASHEM (*Vayikra* 1:9).

The pauper, though, rises to an entirely different level — a level of *mesiras nefesh*, self-sacrifice, not approached by his wealthier friend. As R' Lopian explains, this indigent comes to the *Beis HaMikdash* with a broken heart — all he has is a bit of flour and some oil. He feels depressed, telling himself, "Of what worth am I and my offering?

WEDNESDAY
PARASHAS VAYIKRA

With what am I coming before the King of kings?" And, although he felt badly even before he came to the *Beis HaMikdash,* now, standing with his scant offering in hand, his spirit is completely shattered. He is embarrassed and ashamed, and his whole being prays to Hashem, "Please, Hashem, accept my poor gift with love and favor, as satisfying as if I had brought before You a bull for an *olah,* completely consumed on Your Altar!"

Hashem responds to him, "No, my son — I will not grant your request, that your *minchah* be considered as if you had brought an animal before Me! Rather, I consider your offering to be as if you bound yourself as an *olah* before Me, and offered your life for the sanctification of My Name!"

There is a parallel, concludes R' Lopian, in Torah study. There is a person who, akin to the wealthy, is naturally gifted with a quick grasp, strong intellect, or a powerful memory. He may even — by the grace of Hashem — have all of these attributes! The good fortune he is blessed with allows him to swim in the sea of Talmud, and the Torah he originates is true and beautiful.

But there is another who — paralleling the pauper bringing his *korban minchah* to the *Beis HaMikdash* — has no specific intellectual strength. He struggles to understand each chapter, and before he has reached the second section, he has already almost forgotten the first. So he returns to the first section, exerting himself by reviewing in his mind and with his mouth until the words of Torah become absorbed in his being.

Mishlei, says R' Lopian, describes this man when it says (16:26): נֶפֶשׁ עָמֵל עָמְלָה לוֹ כִּי־אָכַף עָלָיו פִּיהוּ, *The working soul works for itself, when its mouth humbles itself to it.* The verse refers to him as a נֶפֶשׁ, just as it does the pauper who brings the *korban minchah.* He, humbly working to learn and understand the Torah that is so difficult for him, receives the same response from Hashem: "I consider your efforts the equivalent of your sacrificing your נֶפֶשׁ, your *soul,* for the Torah, and I will assist you!" (see also *Sanhedrin* 99b).

HALACHAH OF THE DAY

As we saw yesterday, when two foods of similar taste become mixed, the nonkosher food may become *bateil,* nullified, in a simple majority of kosher food. This rule applies to solid foods that are cold. If, however, a nonkosher liquid has become mixed into kosher food,

**WEDNESDAY
PARASHAS
VAYIKRA**

or a nonkosher solid has been heated and cooked with kosher food, the halachah varies, as we shall see.

Our Sages derived the principle of *bitul* from the verse that states: אַחֲרֵי רַבִּים לְהַטֹּת, *After the majority you shall turn* (*Shemos* 23:2). This verse speaks of the commandment to issue a court verdict based on the majority opinion. The Sages ruled that the characteristics of a mixture likewise follow the majority of its ingredients.

There is disagreement among the *Rishonim* over how exactly *bitul b'rov* works. What are the exact mechanics that allow for a nonkosher food to be eaten within a mix of kosher and nonkosher foods? Let us explore this fascinating topic.

We shall see that, in the opinion of most authorities, *bitul b'rov* is based upon the basic laws of probability. If the majority of the mixture is comprised of kosher food, then the laws of probability dictate that each individual piece separated from the mixture will in all likelihood be kosher.

While this is the view of most *Rishonim,* others contend that *bitul b'rov* has nothing at all to do with the logic of mathematical probabilities. According to these *Rishonim, bitul b'rov* is a unique Torah principle through which a nonkosher food item completely loses its nonkosher identity and becomes a permissible substance.

The ramifications of this dispute are enormous. For example, according to the first opinion, it would be logical to argue that one may not eat the full volume of a mixture containing a nonkosher ingredient. This is because while probability may insure that each individual piece removed from the mix is kosher, if one eats the entire mixture he is certainly ingesting the nonkosher ingredient at some point! According to the second view, however, one may eat the entire mixture — even at one time — since the principle of *bitul* mandates that there is no longer any nonkosher matter present in the mixture at all.

Tomorrow we will explore some of the different positions taken by various *Rishonim* on this fundamental question. We will see that each opinion represents a somewhat different take on the issue, resulting in corresponding differences in halachah.

QUESTION OF THE DAY:
Why is the verse describing the bringing of the minchah written in the singular?

For the answer, see page 268.

פרשת ויקרא

A CLOSER LOOK AT THE SIDDUR

WEDNESDAY
PARASHAS VAYIKRA

Abarbanel (in his commentary to *Avos* 2:13) makes an interesting statement: "Prayer without proper concentration is like a body without a soul." *Sefer Binyan Yehoshua* (in its introduction) quotes the Vilna Gaon, who elaborates on this. He notes that (as we have discussed earlier this week) the prayers were established by the Sages to parallel the offerings that we cannot bring to the *Beis HaMikdash* nowadays. We have also learned that the Mishnah in *Menachos* equates the offerings of the wealthy and the poor, as long as they both intend for the sake of Heaven.

Prayer, says the Vilna Gaon, is the same: With the proper intentions and concentration, it is like the offering of the wealthy; recited without concentration, as empty words, it is similar to the offering of the impoverished.

The rich man brings an *olah*-offering from an animal possessing life and vitality. But the pauper brings the *korban minchah*, the meal-offering. As we mentioned in *A Torah Thought for the Day*, the *minchah*-offering is dead — it possesses no soul. This is the meaning of the *Abarbanel's* statement: Prayer without the proper concentration is like the offering of the pauper, the *korban minchah*. But just as we find that Hashem considers the *minchah*, if it is brought for the sake of Heaven, as the equal of the richest offering, so too is prayer evaluated. Even one who prays without proper concentration will have his prayers accepted by Hashem as long as his intention is to fulfill Hashem's will. He is praying as best as he can, even though he may not even know the meaning of the words he recites. However, since his actions are motivated by his wish to do Hashem's will, his prayers are as valued as those of someone who prays with the deepest concentration according to the prayers' hidden meanings.

The Vilna Gaon's explanation of the *Abarbanel's* statement is referring to someone who is incapable of proper concentration, but still wishes to fulfill Hashem's will. But someone who is capable of concentrating properly on the prayers should certainly make every effort to pray with concentration. *Abarbanel* explains that speech uplifts a person only when it is partnered with thought — otherwise, he argues, what difference is there between the chirping of birds and the mumbling of man? When one recites the prayers by rote, not thinking of their meaning or purpose, he strips them of their spirituality, reducing them to actions performed just as well by an animal. [Of course, as

פרשת ויקרא

WEDNESDAY PARASHAS VAYIKRA

we said earlier, if his intent is for the sake of Heaven and this is all he is capable of, then Hashem accepts his prayers as equal to those of one who prays with the appropriate deliberation.]

In fact, says *Abarbanel,* the Sages decreed that one may not interrupt between the גְּאֻלָה section following the *Shema* and the subsequent *Shemoneh Esrei* prayers because it is so important that one should concentrate upon his prayers. Should there be an interlude between these two sections, then one might lose the focus that he developed during the first part of the prayers!

Sefer Chassidim (46) points out that the prophet Yeshayah already addressed this issue (*Yeshayah* 29:13-14): וַיֹּאמֶר אֲדֹנָי יַעַן כִּי נִגַּשׁ הָעָם הַזֶּה בְּפִיו וּבִשְׂפָתָיו כִּבְּדוּנִי וְלִבּוֹ רִחַק מִמֶּנִּי . . . וְאָבְדָה חָכְמַת חֲכָמָיו וּבִינַת נְבֹנָיו תִּסְתַּתָּר, *The Lord said: Inasmuch as this people has drawn close, with its mouth and with its lips it has honored Me, yet it has distanced its heart from Me . . . the wisdom of its wise men will be lost and the understanding of its sages will become concealed.* When one prays without concentration, it is but lip-service.

פרשת ויקרא

A TORAH THOUGHT FOR THE DAY

THURSDAY
PARASHAS VAYIKRA

וְכָל־קָרְבַּן מִנְחָתְךָ בַּמֶּלַח תִּמְלָח וְלֹא תַשְׁבִּית מֶלַח בְּרִית אֱלֹהֶיךָ מֵעַל מִנְחָתֶךָ עַל כָּל־קָרְבָּנְךָ תַּקְרִיב מֶלַח

You shall salt your every meal-offering with salt; you may not discontinue the salt of your God's covenant from upon your meal-offering; on your every offering you shall offer salt
(*Vayikra* 2:13).

As *Rashi* notes, while the beginning of the verse commands us to salt the *korban minchah*, the meal-offering, the verse concludes with a more general mitzvah of salting all offerings that come atop the Altar. As we have learned, it is improper to offer to Hashem something that one would not give to another person. This, explains *Ibn Ezra* (see also *Rabbeinu Bachya*), is why we salt the various offerings — one would not give his friend unseasoned meat; certainly one should not offer it to Hashem!

Rashi, though, records a better-known reason: Hashem made a covenant during the Six Days of Creation that the earthly waters would be offered on the Altar in the form of sea-salt on the sacrifices and as the water libations on Succos. The exact source of this Midrash is unclear. It is, however, brought in a few places with variations. One of the variants is attributed to an addition to a manuscript version of *Rashi*: When Hashem separated between the lower waters and the upper waters (*Bereishis* 1:6-9), the lower waters burst out crying, and said, "The upper waters are in a place of holiness and purity, while we are in a place of impurity." Hashem appeased them by saying, "My children will bring *korbanos* in holiness and purity and will place salt, which comes from you, on them; they will also perform the water libations, and both of these do not come from the upper waters." Our verse speaks of the salt of that covenant that Hashem had made with the lower waters during the Six Days of Creation.

Rabbeinu Bachya quotes a different Midrashic explanation for this mitzvah: "The world is made up of wilderness, settled areas, and ocean. The ocean stood before the Holy One, Blessed is He, and said, 'Master of the universe: The Torah was given in the wilderness, and the *Beis HaMikdash* was built in a settled area. What will be of me?' Hashem answered, 'The Jewish nation will offer salt with the offerings atop the Altar.' "

But *Kli Yakar* sees a deep symbolism in this mitzvah, and explains

בְּרִית אֱלֹהֶיךָ, *God's covenant*, in the following way: Many people did not believe in one God because they could not submit to the idea that opposites — joy and grief, night and day, fire and water, peace and war — could come from one source. Salt, says *Kli Yakar*, comes from water that is modified by fire (heat). Thus, it is something whose very being embodies two opposites. When we bring it up on the Altar with the *Minchah* (or any other) offering, we, in essence, are testifying to Hashem's reign over the entirety of the world. Our acceptance of Hashem's sovereignty over everything — even the seemingly conflicting — is our covenant with Hashem.

THURSDAY
PARASHAS
VAYIKRA

Chasam Sofer melds the *Ibn Ezra's* explanation with some of the other, more mystical, explanations of the covenant of salt. It is certain, he contends, that the *Ibn Ezra's* interpretation holds true regarding the animal-offerings — they certainly would not be presented to another person without salt, so their proper presentation to Hashem should also be with salt. But what of the *korban minchah*? It consists of fine flour and oil — certainly even sophisticated palates can stomach such food without salt. Why does the *korban minchah* require salt?

It is therefore only regarding the meal-offering, explains *Chasam Sofer*, that the other explanations of מֶלַח בְּרִית אֱלֹהֶיךָ, *the salt of your God's covenant*, enlighten us. This is what the verse means: וְלֹא תַשְׁבִּית מֶלַח בְּרִית אֱלֹהֶיךָ מֵעַל מִנְחָתֶךָ, *you may not discontinue the salt of your God's covenant from upon your meal-offering,* because it your God's covenant, the בְּרִית מֶלַח, that obligates the *minchah* to be brought with salt. But the verse concludes regarding animal-offerings: עַל כָּל־קָרְבָּנְךָ תַּקְרִיב מֶלַח, *on your every offering you shall offer salt,* without invoking the בְּרִית מֶלַח, because the reason for salting animal-offerings is, as *Ibn Ezra* said, because it is improper that meat be offered to Hashem unsalted.

MISHNAH OF THE DAY: ROSH HASHANAH 1:4

The next three Mishnahs discuss the parameters of the permit for witnesses to violate the Sabbath in order to testify before *Beis Din* regarding their sighting of the new moon:

עַל שְׁנֵי חֳדָשִׁים מְחַלְּלִין אֶת הַשַּׁבָּת — To offer testimony *concerning two* of the *months,* the witnesses may *desecrate the Sabbath:*[1] עַל נִיסָן

NOTES

1. The Gemara derives this from *Vayikra* 23:4.

THURSDAY
PARASHAS VAYIKRA

וְעַל תִּשְׁרֵי — *concerning Nissan and concerning Tishrei.*[2] שֶׁבָּהֶן שְׁלוּחִין יוֹצְאִין לְסוּרְיָא — *For in* Nissan and Tishrei *the messengers* of *Beis Din go forth to Surya* to publicize to the Diaspora the exact date of Rosh Chodesh,[3] וּבָהֶן מְתַקְּנִין אֶת הַמּוֹעֲדוֹת — *and in them* (i.e., through determining the proper Rosh Chodesh days for the months of Nissan and Tishrei) *[Beis Din] fixes* the proper days for *the* upcoming *festivals.* וּכְשֶׁהָיָה בֵּית הַמִּקְדָּשׁ קַיָּים — *And when the Holy Temple was in existence,* מְחַלְּלִין אַף עַל כּוּלָן — the witnesses *would desecrate* the Sabbath if necessary *even for all* the other months, מִפְּנֵי תַּקָּנַת הַקָּרְבָּן — *due to the fixing of the proper time for the* additional Rosh Chodesh *offering.*[4]

— NOTES —

2. Although Biblically the witnesses who saw the new moon on the 30th are permitted to desecrate the Sabbath to inform *Beis Din* of their sighting, the Rabbis decreed that for most months the Sabbath not be desecrated. They reasoned that there was no great need to permit desecration of the Sabbath, since in the absence of the Rosh Chodesh Temple offerings the need to declare Rosh Chodesh in its proper time is relatively insignificant. For Nissan and Tishrei, though, which contain the Biblical holidays, the Biblical dispensation remained (*Rashi;* cf. *Rabbeinu Chananel*).

3. However, they may not violate the Sabbath for this. This clause is an indication of the importance attached to these months, and serves as an auxiliary reason for permitting the witnesses to desecrate the Sabbath (*Rashi;* cf. *Baal HaMaor*).

4. On every Rosh Chodesh a *mussaf (additional)-offering* was brought in the Temple (*Bamidbar* 28:11-15). The Mishnah states that during the existence of the Temple it was important to declare Rosh Chodesh in its proper time, so that the additional Rosh Chodesh offering might be brought accordingly. Thus, the Biblical dispensation allowing witnesses to desecrate the Sabbath applied equally with regard to all months (*Rashi; Ritva*).

GEMS FROM THE GEMARA

The Gemara presents an apparent contradiction to our Mishnah:

Do the messengers go forth concerning two months of Nissan and Tishrei and no more? But contrast this with the previous Mishnah, which stated: Concerning six months the messengers go forth! Why then does our Mishnah say that they go forth only concerning two months?

The Gemara answers:

Abaye said: This is what our Mishnah means to say: Regarding all

פרשת ויקרא

THURSDAY PARASHAS VAYIKRA

other months, the messengers depart on the eve of the pronouncement of the sanctification of the new month. However, regarding Nissan and Tishrei, they do not depart until they have heard directly from the mouth of Beis Din, "It is sanctified!" On other months, as soon as it was evident that Beis Din would proclaim Rosh Chodesh, the messengers would immediately depart. For example, if the new moon was sighted clearly on either the 29th day of the month, or the subsequent evening, it was obvious to all that the next day would be proclaimed Rosh Chodesh. In addition, if no witnesses appeared by the night before the 31st of the month, Beis Din would automatically proclaim Rosh Chodesh the next day. In all of these cases, the messengers did not wait until Beis Din actually proclaimed Rosh Chodesh; rather, they departed the day or night before, relatively certain that the next day would be proclaimed Rosh Chodesh (Rashi). Regarding Nissan and Tishrei, since the exact days of the festivals are dependent on the day of Rosh Chodesh, messengers had to be certain that Beis Din would not decide to wait a day before declaring Rosh Chodesh. Therefore, they did not depart until the actual proclamation of Rosh Chodesh by Beis Din. Thus, it is true that the messengers go forth regarding all six months; our Mishnah, however, deals with the occasions that the messengers depart *only after Beis Din's* pronouncement.

The Gemara cites a Baraisa that provides the source for the permit of witnesses to violate the Sabbath in order to testify regarding the sighting of the new moon:

The Rabbis taught in a Baraisa: From where do we know that the witnesses may desecrate the Sabbath to testify with regard to the new month? Scripture states (*Vayikra* 23:4): אֵלֶּה מוֹעֲדֵי ה' מִקְרָאֵי קֹדֶשׁ אֲשֶׁר־תִּקְרְאוּ אֹתָם בְּמוֹעֲדָם, *These are the festivals of* HASHEM, *holy convocations, that you are to designate in their appropriate time*. That is, the verse is interpreted as warning us that the proper time for designating the festivals as "holy convocations" should not be delayed. This refers to Beis Din's proclaiming and sanctifying Rosh Chodesh, as the time of the festivals is directly dependent on the timing of Rosh Chodesh. Thus, the verse teaches that Beis Din must proclaim Rosh Chodesh in the proper time. From this we may infer that witnesses may even desecrate the Sabbath to ensure that Rosh Chodesh is proclaimed in the proper time (*Rashi*).

The Baraisa concludes by excluding the messengers of Beis Din from this permit:

From the above verse it might be thought that just as witnesses

THURSDAY
PARASHAS VAYIKRA

may desecrate the Sabbath so that the festivals will be sanctified in their appropriate time, so too messengers may desecrate the Sabbath so that the festivals will be kept in their designated time. To dispel this idea, Scripture states: אֲשֶׁר־תִּקְרְאוּ, *that you are to designate.* This implies that you may desecrate the Sabbath only with regard to the designation of the festivals, but you may not desecrate the Sabbath so that they will be kept in their designated time.

A MUSSAR THOUGHT FOR THE DAY

In *A Torah Thought for the Day* we discussed some of the reasons behind the mitzvah of salting the *korbanos*. Other reasons are also offered: *Rambam* (*Moreh Nevuchim* 3:46, as explained by *Rabbeinu Bachya* here), for example, explains it as a repudiation of the practices of idolaters, who would deliberately *not* salt their offerings. *Sefer HaChinuch* (mitzvah §119) sees it as an opportunity for a person to influence himself by means of his actions: When the sacrifice is complete it is most effective, and meat without salt, in human terms, is incomplete. Additionally, the preservative qualities of salt allude to the offering's preservative influence upon the person's soul.

We see that this seemingly simple mitzvah has many layers of complexity. This idea is discussed by the *Alter of Kelm,* R' Simchah Zissel Ziv (*Chochmah U'Mussar,* p. 431), in the context of the beginning of *Parashas Beha'aloscha.* There (*Bamidbar* 8:1-3), the Torah relates how Moshe Rabbeinu relayed Hashem's instructions for lighting the Menorah to his brother Aharon. The Torah concludes, saying: וַיַּעַשׂ כֵּן אַהֲרֹן ... כַּאֲשֶׁר צִוָּה ה' אֶת־מֹשֶׁה, *Aharon did so ... as* HASHEM *had commanded Moshe.* Indeed, *Rashi* on the verse quotes *Sifri,* which states that the verse is coming to praise Aharon for not diverging from Hashem's command. This verse, says the *Alter of Kelm,* is hard to understand — would we think that Aharon would not fulfill Hashem's command? What does this mean?

R' Simchah Zissel explains the lesson to be learned, based on a Midrash (*Bereishis Rabbah* 2:7) that says that when Hashem created the world He looked out upon the deeds of the righteous and the deeds of the wicked, but we do not know which He preferred until the verse tells us: וַיַּרְא אֱלֹהִים אֶת־הָאוֹר כִּי־טוֹב, *God saw that the light was good* (*Bereishis* 1:4), referring to the deeds of the righteous. On face value, the Midrash is difficult, for how can there be a question about

פרשת ויקרא

**THURSDAY
PARASHAS
VAYIKRA**

whose deeds — the righteous or the wicked — Hashem prefers.

This Midrash can be understood, says R' Simchah Zissel, when we realize that the wicked also aspire to fulfill mitzvos — but they seek "big" mitzvos, such as saving someone's life or a public demonstration of their piety. The righteous, however, conduct themselves differently. Avraham Avinu, for example, treated his angelic visitors as honored guests, and even though he thought they were simply wandering travelers he bustled around, bestirring himself and his entire household to show them proper hospitality. We see that the righteous treat the smallest mitzvah as if it were the most momentous, as the Sages (Avos 2:1) recommend: הֱוֵי זָהִיר בְּמִצְוָה קַלָּה כְּבַחֲמוּרָה, *Be as scrupulous in [performing] a "minor" mitzvah as [you are] in [performing] a "major" one.*

Why are the righteous so careful with even the most "minor" mitzvos? Because, says R' Simchah Zissel, they — who are aware of the greatness hidden in Hashem's handiwork — understand that there is nothing of no value before Hashem. The wicked, on the other hand, cannot see that hidden portion, and they strive to achieve only those mitzvos that are superficially "great." Thus, the Midrash is saying that Hashem values the seemingly "small" mitzvos of the righteous over the "major" mitzvos of the wicked.

When Aharon was commanded to tip the wicks toward the center post of the Menorah, he approached this task with the same awe as if he were preparing to enter the Holy of Holies on Yom Kippur, because he saw the hidden layers inherent in this seemingly minor mitzvah. The Torah tells us this particular praise of Aharon so that we should take a lesson from him and realize that Hashem considers no action insignificant. In fact, what sometimes seems to us to be of lesser importance, may, in fact, be of greater significance.

We see this lesson, also, in the seemingly "minor" mitzvah of salting the *korbanos,* which is actually incredibly deep and complex. We can use these examples as a means of elevating our own performance of all mitzvos.

QUESTION OF THE DAY:
What similarity is there between salt and suffering?
For the answer, see page 268.

פרשת ויקרא

HALACHAH OF THE DAY

THURSDAY
PARASHAS VAYIKRA

As we have seen, there are two basic views of the mechanics of *bitul b'rov*. While there are those authorities who view *bitul* as a logical derivation of the laws of probability, others contend that *bitul b'rov* is a Torah mechanism whereby nonkosher food is transformed into kosher matter. We will now present some of the different opinions of the *Rishonim* in this matter.

In the opinion of the *Rashba*, *bitul b'rov* is based upon the logical premise that when any part of a mixture is separated from the whole, we may assume that it came from the majority of the material present. Thus, when faced with a mixture of which the majority is kosher food, we may safely assume that each individual piece of food separated from the mix comes from the majority of kosher material. Accordingly, each piece of food removed from the mixture may be eaten. Indeed, even the last remaining piece of the mixture may be eaten by the very same person who has eaten the rest of it. This is because while viewing the final piece as kosher presumes that the nonkosher piece was indeed eaten at some previous point, the fact remains that we still view each individual piece — including the final one — as having being drawn from the kosher majority.

Rashba does, however, concede that one may not eat the entire mixture at *one time,* because if the entire mixture is eaten at the same time, we are forced to concede that the nonkosher portion of the mix is being eaten right now, and this the halachah cannot allow. This is the opinion that is accepted as halachah by most authorities.

There are other *Rishonim* who, while agreeing with *Rashba* as to the mechanics of *bitul,* differ somewhat from his opinion as to the ramifications of this approach. These *Rishonim* are more stringent, and contend that one individual may not eat the entire mixture, even if he desires to eat it one individual piece at a time. Instead, he must leave over a portion of the mixture equal to the size of the original nonkosher food. In this way, we can assume that all the material that was previously removed was drawn from the kosher majority, while the leftover portion represents the nonkosher matter. However, according to these *Rishonim,* even the leftover portion may be eaten by another Jew. While we have noted above that the opinion of the *Rashba* is accepted as halachah, one should, initially, follow this latter opinion, and leave a portion uneaten for another person to eat.

We will discuss two additional opinions on this issue tomorrow.

A CLOSER LOOK AT THE SIDDUR

פרשת ויקרא

THURSDAY
PARASHAS VAYIKRA

There is yet another Midrash regarding the dialogue between Hashem and the earthly waters at the beginning of creation (see *A Torah Thought for the Day*). This Midrash (from *Midrash Aseres HaDibros*) relates that when Hashem divided the world's waters, the lower, earthly waters began crying, "Woe to us, who have not merited to be close to our Creator." They brazenly attempted to rise on high, until Hashem scolded them and restrained them from rising. They then said to Hashem, "You know that we did this for Your glory!" Hashem responded to them, "Since you did this for My honor, know that I will not allow the heavenly waters to sing praise before Me until they receive permission from you." This, concludes the Midrash, is alluded to in the verse (*Tehillim* 93:4) describing the sounds of the earthly waters: מִקֹּלוֹת מַיִם רַבִּים אַדִּירִים מִשְׁבְּרֵי־יָם, *More than the roars of many waters, mightier than the waves of the sea;* only afterwards do the Heavenly waters respond: אַדִּיר בַּמָּרוֹם ה', *You are mighty on high, Hashem!* (See *Rabbeinu Bachya, Vayikra* 2:13.)

This verse is from *Tehillim* Ch. 93, which is recited both in the daily prayers (as the Song of the Day on Friday) and in the Shabbos prayers (as a part of both *Kabbalas Shabbos* and *Pesukei D'Zimrah*). This chapter celebrates Hashem's sovereignty over the world. [According to many commentators, it is specifically referring to the time of the final redemption, when Hashem's greatness will be known to all.] It was therefore chosen to be Friday's Song of the Day because on the first Friday — the sixth day of creation — Hashem completed His work and reigned over the world (*Rosh Hashanah* 31a). Friday's work, explains R' Yaakov Emden, was primarily the creation of Adam, man. That is why this chapter contains 45 words, the numerical value of the word אָדָם, *Adam*.

This psalm is also associated with the day of Shabbos. R' Chaim Yosef David Azulai (known as the *Chida*), in his *Yosef Tehillos* and in *Chomas Anach*, brings an interesting connection between the first verse of the chapter and Shabbos, in the name of the students of the *Arizal*. Chapter 93 of *Tehillim* begins: ה' מָלָךְ גֵּאוּת לָבֵשׁ, *Hashem will have reigned, He will have donned grandeur*. The two words גֵּאוּת לָבֵשׁ are anagrammatic to גּוֹאֵל שַׁבָּת, *redeems for Shabbos*. This, explains *Chida*, alludes to the tradition (see, for example, *Vayikra Rabbah* 3:1) that the ultimate redemption of the Jewish nation will be in the merit of their keeping Shabbos. As we have discussed elsewhere, Shabbos is equal

THURSDAY
PARASHAS VAYIKRA

to all the other mitzvos. When Israel sins, they demonstrate that they do not yet merit the final redemption; but when they keep Shabbos — equal to all the mitzvos — it is as if they are fulfilling the entire Torah, and they then deserve to be redeemed. Indeed, the verse continues: לָבֵשׁ ה׳ עֹז הִתְאַזָּר, H*ashem will have donned might and girded Himself;* and the word הִתְאַזָּר has the numerical value of 613, corresponding to the 613 mitzvos that Hashem considers His people as having performed by properly observing Shabbos.

The word עֹז, *might,* is a direct reference to the Torah, which is referred to by this term elsewhere. Thus, says the *Chida,* when the verse states: אַף־תִּכּוֹן תֵּבֵל בַּל־תִּמּוֹט, *[He] even firmed the world that it should not falter,* we learn that the world's continued existence — *that it should not falter* — is through the merit of the Torah.

A TORAH THOUGHT FOR THE DAY

פרשת ויקרא

FRIDAY
PARASHAS VAYIKRA

אֲשֶׁר נָשִׂיא יֶחֱטָא וְעָשָׂה אַחַת מִכָּל־מִצְוֹת
ה' אֱלֹהָיו אֲשֶׁר לֹא־תֵעָשֶׂינָה בִּשְׁגָגָה וְאָשֵׁם

When a ruler sins, and commits one from among all the commandments of HASHEM *his God that may not be done — unintentionally — and becomes guilty* (*Vayikra* 4:22).

Me'am Loez (verses 25-26), anthologizing a number of commentators, notes that the Torah uses different phrases to introduce the various sections dealing with a sinner's offering. When talking about a standard sin-offering (*chatas*), the Torah says (4:2): נֶפֶשׁ כִּי־תֶחֱטָא בִשְׁגָגָה, *When a person will sin unintentionally*. When referring to the sin of the anointed Kohen, the Torah begins (4:3): אִם הַכֹּהֵן הַמָּשִׁיחַ יֶחֱטָא, *If the anointed Kohen will sin*. In our verse, introducing the sin of the ruler, the Torah begins with: אֲשֶׁר נָשִׂיא יֶחֱטָא, *When a ruler sins* (the word אֲשֶׁר, like כִּי, is translated *when,* but as we will see, it has a different connotation). What is the significance of these variations?

Me'am Loez avers that the three words used here each have a different meaning. The word אֲשֶׁר, *when,* is used to denote something that will definitely happen — unlike כִּי, *when,* which suggests that something either might or might not occur. And the word אִם, *if,* suggests an event that is highly unlikely to take place. So when the Torah introduces the personal sin-offering of any member of the Jewish nation, it uses the word כִּי, for an individual may or may not sin. The anointed Kohen — the high priest — is a holy individual, always cleaving to Hashem. The use of the word אִם is very appropriate when discussing his sin-offering, as it is much less likely that he will sin.

But the נָשִׂיא, *ruler,* is predisposed toward sin! The king of all Israel, who is accustomed to greatness and an elevated station, will certainly feel pride and haughtiness — and such feelings lead directly to sin. So when introducing the sins of the ruler the Torah does not use the words כִּי or אִם, but אֲשֶׁר, *when.* The ruler will almost certainly have occasion to bring this particular offering.

Yet, one might still ask, notes *Me'am Loez,* that verse 27 — also referring to an individual's sin-offering — also uses the word אִם, *if,* suggesting that it is unlikely that an individual will sin: וְאִם־נֶפֶשׁ אַחַת תֶּחֱטָא בִשְׁגָגָה, *If an individual person shall sin unintentionally.* Why does the Torah earlier use the word כִּי for the individual's offering, and here use אִם?

FRIDAY
PARASHAS VAYIKRA

The answer, he explains, is that a person's likelihood of sinning is heavily dependent upon his environment. When one is part of a society that treats its obligations lightly, and often — even unintentionally — people sin, then one is predisposed toward that same lack of gravity that leads to transgression of Hashem's commandments. He will think, "Well, if it were forbidden, then everyone else would certainly be more careful to avoid it!" On the other hand, if one does not see others sinning, it is much less likely that he will sin.

In verse 2, the Torah is talking about the first situation — where one is part of a crowd, and influenced by their actions. There it is likely that he will stumble and commit the same sins as those around him. But in verse 27, the Torah is talking about the other situation. In fact, the very language of the verse corroborates that, for the Torah describes the sinner as נֶפֶשׁ אַחַת, literally, *a single person*. The word נֶפֶשׁ alone would have been appropriate both for the syntax and the content of the verse; the addition of the word אַחַת, *single,* indicates that the Torah is referring to someone acting alone, independent of outside influences. Such a person is, indeed, unlikely to mistakenly sin — hence, the use of the word אִם, *if,* in this verse.

MISHNAH OF THE DAY: ROSH HASHANAH 1:5

The Mishnah discusses under what circumstances witnesses may desecrate the Sabbath to travel to the *Beis Din* in Jerusalem and offer testimony regarding their sighting of the new moon: בֵּין שֶׁנִּרְאָה בַעֲלִיל — *Whether* the new moon *was clearly visible* to everyone, בֵּין שֶׁלֹּא נִרְאָה בַעֲלִיל — *or whether it was not clearly visible* to everyone, מְחַלְּלִין עָלָיו אֶת הַשַּׁבָּת — the witnesses *may desecrate the Sabbath* in order to go to Jerusalem to testify.[1] רַבִּי יוֹסֵי אוֹמֵר — *R' Yose says:* אִם נִרְאָה בַעֲלִיל — *If* the new moon *was clearly visible* to everyone, אֵין מְחַלְּלִין עָלָיו אֶת הַשַּׁבָּת — the witnesses *may not desecrate the Sabbath* in order to go to Jerusalem to testify.[2]

NOTES

1. The Tanna Kamma's opinion is that even when the new moon is clearly visible so that in all probability the members of *Beis Din* and others in their proximity saw it, the witnesses are nevertheless permitted to violate the prohibition against traveling beyond one's Sabbath boundary in order to report their sighting to *Beis Din* (*Rashi* to *Shabbos* 133b).

2. R' Yose's opinion is that since in this case traveling to testify will probably serve no purpose, for in all likelihood other people located closer to *Beis Din* also

---— NOTES ———

sighted the new moon, one may not desecrate the Sabbath because of it (*Rav*).

Both R' Yose and the Tanna Kamma agree that according to Torah law witnesses may desecrate the Sabbath even when the moon is clearly visible. They disagree as to whether or not there is a Rabbinic decree that under such circumstances the witnesses may not desecrate the Sabbath (*Ritva*).

FRIDAY
PARASHAS VAYIKRA

GEMS FROM THE GEMARA

Tangentially, the Gemara cites an Amoraic dispute regarding whether Shlomo HaMelech was as knowledgeable as Moshe Rabbeinu:

Rav and Shmuel disputed this matter. One said: Fifty gates of understanding were created in the world, and all but one were given to Moshe. As the verse in *Tehillim* (8:6) says: וַתְּחַסְּרֵהוּ מְעַט מֵאֱלֹהִים, *But You have made him only slightly wanting in [understanding] Divinity*. The "gates" are the various reasonings for each law in the Torah (*Maharsha* to *Nedarim* 38a; for other explanations, see *Maharal, Chidushei Aggados*). The "one" denied to Moshe refers to the understanding of God's very essence (*Ran* to *Nedarim* 38a; see *Maharal, Chidushei Aggados*).

The Amora who related the aforementioned insight now expounds upon a related verse from *Koheles* (12:10), from which he derives his point of view: בִּקֵּשׁ קֹהֶלֶת לִמְצֹא דִּבְרֵי־חֵפֶץ, *Koheles* (i.e., Shlomo) *sought to find words of delight*. This means that Koheles sought to be as knowledgeable as Moshe; that is, he too wished to be granted the forty-nine gates of understanding. A Heavenly voice came forth and said to him: וְכָתוּב יֹשֶׁר דִּבְרֵי אֱמֶת, *and words of truth are recorded properly* (*Koheles* ibid.), and it is stated (*Devarim* 34:10): וְלֹא־קָם נָבִיא עוֹד בְּיִשְׂרָאֵל כְּמֹשֶׁה, *Never again has there arisen from among the Jewish people a prophet like Moshe*. Thus, this Amora maintains that Shlomo was not granted his request to be as knowledgeable as Moshe.

The Gemara now presents the opinion of the other, dissenting, Amora:

And the other one said: The aforecited verse means that from among prophets one as prominent as Moshe did not arise, but from among kings, one with such prominence did indeed arise. I.e., Shlomo was indeed as knowledgeable as Moshe. However, he was a king, not a prophet, and thus poses no contradiction to the verse that states that Moshe had no equal among the Jewish people. [See *Maharal, Chidushei Aggados,* who discusses the issue of why, when even prophets did not reach the level of

FRIDAY

PARASHAS VAYIKRA

understanding possessed by Moshe, should Shlomo, as a king, have this kind of understanding, which presumably is more appropriate for prophets.]

The Gemara continues:

But if, according to this Amora's interpretation, Koheles was indeed as knowledgeable as Moshe, how do I uphold the verse: בִּקֵּשׁ קֹהֶלֶת לִמְצֹא דִּבְרֵי־חֵפֶץ, *Koheles sought to find words of delight,* which implies that Koheles *sought* to be as knowledgeable as Moshe, but was denied? The interpretation of the verse is that Koheles sought to judge judgments using the wisdom of the heart, without the testimony of witnesses and without the defendant having received proper warning.

According to this interpretation, that which Shlomo sought was to judge on the basis of his understanding, without the backing of witnesses' testimony. Similarly, Shlomo felt that he could determine, through his great wisdom, that the defendant's intention was to perpetrate a crime although he had not been warned (*Maharsha*). [Normally, a warning is a prerequisite for the application of any corporal punishment.]

The Gemara concludes that Shlomo's request was denied:

A Heavenly voice came forth and said to him: וְכָתוּב יֹשֶׁר דִּבְרֵי אֱמֶת, *and words of truth are recorded properly;* and it is stated in the Torah (*Devarim* 17:6): עַל־פִּי שְׁנַיִם עֵדִים . . . יוּמַת הַמֵּת, *Through the testimony of two witnesses . . . the condemned shall be put to death.* I.e., judgment in such matters must be based only upon the testimony of witnesses, and the defendant must have received proper warning.

A MUSSAR THOUGHT FOR THE DAY

In *A Torah Thought for the Day* we discussed the significance of the word אֲשֶׁר, *when,* written in connection with the ruler's sin-offering. The Gemara (*Horayos* 10b, cited by *Rashi*) is also bothered by the language of this verse, and gives a homiletic interpretation to explain the Torah's word choice. It understands that the word אֲשֶׁר can be interpreted as coming from the same root as אַשְׁרֵי, *how fortunate!* In this vein, R' Yochanan ben Zakkai says that the verse indicates to us: "How fortunate is the generation whose ruler brings a sin-offering for his unintentional sin! If the ruler does this, then certainly the common man will do so, and if for an unintentional sin he seeks forgiveness, how much more so for an intentional sin!"

R' Moshe Feinstein (*Darash Moshe,* Vol. 1) infers from this Gemara that it was indeed a challenge for the ruler not to sin (as we have already discussed in *A Torah Thought for the Day*). If, he asks, it is so very difficult for a king to repent his sins and to be careful of his spiritual obligations, then why were we commanded (*Devarim* 17:15): שׂוֹם תָּשִׂים עָלֶיךָ מֶלֶךְ, *You shall surely set over yourself a king*?

FRIDAY
PARASHAS VAYIKRA

It must be, says R' Feinstein, that it is even worse for the Jewish people to be without a king, than to be with a king who at least tries to lead his people according to the way of the Torah. Although he will surely sin, and his pride will deter him from admitting his guilt, there is still a benefit for the people he rules.

R' Feinstein concludes that there is a lesson we must glean from this. There are times when one is presented with two courses of action. When one direction is clearly superior, one should certainly choose it. But sometimes both directions have drawbacks, and one might be tempted to equate them. The Torah here teaches us that in such a situation one should carefully weigh the advantages and disadvantages of each path, and then choose the lesser evil.

R' Shimon Schwab (*Maayan Beis Hasho'evah*) says that the above Gemara's message — about the benefits of a leader's self-scrutiny — applies even in the generations when the Jewish nation's situation seems bleak. The Gemara elsewhere (*Chagigah* 14a) relates that Yeshayah called down eighteen curses upon the Jewish nation, and only calmed himself when he uttered the last one: יִרְהֲבוּ הַנַּעַר בַּזָּקֵן, *the youngster will dominate the elder* (*Yeshayah* 3:5). As the Gemara there explains, this imprecation means that those who are empty of mitzvos will dominate those who are full of mitzvos. But Yeshayah, says R' Schwab, did not, Heaven forbid, hate the Jewish nation — and certainly did not enjoy cursing them! Why did this curse calm him?

There is, he explains, a hidden message in this curse. Yeshayah meant that there will come a time when the young — those empty of mitzvos — will criticize their leaders, the great sages of Israel, saying, "On what basis did you do this thing?" And even though the complainants are themselves not scholars, they will scrutinize the every action of these great men and raise a huge outcry if they find anything objectionable.

This curse calmed Yeshayah. He saw that even in that upcoming terrible age, the elders and leaders would still be wary that their actions be upright and justifiable, so that the lesser elements of the nation not have any basis for revealing their faults. Thus, the youngsters dominating the elderly contained the seed of hope for the Jewish people's future; as the Gemara (*Rosh Hashanah* 25b) puts it: "Fortunate is the generation whose leaders listen to their followers."

HALACHAH OF THE DAY

FRIDAY
PARASHAS VAYIKRA

We continue our discussion of the precise mechanics of *bitul b'rov*.

We saw yesterday that *Rashba* and others understand *bitul b'rov* as a logical derivation of mathematical probability. Thus, in any mixture, we assume that each piece drawn from the whole may be assumed to have come from the majority of the contents. However, while *Rashba* opines that one individual may eat the entire mixture piece by piece, others are of the opinion that one must leave over a portion that will be viewed by halachah as being the nonkosher portion of the mixture. These authorities arrive at this conclusion based on the understanding that to not leave over a portion would be tantamount to conceding that the one who has consumed the mixture has indeed eaten the nonkosher part of the mix as part of the whole. However, we have said that this last portion may be consumed by another individual who did not eat the rest of the mixture. This is because in regard to his eating, we may still assume that whatever he draws from the mixture is being drawn from the majority, kosher, portion.

There are yet other *Rishonim,* notably *Rashi,* who take a more stringent position. They require that one of the pieces of the mixture be set aside not to be eaten by any Jew. This piece should be either discarded or sold to a non-Jew. The halachah will now assume that this is the nonkosher piece, thus rendering the rest of the mix permissible. Indeed, according to these *Rishonim,* once one piece has been discarded, the rest of the mixture may be consumed in its entirety by one individual all at one time. The *poskim* rule that while following this opinion is a meritorious act, it is not a halachic requirement.

A fourth opinion is that of the *Rosh*. *Rosh* takes a more lenient, and indeed radically different, view of the mechanics of *bitul b'rov*. In the opinion of *Rosh, bitul b'rov* has nothing at all to do with mathematical probability or assumptions about where the piece being removed is being drawn from. Rather, according to *Rosh,* nullification through *bitul b'rov* brings about the complete transformation of the nonkosher food into kosher matter. Accordingly, *Rosh* has no problem at all with allowing one individual to consume the entire mixture even at one time. Why not? The laws of *bitul b'rov* have rendered all of the material present in the mixture as being kosher, and therefore permissible.

A CLOSER LOOK AT THE SIDDUR

פרשת
ויקרא

FRIDAY
PARASHAS
VAYIKRA

The last verse in *Tehillim* Ch. 144 appears in the daily prayers as the penultimate verse of *Hodu* and as the second verse of *Ashrei*, while the verse before it is recited by many (along with the rest of the chapter) before *Maariv* at the departure of Shabbos. These two verses read: אַלּוּפֵינוּ מְסֻבָּלִים אֵין־פֶּרֶץ וְאֵין יוֹצֵאת וְאֵין צְוָחָה בִּרְחֹבֹתֵינוּ. אַשְׁרֵי הָעָם שֶׁכָּכָה לּוֹ אַשְׁרֵי הָעָם שֶׁה׳ אֱלֹהָיו, *Our oxen are laden; there is neither defection, nor outburst, nor wailing in the streets. Praiseworthy is the people for whom this is so, praiseworthy is the people whose God is* HASHEM.

As we have translated above, the literal meaning of אַלּוּפֵינוּ is *our oxen* (for a similar usage, see *Devarim* 28:4: שְׁגַר אֲלָפֶיךָ, *the offspring of your cattle*). But some commentators translate the word as coming from the root meaning *ruler*. *Rashi*, for example, explains the phrase אַלּוּפֵינוּ מְסֻבָּלִים as meaning that the leaders of the generation are accepted by the populace. Why are the leaders accepted? Because they make an effort to listen to the common folk, and therefore, as the verse continues: אֵין־פֶּרֶץ וְאֵין יוֹצֵאת וְאֵין צְוָחָה בִּרְחֹבֹתֵינוּ, *there is neither defection, nor outburst, nor wailing in the streets.* [This interpretation translates מְסֻבָּלִים as *tolerated* or *accepted*.] The chapter then concludes by noting the good fortune of the nation that these verses describe: אַשְׁרֵי הָעָם שֶׁכָּכָה לּוֹ, *Praiseworthy is the people for whom this is so!*

The Vilna Gaon (in *Kol Eliyahu*) suggests a novel interpretation here, based on a Gemara (*Bava Metzia* 85a) that says that during the time R' Elazar and R' Yehudah HaNasi were plagued with various afflictions, the world was a better place. Specifically, when R' Elazar was suffering, no person died before his time, and while R' Yehudah HaNasi was sick the world did not lack rain. Hence, when אַלּוּפֵינוּ, *our leaders,* are מְסֻבָּלִים, *weighed down* by affliction, אֵין־פֶּרֶץ, *there is neither defection,* caused by untimely death, *nor outburst, nor wailing in the streets,* both practices common during prayer at times of drought (see *Taanis* 15a). [Here, מְסֻבָּלִים is translated as from the root סבל, *a load*.]

The last verse of the chapter, as we have noted, is recited as part of *Hodu* and *Ashrei*. *Eitz Yosef* explains the verse's meaning in each context. In *Hodu*, he says, the verse follows Hashem's promise to fulfill our requests — הַרְחֶב־פִּיךָ וַאֲמַלְאֵהוּ, *open wide your mouth and I will fill it* (*Tehillim* 81:11). We follow that by noting how fortunate and praiseworthy is the nation that is so guaranteed!

In *Ashrei* this verse is preceded by the verse (ibid. 84:5): אַשְׁרֵי יוֹשְׁבֵי בֵיתֶךָ עוֹד יְהַלְלוּךָ סֶּלָה, *Praiseworthy are those who dwell in Your house;*

FRIDAY

PARASHAS VAYIKRA

may they always praise You, Selah! Here we follow that statement by proclaiming the good fortune of one who is able to do so — to dwell in Hashem's house and to praise Him.

This chapter (144) — according to R' Samson Raphael Hirsch, the last one authored during King David's life — is, as noted above, recited by many before *Maariv* on Motza'ei Shabbos along with *Tehillim* Chapter 67. R' Hirsch states: "We welcome the coming weekdays — along with their struggles and uncertainty, ambition and business, success and failure — with two psalms that were certainly composed to support our refreshed spirit and to implant optimism in our hearts toward every foreseeable goal, both in our personal and communal lives."

QUESTION OF THE DAY:

Which is better — to have a leader who sins and repents, or one who has never sinned at all?

For the answer, see page 268.

A TORAH THOUGHT FOR THE DAY

פרשת ויקרא

SHABBOS PARASHAS VAYIKRA

This week's *Haftarah* begins with Hashem's declaration that the Jewish people were created for the purpose of proclaiming His praises and mastery. The means for doing so are inherent in nature itself, which was created in accordance with Hashem's rules and dictates. After describing the foolishness of those who would replace Hashem with images fashioned by human hands, Hashem reaffirms Bnei Yisrael's selection as His chosen people. He guarantees that as long as we return to the prescribed service of the Temple, we will be forgiven and redeemed.

The intent of creation is the revelation of Hashem's honor and glory. Not only are humans supposed to sing His praises, but every creation sings of Hashem's glory in its own unique way. The *Maadanei Shmuel* explains Psalm 148 as detailing this very concept. First, it records that the heavens sing Hashem's praises (vs. 1-5): הַלְלוּ אֶת־ה׳ מִן־הַשָּׁמַיִם בַּמְּרוֹמִים... כָּל־מַלְאָכָיו... כָּל־צְבָאָו... שֶׁמֶשׁ וְיָרֵחַ... כּוֹכְבֵי אוֹר... שְׁמֵי הַשָּׁמַיִם... יְהַלְלוּ אֶת־שֵׁם ה׳ כִּי הוּא צִוָּה וְנִבְרָאוּ, *Praise* HASHEM *from the heavens... in the heights... all His angels... all His legions... the sun and moon... all bright stars... the most exalted of the heavens... Let them praise the Name of* HASHEM, *for He commanded and they were created.*

Second, it records that the earth and all its creatures sing Hashem's praises (vs. 7-10): הַלְלוּ אֶת־ה׳ מִן־הָאָרֶץ תַּנִּינִים וְכָל־תְּהֹמוֹת. אֵשׁ וּבָרָד שֶׁלֶג וְקִיטוֹר רוּחַ סְעָרָה... הֶהָרִים וְכָל־גְּבָעוֹת עֵץ פְּרִי וְכָל־אֲרָזִים. הַחַיָּה וְכָל־בְּהֵמָה רֶמֶשׂ וְצִפּוֹר כָּנָף, *Praise* HASHEM *from the earth: sea giants and all watery depths; fire and hail, snow and vapor, stormy winds... mountains and all hills; fruitful trees and all cedars; beasts and all cattle, crawling things and winged fowl.*

Third, it records that humans sing Hashem's praises (vs. 11-12): מַלְכֵי־אֶרֶץ וְכָל־לְאֻמִּים שָׂרִים וְכָל־שֹׁפְטֵי אָרֶץ. בַּחוּרִים וְגַם בְּתוּלוֹת זְקֵנִים עִם־נְעָרִים, *Kings of the earth and all governments, princes and all judges on earth; young men and also maidens, old men together with youths.*

Finally, after detailing the praise offerings of inanimate, living, breathing, talking, and thinking creations, the psalm says that the Jewish people have a uniquely exalted praise that transcends all (v. 14): וַיָּרֶם קֶרֶן לְעַמּוֹ תְּהִלָּה לְכָל־חֲסִידָיו לִבְנֵי יִשְׂרָאֵל עַם־קְרֹבוֹ, *And He will have exalted the pride of His nation, causing praise for all His devout ones, for the Children of Israel, His intimate people.* This is the meaning of the opening verse in our *Haftarah* (*Yeshayah* 43:21): עַם־זוּ יָצַרְתִּי לִי תְּהִלָּתִי יְסַפֵּרוּ, *I fashioned this people for Myself, that it might declare My praise.*

SHABBOS

PARASHAS VAYIKRA

One might ask, however: If, in fact, all of creation proclaims the glories and might of Hashem, how are the praises of the Jewish people exalted above all else? What more is there for us to declare that the rest of creation has not yet proclaimed through the simple eloquence of their existence?

The Gemara in *Chullin* (91b) says that the angels in heaven cannot sing שִׁירָה, heavenly *song*, until the Jews sing שִׁירָה on earth. R' Chaim Volozhin, in *Nefesh HaChaim* (1:11), explains that angels waiting to sing *shirah* is not a matter of honor and protocol; instead, our praises are the mechanism that allows the angels to sing their *shirah*. If we do not proclaim Hashem's holiness and uniqueness, then the angels are not able to do so.

Maadanei Shmuel explains that because we are the only ones who study Torah, we are the only ones who can orchestrate all the praises of creation. There is a choir of countless musicians, each singing his unique song, and it is the task of the Jewish people to blend their notes and tones into a single cohesive song worthy of being sung to Hashem. The opening verse of the *Haftarah* establishes our singular ability to conduct this celestial and universal choir.

MISHNAH OF THE DAY: ROSH HASHANAH 1:6

This Mishnah continues the discussion of the previous Mishnah: מַעֲשֶׂה שֶׁעָבְרוּ יוֹתֵר מֵאַרְבָּעִים זוּג וְעִיכְּבָם רַבִּי עֲקִיבָא בְּלוּד — *It once happened that more than forty pairs* of witnesses *passed through Lod* on the Sabbath en route to testify in Jerusalem regarding their sighting of the new moon, *and R' Akiva detained them,* since they would not be needed in *Beis Din.*[1] שָׁלַח לוֹ רַבָּן גַּמְלִיאֵל — *Rabban Gamliel sent* R' Akiva the following message: אִם מְעַכֵּב אַתָּה אֶת הָרַבִּים נִמְצֵאתָ מַכְשִׁילָן לֶעָתִיד לָבֹא — *If you detain the public* from reaching *Beis Din, it will emerge that you are causing them to stumble* by neglecting to testify *in the future.*[2]

NOTES

1. R' Akiva assumed that since so many people witnessed the new moon, it must also have been seen by *Beis Din* and others in the vicinity, so that the extra witnesses were not needed. His actions followed the view of R' Yose, cited in the previous Mishnah (see *Meiri* and *Sfas Emes* to 22a).

2. I.e., if they feel that their traveling is in vain, they will refrain from coming again, even when the new moon is not clearly visible to everyone (*Meiri;* see *Rashash*).

GEMS FROM THE GEMARA

פרשת
ויקרא

SHABBOS
PARASHAS
VAYIKRA

The Mishnah cited an occurrence in which more than forty pairs of witnesses passed through Lod on the Sabbath on their way to testify in Jerusalem regarding their sighting of the new moon. According to the narrative of our Mishnah, R' Akiva prevented them from continuing to Jerusalem, since they would not be needed in *Beis Din*. The Gemara quotes a Baraisa that provides a different perspective of the events:

It has been taught in a Baraisa: R' Yehudah said: God forbid that R' Akiva detained the witnesses. Rather, it was Shezefer, the head official of Gader, who detained them. Although the Mishnah states that R' Akiva detained the witnesses, the Baraisa contends that it was actually Shezefer who detained them. See *Aruch LaNer* who proves that the Mishnah and the Baraisa are indeed arguing.

Alternatively, the Mishnah also agrees with the Baraisa that in actuality Shezefer was the one who detained the witnesses. The intent of the Mishnah that designates R' Akiva as the individual who detained them is to place the blame on R' Akiva, for he lived in the vicinity and did not object to Shezefer's actions (*Misgeres HaZahav*).

The Baraisa concludes its narrative:

Consequently, Rabban Gamliel sent an order, and they deposed Shezefer from his exalted post. As stated in the Mishnah, Rabban Gamliel felt that it was wrong to detain the witnesses, for it would discourage them from traveling to testify on another occasion.

As noted in Mishnah 1:5, in the opinion of R' Yose it is Rabbinically prohibited for witnesses to travel to testify on their sighting a clearly visible new moon. This prohibition is due to the fact that if the moon was clearly visible, in all probability others closer could see it and this would render the violation of the Sabbath by the more distant witnesses unnecessary. The occurrence discussed by our Mishnah and Baraisa was *not* a case of a clearly visible moon. However, due to the fact that so many people had sighted it, R' Akiva applied the logic of R' Yose — that in all probability others closer could see the new moon and this would render the violation of the Sabbath by the more distant witnesses unnecessary (see *Meiri* and *Sfas Emes*).

[That it was not an actual case of a clearly visible moon is derived from the *Yerushalmi's* comment that it is only because there were *forty* pairs that R' Akiva detained them; if there had been only one pair, he would not have done so. Now, if the case was one of a clearly visible moon, and R' Akiva acted in accordance with R' Yose, the number of pairs would be of no consequence, since R' Yose's ruling is unqualified!]

פרשת ויקרא — A MUSSAR THOUGHT FOR THE DAY

SHABBOS
PARASHAS VAYIKRA

The second verse in this week's *Haftarah* states (*Yeshayah* 43:22): וְלֹא־אֹתִי קָרָאתָ יַעֲקֹב כִּי־יָגַעְתָּ בִּי יִשְׂרָאֵל, *But you did not call to Me, Yaakov, for you grew weary of Me, Yisrael*. We may ask: What does the phrase *you grew weary of Me* mean?

The Maggid of Dubno explains the verse using the following analogy. A man purchased merchandise, and paid for it to be delivered. When it arrived, the delivery man was exhausted, due to the excessive weight of the packages. Before unloading, the delivery man explained to the buyer that he had not known how difficult the delivery would be, and feels that he is owed more than the original negotiated price. The buyer agreed that the charge for the delivery was insufficient; however, the merchandise he had purchased was much lighter than the packages being delivered, and therefore what was being delivered could not possibly be the merchandise he had purchased!

So too with Hashem. The *navi* proclaimed: יָגַעְתָּ בִּי יִשְׂרָאֵל, *you grew weary of Me, Yisrael*. The Torah I gave you, and the service I demanded from you, should not have tired you out. If you were serving Me in the way that I intended, you would be joyful, energized, happy, and content. You would not be weary! Clearly, if you are tired from doing the mitzvos, it is not Me that you are honoring or serving!

Shem MiShmuel adds a profound dimension to the understanding of what it means to serve Hashem. "Man is Hashem's agent to accomplish His mitzvos." As *Rabbeinu Yonah* explains in his *Shaarei Teshuvah* (2:21): An intelligent being recognizes that Hashem sent him into this world to keep His Torah and mitzvos, and as such should be solely focused on fulfilling his mission. At the end of days, if he did his job with integrity, he is rewarded like a servant dispatched across the seas who remained completely focused on his king's mission until its successful completion and his return from abroad.

Maadanei Shmuel adds that an agent represents the one who dispatched him. Whatever he does or does not do reflects on his "sender." Moreover, in representing his sender, the messenger utilizes the sender's reputation, authority, and status in accomplishing his mission. To the extent that a person remains focused on his assignment as an agent of Hashem, he will have commensurate strength, energy, joy, and contentment, knowing that he is serving the Creator of heaven and earth. This awareness also controls the degree to which he increases Hashem's honor and glory, and how much he is able to influence every level of the universe. However, if the agent is tired, overwhelmed, or stressed in performing his mission, it proves that he is not working as Hashem's agent, and his mitzvos will not have the power to effect positive changes in the world.

פרשת ויקרא

SHABBOS
PARASHAS VAYIKRA

"Do as I say, not as I do" is the classic educational and parenting refrain. However, it is not a valid teaching platform. In teaching our children and students to serve Hashem, letting them see and realize the ease, energy, and joy with which we daven, learn Torah, and do *chesed* is the single most effective way of ensuring that they will also serve Hashem easily and joyfully.

HALACHAH OF THE DAY

Over the last several days, we have discussed various opinions as to how we understand the workings of *bitul b'rov*. Halachic authorities follow the opinion of the *Rashba*. Thus, in accordance with this opinion, one may not eat at one time all of the pieces of a mixture containing nonkosher material. Additionally, the *Rama* rules that one person should preferably not eat all of the mixture even at separate times. It is considered meritorious to discard or give to a non-Jew a piece from the mixture that is equal in size to the original nonkosher portion of the mixture.

While Torah law dictates that all prohibited foodstuffs are subject to *bitul* in a majority of similar-tasting material — *bitul b'rov* — the Sages required a greater ratio of permissible to prohibited foods for certain prohibited foods that have become mixed in their own type. Among these foods are: *terumah,* the share of produce the Torah requires one to give to a Kohen; *challah,* the Kohen's share of dough; and *bikkurim,* the portion given to the Kohen from the first-ripened fruits of the seven species of fruits for which the Torah praises Eretz Yisrael. The Sages decreed that these items require a ratio of 100 parts of permissible material to one part of prohibited matter in order to become *bateil*.

In addition to the increased ratio required to nullify these items, one must also grant the Kohen a portion corresponding to the original portion of *terumah* etc. that became introduced into the mixture. This is because aside from the fact that these items may not be eaten by a non-Kohen, the Kohanim have a monetary claim to these items that must be repaid. While prohibited matter may become nullified through *bitul b'rov,* monetary claims cannot. Thus, to use the entire mixture would constitute *gezel hashevet,* stealing from the tribe of the Kohanim.

SHABBOS
PARASHAS VAYIKRA

Orlah and *kil'ei hakerem* require a ratio of 200 parts permitted food to one part prohibited matter.

We have now covered the basic guidelines that govern *bitul b'rov*. Tomorrow we will begin to discuss the guidelines that govern *bitul b'shishim*, nullification of taste in a ratio of 60 parts of permissible material to one part of prohibited matter.

A CLOSER LOOK AT THE SIDDUR

This week, we continue our study of the Sabbath morning prayers. Before praying *Mussaf*, on many weeks of the year we recite the prayer of אַב הָרַחֲמִים. This is a memorial prayer, as the text makes clear, for martyrs who died to sanctify Hashem's Name. It was established after the bloody massacres in the times of the Crusades.

It seems from the *Shibbolei HaLeket* that הַזְכָּרַת נְשָׁמוֹת, the *Yizkor* prayers that we recite only on festivals, were originally said primarily on Shabbos, for the following reason: Shabbos is a day of complete rest, a semblance of the World to Come. Accordingly, Shabbos is a day when even the dead have respite from any judgment, so it is befitting to mention them and pray on their behalf, for peace for their souls. There is even a Midrashic source for this in *Parashas Haazinu,* which states: "Therefore we are accustomed to mention the names of the dead that they should not return to Gehinnom, and through pledging to give charity on their behalf they are redeemed from Gehinnom." For some reason, the custom to say *Yizkor* became accepted only on Yom Tov, but the prayer of אַב הָרַחֲמִים is said every Shabbos (except when *Tachanun* would not be recited on the same calendar date if it were a weekday) for the martyrs who died at the hands of the Crusaders.

The penultimate verse in this prayer reads: יָדִין בַּגּוֹיִם מָלֵא גְוִיּוֹת מָחַץ רֹאשׁ עַל אֶרֶץ רַבָּה, *He will judge the corpse-filled nations, He will crush the leader of the mighty land*. Hashem intervenes against the nations who seek to slaughter the Jews; He turns their army into a mass of corpses, and crushes their leader.

There is, however, another layer of meaning in this verse, which is stated in the Midrash. Every time a Jew is killed by Amalek (or any other enemy of the Jews), Hashem takes that spilled blood and dips His cloak into it (so to speak), until His cloak is totally saturated with blood. Then, on the day of judgment, Hashem sits on a stage and "wears" that cloak, showing the enemies the face of every righteous person that they killed, and then takes revenge upon them for their evil deeds. That is the meaning of יָדִין בַּגּוֹיִם מָלֵא גְוִיּוֹת — He judges the nations by showing them all the corpses of the people whose blood they had spilled.

The *Yefei Toar* explains that this is not meant literally, but is rather a metaphor, teaching that the spilled blood of the martyrs is never forgotten. It is as if a constant reminder of it is in front of Hashem, and He is waiting to avenge their deaths.

SHABBOS
PARASHAS VAYIKRA

QUESTION OF THE DAY:

Why does the verse (Yeshayah 43:25) repeat the word אָנֹכִי twice?

For the answer, see page 268.

ANSWERS TO QUESTION OF THE DAY

Sunday:
Netziv writes that the *olah* is a *segulah* for understanding Hashem's ways, and the *shelamim* is a *segulah* for meriting Hashem's kindness.

Monday:
The Altar is invalidated and may not be used until it is repaired.

Tuesday:
A portion of the divided bird would be too insignificant to be worthy of being offered to the King of kings (*Chizkuni*).

Wednesday:
A *minchah* may not be offered in partnership — it must have only one owner (*Maharil Diskin*).

Thursday:
Salt sweetens meat, while suffering sweetens a person's World to Come by causing his sins to be erased.

Friday:
One who has sinned and repented is better, for one who has never sinned cannot understand how to forgive (*Amshinover Rebbe*).

Shabbos:
One time it refers to Hashem having forgiven the generation of the Golden Calf, and the other time it refers to the fact that Hashem will forgive the sinners of every generation (*Radak*).